JESUS
AGAINST
CHRISTIANITY

, , ,

RECLAIMING
THE MISSING JESUS

Jack Nelson-Pallmeyer

TRINITY PRESS INTERNATIONAL
Harrisburg, Pennsylvania

Trinity Press International, P.O. Box 1321, Harrisburg, PA 17105

Trinity Press International is a division of the Morehouse Group.

Cover art: *Head of Christ*, Karl Schmidt-Rottluff. © 2001 Artists Rights Society (ARS), New York/VG Bild-Kunst, Bonn. Erich Lessing/Art Resource, NY.

Cover design: Trude Brummer

Library of Congress Cataloging-in-Publication Data

Nelson-Pallmeyer, Jack.
    Jesus against Christianity : reclaiming the missing Jesus /
Jack Nelson-Pallmeyer.
        p. cm.
    Includes bibliographical references and index.
    ISBN 1-56338-362-4 (alk. paper)
    1. Jesus Christ—Historicity. 2. Christianity—Essence, genius, nature.
I. Title.

BT303.2 .N45 2001
232—dc21   2001027329

Printed in the United States of America

01 02 03 04 05 06   10 9 8 7 6 5 4 3 2 1

CONTENTS

INTRODUCTION

I have always loved mysteries. In a mystery novel, we meet fascinating characters along the way, move through complicated plotlines, and laugh and cry as events unfold on page after page that make it difficult or impossible to set a book down. Clues nestled within texts are sometimes missed and sometimes seen, sometimes crucial and other times irrelevant. The end leaves us exhilarated or exhausted, boasting or baffled, glad to be done or lamenting the final page. *Jesus against Christianity: Reclaiming the Missing Jesus* attempts to solve the mystery of Jesus' disappearance from Christianity. It is a story with obvious clues, hidden clues, and surprise endings. I read most mysteries to escape temporarily from life, but I want to solve the case of Jesus' disappearance in order to make sense out of my life as a person of faith. The goal is not to flee from the world but to find meaning and direction with Jesus as my guide.

Our world is falling apart under the collective weight of gross inequalities, massive injustice, violence, faulty definitions of life's meaning, and distorted faith. Jesus' disappearance from and clash with Christianity is both a mystery and a problem. The mystery concerns how and why Jesus disappeared. The problem is that Christianity is often so at odds with Jesus that it has little to offer in the way of solutions to these problems; it even aggravates many of them. Jesus can help us make sense of God, life, and our role as faithful Christians in a turbulent world if we let him into our lives and our churches.

Jesus is missing and we miss his guidance. He is missing because Christian theologies, creeds, and actions are disconnected from his life as a revelation of God. The Christ of faith is the object of worship and the subject of our creeds and New Testament Gospels. This Christ, however, is often at odds with the historical Jesus and the God revealed through his life. Jesus, who was experienced by some as good news and revelation of God and by others as a subversive threat worthy of scorn and death, has all but disappeared from Christianity. It should not surprise us that Jesus was killed by his enemies. More surprising and at the heart of this book is how Jesus has been distorted by his admirers, from New Testament times to our own.

No mystery novelist's plotline can top the bizarre disappearance of Jesus on his way to becoming the object of Christian devotion. Jesus of Nazareth would wonder why Christians sing carols of his birth in Bethlehem. He might be amazed to see his family tree rewritten to include David in his ancestral line. Would Jesus and his biological brothers and sisters be amused or disgusted by claims that he was born of a virgin based on competition with Rome and a misreading of an obscure verse from an oracle written more than seven hundred years prior to his birth?

How would Jesus make sense out of Christian creeds that ignore his life and confess an ahistorical birth? Like a peanut butter sandwich without peanut butter, the Christian creeds are destined to disappoint. They jump from "born of" to "suffered under," leaving out the most important ingredient. The Christ of faith enshrined in the creeds has literally displaced and rendered the *life* of Jesus meaningless. In this context, the disappearance of Jesus from the creeds, from our churches, and from our lives is a logical, even irresistible progression. If Jesus' life is not important enough to make it into the creeds, then why should it be allowed to shape the content of our faith that, according to creedal logic, is based solely on the experience of the risen Christ?

How would Jesus respond to the Gospel writers deflecting blame for his execution away from Rome and onto the Jews, or later Christians making his executioner, Pontius Pilate, a saint? Would Jesus, who warned about the dangers of wealth, be more scandalized by Christians celebrating his birth with an orgy of consumerism or the date of the celebration itself, which marked the birthday of Mithras, the Roman god and guardian of imperial troops? Jesus preached and lived creative nonviolence. He was executed by the Roman empire. He would be amazed to share his birthday with Mithras, whom he displaced by imperial decree after Emperor Constantine had a dream in which the cross became a sword.

Distorting or ignoring the historical Jesus results in numerous expressions of deformed Christianity. The Jesus of history would be dismayed to hear his name invoked by white militia movements, moral crusaders, anti-gay activists, and right-wing politicians. He would be equally troubled by the accommodating theologies of many wealthy churches where Christ displaces Jesus and the Spirit that guided his life, where church growth eclipses discipleship, and where affluence cripples spirituality and reinforces a deepening social divide. Jesus would wonder why nonviolent activists root his and their own nonviolence in images and expectations of a violent God. Why, he might ask, do people buy WWJD bracelets, WWJD mugs, WWJD shoelaces, WWJD pens, WWJD calendars, WWJD lapel pins, WWJD rings, WWJD T-shirts, WWJD hats, WWJD playing cards, WWJD stuffed animals, and WWJD tote bags without paying attention to my life? Why invoke my name when you have so little interest in the social setting in which I lived, who killed me and why, my confrontation with the powerful forces of oppression, the alternatives I proclaimed and embodied, and the images of God that shaped my life and faith?

Like good detectives we will need to investigate these questions. They point to important historical markers that offer insight into Jesus' faith, his life choices, his opposition to the Rome- and Temple-dominated order, the motives of his murderers, his vision of God's alternative order, and his experience of God. They also contain helpful clues about why Jesus is missing from Christianity. They can help make sense of the contradiction between the obscurity of Jesus on the one hand and the popularity of WWJD bracelets and frequent appeals to his name on the other.

It is very difficult to get an accurate picture of the historical Jesus. Luke Timothy Johnson is widely praised for his criticism of historical Jesus scholarship and his claim that looking to the historical Jesus for guidance in matters of faith is misguided, impossible, or dangerous.[1] The fact that many individuals and groups shape Jesus, Christ, and God in their own image, however, underscores the need to take the historical Jesus seriously. The alternative to a serious probe is to let Jesus or Christ or God be anything to anyone at any time. Thomas Merton asks:

If the "Gospel is preached to the poor," if the Christian message is essentially a message of hope and redemption for the
poor, the oppressed, the underprivileged and those who have
no power humanly speaking, how are we to reconcile ourselves
to the fact that Christians belong for the most part to the rich
and powerful nations of the earth?[2]

Jesus scholar Marcus Borg offers a similar critique: "The dominant values of American life—affluence, achievement, appearance, power, competition, consumption, individualism—are vastly different from anything
recognizably Christian. As individuals and as a culture. . . , our existence
has become massively idolatrous."[3] Borg's criticism is insightful but confusing at one critical point. The values he cites are easily identified with
contemporary American Christianity. I think Borg wants to say that these
values are accepted and reinforced by Christianity but are completely at
odds with the historical Jesus. These values and contradictions could not
be associated with Christianity if Jesus were present rather than missing.
Many expressions of Christianity without Jesus drift like hundreds of
ships without anchors or engines. They weave and bob at the whims of
strong cultural currents or flounder in the stagnant waters of inherited
traditions. In the turbulent seas of social crises that mark life at the
beginning of this new century—social inequality, war, violence, the
absence of meaning, spiritual and physical poverty, and environmental
degradation—the historical Jesus is a missing and therefore unused lifeline of hope.

    When I speak of Jesus against Christianity or say we must reclaim the
missing Jesus, I mean to suggest that Christianity, both in content and
actual practice, is radically disconnected from the Jesus of history. Jesus'
life and faith show us a good deal about what God is like. The images of
God that guided him cannot be reconciled with many other images of
God found in the Hebrew Scriptures and Christian New Testament,
including many portrayals of Jesus or the Christ found within the
Gospels themselves. The substance of Jesus' life must inform the content
of our Christian faith, guide our approach to the Bible, and shape our
images of God.

    Christians owe an enormous debt of gratitude to the New Testament
writers who kept Jesus' subversive memory alive. These writers, however, both reveal and distort Jesus and God. Their insights and perspectives should be treated respectfully, but we must be careful not to idealize
these very human authors. In some cases, their biases overwhelm insights

from the Jesus of history concerning faith and God. It is not uncommon for the New Testament writers, and those of us who follow their lead, to misrepresent Jesus to the point of distorting our understanding of salvation, the resurrection, God, and Christian faith.

Jesus told parables to expose systems of abusive power. Matthew and the other Gospel writers cast heroes in Jesus' story as villains, and they cast as God-figures the abusive power brokers that Jesus exposed. Jesus addressed the deadly consequences of real debt; the Gospel writers soften this with the language of sin. Jesus embodied good news to the destitute; Matthew speaks of spiritual poverty. Jesus broke the relationship between violence and the divine; the Gospel writers often portray Jesus Christ as a vengeful judge sitting in a distant realm next to an equally vengeful and distant God. A monstrous gulf severs and separates Jesus' lived life from the object of Christian devotion, and the consequences for Christian faith and the world are monumental. Christianity without Jesus atrophies our spirituality, subverts the mission of the Church, truncates the individual and collective faith of Christians, distorts God and politics, covers over major issues concerning scriptural authority, and leaves our world in peril.

The distortion of Jesus within Christianity is at the heart of numerous contradictions. None is greater than this: Jesus challenged and was executed by the domination system of his time; many Christians today proclaim the Christ of faith while conforming to, embracing, and receiving rewards from the domination system of our time. Jesus invites us out of the domination system and into an alternative community where abundant life is experienced. Rather than being at odds with imperial injustice as was Jesus, however, Christianity has often functioned as its servant. I share John Dominic Crossan's view that we need to ground our lives and faith in the historical Jesus:

> The earthly Jesus was not just a thinker with ideas but a rebel with a cause. He was a Jewish peasant with an attitude, and he claimed that his attitude was that of the Jewish God. But it was, he said, in his life and in ones like it that the kingdom of God was revealed, that the Jewish God of justice and righteousness was incarnated in a world of injustice and unrighteousness. The kingdom of God was never just about words and ideas, aphorisms and parables, sayings and dialogues. It was about a way of life. And that means it was about a body of flesh and blood. Justice is always about bodies and lives, not just about words and ideas. Resurrection does not mean, sim-

ply, that the spirit or soul of Jesus lives on in the world. And neither does it mean, simply, that the companions or follow-ers of Jesus live on in the world. *It must be the embodied life that remains powerfully efficacious in this world.* . . .There is, then, only one Jesus, the embodied Galilean who lived a life of divine jus-tice in an unjust world, who was officially and legally exe-cuted by that world's accredited representatives, and whose continued empowering presence indicates, for believers, that God is not on the side of injustice—even (or especially) impe-rial injustice. There are not two Jesuses—one pre-Easter and another post-Easter, one earthly and another heavenly, one with a physical and another with a spiritual body. There is only one Jesus, the *historical* Jesus who incarnated the Jewish God of justice for a believing community committed to con-tinuing such incarnation ever afterward.[4]

Christianity has become, in Borg's words, "massively idolatrous" because it has severed its ties to, and articulated a Christ distinct from, the historical Jesus. Without roots in the life and faith of Jesus, Christianity easily recon-ciles God and Christ with the distorted values and priorities of the domi-nant culture that both ignores and accelerates a global crisis of injustice and meaning. *Jesus against Christianity* explores the mystery of how and why Jesus disappeared from Christianity, the troubling religious and historical consequences traceable to his disappearance, and alternatives that place Jesus of Nazareth and our own religious experience at the center of Christian faith. Christianity must allow itself to be criticized, challenged, inspired, and changed by the historical Jesus. The subtitle, *Reclaiming the Missing Jesus,* is meant to convey both Jesus' disappearance from Christianity and the profound sense of loss that accompanies the absence of a loved one. If Jesus is missing, then we must find him for his sake and our own.

One obstacle to finding Jesus is that he may be both missing and unwelcome. A missing person is the object of an intensive search. The community unites and desperately seeks to find that lost person. An unwelcome intruder, on the other hand, is ignored, shunned, or arrested. "It is possible," Robert Funk writes, "that we do not want to readmit Jesus of Nazareth back into Christianity. We probably prefer things as they are."[5] Perhaps. But then again, perhaps not.

I have written this book because the historical Jesus revitalizes my own faith and because I have met many people over the past several years who have expressed a deep hunger for a Jesus-centered faith and spirituality. I hope *Jesus against Christianity* will in some small way help Christians in and outside the churches make sense out of faith, Jesus, God, the Bible, themselves, and a world in crisis. *Jesus against Christianity* is written primarily for:

- People who may be sitting on a reservoir of unasked questions and who are following their faith down new pathways. An atmosphere of dogmatic certainty marks many of our churches and it leads many people into places of silent fear and intimidation.
- People who share a thirst for greater justice and a deeper spirituality but find themselves feeling empty when they try to drink from the wells of traditional faith and theology.
- People who struggle to make sense out of God, faith, and their own lives in the midst of a world torn apart by violence, war, hunger, hate, and inequality.
- People who want to be faithful but find themselves uncomfortable with the creed and feel imprisoned within the walls of doctrinal straitjackets.
- People troubled by the inconsistencies and/or distortions that permeate the Gospels but who are inspired by the life, faith, and ongoing experience of Jesus or the Spirit that guided him.
- People deeply challenged by Jesus' embodiment of love of enemies and profoundly troubled by Christianity's overall embrace of militarization and war.
- People disturbed by a world torn apart by violence, much of it done in God's name.
- People sickened by poverty, challenged by Jesus' message of good news to the poor, and disturbed by Christianity's cozy relationship with wealth and unjust economic systems.
- People who find many promises made in our increasingly secular, consumer culture to be empty, and who long to be part of a community of discipleship where abundant life is experienced and nurtured through spirituality and action.
- People who struggle with the Bible's inspiring and disgusting images of God.
- People who teach their children about a loving God but find themselves censoring many biblical stories, such as Noah's ark, in which a horrible, genocidal flood is attributed to God and covered up (unsuccessfully?) with a rainbow.

- People who find hope and encouragement in Jesus' life, including his willingness to risk and ultimately face death, but who question whether the atonement (God's bloody sacrifice of Jesus as a means of reconciling God with sinful humanity) is an appropriate explanation for Jesus' death or an accurate depiction of a loving God.
- People who can no longer embrace images of God the Almighty Controller of the Universe in the context of a world with so much suffering and evil.
- People who are open to a vision of Christianity that grounds itself in the life and faith of Jesus.

Jesus' status as missing person is rooted in the Christian creeds, is traceable to distortions in the Gospels themselves, and is linked to seriously distorted biblical images of God. It is also reinforced by church theologies, hymns, liturgies, and rituals. At the heart of this book lies my conviction that we must root and reconcile the content of our faith with Jesus' life as a revelation of God and thereby end the radical disjuncture separating Jesus from the Christ. Either Jesus will find a home within Christianity or Christianity will continue to distort God and to undermine its potential to transform lives and to renew the world.

We ignore Jesus to our own peril. This is true not because of biblical portraits of a punishing God or the Gospel writers' threats that Jesus will return as a vindictive judge at the end of history, but because by ignoring the Spirit that guided his life, we close ourselves off from authentic hope. My goal is to ground theological reflection and Christian faith and action in the life and faith of the historical Jesus. This requires a credible and convincing portrait of Jesus. My portrait of Jesus is shaped by insights drawn from a lifetime within the church, participation in an ecumenical faith community committed to peace, justice, and nonviolence, and my own religious experience. I have felt God's embrace and wrestled with God for more than twenty-five years as I have tried to make sense out of God, the Bible, Jesus, and faith in the context of a world torn apart by hunger, poverty, and violence. My portrait also draws on insights from modern scholarship. My intent is to offer a readable and compelling portrait of Jesus consistent with good scholarship without overwhelming readers with unnecessary details, scholarly lingo, and theological trivia. Readers can find abundant clues for further study by examining the footnotes.

Jesus against Christianity sets out to solve the mystery of Jesus' disappearance and to find and welcome Jesus back into our faith and our lives. Chapters 1–10 examine important Jewish traditions and key images and expectations of God found in the Hebrew Scriptures that were part of Jesus' inheritance and socialization as a faithful Jew. This sets the stage for Chapters 11–25, which assess the life and faith of Jesus. These chapters focus on when, why, and how Jesus affirms, reforms, or breaks with his tradition and what it would mean for Christians to let Jesus shape our faith, our understanding of God, and our life and actions in the world.

Notes

1. See Luke Timothy Johnson, *The Real Jesus: The Misguided Quest for the Historical Jesus and the Truth of the Traditional Gospels* (San Francisco: HarperSanFrancisco, 1997) and *Living Jesus: Learning the Heart of the Gospel* (San Francisco: HarperSanFrancisco, 1999). Johnson makes five key arguments. First, historical Jesus scholarship is the work of inferior scholars with bad motives. Second, such scholarship is crippled by limited sources. We cannot know much about Jesus even if we wanted to. Third, given a lack of adequate sources, searchers end up finding a biased Jesus who looks and behaves just like themselves. Fourth, looking for Jesus is a bad idea. The Gospels are faith statements about the resurrected Christ and so the Jesus of history is unimportant to Christian faith. Finally, the search is dangerous because information it reveals threatens Christian orthodoxy and creates doubt among believers.

My brief response to these five criticisms is this: First, good people and good scholars disagree on important matters of faith. It is better to address key issues rather than attack individuals or their motives. Second, we must make the best judgments we can using the sources we have. Differences within the Gospels alone pose many important issues and questions. Third, we all need to be aware of how our biases and presuppositions affect scholarship. This is true, however, whoever is speaking or writing about Jesus, the Bible, Christ, or God. Historical Jesus scholars start with presuppositions. So does Luke Timothy Johnson. Fourth, I find it alarming to suggest that Jesus is unimportant to Christian faith. If this is true, then Jesus may just as well have been a toad. Jesus, in my view, shows us a good deal about what God is or is not like. Finally, Jesus was and is dangerous. That is why he was killed in first-century Palestine and that is why he is unwelcome in many of our churches today. I believe, however, that although much information uncovered through historical Jesus scholarship is disturbing to many, it opens up the possibility of meaningful faith. That is my faith experience and what I see in many of my students. Censorship concerning Jesus seems indefensible, but it happens in our churches all the time.

2. Thomas Merton, *Faith and Violence* (Notre Dame, Ind.: University of Notre Dame Press, 1968), 20.

3. Marcus J. Borg, *Jesus: A New Vision* (San Francisco: Harper & Row, 1987), 195.

4. John Dominic Crossan, *The Birth of Christianity: Discovering What Happened in the Years Immediately after the Execution of Jesus* (San Francisco: HarperSanFrancisco, 1998), xxx, emphasis in original.

5. Robert Funk, *Honest to Jesus* (San Francisco: HarperSanFrancisco, 1996), 22.

1 GOD, JUDAISM, AND JUSTICE

If I had to choose one word that best describes the character of God in the Bible, it would be *violence*. If I could choose a second word, it would be *justice*. Justice was important because the Exodus was understood to be a story of God freeing a people from oppressive, imperial rule. Justice was foundational to the post-Exodus covenant in which the people of Israel agreed to embody God's justice and God agreed to be their God. At times, injustice seemed to sever the ties between Israel and God. Most often, however, it strained their relationship. Injustice or idolatry, alone, together, or in some combination with other forms of unfaithfulness, triggered God's punishing violence. The disobedient people of God became the enemies of God. God the advocate became God the violent judge and executioner.

The vocation of the Jewish people was to embody God's justice in the world. Justice demands specifics, and so the tradition outlined the meaning of justice and applied it to the rigors of daily and national life. Lost within rhetoric concerning sacred scripture is the reality that defining God's justice is always a very human project. Not surprisingly, the specificity with which Judaism named the justice of God was both a profound

1

strength and glaring weakness. I have put troubling issues concerning God and violence on hold until future chapters. This chapter examines justice as a key characteristic of the Jewish God and looks at how the people organized their communal life in response to a God of justice.

JUDGING BETWEEN THE GODS

Psalm 82 describes the relationship between Judaism and justice. Then as now, the name of God or various gods were invoked frequently. Arguments at the time concerned whose God or gods were best. The key question was, When human beings use God to justify what they do or to explain what is happening around them, how can people judge whether God is really being talked about? Let's begin with six contemporary examples:

Example 1. His team trails 80 to 79. Michael, standing at the free throw line, crosses himself, looks at the rim, and shoots. Swish. The ritual is repeated: ball from referee, pause to make the sign of the cross, aim, shoot, swish. In the postgame interview Michael says, "I want to thank God for helping me make the final shots that allowed us to win."

Example 2. Neil and Kathryn receive devastating news that their daughter was killed in a car accident. Neil's brother tries to console them. "I'm sorry," he says, "she was so special that God wanted her with him." A friend, Rafael, walked away from the accident. "God was watching over you," Neil's brother tells him.

Example 3. A quote from Mark Twain's *The War Prayer:*

> Then came the "long" prayer. None could remember the like of it for passionate pleading and moving and beautiful language. The burden of its supplication was, that the ever-merciful . . . Father of us all would watch over our noble young soldiers, and aid, comfort, and encourage them in their patriotic work; bless them, shield them in the day of battle and the hour of peril, bear them in His mighty hand, make them strong and confident, invincible in the bloody onset, help them to crush the foe, grant to them and to their flag and country imperishable honor and glory.[1]

Example 4. When living in Central America, I often heard the phrase, "si Dios quiere" (if God wants). If someone said the harvest would be good or expressed hope that a sick child would recover, then the response was, "si Dios quiere." "If God wants" was not so much an expression of faith as it was a statement of resignation to one's fate.

Example 5. The clinic where John receives medicine is picketed by Christians holding signs that read "AIDS: God's Punishment for Sin."

Example 6. A bumper sticker reads, "God, Guns, and Guts . . . Made America Great."

These references to God raise profound questions about human distortion and the power, sovereignty, and character of God. Each underscores a problem as old as the first human speculation about God: When humans invoke God's name, how do we judge whether God is being talked about? How do we discern real God from false God, God incarnators from God-hustlers? One important biblical response is Psalm 82:

> God has taken his place in the divine council;
>   in the midst of the gods he holds judgment:
> "How long will you judge unjustly
>   and show partiality to the wicked?
> Give justice to the weak and the orphan;
>   maintain the right of the lowly and the destitute.
> Rescue the weak and the needy;
>   deliver them from the hand of the wicked."
>
> They have neither knowledge nor understanding,
>   they walk around in darkness;
>   all the foundations of the earth are shaken.
>
> I say, "You are gods,
>   children of the Most High, all of you;
> nevertheless, you shall die like mortals,
>   and fall like any prince."
>
> Rise up, O God, judge the earth;
>   for all the nations belong to you!

Psalm 82 says justice is the proper measure of God. God chastised and judged the "gods" because they tolerated the oppression of the weak, needy, lowly, and destitute. John Dominic Crossan summarizes the claim being made in this psalm, a claim repeated many times within the Hebrew Scriptures:

Israel's God is the one true God of all the earth and all the nations because this alone is a God of justice and righteousness for those systemically vulnerable, for the weak, the orphan, the lowly, the destitute, and the needy. This God stands against injustice and wickedness because that is the nature and character of this God. The gods and their nations have failed the wretched of the earth.[2]

A God that does not promote justice is not worthy of being God. A person who invokes God's name but is not working for justice is a God hustler. Psalm 82 does not allow justice to be an abstraction. The authentic God gives justice to the weak and the orphan, maintains the right of the lowly and the destitute, rescues the weak and the needy, and delivers vulnerable and oppressed groups from the hand of the wicked. Justice is God's character embodied in human relationships and national life. Injustice clashes sharply with a people whose identity is forged in covenant with a just God. Crossan makes this point in relation to the Exodus, in which the pharaoh is defeated and slaves freed:

The problem is, of course, that when God is revealed by freeing doomed slaves from imperial control, the future is set on a collision course with domination, oppression, and exploitation—even when those actions are exercised by a people on itself. In the biblical texts, accusations of injustice are made against the rich and powerful within Judaism itself. That is because Jews were then in charge of their own people and land. In the post-biblical texts, accusations of injustice are made against the pagan nations, the great empires, and the imperial gods. That is because they were then in charge of the Jewish people and the Jewish land. But what is always at stake is the Jewish God of justice, who stands against injustice, against unjust individuals, against unjust empires, and against unjust gods.[3]

This, in my view, is an idealized reading of the Exodus that I challenge in future chapters. It reflects many voices within the tradition, however, which assert that justice is the issue for people who claim to be in relationship with a just God. The meaning of justice narrowed considerably. Time and time again the biblical writers said that God's justice means *equality*. Justice and equality or justice as equality reflect the character of God.

JUSTICE AS EQUALITY

Throughout the biblical narrative, land, oppression, debt, and slavery are the issues around which justice and faithfulness are embodied or denied. Exodus 3:7–8 says:

> Then the LORD said, "I have observed the misery of my people who are in Egypt; I have heard their cry on account of their taskmasters. Indeed, I know their sufferings, and I have come down to deliver them from the Egyptians, and to bring them up out of that land to a good and broad land, a land flowing with milk and honey."

The author of this text says a just God heard the cry of an oppressed people, came to deliver them, and promised them a good land. Questions arose following the Exodus encounter. How were people to respond to a God of justice who delivered them from oppression? How were they to structure their life together once they gained control of their own land? The answers seemed clear. A just God required the people of God to take on the vocation of justice. Their social order was expected to reflect, promote, establish, and maintain justice and equality. Justice was possible when land ownership was distributed evenly, interest forbidden, and debts periodically canceled. At set intervals, the cycles of poverty were to be interrupted or broken. Laws that defined the people's proper relationship to land, debt, interest, and slavery were at the heart of the covenant. If the people obeyed them, things would go well. If not, there would be problems. A passage in Nehemiah reveals the relationship between crisis, debt, slavery and loss of land: "Now there was a great outcry of the people and of their wives against their Jewish kin. For there were those who said, 'With our sons and our daughters, we are many; we must get grain, so that we may eat and stay alive'" (5:1–2).

A food crisis provides the powerful with an opportunity to exploit the needy. The powerful could be foreign rulers or, as in this case, other Jews. Those who are well placed and well fed have sufficient food and influence to turn a crisis into unjust gain. They force the desperately hungry to put up their land as collateral: "There were also those who said, 'We are having to pledge our fields, our vineyards, and our houses in order to get grain during the famine'" (5:3). Interest rates rise along with the desperation of the borrower: "And there were those who said, 'We are having to borrow money on our fields and vineyards to pay the king's tax'" (5:4).

After borrowing to the hilt against limited assets, pledging and losing everything, including their land, they sell their children into slavery and give their daughters up for rape: "Now our flesh is the same as that of our kindred; our children are the same as their children; and yet we are forcing our sons and daughters to be slaves, and some of our daughters have been ravished; we are powerless, and our fields and vineyards now belong to others" (5:5).

There will always be opportunity to capitalize on calamity because you cannot legislate against famine or other disasters, and no people can construct a social system immune from crisis. Constructing a social system based on the justice of God, however, can limit that opportunity:

> I was very angry when I heard their outcry. . . . I brought charges against the nobles and the officials; I said to them, "You are taking interest from your own people." And I called a great assembly to deal with them, and said to them, "As far as we were able, we have bought back our Jewish kindred who had been sold to other nations; but now you are selling your own kin, who must then be bought back by us!" They were silent, and could not find a word to say. So I said, "The thing that you are doing is not good. Should you not walk in the fear of our God, to prevent the taunts of the nations our enemies? Moreover I and my brothers and my servants are lending them money and grain. Let us stop this taking of interest. Restore to them, this very day, their fields, their vineyards, their olive orchards, and their houses, and the interest on money, grain, wine, and oil that you have been exacting from them." Then they said, "We will restore everything." (5:6–12)

A famine results in a crisis of faith because charging interest, taking possession of land and reducing neighbors to slavery are antisocial, ungodly behaviors. They directly violate the character of a just God who demands equality as an embodiment of divine love. How do you construct a social system based on the justice of God? According to these texts, you establish principles based on the character of God and specify meaning through laws and ordinances that address issues of land, interest, and slavery. A social system so constructed makes exploitation contrary to the will of God and against the law.

Nehemiah addressed a people who had recently returned from captivity in Babylon (fifth century B.C.E.), but he drew on law codes that were written centuries earlier. The sabbatical year provisions described in Leviticus 25 and Deuteronomy 15, by way of example, are proposals that address the cycles of poverty. Every seven years debts are to be canceled (Deut 15:1, 7–9) and slaves freed (Deut 15:12). The sabbatical year is also one of rest for the land (25:3–5). Crossan describes the relationship between Sabbath and equality:

> The sabbath day represents a temporary stay of inequality, a day of rest for everyone alike, for animals and humans, for slaves and owners, for children and adults. Why? Because that is how God sees the world. Sabbath rest sends all alike back to symbolic egalitarianism. It is a regular stay against the activity that engenders inequality on the other days of the week. The sabbath year is to years as the sabbath day is to days. Every seventh year is also special. It represents another stay against inequality.[4]

Norman Gottwald offers a less idealized reading of these texts. The laws or codes "do not resolve into a single harmonized system but reflect relief measures proposed or practiced in various Israelite circles over some hundreds of years." They testify to deep and ongoing problems in the social order. "Taken together," he writes, "they attest to a political economy that repeatedly generated tax and debt burden that led to loss of land and impoverishment for sizeable numbers of people, and in turn, undermined communal stability. They also," he continues, "attest to frequent efforts to ameliorate the baleful effects of this economic impoverishment, or even to actually halt the economic juggernaut that caused them."[5]

Pressure for relief sometimes came from below. More often than not, however, as Gottwald notes, it was kings and priests who initiated relief efforts in order to diffuse tensions that threatened their interests and power.[6] The jubilee provision may have originated as a priestly initiative offered for largely self-serving reasons. Every fifty years was to be a super-sabbatical or jubilee (Leviticus 25) in which each family returned to its inheritance. Gottwald suggests that the "initial jubilee could have been proposed as the framework within which to restore former holdings" to members of the Jewish elite as their captivity in Babylon ended and they returned to Judah:

> The 50 years between the fall of Jerusalem in 587 and the edict of Cyrus in 538 could have been the historical impetus to begin

the jubilee programme with all possible speed following the restoration of Judah. The jubilee programme can thus be viewed as the political and economic ploy of the Aaronid priests to achieve leadership in restored Judah by dispensing benefits to a wide swath of the populace, presumably with civil and military support from the Persians.[7]

The jubilee program, Gottwald notes, would have been "attractive for returning exiles whose land had fallen into other hands in their absence." If enacted it would have shored up the popularity of priests and been of economic benefit to them. Gottwald continues:

Often overlooked in assessing the jubilee is the economic role of the priests. It is noteworthy that houses and land in walled cities are exempt from the jubilee. Within the fortified administrative and commercial centres, the priests functioned as temple officials, tribute gatherers and profitable entrepreneurs. . . . [J]ubilee does not probe the reasons for Israelites becoming impoverished, which would include not only Persian taxes but also tithes and offerings taken by the priests. It should not be surprising that a century after the edict of Cyrus, Nehemiah found debt and debt slavery rampant in Judah, threatening the foundations of "social peace."[8]

Some provisions of the jubilee were less progressive than the more ancient Sabbath laws and may have actually hurt impoverished peasants:

Unlike the related provisions of Exodus and Deuteronomy, Leviticus 25 does not include remission of debts or release of debtor slaves every seven years. It does, however, incorporate the seventh year fallow of Exodus. The jubilee programme posits the benign cooperation of God in providing a bounteous sixth-year harvest to feed the community over the two or more years before crops are once again harvested after the seventh-year fallow. This optimism defies the irregularity of drought conditions which occur on the average of every two to four years. It also overlooks the inflation of food prices in conditions of scarcity. The jubilee programme further premises sufficient prosperity for debtors and debtor slaves to be able to work their way to solvency and freedom long before the next jubilee. Moreover, it assumes that creditors will honour the solidarity of the community and facilitate this mandated recovery of land and personal freedom. There is a large measure of naiveté in thinking that those destitute enough to lose land and freedom would be able to recover their losses. . . . For most debtors and debt slaves, the jubilee would be their only salvation. Indeed, the plight of those in the majority who suffered loss more than seven years before the next jubilee could be far worse under the jubilee release than under the seven-year releases of debts and debtor slaves granted in Exodus and Deuteronomy.[9]

The jubilee, in other words, may have been introduced with priestly interests rather than God's justice in mind. With the passage of time, however, and when wedded to other Sabbath provisions involving debt forgiveness and remission of slaves, it became an expressive symbol of God's intended justice. By the time of Jesus, jubilee visions and assumptions clashed sharply with the Rome and Temple dominated order in which land ownership was concentrated and peasant marginalization permanent. In the context of Roman commercialization of land in first-century Palestine, jubilee was a powerful ideal by which social systems and rulers were judged. The jubilee embodied and symbolized God's intent. Jesus called on memories of jubilee to remind families in Israel that God's will is that all people have access to land. If people lost land, or had it stolen through usury or violence, they would not be permanently dispossessed, indebted, or enslaved. "In this year of jubilee you shall return, every one of you, to your property" (Lev 25:13). Human justice, equality, freedom, and landedness were manifestations of God's will.

Unequal distribution of land (or wealth) over time creates systemic problems. Jubilee as ideal, critique, and promise presumes and mitigates against structural injustices that evolve within all social systems. God's justice requires a systemic response to inequality as a matter of faithfulness. Land belonged to God, and ownership was always provisional (Lev 25:23). Other covenantal codes banned the charging of interest in transactions between Israelites (Exod 22:25; Deut 23:19). This increased the likelihood of an egalitarian social order. People who were inclined not to share as the year of debt forgiveness approached were instructed to be generous: "Do not be hard-hearted or tight-fisted toward your needy neighbor. You should rather open your hand, willingly lending enough to meet the need, whatever it may be" (Deut 15:7–8).

The justice of God was institutionalized through mechanisms that insured debt forgiveness, freedom, no charging of interest, free giving, and rights and restoration to land. The justice of God held the promise that "there will . . . be no one in need among you" (Deut 15:4). An ideal social order was unlikely, however, and so we find this admonition: "Since there will never cease to be some in need on the earth, I therefore command you, 'Open your hand to the poor and needy neighbor in your land'" (Deut 15:11).

CONCLUSION

Important segments of the Jewish tradition understood justice to be the proper measure of God and the clearest expression of faithfulness to God. God's justice is central to the character of God, and the people of God are expected to embody justice and equality in their social relations. In biblical times, the most pressing arenas in which justice and injustice, equality and inequality, God and not-God were defined had to do with land, debt, interest, and slavery. Jesus built on the Jewish vision of a just God. He was close to many aspects of the God and justice tradition set forth in Psalm 82 and elsewhere in the Hebrew Scriptures, although, as we will see, even here there are differences. There are other aspects of the Jewish tradition, however, that are far less inspiring. How are we to make sense out of the numerous and contradictory metaphors and images of God found in the Bible, including the dominant image of God the pathological killer?

Notes

1. Mark Twain, *The War Prayer* (New York: Harper & Row, 1971).
2. John Dominic Crossan, *The Birth of Christianity* (San Francisco: HarperSanFrancisco, 1998), 208.
3. Ibid., 184.
4. Ibid., 189.
5. Norman Gottwald, "The Biblical Jubilee: In Whose Interests?" in *The Jubilee Challenge: Utopia or Possibility*, ed. Hans Ucko (Geneva: WCC Publications, 1997), 34.
6. Ibid., 35.
7. Ibid., 36–37.
8. Ibid., 37–38.
9. Ibid., 35–36.

2 DIVERSE AND CONTRADICTORY IMAGES OF GOD

It may be impossible to portray God accurately, but this has not stopped people from trying throughout history. This chapter examines diverse biblical metaphors for God and their implications for our faith journeys. The problem of describing God is aggravated by appeals to authoritative scriptures that present many incompatible images. The Bible is a reservoir of diverse, troubling, and contradictory metaphors for God. God is often at odds with God, and human actions rooted in "God's will" are often despicable and deadly.

Marcus Borg offers a summary of biblical images of God. Reflecting the realm of political leadership, God is portrayed as king, lord, warrior, judge, and lawgiver. Images from everyday life include builder, gardener, shepherd, potter, doctor or healer, father, mother, lover, wise woman, old man, woman giving birth, and friend. Drawing on nature and inanimate objects, God is described as eagle, lion, bear, hen, fire, light, cloud, wind, breath, rock, fortress, and shield.[1] Psalm 82 makes justice and equality the proper measure of God. Other biblical portraits include creator, sustainer, and redeemer. God is described through the feminine image of Womanly Wisdom or Sophia. Wisdom is sometimes equated with God or is a name for God. At other times, she is God's companion and coworker.

The waters are muddied further when Jesus is added to the mix. Jesus, who blesses peacemakers and teaches love of enemies, cannot be reconciled easily with God as holy warrior or violent judge. The historical Jesus embraced, ignored, jettisoned, or revolutionized various images of God that were part of his inherited tradition. If we take his life and faith seriously, then Jesus can help us discern what God is and is not like.

Biblical images—extraordinary in light of their number, diversity, and contradictory nature—have important implications for people of faith and for any effort to revision Christianity with Jesus' life and faith at the center. Six will be addressed here.

LIMITS OF LANGUAGE

Diverse images and metaphors remind us that all human efforts to name God are limited. The multiplicity of names and conflicting images for God within and outside the Judeo-Christian tradition tell us that the search for religious meaning is widespread. They also reflect the inadequacy of our language about the divine. The nineteenth-century German philosopher Ludwig Feuerbach explained diverse portraits of God in light of the projections, wishes, and needs of humanity.[2] Different gods and different characteristics of the same God reflect diverse human needs and distinctive imaginations. Feuerbach's contemporary, Karl Marx, agreed. "Man makes religion," Marx wrote, "religion does not make man." Marx drew a sociological conclusion based on the role and impact of religion within oppressive societies. "Religion is the sigh of the oppressed creature," he wrote, "the heart of a heartless world, just as it is the spirit of spiritless conditions. It is the opium of the people."[3] For Marx, religion was like a drug that diverted attention from the social causes of human misery. It served the interests of the upper classes and robbed the oppressed of authentic hope.

Humans project many things onto God, and religion can and does function as an opiate. I believe, however, that Marx and Feuerbach were wrong about God. God is more than a human construct, but our images of God are not. God is real, but descriptions of God, including those drawn from biblical images and metaphors, are limited, flawed, and often wrong.

NAMES AND METAPHORS ARE NAMES AND METAPHORS

The volume, diversity, and contradictory nature of biblical metaphors for God remind us never to confuse our names for and images of God with God. Metaphors say what God is like in someone's or some community's religious experience. Metaphors do not tell us what God is. God is not a male being with one or more children, but in the experience of the writer or the community or a part of the community that he or she represents, God can be described as like a father. God is not a woman who gives birth, but is sometimes experienced in ways that allow people to associate God with a mother who loves, nurtures, and caresses her children or like an angry mother bear robbed of her cubs (Hos 13:8). God is like a mother. When a biblical writer refers to God as a rock, he or she is not saying that God is a piece of stone but that in times of uncertainty and distress, God is a firm foundation wherein to ground one's hope. God is like a rock. "It is vital that we remind ourselves constantly," Virginia Ramey Mollenkott writes, "that our speech about God, including the biblical metaphors of God as our Father and all the masculine pronouns concerning God, are figures of speech and are not the full truth about God's ultimate nature. But on the other hand," she continues, "we would be no more accurate to assume that God is really our Mother than to assume literal fatherhood."[4]

METAPHORS, POWER, AND BIAS

Images drawn from the realm of political leadership and everyday life are culturally bound or determined. Politics and culture are often driven and determined by unequal power relationships. They are subject to bias, manipulation, and error. Human beings often distort God. For example, people easily confuse justice and revenge and then project their confusion onto God. We deform God's image whenever we conform it to unjust political, cultural, and social systems. This can be illustrated with reference to the metaphor of God the Father. God the Father is a conflictual metaphor within scripture. It often reflects and reinforces the abusive patriarchal family and political structure that characterized Israelite society. It mirrors the social world of patriarchy in which religion reinforces the power of men over women. God the Father is closely tied to other images of God as king or judge. Marcus Borg writes:

Put most compactly, God is imaged as a male authority figure
who is the ruler of the universe. As with an earthly king, images
of domination and subjection are central to this model. The
model has profound consequences for our images of ourselves,
the internal dynamics of the religious life, and the world.[5]

Images of God the Father, King, or Judge flow from and legitimate male
power within society. They reinforce abusive power within the family,
within religious and political institutions, and within the economy.
"Without doubt," Elisabeth Schüssler Fiorenza writes, "the Bible is a *male
centered* book."[6] Virginia Ramey Mollenkott observes that "we forget that
God-as-Father is a metaphor, a figure of speech, an implied comparison
intended to help us relate to God in a personal and intimate way."[7] As a
result, patriarchal images of God are used to bolster male power and privilege. Powerful men continue to justify an all-male priesthood based on
religious "facts": God the "Father" was incarnate in a "Son" who appointed
only male disciples.

Jesus of Nazareth challenges and subverts the traditional meaning
assigned to God the Father and the abusive power of real fathers within
the patriarchal household. Let's start with real fathers in ancient Near
Eastern society, who at the time held almost dictatorial power within families. "The family," in Walter Wink's definition, "is the most basic instrument of nurture, social control, enculturation, and training in society."
During the time of Jesus it was "deeply imbedded in patriarchy, and served
as the citadel of male dominance, the chief inculcator of gender roles, and
a major inhibitor of change."[8] God tells Moses that the community must
kill children who curse their parents (Lev 20:9). Jesus, in sharp contrast,
says that his followers must hate father and mother (Luke 14:26; Matt
10:37). As Crossan notes, "the point of Jesus' attack on the family" has
nothing to do with the "usual explanation that families will become
divided as some accept and others refuse faith in Jesus. . . . *The attack has
nothing to do with faith but with power.* The attack is on the Mediterranean
family's axis of power."[9] In this context, Jesus calls forth a new family, not
limited to blood ties, but rather linked to living out God's will in the
world. When told that his mother and brothers are looking for him, Jesus
responds: "Here are my mother and my brothers! Whoever does the will
of God is my brother and sister and mother" (Mark 3:34b–35).

Citing Matt 23:9 ("call no one your father on earth, for you have one
Father—the one in heaven"), Wink notes that in "the new family of Jesus
there are only children, no patriarchs."[10] Here we see the connection

between Jesus' rejection of the patriarchal image of God the Father that dominated the tradition, his undermining of patriarchy within real families, and his alternative use of the same metaphor. Jesus uses the language of Father to describe what God is like but with different intent and meaning. As Schüssler Fiorenza explains:

> The saying of Jesus uses the "father" name of God not as a legitimation for existing patriarchal power structures in society or church but as a critical subversion of all structures of domination. . . . Neither the "brothers" nor the "sisters" in the Christian community can claim the "authority of the father" because that would involve claiming authority and power reserved to God alone.[11]

When Jesus uses "Father" imagery to name God, however, he is doing more than assigning power to God that had been claimed by abusive human fathers. He is redefining the meaning of power itself. Jesus refers to God as Father, or more informally as Daddy (Abba). Father/Abba language reflects the intimacy of Jesus' relationship with an intimate God. God, according to Jesus, is not a powerful, finger-pointing, male authority figure, emotionally removed and ruling from afar with an iron fist. Jesus' intimacy with the intimate Father/Abba, as we will see in future chapters, is the spiritual ground from which he challenges and undermines the abusive power that characterized the patriarchal household, Roman rule, and the Temple establishment and that infected and distorted the character of God within the tradition. The intimate tie between Abba and Jesus and the intimacy of Abba are the foundations from which Jesus breaks a deadly and disastrous linkage between violence and the divine. It is a linkage permeating human history from biblical times to our own. Jesus uses but subverts the traditional metaphor of God the "Father." His use of the metaphor has nothing to do with either the gender of the divine or the divinity of the offspring. It challenges abusive power within real households and calls into question all metaphors that project abusive power onto God.

RELIGIOUS EXPERIENCE

Diverse and competing biblical images of God reinforce the need to take our own religious experience seriously. It is a mistake to think that Jesus, the Bible, church dogma, or anything else can provide us with a spiritual road map that can substitute for our own faith journeys. God did not speak only or even primarily in the past. The Spirit of God is available to us now. Scripture is important, but we do not know or experience God primarily through scripture (what the Bible says about God) or tradition and dogma (what others tell us we should believe about faith and God). John Shelby Spong observes:

> It is almost typical of religious people to make idols out of their religious words. Perhaps in their quest for security, they identify their concept of God with God. When that concept is challenged, they think God is being challenged. That is why no concept of God can ever be more than a limited human construct, and personal words about God, we must learn to admit, reveal not God but our own yearning. . . . [A]ll Bibles, creeds, doctrines, prayers, and hymns are nothing but religious artifacts created to allow us to speak of our God experience at an earlier point in our history.[12]

Biblical metaphors are a well from which we can draw as we try to make sense of God in light of our own journeys of faith. They also give us permission to search out metaphors for God that reflect and enrich religious experience. Not all metaphors, however, are equal or even helpful. We should not be bound by metaphors found in the Hebrew and Christian Scriptures, nor can we allow them to serve as blind guides. The Bible tells us more about human beings than it does about God, and it does so even when it claims to be talking about God. Revelation within the biblical story, in my view, is rare, and it is often overwhelmed by distorted human projections. The Bible is both sacred and dangerous. It is sacred because God is revealed partially within the experiences of those responsible for its pages. That is why many of us return to it day after day and year after year in search of meaning and guidance. It is also a dangerous book because we often ascribe divine will to the many human distortions it contains. We undermine the sacredness of the Bible and fuel its dangers whenever we fail to discern the difference between distortion and revelation, whenever we give its words and its writers too much authority, or whenever we abandon or fail critically to examine the content of its pages. Stated simply, the Bible can inform our religious experience, but it is often wrong about God. Marcus Borg reminds us that the images of God we embrace matter:

> How are we to think of God? Some intellectual questions may not matter much, but this one has major consequences. What is

our concept of God (or the sacred, or Spirit, terms that I use interchangeably)? By "concept of God," I simply mean what we have in mind when we use the word God. All of us have some concept of God, whether vague or precise and whether we are believers or nonbelievers. My central claim is very direct: our concept of God matters. It can make God seem credible or incredible, plausible or highly improbable. It can also make God seem distant or near, absent or present. How we conceptualize God also affects our sense of what the Christian life is about. Is the Christian life centrally about believing, or is it about a relationship? Is it about believing in God as a supernatural being separate from the universe or about a relationship to the Spirit who is right here and all around us? Is it about believing in a God "out there" or about a relationship with a God who is right here?[13]

The images and metaphors we choose will determine our answers to many important questions. Is God concerned about justice and equality? If so, how does God express this concern? Is God violent or nonviolent? Merciful or judging? Can God be all of the above? Is God compassionate? Holy? Both? Is holiness always compatible with justice? Is God powerful? If so, what is God's power like? Is it expressed as superior violence? Redeeming love? Is God's mercy compatible with God's justice? Is God a theistic being inhabiting a space out there or the spiritual ground that envelops all of life?

These and related questions force us to be honest about five things. First, concepts of God rooted in biblical images and metaphors are often in conflict with each other. Second, not all biblical images of God are equally valid or valuable. Third, we must discern and choose between competing images of God with full awareness that our choices matter because our images of God affect the content and character of our faith. Fourth, Jesus can inform but cannot substitute for our own religious experience. Fifth, our religious experiences can be windows into the divine, but they too must be guided by a healthy dose of skepticism because our windows have plenty of smudges.

JESUS AND GOD

As Christians, we must be attentive to images of God that guided Jesus. Liberation theology suggests that faith *in* Jesus will be distorted unless we pay attention to the faith *of* Jesus.[14] Robert Funk has written that he is more interested in what Jesus reveals to us about God than he is in Christian claims that Jesus is God.[15] I am interested in both. At a minimum, we cannot make sense out of later Christian claims that Jesus is divine without fully probing the divine image Jesus embraces and reveals. Amidst incompatible metaphors and images, Jesus helps us see what God is and is not like. Intimate Abba is provocatively distinct from abusive Patriarchal Father or Judge. So also is the linkage of "kingdom" to mustard seed, a metaphor that offers an intentionally jolting contrast to Jewish expectations and our own.

I am also interested in the images and metaphors used by the Gospel writers to tell their versions of the Jesus story. One reason I speak of Jesus *against* Christianity is that the Gospel writers and Paul, as we will see, use many images and metaphors for God and Jesus that Jesus himself rejected. Jesus, who teaches forgiveness of others as a faithful response to the character of God, is often portrayed as a violent judge. Jesus, the practitioner of nonviolence, becomes a mouthpiece for the apocalyptic violence and vengeance of God. These and other contradictions point to the profound inadequacy of ignoring the historical Jesus. They also speak against tidy distinctions between the Jesus of history and the Christ of faith, or the pre-Easter and post-Easter Jesus. The "Christ of faith" declared within the New Testament often violates what the historical Jesus tells us about God elsewhere in the New Testament. Luke Timothy Johnson resolves this dilemma by refusing to acknowledge a problem. In a chapter entitled "The Continuing Mystery," he writes:

> The diversity of images of Jesus in the New Testament is indeed dazzling. What multiple associations are generated by each of the separate titles given to Jesus in these writings: teacher, Messiah, king, prophet, priest, Lord, Son of man, Son of God, first-born of the dead, amen. Savior, redeemer, servant, Righteous One, Son of David, Word, overseer, judge, advocate, witness, friend. And how much more complex those associations become when put into a variety of combinations by each composition. There are also the many metaphors and metonymies applied to Jesus—lamb, shepherd, door, vine, light, bread, water, blood, temple, spirit, anchor, stone, builder—which are also combined in intricate ways. It is impossible to select one of these titles or metaphors as more central than the others. They are all put in play by the compositions themselves for our learning of Jesus. None of them captures all

of Jesus; none is without some truth concerning Jesus. We are incredibly enriched precisely by their abundance and diversity, and we would be impoverished by the loss of any of them.[16]

This smorgasbord approach reduces theology to the art of bludgeoning square pegs into round holes and it does a fundamental disservice to Jesus. My point here is to stress that amidst competing biblical metaphors and images we must pay careful attention to Jesus, or more accurately, to incompatible portraits of Jesus presented in the Gospels. We should also look carefully at how the Gospel writers reflect or distort Jesus' images of God when they tell their versions of the Jesus story.

The historical Jesus can help judge the authenticity of our religious experience and help us choose between diverse biblical images and portraits of God. Jesus' life is a lens through which we see the divine, the world, scripture, and our life as people of faith. It unmasks human prejudice and distortion sanctified by reference to the divine. When Augustine meets God in his mind, says he has "attained the eternal wisdom which abides beyond all things," and then portrays God as terrifying and terrible; when he says he was touched by God who set him "on fire to attain that peace which was yours" and then portrays women as "the cause of Adam's sin and the companion of his damnation," then we have reason to doubt his religious claims. According to Tertullian and Augustine, the Son of God had to die because of Eve's sin. "What is the difference," Augustine wrote, "whether it is in a wife or a mother, it is still Eve the temptress that we must beware of in any woman."[17] As Karen Armstrong notes, for Augustine, woman's "only function was the childbearing which passed the contagion of Original Sin to the next generation, like a venereal disease."[18] That is why Augustine insisted the virgin birth had to be literally true because otherwise Jesus would not have been the perfect sacrifice required by God. What kind of tormented mind and deformed images of God gave rise to such distortions? Augustine's God-talk can be challenged by Jesus' life and faith.

The Crusades offer another example of why it is important to pay attention to the specifics of Jesus' life, including his images of God:

> The first Crusaders had seen their expedition to the Near East as a pilgrimage to the Holy Land, but they still had a very primitive conception of God and of religion. Soldier saints like St. George, St. Mercury and St. Demetrius figured more than God in their piety. . . . Jesus was seen as the feudal lord of the Crusaders rather than as the incarnate Logos: he has summoned his knights to

recover his patrimony—the Holy Land—from the infidel. As they began their journey, some of the Crusaders resolved to avenge his death by slaughtering the Jewish communities along the Rhine Valley. . . . it seemed simply perverse to many of the Crusaders to march 3,000 miles to fight the Muslims, about whom they knew next to nothing, when the people who had—or so they thought—actually killed Christ were . . . on their very doorsteps.[19]

Between these and other tragedies stands the long-ignored historical Jesus, who shows us what God is and is not like. Faith informed by Jesus, in other words, could have put the break on such deadly nonsense linking God to the Crusades and to Augustine's hatred of women and sex. Closer to home, if someone cites religious experience or scripture as a basis for killing or discriminating against homosexuals, then we can deny the validity of their claim and the implied image of God on which it is founded. We can do so based on human decency, our understanding of Jesus, and our critical appraisal of scriptural authority. Vile and violent biblical metaphors for God such as holy warrior, or others that we or others may invent as part of our religious experience, can be measured and judged, embraced or discarded in reference to Jesus' life as a revelation of God.

DOMINANT CHARACTER

A final implication that flows from the diversity and large number of images and metaphors is that they tend to obscure that the overwhelming portrayal of God in the Bible is as a brutal killer and punishing judge. God, as I will discuss in future chapters, orders people to execute children who curse their parents; sends forth she-bears to maul children who insult a prophet; punishes disobedient people by reducing them to cannibalism; orders the murder of all men, women, and children after battle; drowns nearly all of creation and humanity in a punishing flood; sends imperial armies to slaughter sinful people; promises eternal punishment for those who do not feed the hungry; and demands human sacrifice, recants, and then requires the bloody sacrifice of Jesus as atonement for human sin and as a means to reconciliation. None of this makes sense in light of the God embraced by the historical Jesus.

The point here is that God's cruel violence is downplayed or ignored when we emphasize the diverse and large number of biblical metaphors used to describe God. It is as if we describe a forty-foot-tall man by noting a great variety of characteristics: he has two eyes, hands, and feet; his hair is short and gray; he has a mustache; his eyes are blue and he is wearing glasses; he has a ring on the index finger of his left hand and a wart on his right thumb; he is wearing blue jeans with a small stain by the right knee and sneakers on his feet.

Missing from this description is that this man is tall. He is in fact gigantic and despite everything else we might say about him, it is his size that dominates. Reading the lengthy description above obscures this man's dominant characteristic. His overwhelming height gets lost in the length and detail of our portrayal. In a similar way, the numerous and diverse images of God named earlier divert attention from the fact that the overwhelming image of God in the Bible is that of a brutal, violent, and vengeful judge. In a world being torn apart by violence, there is no more urgent task than to counter the Bible's frequent and nauseating portraits of a ruthless and violent deity. The cruelty of God, however, is a problem that almost no one is willing to face squarely, including Christian interpreters. Two examples can illustrate this point adequately for now.

While reading Virginia Ramey Mollenkott's insightful book *The Divine Feminine: The Biblical Imagery of God as Female,* it seemed to me that she was so determined to lift up female images of God that she turned a blind eye to despicable characteristics that infect male and female images alike. Hosea 13, which in the New Revised Standard Version carries the caption, "Relentless judgment on Israel," uses metaphors of wild animals to describe God, who is about to devour the people because of their unfaithfulness. Verse 8 reads: "I will fall upon them like a bear robbed of her cubs, and will tear open the covering of their heart; there I will devour them like a lion, as a wild animal would mangle them."

Mollenkott defends this brutal image (and another in which a she-bear mauls forty boys for insulting a prophet in 2 Kings 2:24) because it overcomes stereotypes. "Understandably," she writes, "Hosea's image of an infuriated female God has never achieved the popularity of the gentler, more sentimental imagery of God as a loving and self-sacrificing Mother. . . . Precisely because the image of God as a savagely angry Mother Bear breaks all our stereotypes of how a woman (especially a mother) ought to behave it is an important image of our time."[20]

A second example is from John Dominic Crossan's description of Elijah and Elisha defending widows as part of their broader commitment to a Jewish God of justice:

But those two prophets not only helped widows and orphans, they also ruthlessly opposed the local pagan god Baal and toppled a Jewish dynasty that had accepted his worship. All of that went together, from their viewpoint. The Jewish god Yahweh was a divinity demanding traditional righteousness and justice. The pagan god Baal presumed a far less egalitarian society. Different divinities begat different monarchies, and those begat different rights and justices.[21]

Crossan does not mention that the "different rights and justices" begat by Yahweh apparently included Elijah's right to murder all the priests of Baal following a contest between them: "When all the people saw it [the fire of Yahweh, which consumed a burnt offering], they fell on their faces and said, 'The LORD indeed is God; the LORD indeed is God.' Elijah said to them, 'Seize the prophets of Baal; do not let one of them escape.' Then they seized them; and Elijah brought them down to the Wadi Kishon, and killed them there" (1 Kings 18:39–40).

Although Crossan uses the adverb "ruthlessly" in the above description, his treatment trivializes violence under the cover of liberation themes, a problem I will return to in later discussions of the exodus tradition. God's cruelty and propensity for violence are censored by many Christians, but the despicable characteristics that get attached to God throughout the Bible are undeniable. We may choose to ignore the violence of God at the heart of the Hebrew Scriptures and the New Testament because we have set our sights on liberation themes, or female images, or for any number of reasons. The consequence of our silence is that like any untreated pathology, it rears its ugly head and causes a great deal of destruction. It contributes mightily to human violence and the problem of war. It also helps explain why and how Christianity for all practical purposes is disconnected from Jesus. We must acknowledge, understand, and eventually rid ourselves of God the pathological killer or we won't be able to make sense out of the Bible, the justice tradition, Jesus as a revelation of God, or our own propensity to embrace redemptive violence in the name of the Divine.

Notes

1. Marcus Borg, *The God We Never Knew* (San Francisco: HarperSanFrancisco, 1997), 58.

2. Lewis M. Hopfe, *Religions of the World*, 6th ed. (Upper Saddle River, N.J.: Prentice-Hall, 1994), 10.

3. Quoted in Hopfe, *Religions of the World*, 11.

4. Virginia Ramey Mollenkott, *Women, Men, and the Bible* (New York: Crossroad, 1992) 53.

5. Borg, *God We Never Knew*, 62.

6. Elisabeth Schüssler Fiorenza, *But She Said: Feminist Practices of Biblical Interpretation* (Boston: Beacon Press, 1992), 53, emphasis in original.

7. Mollenkott, *Women, Men, and the Bible*, 40, emphasis in original.

8. Walter Wink, *Engaging the Powers: Discernment and Resistance in a World of Domination* (Minneapolis: Fortress Press, 1992), 118.

9. John Dominic Crossan, *Jesus: A Revolutionary Biography* (New York: HarperCollins, 1995), 59–60, emphasis in original.

10. Wink, *Engaging the Powers*, 119.

11. Elisabeth Schüssler Fiorenza, *In Memory of Her: A Feminist Theological Reconstruction of Christian Origins* (New York: Crossroad, 1983), 151.

12. John Shelby Spong, *Why Christianity Must Change or Die* (San Francisco: HarperSanFrancisco, 1998), 58.

13. Borg, *God We Never Knew*, 11.

14. See, for example, Jon Sobrino, S.J., *Christology at the Crossroads* (Maryknoll, N.Y.: Orbis Books, 1978).

15. Robert Funk, *Honest to Jesus* (San Francisco: HarperSanFrancisco, 1996), 11.

16. Luke Timothy Johnson, *Living Jesus: Learning the Heart of the Gospel* (San Francisco: HarperSanFrancisco, 1999), 198.

17. Quoted in Karen Armstrong, *A History of God* (New York: Ballantine Books, 1993), 121, 123–24.

18. Armstrong, *History of God*, 124.

19. Ibid., 197.

20. Virginia Ramey Mollenkott, *The Divine Feminine: The Biblical Imagery of God as Female* (New York: Crossroad, 1983), 51–52.

21. John Dominic Crossan, *The Birth of Christianity* (San Francisco: HarperSanFrancisco, 1998), 199.

CAN THIS REALLY BE GOD? PART 1
Land Thievery, Genocide, and Other Tales

I painted a picture of a God of justice and equality in chapter 1. Chapter 2 summarized many diverse and oftentimes incompatible images and metaphors for God. Chapters 3–5 focus on some of many violent and disturbing biblical portraits of God.

CHILD ABUSE FROM THE PULPIT

It was an unforgettable children's sermon. After many years I can name it now as child abuse from the pulpit. The setting was the mid-1970s at a suburban Lutheran church similar to the one I grew up in as a child. I should have known something was wrong when the pastor, a large and imposing figure, stood in the pulpit. He was like a mountain lion waiting to pounce on unsuspecting prey. He must not have been the regular pastor or the children would never have approached him willingly. "You are sinful, evil creatures," he began his verbal lashing. "You are worthless like a rotten apple and you deserve God's wrath." Smiles disappeared quickly as these innocent children absorbed blow after verbal blow, cowering beneath the weight of the pastor's hateful words. "You deserve to rot in hell," he continued. "God should throw you into a fire." The religious tongue-lashing was a lengthy preface to what this pastor considered his grace-filled punch lines. "You are worthless and rotten and deserve to rot in hell," he repeated, "but," he paused for effect, "God loves you so much that he sent his Son to die for your sins. And so you miserable, sinful children who deserve to be swallowed up by God's anger and rot in hell will not do so. Jesus died for your sins and you are forgiven. Amen."

This scene is permanently etched in my memory and I can only hope the children have forgotten it. The abusive rhetoric of this pastor will rightfully repulse many readers. His hateful words, theology, and brutal images of God, however, are supported by numerous passages in both the Hebrew Scriptures and the Christian New Testament. Those who express surprise at such a link probably do so for one of the following reasons. First, they may never have been associated with fundamentalist churches where such abusive rhetoric is common. Second, few Christians have read the Bible cover to cover. Those who read it selectively can live with a kind of biblical innocence that blocks out the pathology of God. Third, Christian interpreters ignore or downplay unpleasant images of God. Fourth, a great deal of censorship occurs within the church. Lectionaries that determine which Bible verses are read each Sunday in our churches, for example, often screen out God's pathology verse by verse and passage by passage. Pastors and priests do the same when they determine what is or is not a worthy sermon topic. Finally, many stories, such as Noah and the flood and Joshua and Jericho (discussed below), have been sanitized through art, interpretation, and familiarity.

SEVEN TROUBLING IMAGES OF GOD

Troubling Image of God 1: God Orders the Murder of Disobedient Children

> The Lord spoke to Moses, saying: "Say further to the people of Israel: . . . All who curse father or mother shall be put to death; having cursed father or mother, their blood is upon them" (Lev 20:1–2a, 9).

The injunction to kill disobedient children is fleshed out in other passages. In Deuteronomy, God commands the community to stone rebellious sons in order to "to purge the evil from your midst" (20:18–21). In 2 Kings, the prophet Elisha takes offense when some small boys call him

"baldhead." He curses them "in the name of the LORD" and immediately
two she-bears come out of the woods and maul forty-two boys (2:23–24).
David Penchansky writes in *What Rough Beast?* "that most interpretations
of this passage are primarily 'spin control.'" Frequently, "interpreters have
ignored this admittedly brief passage or they have imposed outlandish
interpretations to protect the reputation of YHWH." He continues:

> Complicity between Elisha and YHWH to accomplish the
> prophet's revenge on the youngsters is most consistent with a
> theme I have been tracing throughout this book, that God is
> dangerous and unpredictable, and might likely act in a jeal-
> ous, selfish, petulant, bitter, vengeful, and spiteful way. . . .
> What kind of god kills children because they show disrespect
> to his prophet? God appears to be petty, selfish, vain, and eas-
> ily angered, and overreacts in judgment and frequently regrets
> his actions.[1]

Troubling Image of God 2: A Means Test to Measure Faith: Willingness to Murder Our Children

> [God] said, "Take your son, your only son Isaac, whom you love,
> and go to the land of Moriah, and offer him there as a burnt
> offering on one of the mountains that I shall show you." . . . He
> bound his son Isaac, and laid him on the altar, on top of the
> wood. Then Abraham reached out his hand and took the knife
> to kill his son. But the angel of the LORD called to him from
> heaven, and said, "Abraham, Abraham!" And he said, "Here I
> am." He said, "Do not lay your hand on the boy or do anything
> to him; for now I know that you fear God, since you have not
> withheld your son, your only son, from me" (Gen 22:2, 9b–12).

Imagine the psychological trauma for father and son and for the voice-
less mother whose anguish is left out of the story. We should also consider the trauma our children experience when hearing such a tale.
Telling them that this was only a test (v. 1) or that the intent of the story
(as edited) is to criticize human sacrifice to the gods may not sufficiently
ease their emotional distress. Isaac, after all, was saved because Abraham
demonstrated the appropriate level of fear, an insight consistent with the
children's sermon recounted above. It is also likely that at various points

in its history the people of Israel practiced child sacrifice and that "in the original version of this story Isaac was actually sacrificed."[2]

There is also a troubling inconsistency. This story was edited during a period in which child-sacrifice was no longer considered pleasing to God, and yet Western Christianity interprets the death of Jesus in a sacrificial manner. John's Gospel introduces Jesus as "the Lamb of God" (1:29) and Jesus, according to the dominant Christian theologies of our time, is sent by God to die. The blood sacrifice of "God's only Son" is necessary to reconcile sinful humanity to God. Jesus' political murder at the hands of the Romans is interpreted through the lens of atonement. Jesus, who spoke of intimate Abba (Daddy), is the victim of Divine child abuse.

Troubling Image of God 3: An Angry, Punishing God Destroys the Earth

> And God said to Noah, "I have determined to make an end of all flesh, for the earth is filled with violence because of them; now I am going to destroy them along with the earth. . . . " *He blotted out every living thing that was on the face of the ground, human beings and animals and creeping things and birds of the air; they were blotted out from the earth.* Only Noah was left, and those that were with him in the ark (Gen 6:13, 7:23, emphasis added).

This image of God brings to mind a Dr. Strangelove-type maniac held up in a well-stocked bomb shelter with his finger poised on a nuclear trigger. The earth is filled with too much violence and so God violently destroys the earth and most of its inhabitants. We ignore the horrific violence of God at the heart of the flood story by focusing our attention on the rainbow promise that God will never again destroy the inhabitants of the earth: "When the bow is in the clouds, I will see it and remember the everlasting covenant between God and every living creature of all flesh that is on the earth" (Gen 9:16). Promises, as the old saying goes, are made to be broken. Zephaniah announces God's undoing of the rainbow promise to Judah during the reign of King Josiah:

> I will utterly sweep away everything
>   from the face of the earth, says the LORD.
> I will sweep away humans and animals;
>   I will sweep away the birds of the air
>   and the fish of the sea.

I will make the wicked stumble.
 I will cut off humanity
  from the face of the earth, says the LORD (Zeph 1:2–3).

God has a short memory or everlasting is not a very long time or there are not enough rainbows.

Troubling Image of God 4: God the Land Thief

On that day the LORD made a covenant with Abram, saying, "To your descendants I give this land, from the river of Egypt to the great river, the river Euphrates, the land of the Kenites, the Kenizzites, the Kadmonites, the Hittites, the Perizzites, the Rephaim, the Amorites, the Canaanites, the Girgashites, and the Jebusites" (Gen 15:18–21).

God is here depicted as a determined and powerful land thief. As the Reform Jewish writer Regina M. Schwartz notes, "over and over the Bible tells the story of a people who inherit at someone else's expense."[3] How would we respond to a group of Mexicans invading the United States and claiming the land as their inheritance based on God's promises? If that seems far-fetched, then imagine the reverse, which actually happened. We should also recall how our ancestors nearly wiped out native peoples and then continued onward and outward. Consider these words from U.S. Senator Albert J. Beveridge of Indiana in an 1898 speech:

God has . . . made us the master organizers of the world to establish system where chaos reigns. He has given us the spirit of progress to overwhelm the forces of reaction throughout the earth. He has made us adept in government that we may administer government among savage and senile peoples. Were it not for such a force as this the world would relapse into barbarism and night. And of all our race He has marked the American people as His chosen nation to finally lead in the regeneration of the world. This is the divine mission of America, and it holds for us all the profit, all the glory, all the happiness possible to man.[4]

A defense of God the land thief is implicit in both the biblical text and the quote above: It is okay for God's chosen people to steal land from pagans because they are pagans. They worship false gods. They, always defined as the other, are savage peoples, barbarians. These are but variations on the theme popularized during the Cold War in which anything was justified in the name of fighting godless communism. It was okay to kill "communists" even if they were in fact priests and nuns or doctors or peasants who were communists only in the eyes of their enemies. Returning to the Bible, consider this passage from Deuteronomy:

> When the LORD your God brings you into the land that you are about to enter and occupy, and he clears away many nations before you—the Hittites, the Girgashites, the Amorites, the Canaanites, the Perrizzites, the Hivites, and the Jebusites, seven nations mightier and more numerous than you—and when the LORD your God gives them over to you and you defeat them, then you must utterly destroy them. Make no covenant with them and show them no mercy. . . . But this is how you must deal with them: break down their altars, smash their pillars, hew down their sacred poles, and burn their idols with fire. For you are a people holy to the LORD your God; the LORD your God has chosen you out of all the peoples on earth to be his people, his treasured possession (7:1–2, 5–6).

The image of God as land thief is more problematic when we remember that pagans are people too. They create art, sing songs, worship, harvest, and live from the land. Richard Elliott Friedman explains:

> The dominant religion across the ancient Near East was pagan religion. Pagan religion was not idol worship, as formerly it was thought to be. . . . We can read the pagan hymns, prayers, and myths; we can see the places where they worshiped; and we can see how they depicted their gods in art. Pagan religion was close to nature. People worshiped the most powerful forces in the universe: the sky, the storm wind, the sun, the sea, fertility, death. The statues they erected were like the icons in a church. The statues depicted the god or goddess, reminded the worshiper of the deity's presence.[5]

A disturbing story in Judges 11 unites troubling images of God 2 (faith tested through willingness to engage in human sacrifice) and 4 (God as land thief) while raising the additional problem of God's violence in service to land-thievery. It is an account of "Jephthah the Gileadite, the son of a prostitute, ... a mighty warrior" (v. 1) who is recruited to fight the Ammonites on behalf of the Israelites. The basic plot line is that the people of Israel are preparing for war with the Ammonites whose land they are accused of stealing. They will let Jephthah rule over them if he defeats the Ammonites. The problem, according to the Ammonite king, is that "Israel, on coming from Egypt, took away my land from the Arnon to the Jabbok and to the Jordan." The solution he proposes seems reasonable: "now therefore restore it peaceably" (11:13). Jephthah refuses:

> The LORD, the God of Israel, has conquered the Amorites for the benefit of his people Israel. Do you intend to take their place? Should you not possess what your god Chemosh gives you to possess? And should we not be the ones to possess everything that the LORD our God has conquered for our benefit?" (vv. 23–24).

Instead of restoring the land to the Ammonite king or pursuing other peaceful means, Jephthah claims the land as gift by divine appropriation. He then makes a deal with the Lord, who has a reputation as a tribal deity willing to conquer others for the benefit of Israel. Grant me victory over my enemy, Jephthah tells God, and I will offer you a human sacrifice (11:30–33a):

> And Jephthah made a vow to the LORD, and said, "If you will give the Ammonites into my hand, then whoever comes out of the doors of my house to meet me, when I return victorious from the Ammonites, shall be the LORD's, to be offered up by me as a burnt offering." So Jephthah crossed over to the Ammonites to fight against them; and the LORD gave them into his hand. He inflicted a massive defeat on them.

The victorious warrior returns home. His daughter celebrates his victory with dancing and timbrels. Jephthah's victory, however, is her defeat. Yahweh promised to settle a land dispute with violence, and he delivered a bloody victory over the Ammonites on the battlefield. Jephthah promised a human sacrifice to Yahweh on the home front, and he delivers his daughter up for slaughter. As so often happens when a male warrior and a male deity plan together, the result is violence against women. Jephthah's daughter, who is nameless throughout the story, "returned to her father, who did with her according to the vow he had made" (v. 39b).

We are not told whether it was the bloody conquest, the land thievery, or the sacrifice of an innocent young woman that most pleased Yahweh. We are left, however, with troubling images of God in which Yahweh the land thief delivers bloody victory on the battlefield and in turn receives the bloody sacrifice of an unnamed daughter. Phyllis Trible includes this story in her *Texts of Terror*. "Under the power of the vow," she writes, "the daughter has breathed her last. My God, my God, why hast thou forsaken her?"[6]

Troubling Image of God #5: A Land-Thieving God Orders Humans to Commit Genocide

> Thus Israel settled in the land of the Amorites. Moses sent to spy out Jazer; and they captured its villages, and dispossessed the Amorites who were there. Then they turned and went up the road to Bashan; and King Og of Bashan came out against them, he and all his people, to battle at Edrei. But the LORD said to Moses, "Do not be afraid of him; for I have given him into your hand, with all his people, and all his land. You shall do to him as you did to King Sihon of the Amorites, who ruled in Heshbon." So they killed him, his sons, and all his people, until there was no survivor left; and they took possession of his land (Num 21:31–35).

The biblical writers often couple God-ordained land theft with divinely sanctioned genocide. "You must utterly destroy them . . . show them no mercy" (Deut 7:2). The book of Joshua indicates that God deliberately hardened the hearts of other groups inhabiting the land in order to facilitate extermination during warfare: "For it was the LORD's doing to harden their hearts so that they would come against Israel in battle, in order that they might be utterly destroyed, and might receive no mercy, but be exterminated, just as the LORD had commanded Moses" (Josh 11:20). Sometimes the murder pleasing to God is slightly less sweeping:

> The LORD spoke to Moses, saying, "Avenge the Israelites on the Midianites. . . . They did battle against Midian, as the LORD had commanded Moses, and killed every male. . . . The Israelites took the women of Midian and their little ones captive; and they took all their cattle, their flocks, and all their goods as booty. All their towns where they had settled, and all their encampments, they burned, but they took all the spoil and all the

booty, both people and animals. . . . Moses became angry with
the officers . . . who had come from service in the war. Moses
said to them, "Have you allowed all the women to live? . . . Now
therefore, kill every male among the little ones, and kill every
woman who has known a man by sleeping with him. But all the
young girls who have not known a man by sleeping with him,
keep alive for yourselves" (Num 31:1–2, 7, 9–11, 14–15, 17–18).

Moses orders the murder of all the male children (the men are already
dead) and all the women except virgins. One needs little imagination to
realize that many would not be virgins for long. Moses is angry with the
officers because they have not been ruthless enough to please God. This
could result in the congregation being punished by plague (Num 31:16),
as God was known to do in a variety of other settings. Plagues, in fact,
seem to be one of God's favorite deadly instruments. When the men
Moses sent out "brought an unfavorable report about the land [they] died
by a plague before the LORD" (Num 14:37). When the people grumbled
about having only quail to eat "the anger of the LORD was kindled against
the people, and the LORD struck the people with a very great plague"
(Num 11:33). Pharaoh and the Egyptians had a good deal of experience
with God-induced plagues: water turned to blood, frogs, gnats, flies, dis-
eased livestock, boils, thunder and hail, locusts, darkness, and the killing
of the firstborn (Exod 7–11).

We teach our children to sing "Who Built the Ark" and "Joshua Fought
the Battle of Jericho," but we leave out scenes of drowning humanity and
bloody carnage. The historical defeat of Joshua's enemies is cast in light
of divine will and action:

So the people shouted, and the trumpets were blown. As soon as
the people heard the sound of the trumpets, they raised a great
shout, and the wall fell down flat; so the people charged straight
ahead into the city and captured it. Then they devoted to
destruction by the edge of the sword all in the city, both men and
women, young and old, oxen, sheep, and donkeys (Josh 6:20–21).

Another link between the image of God as land thief and God-
sanctioned genocide is recorded in Deuteronomy:

The LORD said to me, "Do not fear him, for I have handed him
over to you, along with his people and his land." . . . And we

utterly destroyed them . . . in each city utterly destroying men, women, and children. But all the livestock and the plunder of the towns we kept as spoil for ourselves (3:2a, 6–7).

Troubling Image of God 6: God Is a Holy Warrior Capable of Genocide with or without Human Hands

Moses said, "Thus says the LORD: About midnight I will go out through Egypt. Every firstborn in the land of Egypt shall die, from the firstborn of Pharaoh who sits on his throne to the firstborn of the female slave who is behind the handmill, and all the firstborn of the livestock. Then there will be a loud cry throughout the whole land of Egypt, such as has never been or will ever be again" (Exod 11:4–6).

The biblical writers often describe humans as instruments of divinely sanctioned genocide. Deuteronomy 20 summarizes this view with simplistic horror: "But as for the towns of these peoples that the LORD your God is giving you as an inheritance, you must not let anything that breathes remain alive. You shall annihilate them" (vv. 16–17a). In the killing of the firstborn, which gave rise to the Jewish feast of Passover, genocide needs no human agency. The killing of the firstborn is an episode in the broader Exodus account. According to popularized versions of the Exodus (which I will challenge in the next chapter) a people, burdened and oppressed by Pharaoh, cry out for freedom. God hears their cry and promises to liberate them. God begins to actualize this promise by passing over the houses of the Israelites (they placed blood from the sacrifice of a lamb without blemish on their doorposts and lintel to alert God to their whereabouts) while murdering the firstborn of all Egyptians. God's murder of the firstborn, according to the book of Exodus, is done in service to this broader liberation project. God's violence, in other words, is understood as a central component of God's justice.

God wipes out all firstborn Egyptians, but freedom still seems an unlikely prospect. Maybe slavery isn't so bad after all and freedom not all it's cracked up to be. When things get difficult, the people grumble to Moses with biting sarcasm: "Was it because there were no graves in Egypt that you have taken us away to die in the wilderness?" (Exod 14:11).

The people's fears seem justified because the Egyptians have all the chariots. According to the Exodus account, however, God's violence is

sufficient for the task of freedom. The oppressors falter when God
secures the people's liberation at the crossing of the Reed (Red) Sea.

> But Moses said to the people, "Do not be afraid, stand firm, and
> see the deliverance that the LORD will accomplish for you today;
> for the Egyptians whom you see today you shall never see again.
> The LORD will fight for you, and you have only to keep still." . . .
> The Egyptians pursued, and went into the sea after them, all of
> Pharaoh's horses, chariots, and chariot drivers. At the morning
> watch the LORD in the pillar of fire and cloud looked down upon
> the Egyptian army, and threw the Egyptian army into panic. He
> clogged their chariot wheels so that they turned with difficulty.
> The Egyptians said, "Let us flee from the Israelites, for the LORD
> is fighting for them against Egypt. . . . So Moses stretched out
> his hand over the sea, and at dawn the sea returned to its nor-
> mal depth. As the Egyptians fled before it, the LORD tossed the
> Egyptians into the sea. The waters returned and covered the
> chariots and the chariot drivers, the entire army of Pharaoh that
> had followed them into the sea; not one of them remained
> (Exod 14:13–14, 23–25, 27–28).

Troubling Image of God 7: God Destroys God's People

Three citations from the prophets should sufficiently illustrate this point.
Each describes how God behaves when God's people act unjustly:

> Then Jeremiah said to them: Thus you shall say to Zedekiah:
> Thus says the LORD, the God of Israel: I am going to turn back
> the weapons of war that are in your hands and with which you
> are fighting against the king of Babylon and against the
> Chaldeans who are besieging you outside the walls; and I will
> bring them together into the center of this city. I myself will
> fight against you with outstretched hand and mighty arm, in
> anger, in fury, and in great wrath. And I will strike down the
> inhabitants of this city, both human beings and animals; they
> shall die of a great pestilence (Jer 21:3–6).

God here is depicted as a holy warrior fighting against God's chosen people. A similar passage from Isaiah reads:

> I myself have commanded my consecrated ones,
>   have summoned my warriors, my proudly exulting ones,
>   to execute my anger [against the people of Israel].
>
> They come from a distant land,
>   from the end of the heavens,
> the LORD and the weapons of his indignation,
>   to destroy the whole earth.
>
> See, the day of the LORD comes,
>   cruel, with wrath and fierce anger,
> to make the earth a desolation,
>   and to destroy its sinners from it.
>
> Whoever is found will be thrust through,
>   and whoever is caught will fall by the sword.
> Their infants will be dashed to pieces
>   before their eyes;
> their houses will be plundered,
>   and their wives ravished.
> See, I am stirring up the Medes against them . . . (Isa 13:3, 5, 9, 15–17a).

In the book of Lamentations (4:4, 9–11), God reduces the people to cannibalism. This must rank as one of the most disturbing passages in the Bible:

> The tongue of the infant sticks
>   to the roof of its mouth for thirst;
> the children beg for food,
>   but no one gives them anything.
>
> Happier were those pierced by the sword
>   than those pierced by hunger,
> whose life drains away, deprived
>   of the produce of the field.
>
> The hands of compassionate women
>   have boiled their own children;
> they became their food
>   in the destruction of my people.

The LORD gave full vent to his wrath;
    he poured out his hot anger,
and kindled a fire in Zion
    that consumed its foundations.

Tongues stick to the roof of the mouths of thirsty children, children beg for food but receive none, the fields yield no produce, compassionate women boil their children for food, and the people of God long to be killed with swords. Why? According to the "Holy Bible," it is because the "LORD gave full vent to his wrath," "poured out his hot anger" and "kindled a fire in Zion." God is cruel, violent, wrathful. God destroys sinners and God's fierce anger makes the earth desolate. God reduces the people to cannibalism and seems to take pleasure at the thought of infant stew. Infants are dashed to pieces. Wives are raped by armies doing God's dirty work. This is what God does to God's chosen people. God is known to others as a genocidal land thief and murderer. In retrospect, the images of God behind the vile children's sermon seem almost tame compared to the large stockpile of pathological possibilities. If this is God, then count me among the atheists.

THE PATHOLOGY OF GOD

There are two contact points in Webster's definition of pathology that lead me to choose this word to describe God's dominant character in the Bible. Pathology is defined as "deviation from propriety."[7] If we behaved like God often does in the Bible or did what God tells us to do within its pages, then our "deviation from propriety" would lead us straight to jail and we would stay there for a very long time. To repeat a prior illustration, anyone who advocated killing disobedient children, as God does in Leviticus and Deuteronomy, would and should be considered mentally ill, and those who went beyond words to murder should be imprisoned.

A second contact point with Webster's definition is pathology's link to disease. Mass murder moves on a spectrum from deviancy to disease, and mass murderers are known as "pathological" killers. God in much of the Bible shares troubling characteristics with such killers, including an overwhelming obsession with abusive, deadly violence.

One defense of God's abusive violence is that God is God and therefore can do or say anything. Another wraps God's pathology in a shroud of mystery. There are, according to this view, some things too mysterious for us to understand. We can also respond to God's pathology simply by ignoring how God's destructive violence is etched graphically onto page after page of the Bible. None of these approaches is the least bit helpful. The issue is not whether God can do what God likes or whatever pleases God. The fundamental question for people of faith is, What is God like? Or in our present context, Is God really as violent and vile as the biblical writers say?

CONCLUSION

Troubling images of God cascade from biblical texts like waterfalls after a violent storm. God's repugnant words and pathological behavior are so widespread as to be considered normative behavior for God! But let me be clear about what I am doing and why. I am *not* making a case that God is a pathological killer. I am saying that the biblical writers often portray God as a pathological killer. I am not arguing in favor of more vile children's sermons. I am saying that many biblical portraits of God can be called on to justify such sermons. The troubling truth is that the pastor's abusive rhetoric is rooted in images of God that are widespread within the Bible, both Old Testament and New. Our task is to confront and challenge rather than to ignore or embrace these terrifying images of God and to explore whether Jesus' faith and images of God are in harmony with or deviate from them.

Notes

1. David Penchansky, *What Rough Beast? Images of God in the Hebrew Bible* (Louisville, Ky.: Westminster John Knox Press, 1999), 82, 86.

2. Richard Elliott Friedman, *Who Wrote the Bible?* (San Francisco: HarperSanFrancisco, 1987), 257.

3. Regina M. Schwartz, *The Curse of Cain: The Violent Legacy of Monotheism* (Chicago: University of Chicago Press, 1997), x.

4. Quoted in John M. Blum et al., *The National Experience: A History of the United States* (New York: Harcourt Brace Jovanovich, 1963), 533.

5. Friedman, *Who Wrote the Bible?* 34–35.

6. Phyllis Trible, *Texts of Terror: Literary-Feminist Readings of Biblical Narratives* (Philadelphia: Fortress Press, 1984), 106.

7. *Merriam-Webster's Collegiate Dictionary*, 10th ed. (Springfield, Mass.: Merriam-Webster, 1996).

4 | CAN THIS REALLY BE GOD? PART 2
The Exodus Is not a Story of Liberation

I studied with Gustavo Gutierrez, the Peruvian liberation theologian, who placed the Exodus at the center of Christian theology. The idea that liberation was central to God's character and to the mission of the church profoundly shaped my faith. I lived in Nicaragua from 1984 to 1986 and have been a frequent visitor to Central America since. The liberation thrust of the Exodus seemed to come alive in the experiences of people whose hunger and poverty were products of a long history of oppressive rule often connected to the distorted policies and practices of the United States.[1]

Until recently, I focused on liberation themes in the Exodus account while turning my eyes from other troubling issues. I can no longer do so. Hence, let me note three challenges to the Exodus account. First, in real history, in sharp contrast to expectations and promises rooted in liberation interpretations of the Exodus, those who use violence and expect divine aid are often slaughtered. Second, I believe Jesus challenges the link between God and violence. This link is the central theme in the exodus and, in my view, the central problem confronting people of faith today, including Jews, Christians, and Muslims. Third, and the subject of this chapter, is that the book of Exodus itself does not conform to and in fact shatters the liberation lens that guides many modern interpretations of the Exodus.

DOES GOD'S JUSTICE DEPEND ON GOD'S VIOLENCE?

The first challenge to a liberation reading of the Exodus is the story's reliance on God's deadly violence as the means to God's justice. The way to overcome injustice and oppression, the book of Exodus says, is through redemptive violence, executed directly by God or through human hands:

> The LORD is a warrior; the LORD is his name. Pharaoh's chariots and his army he cast into the sea; his picked officers were sunk in the Red Sea (15:3–4). I will hand over to you the inhabitants of the land, and you shall drive them out before you (23:31b).

One problem with linking God's justice to God's violence is that people nearly always claim that justice and God are on *their* side. The centrality of justice and equality within the tradition should allow us to presume a Christian commitment to justice. The question for Christians concerns means. How does God work for justice? How should we? More specifically, does Jesus see God's violence or divinely sanctioned human violence as a necessary means to God's justice? The book of Exodus affirms very explicitly that God's violence or God-sanctioned human violence are the primary means by which God works for justice. The Gospel writers present conflicting information concerning Jesus, God, and violence. We must choose between their incompatible claims. If we answer, "No, Jesus does not see God's violence as a necessary component of God's justice," then our images of God and the content of our Christian faith will be very different than if we answer, "Yes."

CRACKS IN THE OPPRESSED VERSUS OPPRESSOR PARADIGM

A second concern that challenges traditional interpretations of the Exodus as a story of God's liberating violence on behalf of an oppressed people is that issues, then and now, are more complicated than the tidy division separating oppressed from oppressors. The Exodus paradigm that God's violence overcomes oppression is problematic for several reasons. We can first note how frequently modern conflicts are cast in God-talk in which human violence is justified in the name of God. We can also recall our own history in which near genocide of native peoples was justified theologically: God gave the land of the Canaanites to the Israelites/God gave the land of native peoples to European settlers. The writers of the book of Exodus paint a picture of God as a violent, murderous, genocidal land thief. The people displaced or killed by "God's chosen people" were targeted for divinely sanctioned slaughter. Neither bloody history nor the biblical accounts themselves allow us to see the Exodus as a story of God united with the oppressed against evil oppressors.

One defense of God stresses the historical inaccuracy of biblical accounts that portray conquest of the land through genocide. This defense challenges certain aspects of the Exodus story without challenging the basic liberation paradigm.[2] "Conquering the Canaanites," as Regina M. Schwartz writes, "was a fantasy of an exiled people."[3] This fantasy was recorded as history and inserted into the text by later writers. As Schwartz notes, however, when scholars recreate "historical versions of Israel's taking the promised land" they "turn out to be less violent, less oppressive, and less morally repugnant that the version in the biblical narrative." These efforts, however, cannot hide the "historian's sleight of hand" and cannot overcome the question "of ethical accountability."[4]

> And what about the biblical narrative? Should we hold it culpable for emblazoning this desire for land acquisition on its readers, inscribing deep into our culture the primordial myth of an exodus that justifies conquest? From one perspective—that of history of the text—the conquest narrative is only a wild fantasy written by a powerless dispossessed people who dream of wondrous victories over their enemies, of living in a land where milk and honey flow, and of entering that land with the blessing and support of an Almighty Deity. But from another perspective—that of the text's political afterlife—there is another story that is less appealing and considerably less innocent, telling of creating a people through the massive displacement and destruction of other peoples, of laying claim to a land that had belonged to others, and of conducting this bloody conquest under the banner of divine will.[5]

Like plutonium, theological distortions have an afterlife. They feed destructive historical patterns in which one people, with God's blessing, destroys another.

The oppressed versus oppressor paradigm also breaks down because the Exodus texts themselves do not conform to a reading in which God is said to take sides with the oppressed in a struggle for liberation. They portray God as tribal, brutal, and ethnically partial. Even the dogs carry out "God's will" by distinguishing between Israelites and Egyptians: "But not a dog shall growl at any of the Israelites—not at people, not at animals—so that you may know that the LORD makes a distinction between Egypt and Israel" (11:7). Animals escape the violence of God, only if they belong to Israelites:

> The hand of the LORD will strike with a deadly pestilence your livestock in the field: the horses, the donkeys, the camels, the herds, and the flocks. But the LORD will make a distinction between the livestock of Israel and the livestock of Egypt, so that nothing shall die of all that belongs to the Israelites (9:3–4).

The oppressed versus oppressor model breaks down further when we consider God's murder of the firstborn. Those killed range "from the firstborn of Pharaoh who sits on his throne to the firstborn of the female slave who is behind the handmill, and all the firstborn of the livestock" (11:5). The firstborn of *all* Egyptians, whether they be slaves who are undoubtedly oppressed under the pharaoh's rule or the oppressive pharaoh himself, are killed. *All* Israelites, no matter whether they be oppressed or collaborators with oppressors, are spared. God's "liberating" murder of the firstborn pits oppressed Israelites against oppressed Egyptian slaves because of ethnic or national identity.

The tendency to justify mass murder in response to a demonized leader is revealed in these texts and in our own recent history. In the aftermath of the Gulf War, Lance Morrow wrote in *Time* that "Americans almost unconsciously regard the victory as a kind of moral cleansing: the right thing. But reality and horror have not been rescinded." Earlier in the essay he stated:

> It is not inconsequential to kill 100,000 people. That much life suddenly and violently extinguished must leave a ragged hole somewhere in the universe. . . . The victors have not given them much thought. Still, killing 100,000 people is a serious thing to do. It is not equivalent to shooting a rabid dog, which is, down deep, what Americans feel the war was all about, exterminating a beast with rabies. . . . They were ordinary people: peasants, truck drivers, students and so on. They had

the love of their families, the dignity of their lives and work. . . .
The secret of much murder is to dehumanize the victim, to
make him alien, to make him Other, a different species. . . . To
kill 100,000 people and to feel no pain at having done so may
be dangerous to those who did the killing. It hints at an
impaired humanity.[6]

Returning to the Exodus texts, the violence and solidarity of God manifested through barking dogs and murder are based not on justice for
oppressed people but on ethnic or national identity. The liberation framework breaks down further and the ethnic lens comes into sharper focus
when we take a closer look at Lev 25:39–46, which outlines the sabbatical provisions of debt forgiveness, freedom of slaves, and jubilee. These
provisions apply to Israelites alone:

If any [Israelites] who are dependent on you become so impoverished that they sell themselves to you, you shall not make
them serve as slaves. They shall remain with you as hired or
bound laborers. They shall serve with you until the year of the
jubilee. Then they and their children with them shall be free
from your authority; they shall go back to their own family and
return to their ancestral property. For they are my servants,
whom I brought out of the land of Egypt; they shall not be sold
as slaves are sold. You shall not rule over them with harshness,
but shall fear your God. As for the male and female slaves whom
you may have, it is from the nations around you that you may
acquire male and female slaves. You may also acquire them from
among the aliens residing with you, and from their families that
are with you, who have been born in your land; and they may
be your property. You may keep them as a possession for your
children after you, for them to inherit as property. These you
may treat as slaves, but as for your fellow Israelites, no one shall
rule over the other with harshness.

The Exodus cannot be about God's liberating violence on behalf of
slaves when God's murder of the firstborn includes Egyptian slaves and
when the Holiness Code authorizes the Israelites to acquire slaves among
resident aliens and from surrounding nations. These texts force us to
challenge idealized readings that focus on a liberation-oppression paradigm, including the notion of God's liberating violence. They also com-

pel us to add xenophobia, irrational hatred of other races or groups, to our list of despicable characteristics of God.

SUPERIOR VIOLENCE PROVES GOD IS GOD

A third challenge to a liberation reading of the Exodus is that according to the book of Exodus God is God because of superior violence. "Now I know that the LORD is greater than all gods, because he delivered the people from the Egyptians, when they dealt arrogantly with them" (18:11). After describing God's furious violence consuming Israel's adversaries like stubble, the Song of Moses continues: "Who is like you, O LORD, among the gods? Who is like you, majestic in holiness, awesome in splendor, doing wonders? You stretched out your right hand, the earth swallowed them. . . . Terror and dread fell upon them" (Exod 15:11–12, 16a).

The conviction that God proves to be God through superior violence is deeply rooted in the scriptures. Superior, brutal, avenging, hateful violence directed against the enemies of Israel, disobedient Israelites, or all of creation is what proves that God is God.

> Has any god ever attempted to go and take a nation for himself from the midst of another nation, by trials, by signs and wonders, by war, by a mighty hand and an outstretched arm, and by terrifying displays of power, as the LORD your God did for you in Egypt before your very eyes? To you it was shown so that you would acknowledge that the LORD is God; there is no other besides him (Deut 4:34–35).

The book of Ezekiel confirms that God is God because of superior violence. The phrase (or a variation of the same) "then you shall know that I am the LORD" is used at least sixty-five times, mostly in a context similar to these representative passages. "Those far off shall die of pestilence; those nearby shall fall by the sword; and any who are left and are spared shall die of famine. Thus I will spend my fury upon them. And you shall know that I am the LORD" (6:12–13a). "My anger shall spend itself, and I will vent my fury on them and satisfy myself; and they shall know that I, the LORD, have spoken in my jealousy, when I spend my fury on them (5:13).

We know God is God because of terrifying violence directed against the disobedient people of God or their enemies. Superior violence not only proves that God is God, it is a manifestation of God's holiness (see

Exod 15:11) and glory. Isaiah 6:3 presents God as gloriously violent: "Holy! Holy! Holy is Yahweh Sabaoth [the god of the armies]. His glory fills the whole earth." Returning to the Exodus account, God says:

> Then I will harden the hearts of the Egyptians so that they will go in after them; and so I will gain glory for myself over Pharaoh and all his army, his chariots, and his chariot drivers. And the Egyptians shall know that I am the LORD, when I have gained glory for myself over Pharaoh, his chariots, and his chariot drivers (Exod 14:17–18).

Superior violence demonstrates glory over Pharaoh, his army, and Egypt's gods: "For I will pass through the land of Egypt that night, and I will strike down every firstborn in the land of Egypt, both human beings and animals; on all the gods of Egypt I will execute judgments: I am the LORD" (12:12).

The violence of God is justified within the oppressed versus oppressor paradigm because Yahweh, unlike all other gods, uses violence to defeat rather than to shore up empire. Imperial wisdom says the gods bless empires and that is why they are powerful. The defense of God's "liberating violence" links traditional gods with oppressive empires and the God of the Bible with the anti-imperial struggles of oppressed slaves. The implication is that God's violence is a necessary component of God's justice because it is part of the people's struggle against imperial politics and religion. This is the perspective of many progressive Christian activists and interpreters.

John Dominic Crossan illustrates the tendency to downplay God's violence by subordinating it to a broader justice agenda. Crossan says, as noted previously, that Elijah and Elisha had defended widows and orphans while "ruthlessly" opposing "the local pagan god Baal." These "went together, from their viewpoint," he claims, because the "Jewish god Yahweh was a divinity demanding traditional righteousness and justice. The pagan god Baal presumed a far less egalitarian society."[7] God and human violence are justified because they are subordinated to a broader fight for an egalitarian society on behalf of an egalitarian deity. A second example is Crossan's claim that "when God is revealed by freeing doomed slaves from imperial control the future is set on a collision course with domination, oppression, and exploitation."[8] Violence is again seen as the necessary means by which God or the people of God thwart empires and seek justice.

I believe Crossan is right in saying that authentic God and faith inevitably clash with the forces of domination. The Exodus, however, does not fit this view of God aligned with doomed slaves and against imperial control and assertions that it does often justify violence done in God's name. Traditional Exodus interpretations say that God's liberating violence and human violence in service to a just God are good and necessary, while imperial violence, justified by empires and their gods, is bad. According to the oppressed versus oppressor model, God's successful liberating violence frees slaves, defeats Pharaoh, and proves that God is God.

This anti-imperial thrust may seem compelling, but it breaks down due to historical abuse and within the text itself. It collapses in the face of many biblical texts and promises. Third Isaiah promises a scattered, oppressed people that they will one day be *the* imperial nation.[9] The "wealth of the nations shall come to you," the prophet promises. "For the nation and kingdom that will not serve you shall perish; those nations shall be utterly laid waste" (Isa 60:5b, 12). Second Isaiah says much the same thing (45:14a, 17):

> Thus says the LORD:
> The wealth of Egypt and the merchandise of Ethiopia,
>   and the Sabeans, tall of stature,
> shall come over to you and be yours,
>   they shall follow you;
>   they shall come over in chains and bow down to you.
>
> But Israel is saved by the LORD
>   with everlasting salvation;
> you shall not be put to shame or confounded
>   to all eternity.

Second Isaiah goes on to describe Babylon's coming humiliation. God declares, "I will take vengeance, and I will spare no one. Our Redeemer— the LORD of hosts is his name—is the Holy One of Israel" (47:3b–4). There is not one shred of anti-imperial pretension in these promises, only the promise of revenge and a hoped-for reversal.

The presumption of God's anti-imperial stand within the Exodus story is further undermined by the biblical hero Joseph who is featured prominently in Genesis as a servant of Pharaoh. Joseph has a cozy relationship with empire and is blessed by God. His memory casts a shadow over the book of Exodus. The first chapter introduces a conflict with the words:

"Now a new king arose over Egypt, who did not know Joseph" (Exod 1:8). This passage points us back to Joseph's relationship to God and to Pharaoh (a king who did know Joseph) in the Genesis account. God, according to Gen 45:8, made Joseph "a father to Pharaoh, and lord of all his house and ruler over all the land of Egypt."

We will soon see how Joseph paved the way for the oppression of both Israelites and Egyptians through his use of food as a weapon. Already, however, we see that God is not hostile to empire as the Exodus paradigm of oppressed versus oppressor strongly asserts. God is said to have blessed Joseph who rules on behalf of Pharaoh. Joseph's father (Jacob) blesses Pharaoh. Pharaoh in turn allows Jacob and Joseph's brothers to settle "in the land of Egypt, in the best part of the land" (47:11). No human or divine character in the story is the least bit hostile to empire. All benefit from and have a role in imperial power that has many rewards. Joseph pleases both God and Pharaoh and pleases God by serving Pharaoh. With God's blessing he enriches Pharaoh and dramatically expands the power of the Egyptian empire. In Joseph's skillful hands, famine is an instrument of oppression. Step 1 is to get all the money:

> Now there was no food in all the land, for the famine was very severe. The land of Egypt and the land of Canaan languished because of the famine. Joseph collected all the money to be found in the land of Egypt and in the land of Canaan, in exchange for the grain that they bought; and Joseph brought the money into Pharaoh's house (47:13–14).

Step 2 is to take control of all the livestock:

> When the money from the land of Egypt and from the land of Canaan was spent, all the Egyptians came to Joseph, and said, "Give us food! Why should we die before your eyes? For our money is gone." And Joseph answered, "Give me your livestock, and I will give you food in exchange for your live-stock, if your money is gone." So they brought their livestock to Joseph; and Joseph gave them food in exchange for the horses, the flocks, the herds, and the donkeys. That year he supplied them with food in exchange for all their livestock (47:15–17).

Step 3 is to enslave all Egyptians and take their land:

> When that year was ended, they came to him the following year, and said to him, "We can not hide from my lord that our money is all spent; and the herds of cattle are my lord's. There is nothing left in the sight of my lord but our bodies and our lands. Shall we die before your eyes, both we and our land? Buy us and our land in exchange for food. We with our land will become slaves to Pharaoh; just give us seed, so that we may live and not die, and that the land may not become desolate." So Joseph bought all the land of Egypt for Pharaoh. All the Egyptians sold their fields, because the famine was severe upon them; and the land became Pharaoh's. As for the people, he made slaves of them from one end of Egypt to the other (47:18–21).

The book of Exodus picks up the story shortly after Joseph's use of food as a weapon on behalf of Pharaoh. It begins with a report that "the Israelites were fruitful and prolific; they multiplied and grew exceedingly strong, so that the land [Egypt] was filled with them" (1:7). The story begins, in other words, not with a portrait of vulnerable Israelites but rather with a privileged, prolific, and powerful people poised to take over a land that is not their own.

The Genesis texts imply that Joseph's relatives prospered during and after the time in which Joseph served Pharaoh and brutally used food as a weapon so that all Egyptians became penniless, landless slaves (Gen 47:27). Pharaoh, as noted previously, had given Joseph's relatives the best land in Egypt. Oppression is always wrong, and unless its causes are rooted out it always resurfaces within an inevitable spiral of violence. In the context of Joseph's brutal oppression of the Egyptians on behalf of Pharaoh and the Israelites favored treatment over their enslaved Egyptian counterparts, it is understandable why a new king who did not know Joseph might fear the powerful Israelites and even oppress them. A policy of repressing Israelites may have had broad public support among oppressed Egyptians who would have viewed persecution of Israelites as justified retribution for past wrongs. Egyptian resentment against the prolific and powerful Israelites who occupied Egypt's best lands while Egyptians were landless boiled over into violence against the beneficiaries of Joseph's oppressive rule.

Placing the Exodus in the context of Joseph's service to Pharaoh and successful food weapon strategy can help us see the cycles of violence and oppression at the heart of many conflicts. It is a necessary corrective to idealized versions of the Exodus centered in the oppressed versus oppressor story line. It moves us, as it should, far away from the notion of the liberating violence of Yahweh in service to a broader liberation agenda and towards an understanding of the spiral of violence that lies at the heart of all oppressive rule, whether Egyptian, Israeli, Roman, Salvadoran, or American. If we idealize the Exodus tradition, then we ignore powerful lessons that could be learned about cycles of violence and oppression and about human distortions of God. We also make it difficult if not impossible to understand Jesus and Jesus' experience of God in relation to the spiral of violence in first-century Palestine.

Stories in which God's servant Joseph blesses Pharaoh, rules Egypt, uses food as a weapon, and robs all Egyptians of their money, cattle, land, and freedom are incompatible with traditional interpretations of the Exodus. They undermine claims that God's liberating violence is a necessary feature of God's justice. God cannot with integrity bless empire and oppression in the Joseph accounts and then be heralded as a distinctive, anti-imperial deity in the Exodus.

The images of God in the book of Exodus have more to do with human distortion and tribal and ethnic biases than with divine inspiration. It is okay for Joseph and other Israelites to cooperate with and benefit from Pharaoh's rule at the expense of impoverished Egyptians. It is not okay for Pharaoh to oppress Israelites. It is okay for Israelites to have slaves from foreign nations and from among resident aliens (and for God to murder Egyptian slaves as part of the killing of the firstborn) but it is not okay for Israelites to be enslaved by foreigners or to hold other Israelites as slaves. These abuses of power and ethnically based distinctions clash sharply with the Exodus paradigm that Yahweh's opposition to empire, slavery, and injustice separates Yahweh from other gods. They also undermine claims that Yahweh's violence is justifiable because it is liberating violence that breaks traditional links between religion and empire, God and oppression.

We can now return to the disturbing problem that the book of Exodus reveals: that God is God because of superior violence. Exodus 14:17–18 says that it is God who hardens Pharaoh's heart and thereby blocks the desired liberation. Why does God demand and then prevent liberation? This question can be answered on three levels. Some of the Israelites who eventually made their home in Canaan were probably slaves in Egypt. It is likely that something went wrong at the level of history.

Perhaps freedom took longer than anticipated. Delayed freedom posed a theological problem for a people who proclaimed God to be powerful, in control of history, and on their side. People explained the discrepancy between God's capacity to free them and the absence of freedom by asserting that God hardened Pharaoh's heart.

The third level of probing flows from the text itself, which says that God demands and then prevents liberation by hardening Pharaoh's heart because God wants an opportunity to demonstrate superior violence. Why? Because superior violence proves that God is God and makes God's glory clear to all. "I will harden Pharaoh's heart, and he will pursue them, so that I will gain glory for myself over Pharaoh and all his army; and the Egyptians shall know that I am the LORD. And they did so" (14:4). The same point is made when God instructs Moses to tell Pharaoh why God had let Pharaoh live:

> For this time I will send all my plagues upon you yourself, and upon your officials, and upon your people, so that you may know that there is no one like me in all the earth. For by now I could have stretched out my hand and struck you and your people with pestilence, and you would have been cut off from the earth. But this is why I have let you live: to show you my power, and to make my name resound through all the earth (9:14–16).

God hardens Pharaoh's heart in order to create an opportunity to prove that God is God through superior violence. Hardness of heart is God's pretext to demonstrate power, holiness, and glory through violence. This is not only an ancient impulse. The United States dropped a nuclear bomb on Hiroshima and a second one on Nagasaki at the end of World War II, not to defeat the Japanese but to send a message to the Soviet Union. General Colin Powell, when head of the Joint Chiefs of Staff, reportedly said shortly after the Berlin Wall came crashing down and on the eve of the U.S. invasion of Panama that "we have to put a shingle outside our door saying superpower lives here no matter what the Soviets do, even if they evacuate all of Eastern Europe."[10] The 1991 Gulf War offers another example. Iraq agreed to pull its troops from Kuwait and when its soldiers retreated they were slaughtered. The U.S. "turkey shoot" in Iraq was a deadly advertisement for sophisticated weapons. The Pentagon produced its own rock video about the effectiveness of these weapons, and U.S. arms sales increased dramatically.

GOD'S SUPERIOR VIOLENCE INSPIRES BELIEF

The idea that God is God because of superior violence and that superior violence is an expression of God's holiness and glory is deeply troubling. In the book of Exodus, it is superior violence that inspires belief in God, and God uses superior violence to inspire belief. God's superior violence prompts worship and inspires rituals. "Israel saw the great work that the LORD did against the Egyptians. So the people feared the LORD and believed in the LORD and in his servant Moses" (14:31). Exodus 12:23–27 reads:

> For the LORD will pass through to strike down the Egyptians; when he sees the blood on the lintel and on the two doorposts, the LORD will pass over that door and will not allow the destroyer to enter your houses to strike you down. You shall observe this rite as a perpetual ordinance for you and your children. When you come to the land that the LORD will give you, as he has promised, you shall keep this observance. And when your children ask you, "What do you mean by this observance?" you shall say, "It is the passover sacrifice to the LORD, for he passed over the houses of the Israelites in Egypt, when he struck down the Egyptians but spared our houses." And the people bowed down and worshiped.

A God of superior violence begets violence among followers, including and especially among priestly factions who vie for authority to mediate between humans and God. According to one strand of the tradition that sought to denigrate Aaron and lift up Moses (and priests aligned with Moses), the Levites ordained themselves through violence (Exod 32:26–29):

> Then Moses stood in the gate of the camp, and said, "Who is on the LORD's side? Come to me!" And all the sons of Levi gathered around him. He said to them, "Thus says the LORD, the God of Israel, 'Put your sword on your side, each of you! Go back and forth from gate to gate throughout the camp, and each of you kill your brother, your friend, and your neighbor.'" The sons of Levi did as Moses commanded, and about three thousand of the people fell on that day. Moses said, "Today you have ordained yourselves for the service of the LORD, each one at the cost of a son or a brother, and so have brought a blessing on yourselves this day."

Real God is separated from false god(s) by the efficacy of violence. First Kings describes a competition between two prophets representing two gods. Elijah wins the competition and presumes his right to express victory through violence. In this instance the issue is not an inner dispute between the priests of Aaron and the priests of Moses. It is a situation in which different gods and different peoples attempt to inhabit the same space.

First Kings describes a deadly conflict pitting the prophets of Baal, a Canaanite god who controlled agriculture and fertility, against the prophets of Yahweh. Many Israelites worshiped Baal. Perhaps they were struck by similarities between various Canaanite gods and Yahweh, or maybe they were intimidated by the fact that all the prophets of Yahweh except Elijah had been murdered.

Elijah suggests a way to settle the dispute. He and his adversaries each take a bull, lay it on piles of wood and call on the name of their respective god to light the fire:

> So they [the prophets of Baal] took the bull that was given them, prepared it, and called on the name of Baal from morning until noon, crying, "O Baal, answer us!" But there was no voice, and no answer. They limped about the altar that they had made. At noon Elijah mocked them, saying, "Cry aloud! Surely he is a god; either he is meditating, or he has wandered away, or he is on a journey, or perhaps he is asleep and must be awakened" (1 Kings 18:26–27).

Elijah, for dramatic purposes, douses his wood. He wins the competition between the gods when the fire of the Lord consumes the burnt offering and the water lining the trench:

> When all the people saw it, they fell on their faces and said, "The LORD indeed is God; the LORD indeed is God." Elijah said to them, "Seize the prophets of Baal; do not let one of them escape." Then they seized them; and Elijah brought them down to the Wadi Kishon, and killed them there (18:39–40).

In the book of Exodus we have the troubling claim that God is God and proves it in competition with other gods through superior violence. Here we have the logical corollary: those who win the competition between the gods, whether through superior violence, as in the Exodus, or a consuming fire, as in 1 Kings, presume the right to violently destroy their adversaries. Violence both redeems and is an instrument of revenge.

SALVATION UNDERSTOOD AS DEFEAT OF ENEMIES

I am concerned about the definition of salvation that emerges out of the common interpretation of the Exodus as a story of God's liberating violence on behalf of an oppressed people. The book of Exodus, many psalms, and much of the Hebrew Scriptures define salvation as the defeat of enemies.

> Thus the LORD *saved* Israel that day from the Egyptians; and Israel saw the Egyptians dead on the seashore (Exod 14:30, emphasis added).

> Then Moses and the Israelites sang this song to the LORD:
> "I will sing to the LORD, for he has triumphed gloriously;
>   horse and rider he has thrown into the sea.
> The LORD is my strength and my might,
>   and he has become *my salvation*. . . .
> The LORD is a warrior;
>   the LORD is his name.
> Pharaoh's chariots and his army he cast into the sea. . . ."
>   (Exod 15:1–3a,4a, emphasis added).

> Foreigners lost heart,
>   and came trembling out of their strongholds.
> The LORD lives! Blessed be my rock,
>   and exalted be the God of *my salvation*,
> the God who gave me vengeance
>   and subdued peoples under me;
> who delivered me from my enemies . . . (Ps 18:45–48a, emphasis added).

> It will be said on that day,
>   Lo, this is our God; we have waited for him, so that he might
>   *save us*.
>   This is the LORD for whom we have waited;
>   let us be glad and rejoice in his *salvation*.
> For the hand of the LORD will rest on this mountain.
> The Moabites shall be trodden down in their place
>   as straw is trodden down in a dung-pit (Isa 25:9–10, emphasis added).

CONCLUSION

The centrality of God's violence in the Exodus account raises many questions and concerns. Is God's violence a necessary component of God's justice? Can we interpret the Exodus through the lens of oppression and liberation without asking about the murder of the firstborn Egyptian slaves? Can we justify land theft without remembering falsified history and distorted theology? Can we say that God breaks the link between God and empire without closing our eyes to Joseph's role in enslaving Egyptians on behalf of Pharaoh? Can we ignore those in Canaan who, according to the text, were displaced and murdered by divine mandate? Can we fail to see parallels in present-day conflicts between Palestinians and Israelis, or within our own historical legacy of genocide against native peoples justified through appeals to God and manifest destiny? Is God a violent, murderous, and genocidal land thief? Is God really God because of superior violence? Does God need and create opportunities to express superior violence as a measure of God's holiness and glory? Does God use superior violence to inspire belief? Is salvation to be understood as annihilation, defeat, or vengeance against enemies?

The answer to each question, according to the book of Exodus and numerous other biblical texts, is unhesitatingly Yes. My answer, based on the history of violence and the life and faith of Jesus, is resoundingly No. The concerns raised during this detour into the Exodus account press forward the problem of God's pathology. The problem intensifies as we examine troubling images of God within the New Testament.

Notes

1. See Jack Nelson-Pallmeyer, *School of Assassins* (Maryknoll, N.Y.: Orbis Books, 1998).

2. Regina M. Schwartz, *The Curse of Cain: The Violent Legacy Of Monotheism* (Chicago: University of Chicago Press, 1997), x.

3. Ibid., 4.

4. Ibid., 61.

5. Ibid., 57.

6. Lance Morrow, "A Moment for the Dead," *Time*, 1 April 1991.

7. John Dominic Crossan, *The Birth of Christianity* (San Francisco: HarperSanFrancisco, 1998), 199.

8. Ibid., 184.

9. Many scholars believe the book of Isaiah reflects the work of three distinct writers who wrote in different historical contexts.

10. Quoted by Michael Klare, "Facing South: The Pentagon and the Third World in the 1990s," a talk given at the University of Minnesota, 5 October 1990.

5 CAN THIS REALLY BE GOD? PART 3
Troubling Images of God from the New Testament

The troubling images of God described thus far have been drawn from the Hebrew Scriptures. This could lead to the false impression that the "Jewish God" of the Hebrew Bible is distinct from the "Christian God" of the New Testament, with the "Jewish God" being bad or violent and the "Christian God" being good or nonviolent. Many positive images of God discussed in chapter 1 are affirmed in the life and faith of Jesus, and many pathological images of God rejected by Jesus carry over into the New Testament and receive prominent place in Gospel interpretations of Jesus. The present chapter addresses the pathology of God deeply imbedded in the Christian New Testament.

CONTINUITY

There is a basic continuity of themes between the Hebrew Scriptures and the Christian New Testament. Four examples should be sufficient to warn against erecting a wall separating Jesus from his Jewish roots or from idealizing New Testament portraits of God in contrast with the Hebrew Scriptures. The first is the Feast of Passover that commemorates the defeat of Israel's enemies. God's redemptive violence is reenacted and reaffirmed through the remembrance of God's murder of firstborn Egyptians and sparing of Israelites as part of God's liberation project. The Gospels set the execution of Jesus at or near Passover, a time of great tension between the Jews and the Romans. The fact that Jesus is executed by order of an imperial official during a period of oppression creates a sense of parallelism between Passover's original Exodus setting and oppression in first-century Palestine.

A second example of continuity in themes is Mary's song, which was carefully crafted in relation to Hannah's prayer. Both Hannah and Mary anticipate or celebrate defeat of enemies and the reversal of fortunes made possible by God's saving acts:

Hannah prayed and said,
"My heart exults in the LORD;
   my strength is exalted in my God.
My mouth derides my enemies
   because I rejoice in my victory. . . .
The bows of the mighty are broken,
   but the feeble gird on strength.
Those who were full have hired themselves out for bread,
but those who were hungry are fat with spoil" (1 Sam 2:1, 4–5a).

And Mary said,
"My soul magnifies the Lord,
   and my spirit rejoices in God my Savior. . . .
He has shown strength with his arm;
   he has scattered the proud in the thoughts of their hearts.
He has brought down the powerful from their thrones,
   and lifted up the lowly;
he has filled the hungry with good things,
   and sent the rich away empty" (Luke 1:46–47, 51–53).

A third example of continuity is a coded story in Mark's Gospel modeled on the destruction of Pharaoh's army in the Reed Sea. The story is cast in terms of a confrontation between Jesus and a demon named

Legion. It reflects the dreams of a Jewish revolutionary in Roman occupied Palestine, where Roman soldiers (two thousand soldiers make up a legion) maintained imperial control. Watch what happens to "Legion" at the end of the confrontation and note its parallels with the Reed Sea account:

> Then Jesus asked him, "What is your name?" He replied, "My name is Legion; for we are many." He begged him earnestly not to send them out of the country. Now there on the hillside a great herd of swine was feeding; and the unclean spirits begged him, "Send us into the swine; let us enter them." So he gave them permission. And the unclean spirits came out and entered the swine; and the herd, numbering about two thousand, rushed down the steep bank into the sea, and were drowned in the sea" (Mark 5:9–13).

Two thousand spirits occupied Legion at a time when Roman legions occupied Palestine. In Mark's coded version they beg not to be sent out of the country. They end up in a herd of swine (the most unclean animal for Jews) at the bottom of the sea. This story reminds us that the New Testament reflects an ongoing struggle concerning expectations and images of God. Many of Jesus' contemporaries expected God to defeat Roman soldiers as part of a salvation plan just as God had defeated the oppressive armies of Pharaoh. Some followers clearly believed Jesus was the one to free Israel from Roman imperialism. The story of Legion, whatever its origin, placed Jesus in continuity with the tradition linking the violence of God to the justice of God.

A fourth point of continuity between the Hebrew Scriptures and Christian New Testament is the integration of Exodus themes within baptism rituals. John baptized people in the river Jordan, the river that, according to foundational lore, the Israelites crossed to live freely in the Promised Land. Baptism symbolized and reenacted this freedom crossing. The radical political implications, liberation themes, and troubling issues of God's violence may have disappeared from our consciousness, but they are firmly rooted in our baptism rituals. The baptism service in the *Lutheran Book of Worship* includes the following prayer affirming God's pathological violence: "By the waters of the flood you condemned the wicked and saved those whom you had chosen, Noah and his family. You led Israel by the pillar of cloud and fire through the sea, out of slavery into freedom of the promised land."[1]

THE PATHOLOGY OF GOD CONTINUED

The New Testament is filled with images of God consistent with the pathology of God described earlier based on Hebrew scriptural accounts.

Troubling Image of God 8: God as Wrathful Judge— New Testament Style

> But when he saw many Pharisees and Sadducees coming for baptism, he said to them, "You brood of vipers! Who warned you to flee from the wrath to come? Bear fruit worthy of repentance. . . . Even now the ax is lying at the root of the trees; every tree therefore that does not bear good fruit is cut down and thrown into the fire. . . . His [God's or perhaps one chosen by God] winnowing fork is in his hand, and he will clear his threshing floor and will gather his wheat into the granary; but the chaff he will burn with unquenchable fire" (Matt 3:7–8, 10, 12).

John the Baptist expects a new intervention of God to rectify present injustices. God's action, according to John, will be soon, violent, and deadly. As in the Exodus account, it will also be selective, rewarding God's favored and brutally punishing others. According to John, God is angry, wrathful, and fully capable of punitive violence.

Matthew's Jesus sometimes shares the Baptist's wrathful images of God: "Every tree that does not bear good fruit is cut down and thrown into the fire" (7:19). "You snakes, you brood of vipers! How can you escape being sentenced to hell?" (23:33). Matthew builds on this association between Jesus and the wrath of God by presenting Jesus as an end-time judge associated with the "Son of Man," an apocalyptic figure (discussed in future chapters) that evolved from the book of Daniel. Apocalypticism included the expectation of a new, decisive, and imminent violent coming of God to destroy the wicked and vindicate the good. Matthew's Jesus (his portrayal of Jesus within history) and Matthew's Christ (his portrayal of the resurrected Jesus who will return to judge the world) often display characteristics similar to God the pathological judge we met in Jeremiah, Lamentations, and Isaiah. Each punishes, or threatens to punish, injustice within or at the end of history. At the close of Matthew's great judgment parable, those who did not feed the hungry or clothe the naked (presumably both people and nations) "will go away into eternal punishment, but the righteous into eternal life"

(25:46). God, who is wrathful, selectively violent, angry, and judging, warrants fearful obedience.

Troubling Image of God 9: God Kills Those Who Withhold a Portion of the Proceeds from a Land Sale

God, according to the Exodus story, is a land thief. In the book of Acts, God is a petty murderer who kills those who withhold the proceeds from a voluntary land sale. Ananias and Sapphira sell their land and give most of the proceeds to the faith community. Their generosity is not rewarded. God wants all the money. By keeping some of it for themselves they are guilty of putting "the Spirit of the Lord to the test" (Acts 5:9). One should not put the Spirit of the Lord to the test any more than young boys should call a prophet "baldhead." After Ananias is told that he lied to God when he withheld part of the proceeds from the land sale, "he fell down and died. And great fear seized all who heard of it" (5:5). His wife Sapphira suffers a similar fate. In light of this image of God, we may wish to reconsider our tithing.

Troubling Image of God 10: God the Violent Avenger of Injustice

The book of Revelation offered powerful testimony to people of faith who were asked to stand firm against or come out of empire.[2] It is filled with so much blood and gore that one needs a thick skin to read it. The violence of God, in Revelation as in traditional readings of the Exodus, is understood as the redemptive key for those suffering persecution at the hands of oppressive empires. The message, however, is not so much that of liberation but vindication. Several passages illustrate how troubling images and expectations of God found in the Hebrew Scriptures are mirrored in the book of Revelation:

> When he opened the fifth seal, I saw under the altar the souls of those who had been slaughtered for the word of God and for the testimony they had given; they cried out with a loud voice, "Sovereign Lord, holy and true, how long will it be before you judge and avenge our blood on the inhabitants of the earth?" (6:9–10).
>
> Then the sixth angel blew his trumpet, and I heard a voice from the four horns of the golden altar before God, saying to

the sixth angel who had the trumpet, "Release the four angels who are bound at the great river Euphrates." So the four angels were released, who had been held ready for the hour, the day, the month, and the year, to kill a third of humankind (9:13–15).

"We give you thanks, Lord God Almighty,
    who are and who were,
for you have taken your great power
    and begun to reign.
The nations raged,
    but your wrath has come,
    and the time for judging the dead,
for rewarding your servants, the prophets
    and saints and all who fear your name,
    both small and great,
and for destroying those who destroy the earth" (11:17–18).

Then another angel, a third, followed them, crying with a loud voice, "Those who worship the beast and its image, and receive a mark on their foreheads or on their hands, they will also drink the wine of God's wrath, poured unmixed into the cup of his anger, and they will be tormented with fire and sulfur in the presence of the holy angels and in the presence of the Lamb" (14:9–10).

Therefore her plagues will come in a single day—
    pestilence and mourning and famine—
and she [Babylon] will be burned with fire;
    for mighty is the Lord God who judges her (18:8).

The slippery slope described in relation to the Exodus account's linkage between justice and divinely sanctioned violence is apparent throughout the book of Revelation. The images and characteristics of God commonly used to fortify Revelation's appeal to resistance and promise of vindication are troubling. We encounter many familiar themes and images of God: God is wrathful and full of fury; God feeds on fear and is willing and capable of destroying humanity; God is a powerful, violent, vengeful judge; God executes enemies; and God's salvation and glory are rooted in violence.

In the case of Noah, God's genocide is covered over with the promise of a rainbow. In the case of the book of Revelation, God's pathological violence is downplayed by focusing on the promise of "a new heaven and a new earth" in Revelation 21:

> Then I saw a new heaven and a new earth; for the first heaven and the first earth had passed away, and the sea was no more. And I saw the holy city, the new Jerusalem, coming down out of heaven from God, prepared as a bride adorned for her husband. And I heard a loud voice from the throne saying,
>
>> "See, the home of God is among mortals.
>> He will dwell with them as their God;
>> they will be his peoples,
>> and God himself will be with them;
>> he will wipe away every tear from their eyes.
>> Death will be no more;
>> mourning and crying and pain will be no more,
>> for the first things have passed away."
>
> And the one who was seated on the throne said, "See, I am making all things new." Also he said, "Write this, for these words are trustworthy and true." Then he said to me, "It is done! I am the Alpha and the Omega, the beginning and the end. To the thirsty I will give water as a gift from the spring of the water of life" (vv. 1–6).

This is a powerful vision to be sure. I cried when I heard these verses read at the funeral of a young man at my church who died in a tragic rafting accident. The promise of no more tears and no more death is a comforting message when we are shedding so many tears amidst a senseless death. At another level, however, the image of a "new heaven and a new earth" is troubling. First, this image is drawn from Isaiah (65:17; 66:22), who says that all nations will serve and bring all their wealth to Israel. He promises that "the day of vengeance of our God" is coming (61:2b) and that those who "forsake the LORD" are destined "to the sword" (65:11–12). The verses following the promise of "a new heaven and the new earth" in chapter 66 include these words, which are the final words in the book of Isaiah: "And they shall go out and look at the dead bodies of the people who have rebelled against me; for their worm shall not die, their fire shall not be quenched, and they shall be an abhorrence to all flesh."

Another troubling feature of Revelation's promise of a new heaven and a new earth is that it seems to be predicated on having given up on this earth. Equally problematic, the verses that immediately follow this promise bring us back to troubling images of God encountered throughout the rest of the book:

> Those who conquer will inherit these things, and I will be their God and they will be my children. But as for the cowardly, the faithless, the polluted, the murderers, the fornicators, the sorcerers, the idolaters, and all liars, their place will be in the lake that burns with fire and sulfur, which is the second death (21:7–8).

It is hard to reconcile the vision of the first six verses with the pathology of God evident in the final two unless we embrace the relationship between God's justice and God's punitive violence. Walter Wink summarizes the tone of Revelation:

> The Book of Revelation . . . despite its penetrating insights about the Domination System, is filled with a craving, not for redemptive violence, but something even worse: punitive violence, to be carried out by God, of course, so that John himself keeps his own hands clean. We are a long, long way from Jesus here.[3]

CONCLUSION

These New Testament references to the pathology of God, like their Hebrew Scripture counterparts, raise serious questions about scriptural authority. They force us to make decisions about what is God and what is not God and how to decide. It is not a problem of the Old Testament God versus the New Testament God. The pathology of God described extensively in reference to the Hebrew Scriptures is firmly attested within the New Testament as well. The problem is that the Old and New Testaments both reveal and distort God. We will need to make sense of Jesus as a revelation of God precisely in this context.

Many years ago as a seminary student on retreat, I sat by a fireplace reading my Bible. I had my pen in hand, ready to highlight passages or paragraphs that struck me as particularly important or meaningful. On this occasion, another student saw me underlining in my Bible. He apparently knew of a passage that made writing in the Bible a punishable offense. "What are you doing?" he screeched, unable to conceal his rage. I looked up and said simply, "I'm crossing out the parts I don't like."

At the time, this was a witty response to a hostile question. Today it is more. The biblical portraits of God as murderous, wrathful, hateful, and venomous are so widespread that they leave us no choice but to cross out parts of the Bible, not through disingenuous silent censorship but through conscious choices guided by clear and transparent criteria. We must read the Bible with eyes wide open. When human beings invoke God's name, or write about God, or describe what God is like, we must judge whether God is really being talked about. The pathological portraits of God painted by the biblical writers force us to be discerning readers, with the life and faith of Jesus as our guide.

Notes

1. *Lutheran Book of Worship* (Minneapolis: Augsburg Publishing House; Philadelphia: Board of Publication, Lutheran Church in America, 1979), 22.

2. Wes Howard-Brooke and Anthony Gwyther, *Unveiling Empire: Reading Revelation Then and Now* (Maryknoll, N.Y.: Orbis Books, 1999).

3. Walter Wink, *Engaging the Powers: Discernment and Resistance in a World of Domination* (Minneapolis: Fortress Press, 1992), 136.

6 THE MANY GODS OF MONOTHEISM

Why the Bible Is Often Wrong about God

An overwhelming body of biblical material says that God is willing and capable of murderous, wrathful, hateful deeds, including genocide or near destruction of God's people, all nations, and the earth itself. People of faith have little choice but to make a choice: *either God is a pathological killer because the Bible says so, or the Bible is sometimes wrong about God.* God's pathology is downplayed or ignored for a variety of reasons, including the cowardice of interpreters. Perhaps God's pathology gets buried beneath an avalanche of diverse and numerous biblical images and metaphors. Maybe it is ignored because many people have not read the Bible cover to cover, or because most of us do not experience God as vile and violent. Perhaps unpleasant passages are ignored because all we want to know is that God exists and that we are going to heaven. Some accept God's pathology because they believe God's violent power is essential to counter evil and establish justice. Many of us sanitize God's pathology through quaint stories, songs, and pictures of rainbows and arks. Perhaps our fear of raising questions of biblical authority leads us to say that if something is in the Bible then it must somehow be true. Or maybe, despite the fact that God's pathology is a problem for Christians,

Jews, and Muslims, in the aftermath of the Holocaust we prefer silence because we do not want to risk charges of anti-Semitism.

There is also the tendency for religious authorities to uphold doctrinal certainties in an uncertain, changing, and pluralistic world. Concerned that interreligious and interdenominational dialogue might water down the Catholic Church's claim to exclusive and ultimate truth, the Vatican's Offices of the Congregation for the Doctrine of the Faith recently issued a chilling statement that included the following:

> The Church's tradition . . . reserves the designation of inspired texts to the canonical books of the Old and New Testaments, since these are inspired by the Holy Spirit. Taking up this tradition, the Dogmatic Constitution on Divine Revelation of the Second Vatican Council states: "For Holy Mother Church, relying on the faith of the apostolic Testaments, whole and entire, with all their parts, on the grounds that, written under the inspiration of the Holy Spirit . . . they have God as their author, and have been handed on as such to the Church herself." These books "firmly, faithfully, and without error, teach that truth which God, for the sake of our salvation, wished to see confided to the Sacred Scriptures."[1]

It is hard to explore God's pathology when the texts being considered are understood to have been written by God. Whatever the reasons for downplaying God's violence, it is clear that day by day, week by week, and year by year, God's pathology is censored by pastors, theologians, church editors, religious publishers, and parents.

If we believe that God is as vile, hateful, and murderous as much of the Bible says, then let us tell our children that the God to whom we teach them to pray orders us to kill them if they talk back to us. I am not sure how to explain why we have not yet killed them, because the Bible says clearly that disobedience invites God's wrath. Let us warn them against insulting their elders, because God may send one or more bears from the woods to devour them. We could modernize the threat by saying that God might send a car to run them down or a vicious dog to tear them to pieces. On the occasion of the next thunderstorm let us read our children the story of Noah and the flood. Maybe we have displeased God sufficiently to undo the rainbow promise. If the rain stops and they have not been sufficiently frightened into good behavior, then we could tell them that God is flexible and might use nuclear war.

If our children are not eating good food and if images of starving children elsewhere do not get them to join the clean plate club, then we could tell them that an angry God may reduce them to cannibalism. And if they decline to participate in this year's food drive and thereby neglect to help the needy, we could remind them that Jesus' penalty for such indifference is eternal punishment. When they ask how we know these things and why God and Jesus would do them, we can point to the Bible, chapter and verse.

The absurdity of the above suggestions illustrates why we must challenge scriptural authority. The Bible is sometimes wrong about God. Once we state the obvious we can begin the important task of discerning between revelation and distortion. Jesus did the same in relation to his inherited tradition. Why do the biblical writers portray God in despicable ways? In chapters 8 and 9, I examine how the experience of exile or loss of land or freedom influenced portrayals of God as violent, wrathful, and genocidal. The present chapter and chapter 7 approach the "Why?" question differently. They challenge the widely held view that the Bible tells the story of one God. The false assumption of biblical monotheism turns out to be fertile ground in which the pathologies of God are rooted.

THREE CHALLENGES TO JEWISH MONOTHEISM

The idea that the Bible tells the story of "one God" is the source of many distortions about God and Jesus. In fact, Jewish monotheism can be challenged on three levels. First, numerous biblical texts presume the existence of many gods. The first commandment says, "You shall have no other gods before me" (Deut 5:7). This verse, like Ps 82, says other gods are real but demands that they be subordinated to Israel's God. This was the purpose of the covenant between God and Israel. Karen Armstrong writes:

> The idea of the covenant tells us that the Israelites were not yet monotheists, since it only made sense in a polytheistic setting. The Israelites did not believe that Yahweh, the God of Sinai, was the *only* God but promised, in their covenant, that they would ignore all the other deities and worship him alone. It is very difficult to find a single monotheistic statement in the whole of the Pentateuch. Even the Ten Commandments delivered on Mount Sinai take the existence of other gods for granted.[2]

The presumption of multiple gods is also clear in Psalm 137. Exiled following Judah's crushing defeat at the hands of the Babylonian empire in 587 B.C.E., the people had to reassess their lives and their God. The psalmist assumes that Israel's God, Yahweh, is a tribal and territorial deity:

> By the rivers of Babylon—
>   there we sat down and there we wept
>   when we remembered Zion.
> On the willows there
>   we hung up our harps.
> For there our captors
>   asked us for songs,
> and our tormentors asked for mirth, saying,
>   "Sing us one of the songs of Zion!"
>
> How could we sing the LORD's song
>   in a foreign land?
> If I forget you, O Jerusalem,
>   let my right hand wither! (Ps 137:1–5).

The psalmist says Yahweh is God both of and in Judah whose capital is Jerusalem. You cannot sing songs to Yahweh in Babylon because Yahweh is in Judah and will not hear them. What is more, at this time both the city and the temple (God's dwelling place) lay in ruins.

The overwhelming disaster prompts a faith crisis. Some explanation must be found for the destruction and how it relates to Yahweh. One logical impulse is to assimilate. The gods of Babylon by virtue of Judah's defeat are powerful and effective. Judah's defeat is Yahweh's defeat. Yahweh is an ineffectual deity that should be abandoned. Another option is to declare Yahweh more than a territorial deity. Yahweh can be worshiped even in a foreign land. Yahweh is powerful, is in charge, and is the one who did this to us. Yahweh used a foreign empire to punish us for our sins. Don't assimilate. Adapt, figure out what we did wrong, be faithful, hold on to our traditions, and wait for Yahweh to act again.

My point here is to note that the presumption of Psalm 137 is that there are many gods. Until very late in the tradition, Israel's God was understood by some to be the *best* God among a variety of competitors. Best is often determined by superior violence, and salvation is often defined as defeat of one's enemies and their gods. No wonder being crushed by a foreign empire challenged the integrity of God. One common response was to wait for God to provide an opportunity for revenge against one's enemies: "O daughter Babylon, you devastator! Happy shall they be who pay you back what you have done to us! Happy shall they be who take your little ones and dash them against the rock!" (137:8–9).

A second challenge to the widespread view that the Bible tells the story of one God is that the book of Genesis has two creation stories about two distinct deities. Stating the problem simply, one plus one does not equal one. Two deities do not add up to one God. The two creation stories in Genesis reflect the experiences and perspectives of different priestly writers, different communities of faith, and different gods. These two gods share some common characteristics, and their competing portraits are drawn in relation to some parallel stories and characters. Overall, however, their characters are different enough as to make them impossible to reconcile. We cannot, in other words, dismiss the problem of two gods by saying that the two creation stories are about the same God known by two different names.

In Genesis 1, God (Elohim) creates the heavens and the earth. Elohim looks upon creation and pronounces it very good. In this account, human beings are said to be created in Elohim's image, although we are given no clue about what this means. Elohim seems removed but pleased. In Genesis 2, it is not Elohim but the "LORD God" (Yahweh) who creates the earth and the heavens. In the first creation story, creation of heaven precedes the creation of earth. The second creation story reverses this order. This seems appropriate because Elohim is cosmic, distant, and removed, while Yahweh, at least in the creation account, is more earthy and humanlike.[3]

If Elohim in the Genesis 1 account is removed but pleased, then Yahweh in Genesis 2 is near but unhappy, more humanlike but inhumane. Yahweh plants a garden, walks in the garden, speaks to the humans, and even makes clothing for them. Characteristics of Yahweh such as walking with or near humanity are completely foreign to Elohim, highlighting that these creation stories are dealing with two distinct deities.

Yahweh may be close to Adam and Eve, but familiarity breeds contempt. The story line shifts abruptly in the direction of sin and punishment. The hint of compassion one sees as Yahweh makes garments for Adam and Eve is quickly overwhelmed by their expulsion from the garden. Although distinct deities, Elohim and Yahweh share many characteristics associated with the pathology of God described in previous chapters. This is evident in the stories concerning Cain and Abel, and Noah and the flood. The first offering described in Genesis is a source of controversy and leads to murder. Cain kills his brother Abel in a jealous rage after Yahweh rejects Cain's but accepts Abel's offering (Gen 4). It is the beginning of the end of humanity. In one of the great ironies of the Hebrew Scriptures, Yahweh threatens a sevenfold vengeance against anyone who kills the murderous Cain (4:15), and then Yahweh himself nearly wipes out all of creation through a genocidal flood (Gen 7). A potentially powerful statement against human revenge is undermined by Yahweh's violence.

We are not told why Cain's offering of fruits from the soil is unacceptable, although Yahweh had cursed the ground previously in response to Adam and Eve's sin and promised a harvest of thorns and thistles (3:17–18). Abel, a keeper of sheep, fares better. Once again, no reason is given. Regina M. Schwartz notes that the "sacrifices of Cain and Abel suggest . . . an offering to ward off divine wrath, to encourage the deity's favor, to invoke his blessings of prosperity."[4] The image of Yahweh is not loving or compassionate but violent and unpredictable. Offerings are human attempts to appease a wrathful deity, but success is apparently a crap shoot. Abel succeeds. Cain fails. The text does not say why. It gives the impression that God is violent, petty, arbitrary, and to be feared. The stakes get increasingly high as God's violence bursts out of control throughout biblical history.

Why would God like an animal offering and dislike fruits from the soil? There are three likely factors. First, some of Yahweh's followers were nomads who projected their biases against agriculturalists onto Yahweh. Second, before becoming a nation, the peoples that became "Israel" were probably part of independent tribes or groups that eventually formed a confederation. Agriculture (associated with first fruits) supported cities. Cities were centers of power for centralized empires (such as Pharaoh's Egypt). Centralized empires legitimated their oppressive rule with appeals to the gods. Nomadic people lived as independently as possible at the fringes of empire. Yahweh's acceptance of animal sacrifice may signify the importance of the Yahweh cult to these independent tribes, and Yahweh's rejection of first fruits may indicate conflict between God, city, and empire.

A third possible explanation for Yahweh's different responses to Cain and Abel's offerings places rejection of first fruits in a broader context of competition between different gods or different understandings of what pleases God. The Canaanite fertility god Baal was worshiped widely because he was thought to make crops grow. Many Israelites as well as other residents of Canaan celebrated Baal's role in agricultural abundance through rituals having to do with first fruits of the land. The writer of this account may have thought that was a bad idea.

These explanations do not make the story less troubling. They point to the broader danger that humans often project biases onto God. These biases frequently lead to violence as different groups claim to be the authentic voice for their god among the gods, and after monotheism finally takes hold, for the *only* true God. Schwartz argues that violence is rooted in the assumption of scarcity that permeates the Hebrew Scriptures, infects common images of God, and lies at the heart of monotheism itself:

> What would have happened if he had accepted both Cain's and Abel's offerings instead of choosing one, and thereby promoted cooperation between the sower and the shepherd instead of competition and violence? What kind of God is this who chooses one sacrifice over the other? This God who excludes some and prefers others, who casts some out, is a monotheistic God—monotheistic not only because he demands allegiance to himself alone but because he confers his favor on one alone.[5]

This view of limited blessing is repeated, Schwartz notes, when Jacob steals his brother's blessing; there are no blessings. "There is not enough divine favor, not enough blessing, for both Jacob and Esau. One can prosper only at the other's expense."[6]

After the Cain and Abel episode and before the story of Noah and the flood, Elohim makes another brief appearance, reiterating that humankind is created in God's image, both male and female (5:1–2). Yahweh then reemerges along with a terrifying image of the divine. The story line is simple. Wickedness warrants and receives God's wrath. Righteousness results in God's blessing. Disobedience means destruction.

> The LORD [Yahweh] saw that the wickedness of humankind was great in the earth. . . . And the LORD was sorry that he had made humankind on the earth, and it grieved him to his heart. So the LORD said, "I will blot out from the earth the human beings I have created—people together with animals and creeping things and birds of the air, for I am sorry that I have made them" (6:5–7).

In the verses that follow we are told that Noah, who was "righteous" and "blameless," found favor both with Yahweh and Elohim (Gen 6:8–9).

Any hope that the cosmic Elohim, who deemed creation good and created humankind in "God's" image, would be more compassionate than
the imminent Yahweh, who walks in the garden, grieves to his heart, but
is petty and punishing, is dashed quickly. Elohim reenters the story and
says to Noah with chilling detachment, "I have determined to make an
end of all flesh, for the earth is filled with violence because of them; now
I am going to destroy them along with the earth" (6:13).

These stories may function mythologically to portray a good beginning (creation), bad human conduct (sin), and a fresh start (inhabitants of
the ark start over). Unfortunately, however, mythology collapses under
the weight of real human violence rooted in violent images of God. How
is God's unimaginable genocide, willfully carried out in one account by
the God Elohim and in another account by the God Yahweh, going to rid
the earth of violence? It is a question left unasked when we place crayons
in the hands of Sunday school children and ask them to draw a rainbow.

Neither Elohim nor Yahweh in the Genesis accounts sees any relationship between means and ends. Elohim instructs Noah to build an ark.
Elohim's instruction reflects a pattern that will repeat itself hundreds of
times within a variety of biblical stories: God's horrible destruction of
humanity is theologically explained as punishment for sin or disobedience and then followed by a promise. "For my part, I am going to bring
a flood of waters on the earth, to destroy from under heaven all flesh in
which is the breath of life; everything that is on the earth shall die. But I
will establish my covenant with you" (6:17–18a). These words are spoken
by Elohim, but the redactor's pen has brought two gods, Elohim the cosmic, transcendent deity, and Yahweh the imminent but equally destructive god, together in a common genocidal plot.

The images and characteristics of Elohim and Yahweh should make us
cringe. These gods function like abusive alcoholic fathers. They beat up
on spouse and children and then follow their abusive behavior with promises that rarely if ever include actions of remorse. I recount these images
here, however, to do more than reinforce the deep association between
God and deadly violence. They illustrate that the assumption of Jewish
monotheism is undermined from material placed by later writers at the
very beginning of the Hebrew Scriptures that depict two distinct deities.
One god + one god = one God is bad math that makes for bad theology.
Simple appeals to Jewish monotheism make little sense in such a context.

Postcreation story accounts complicate the situation further. Karen
Armstrong notes that among the patriarchs alone we are probably dealing with three different deities:

We are so familiar with the Bible story and the subsequent history of Israel that we tend to project our knowledge of later Jewish religion back onto these early historical personages. Accordingly, we assume that the three patriarchs of Israel— Abraham, his son Isaac and his grandson Jacob—were monotheists, that they believed in only one God. . . . [I]t is probably more accurate to call these early Hebrews pagans who shared many of the religious beliefs of their neighbors in Canaan. They would certainly have believed in the existence of such deities as Marduk, Baal and Anat. They may not all have worshipped the same deity: it is possible that the God of Abraham, the "Fear"or "Kinsman" of Isaac and the "Mighty One" of Jacob were three separate gods. . . . It is highly likely that Abraham's God was El, the High God of Canaan. The deity introduces himself to Abraham as El Shaddai (El of the Mountain), which was one of El's traditional titles. Elsewhere he is called El Elyon (The Most High God) or El of Bethel. The name of the Canaanite High God is preserved in such Hebrew names as Isra-El or Ishma-El.[7]

The third challenge to the assumption of Jewish monotheism is that Judaism's "one" God turns out to be a reflection or compilation of many gods. This is different than saying that the one God of Judaism can be described with many metaphors. We get closer to the truth if we see the "one God" as having a multiple personality, and unfortunately, as chapters 3–5 revealed, oftentimes a multiple personality disorder. Even this, however, does not go far enough in describing the way in which many gods make up the "one" God of Judaism.

The "God" we encounter in the Bible is the product of many fusions with other ancient gods. The character of God in the Bible, in other words, is shaped by the characteristics of other prevalent deities. In the Hebrew Scriptures, God is sometimes El, sometimes Baal, sometimes Yahweh, sometimes Elohim (who is El with another name or El who has undergone changes in both name and temperament), and sometimes Yahweh who is Elohim by another name. Monotheism in such a context is always messy if not impossible. God emerges in the Hebrew Scriptures as a composite character shaped by Canaanite fertility gods, personal gods common to Egypt and Canaan, Tiamat (the cosmic destroyer of Babylonian mythology) and other violent Babylonian deities such as Marduk, and the Canaanite warrior god Baal, among others. Each of these gods is part of the evolution of God evident in the Hebrew Scriptures. Each shapes the character of this fused and therefore confusing God. The key point is that any talk of monotheism (the idea of one God, exclusive or above all other gods) makes little sense without first acknowledging that the "one God" is a fusion of many gods.

Let me illustrate the evolution of the Jewish God through a somewhat different example involving the issue of life after death. For approximately a thousand years Judaism had no concept of an afterlife. As a result, God's judgment was always for the living within history. The idea of God's judgment of the dead outside of history, in which the righteous would be rewarded and the unrighteous sent to a more or less permanent place of torment, can be traced to Zoroastrianism, the religion of the Persian empire. Persian influence grew as a result of its defeat of Babylon around 539 B.C.E. Some Jews, as evidenced in Isaiah 45, declared the Persian leader Cyrus, who defeated the Babylonians and allowed the exiled Jews to return to Judah, the Messiah, that is, God's anointed one. Judaism appropriated the concept of life after death from Zoroastrianism, the dominant Persian religion. Zoroastrianism is also an important source of Christianity's horrific portrayal of hell.[8]

DIFFERENT SOURCES, DIFFERENT GODS

Before discussing how confusing the competing god-talk and god-claims would have been to the people of Israel, let me include a few paragraphs on competing sources or writers that shaped the content of the Torah (the first five books of the Hebrew Scriptures). Many scholars believe Genesis, Exodus, Leviticus, Numbers, and Deuteronomy were shaped primarily by five different pens, writers, or schools of thought. These five writers describe more than one god, as the discussion of the two creation stories makes clear. Even when they use the same name for God they often saddle God with irreconcilable characteristics. According to one writer, God is capable of mercy, while for another writer God is never merciful. Both writers cannot be right, and both images of God cannot be true.

The general thrust of information concerning sources is many decades old. (Much of what follows is gleaned from *Who Wrote The Bible?* by Richard Eliott Friedman.) Scholars designate the five key writers of the Torah as E, J, P, D, and R. By the eighth century B.C.E., the Israelites inhabited two separate kingdoms within Canaan. The E writer came from the northern kingdom, Israel, and wrote about this territory, its peoples, and its god. The E writer tells the story of the God Elohim, in all likelihood the high Canaanite god, El. E always refers to the deity as Elohim until Moses is introduced into the story. From Moses on, E refers to God as Yahweh, although E's Yahweh has the characteristics of Elohim.

Elohim is the subject of the Genesis 1 account of creation, although P not E is the author of this account. E was probably written between 922 and 722 B.C.E., before Israel was destroyed by the Assyrian empire.[9] When Assyria conquered Israel in 722, Israel disappeared as a nation. The people who inhabited this territory are known as the lost tribes of Israel. Some Israelites fled from the North (Israel) to the South (Judah) in the context of the Assyrian conquest. They probably brought with them their sacred text that described the people's relationship with Elohim.

The J writer tells the story of a different God, Yahweh. Yahweh, the subject of the second creation story in Genesis, may have been associated with a liberation tradition among freed slaves from Egypt who later joined with other inhabitants in Canaan in what became the southern kingdom, Judah. J is concerned with the God Yahweh's relationship to the people and territory of Judah. Yahweh and Elohim share many pathological tendencies, as we saw above, but they are very different deities. The J author sometimes describes Yahweh with human qualities, unlike the cosmic, transcendent Elohim. Yahweh, unlike Elohim, is on occasion capable of regret and is sometimes referred to as merciful and gracious. Like E, J was written prior to Israel's destruction by the Assyrians, probably sometime between 848 and 722.[10] Judah survived the Assyrian assault. The writings of E and J were combined sometime shortly after the Assyrian empire destroyed Israel. That is why we find two gods, Elohim and Yahweh, imbedded in the same stories and texts.

A third author, P, is visible throughout the Torah. The P writer is familiar with the writings of both J and E in their combined form (JE). P composed an alternative to JE because from P's vantage point, JE did not adequately portray God or the proper role of priests. P was probably written sometime between 722 and 609.[11] P is so named because of P's particular interest in priests and things of concern to priests. P material dominates the Torah. It contains "stories about priests, laws about priests, matters of ritual, sacrifice, incense-burning, and purity, and concern with dates, numbers, and measurements."[12] Both early P and E refer to God as Elohim, although P like E later adopts the name Yahweh. P, J, and E project many pathological characteristics onto God. P's God and J's God, however, are different deities with different characteristics who relate to human beings in different ways. P, like E, depicts God as a distant, cosmic, transcendent judge and controller of the universe.

It is difficult to harmonize any of the stories we are considering with the quality of mercy. Both Yahweh and Elohim are the subject of flood stories that wipe out nearly all of humanity. The J writer, however, associates words such as *mercy*, *pardon*, and *forgiveness* with Yahweh and occasionally depicts Yahweh relenting from his intention to destroy. Not so with P. "In the P text, there is not a single reference to God as *merciful*. The very words 'mercy,' 'grace,' 'faithfulness,' and 'repent' never occur."[13]

The D writer's voice is evident throughout the book of Deuteronomy. D explains Israel's blessing as a result of faithfulness and Israel's destruction at the hands of foreign empires as a consequence of unfaithfulness and idolatry. Other key themes in D are where and how best to worship Yahweh, the Davidic covenant, Yahweh's rewards for fidelity, and exile as punishment for sin. The D writer may also be the author of most or all of Joshua, Judges, 1–2 Samuel, and 1–2 Kings.[14]

The final pen or voice visible in the Torah is that of a final redactor (R). The Torah, like many other parts of the Bible, is the end product of a careful editor. Redactors weave together diverse strands of tradition, myths, events, and meanings into a more or less common story. Perhaps less generously it can be said that redactors sometimes create a more or less common story within which they defend their particular interests by positioning their God, their perspectives on religious and political problems, and their privileged institutional position favorably within the text. The final redactor of the Torah is another P voice that edited and combined JE, P, and D sometime around 440 B.C.E. Friedman thinks the final redactor was Ezra, an influential priest, scribe, and lawgiver placed in power in Judah by the Persian emperor following Persia's defeat of Babylon.[15]

R and P share similar concerns and images of God. The fact that a P redactor gets the last word helps explain why the P voice gets the first word. P's perspective is prominent and privileged within the overall narrative, including P's placement of the God Elohim's role in creation at the beginning of the Genesis account.

CONCLUSION

The widespread assumption that the Bible speaks of "one God" is undermined by numerous scriptural passages that presume the existence of other gods, by two creation accounts written about two distinct deities, and by clear indications that the character of the "one God" is shaped by numerous other deities and religions. The five writers behind the Torah describe more than one god, and even when using the same name for God they often describe God in incompatible ways. God, for example, cannot be both merciful and not merciful. We must choose. The people of Israel also had to make choices between competing claims about God or gods. The difficulty of these choices can help us better understand the pathology of God.

Notes

1. From the introduction to the declaration, "Dominus Iesus," issued by the Offices of the Congregation of the Doctrine of the Faith, 6 August 2000.

2. Karen Armstrong, *A History of God* (New York: Ballantine Books, 1993), 23, emphasis in original.

3. Richard Elliott Friedman, *Who Wrote the Bible?* (San Francisco: HarperSanFrancisco, 1987), 59–60, 236–241.

4. Regina M. Schwartz, *The Curse of Cain: The Violent Legacy of Monotheism* (Chicago: The University of Chicago Press, 1997), 2.

5. Ibid., 3.

6. Ibid., 4.

7. Armstrong, *A History of God*, 14.

8. Lewis M. Hopfe, *Religions of the World*, 6th ed. (Upper Saddle River, N.J.: Prentice-Hall, 1994), 253–55.

9. Friedman, *Who Wrote the Bible?*, 87.

10. Ibid.

11. Ibid., 210.

12. Ibid., 52–53.

13. Ibid., 196–97, emphasis in original.

14. Ibid., 130.

15. Ibid., 233.

7 MESSY MONOTHEISM
False Portraits of God and Scripture

The biblical accounts reflect different writers and different gods. Some people worshiped El. Some called El "Elohim." Some worshiped Yahweh. Some worshiped El thinking that Yahweh and El were different names for the same God. Some worshiped El, Baal, and Yahweh. Some changed Elohim's name to Yahweh but maintained Elohim's cosmic distance and merciless character. E, J, P, D, and R were all priestly voices. Some priests said you could sacrifice to Yahweh only in Jerusalem. Others disagreed. Some said when you sacrificed to Yahweh outside of Jerusalem you were really sacrificing to El. Others disagreed. Some sacrificed directly and openly to El. Others thought doing so prompted God's punishing violence. Some spoke of Yahweh as close and personal. Others said Yahweh was distant. Some said Yahweh was merciful. Others understood Elohim who underwent a name change (Yahweh) to be without mercy. Some spoke about Levites and priests as the same thing. Others said Levites were subordinate to priests linked to Aaron. Others denied the legitimacy of priests tied to Aaron and asserted that ties to Moses were necessary for divine approval. These conflicts led to violence and fed the pathology of God as adversaries claimed divine approval.

IMPLICATIONS

The language in the previous paragraph is necessarily awkward and clumsy because the Hebrew Scriptures portray messy monotheism. By "messy monotheism" I mean that multiple gods and personalities of the gods frame the biblical story. Acknowledging messy monotheism frees us to examine our inherited images of God, the scriptures on which they depend, and the life and faith of Jesus as revelations of God. The uncritical endorsement of biblical monotheism results in a false picture of God. It carries the mistaken assumption that we can identify the one God of the Hebrew Scriptures. It also distorts our approach to scripture. We give scripture too much authority when we treat it as the definitive word about this "one" God or when the Vatican's Congregation for the Doctrine of the Faith upholds the absurd conviction that God, through the Holy Spirit, is the "author" of the Old and New Testaments.

The practical consequences of taking messy monotheism seriously can be illustrated with a seemingly abstract example. Christians presume that Jesus is the only Son of the one God of the Hebrew Bible. But which God is Jesus' "Father"? Is Jesus the "Son" of P's merciless God and/or P's God of the sabbatical and jubilee tradition? Is Jesus' "Father" the God of P and D who orders children murdered for disobeying their parents? Is Jesus the "Son" of the cosmic, transcendent Elohim? Is Jesus' "Father" P's Yahweh or J's Yahweh? Or is Jesus the "Son" of a composite deity who reflects violence once associated with Tiamat, Marduk, and Baal?

Many interpreters cite "scriptural authority" to avoid these questions. I suggest the following guidelines to help us approach them. First, we cannot not answer them. Calling Jesus "God's Son" without acknowledging the reality of messy monotheism is unhelpful and misleading. If someone looked at me and told a stranger that I am "his mother's son," the stranger would be in the dark until he or she learned what my mother is like. "His mother's son" would mean something completely different depending on whether the person using this phrase had experienced my mother as friend or tyrant. In a similar way, the language of "God's Son" forces us to probe the images and experiences of God that guided the biblical writers.

The need to clarify images and experiences also moves in the other direction. If someone described my mother by saying, "She's just like her son," then we would need to know what the son is like from the perspective of the person who offered the comparison. Translating these

analogies to the realm of faith means that images of God are important
in our efforts to make sense out of Jesus, and the life and actions of Jesus
are important as we try to make sense out of God. We must also know
who is speaking and what that person's experience of God or Jesus may
have been.

Second, silence concerning messy monotheism is the functional equivalent to answering "all of the above." Silence allows us to embrace God
the pathological killer. It associates monotheism with the fusion of
almost every and any characteristic of competing gods. God (Yahweh)
cannot be both merciful (J's perspective) and incapable of mercy (P's perspective). Writing off these contradictions under the rubric of "mystery"
is not helpful either. We must choose between gods and/or between
competing images of God.

Third, if we cannot not answer and if the answer cannot be "all of the
above," then we are forced back to the question pressed upon us by
messy monotheism and our Christian faith. If there is no such thing as
the "one God" of the Hebrew Bible, then what does it mean to say that
Jesus is the "Son of God"? In the Hebrew Bible, we encounter different
gods, different names for God, different characteristics of God, and different priestly factions. How in the midst of messy monotheism are we
to make sense out of claims that Jesus is God's Son?

Fourth, in seeking answers to these questions we need to avoid the pitfall of viewing "Son of God" as a biological category rooted in a miraculous virgin birth. I agree with Crossan, who says that the "virginal
conception of Jesus" is a "confessional statement about Jesus' status and
not a biological statement about Mary's body."[1] "Son of God" is also a
confessional statement concerning Jesus' intimacy with God and not a
gender statement about Jesus or God.

By confusing confessional claims of status with biological claims concerning Mary's body and God's gender, the church has distorted both
God and Jesus. The confusion is rooted in the dangerous move from
"Father" as metaphor to the image of "Father" as actual parent. The
problem is aggravated further by our clinging to an archaic first-century
understanding of God as a theistic being living in the sky. The shift from
metaphor—God is like a Father—to biological miracle—God is the
Father of Jesus who was born of the virgin Mary—to Trinitarian formulations—Father/Son as persons in the Trinity—all build on ahistorical
virgin birth accounts enshrined in Christian creeds.

Three tragic consequences linked to the widespread adoption and mis-
use of "Son of God" language will be named here. First, the virgin birth

is understood as biological miracle because male interpreter's were/are obsessed with women's presumed role in passing on original sin through sex and childbirth and because of God's presumed pathology. A violent, punishing deity, according to Augustine and others indebted to him, could only be pacified with a perfect sacrifice, a Hitleresque-type perfect specimen. Jesus *had* to be born of a virgin in order to break the cycle by which women passed on sin from generation to generation in order properly to appease a bloodthirsty deity. Without the virgin birth, the sacrifice would not have been perfect because Jesus would not have been born without sin. The rift between God and humanity, therefore, would not have been mended. When it was finally discovered that women had eggs and were more than divine incubators, the Catholic Church insisted, for the same reasons as noted above, that Mary had herself been immaculately conceived.[2] The images of both women and God that lie behind biological interpretations of the virgin birth are both offensive and problematic.

A second consequence of confusing confessional status with biological claims is female exclusion from the Catholic priesthood. The prohibition of women as priests is based on the presumed will of a male deity. God the "Father" is male. God's Son Jesus was male. Mary the mother of God's Son needed the intervention of a male deity to prevent her from passing sin onto Jesus. The passive Mary serves as divine incubator for a male God's seed. According to male interpreters of the tradition, God's Son Jesus appointed a male, Peter, to head the church, and selected all male disciples. Given this logic, women cannot be priests.

A third troubling consequence of confusing confessional status with biological claims is that the shift from "Father" as metaphor to an emphasis on a male God's role in biological miracle has meant female exclusion from the divine image. By elevating one metaphor for God (Father) to the Trinity and by transforming that metaphor into a biological category, privileged male interpreters robbed the Godhead of feminine images. Feminine images of God were downplayed, disappeared, or were deflected onto Mary, where they languish safely at the sidelines of Christian faith or take on a life of their own, as in Mariology, far removed from God as revealed through the historical Jesus.

I will return to the virgin birth in later chapters. My point here is to stress that messy monotheism makes traditional "Son of God" language inappropriate and misleading. Even if we accept the distorted view of the "Father's" role in a biological miracle, our questions would not go away. The Jewish view that "son" or "daughter" of God signifies relationship to the divine and not biology is more helpful, but we must still make sense out of competing claims and competing images of God. Which God provided the divine equivalent to male sperm? Is Jesus the "Son of God" in close relationship to Elohim or Yahweh, P's Yahweh or J's Yahweh, a God capable or incapable of mercy?

Finally, troubling questions posed by messy monotheism require us to pay close attention to Jesus as a revelation of God. Specifically, we must focus on the images and experiences of God that guided Jesus, value but place limits on our own religious experience, and explore the ways in which the Bible reveals and distorts both God and Jesus.

JESUS AND MESSY MONOTHEISM

We can make the discussion of Jesus and messy monotheism concrete by looking at his relationship with images of God found in the P writings. We begin with a point of convergence. P authored the Holiness Code (Leviticus 17–26), which says that a just God requires justice as equality among the people of God. Justice issues such as debt forgiveness, freedom from slavery, free giving, and the jubilee practice of restoration to the land are featured prominently by P. The fact that P positions justice centrally within the Holiness Code has prompted some biblical scholars, including John Dominic Crossan, to suggest that God's justice and God's holiness are essentially the same thing or to imply that they are fully compatible:

> [When] the priests articulated traditional law, *they did not substitute holiness and purity for justice and righteousness, they combined them both together.* Indeed, that combination of justice and purity in the Holiness Code at Leviticus 25 contains one of the most radical proposals for social equality anywhere in the entire Bible.[3]

Crossan, in my view, idealizes the justice tradition, harmonizes it with holiness, and downplays conflicts between holiness and justice. By conflating justice and holiness we lose sight of the ways in which Jesus embraced, reformed, and rejected key aspects of his tradition. Jesus, as Crossan and others have written, was probably an illiterate peasant in a society marked by an illiteracy rate of 95–97 percent.[4] Jesus most certainly believed in one God and did not know details concerning the different writers behind the Torah. He was fully aware, however, of competing portrayals of God within the tradition and competing expectations of what God was capable of doing within his particular historical period. We must pay attention to the ways in which Jesus wrestled with the many competing images and expectations of God that greeted him as a Jew.

In the case of the Sabbath and jubilee traditions of Leviticus 25, Jesus seems to have embraced much of P's justice of God perspective. Many of his parables address issues centrally featured by P, including land, interest, and debt. Jesus, however, rejected many other images of God penned by P both within and outside the Holiness Code. Three examples illustrate key differences between Jesus and P. P's God tells Moses to execute children who curse their parents (Lev 20:9). This divine mandate is found in the same Holiness Code that outlines the sabbatical and jubilee legislation. Jesus, on the other hand, says whoever does not "hate father and mother . . . cannot be my disciple" (Luke 14:26). This striking contrast leads to the question posed by messy monotheism: Is Jesus' "Father" P's God of justice or P's vindictive killer of children? The answer cannot be both. A similar irreconcilable conflict between Jesus and P concerns Sabbath regulations. The Holiness Code says clearly that no work is to be done on the Sabbath (Lev 23:3). P's God demands that violators be killed:

> When the Israelites were in the wilderness, they found a man gathering sticks on the sabbath day. Those who found him gathering sticks brought him to Moses, Aaron, and to the whole congregation. They put him in custody, because it was not clear what should be done to him. Then the LORD said to Moses, "The man shall be put to death; all the congregation shall stone him outside the camp." The whole congregation brought him outside the camp and stoned him to death, just as the LORD had commanded Moses (Num 15:32–36).

Jesus, in sharp contrast to this "divine order," healed on the Sabbath because fidelity to God required it. When Jesus worked on the Sabbath, he made it clear that holiness and justice were not the same thing and were often in conflict (Luke 13:10–17; Mark 3:1–6). Jesus' experience of God led him to heal on the Sabbath. P's God demanded holiness understood as strict Sabbath obedience. Religious authorities faithful to P's God killed a man who gathered sticks and sought to kill Jesus who in faithfulness to God healed on the Sabbath in violation of Sabbath holiness codes. These conflicts suggest it makes little sense to consider P's God to be Jesus' "Father."

A third contradiction between P and Jesus concerns images of God and relationship to enemies. P writes:

> If you follow my statutes and keep my commandments and observe them faithfully, I will give you your rains in their season, and the land shall yield its produce, and the trees of the field shall yield their fruit. . . . You shall give chase to your enemies, and they shall fall before you by the sword. . . . But if you will not obey me . . . I will bring terror on you; consumption and fever that waste the eyes and cause life to pine away. You shall sow your seed in vain, for your enemies shall eat it. I will set my face against you, and you shall be struck down by your enemies; your foes shall rule over you, and you shall flee though no one pursues you. And if in spite of this you will not obey me, I will continue to punish you sevenfold for your sins (Lev 26:3–4, 7, 14, 16–18).

In contrast to these aspects of the Holiness Code and much of what the Hebrew Scriptures and New Testament say concerning God and enemies, Jesus says in Matt 5:43–45:

> You have heard it that it was said, "You shall love your neighbor and hate your enemy." But I say to you, Love your enemies and pray for those who persecute you, so that you may be children of your Father in heaven; for he makes his sun rise on the evil and on the good, and sends rain on the righteous and on the unrighteous.

This startling contrast between Jesus and P is rooted in different images and expectations of God. The association of Yahweh with defeat of enemies was so widespread in the tradition that Jesus' teaching concerning enemies and the images of God raised challenges that extended well beyond P. I will look more closely at this radical departure in future chapters. We can say here that when Jesus expressed his intimate connection to his "Father" who "sends rain on the righteous and on the unrighteous," he broke with P's understanding of God. Whatever meaning we attach to a phrase such as "Son of God," it is clear that Jesus is not the Son of P's God. Jesus' life, faith, teaching, and action force us to make decisions between true God and not God. Jesus provides profound challenges to the Bible and to scriptural authority, and he helps us wade through the wide variety of images, names, and characteristics of God. The above examples show Jesus in harmony with much of the Sabbath and jubilee tradition of P but in bitter conflict with other P perspectives.

We need different interpretive keys if we are to satisfactorily answer what it means that Jesus is the "Son of God." This is true because the Hebrew Scriptures tell the story of many gods with competing names, characteristics, and desires. Is Jesus' "Father" a God who orders us to kill disobedient children, or one who sees challenging abuses within patriarchal households as essential for discipleship? Is Jesus the Son of a God who orders us to kill those who gather sticks on the Sabbath, or one who is imitated and glorified through illegal Sabbath healings? Is Jesus' divine Parent a God who crushes enemies, or the one who loves enemies and invites followers to do the same? These questions can be answered adequately if we shift our attention to the historical Jesus and if we let our approach to scripture be guided by the substance of his life and faith.

This leads to one other important point. Many Christian interpreters speak of the Jesus of history and the Christ of faith or the pre-Easter and post-Easter Jesus. These distinctions suggest there are two Jesuses. One is a real human being who lived in history. The other is experienced by followers after his death and resurrection. The New Testament writers confess that this second Jesus, known as Savior or Christ, is Lord. The church worships the second Jesus today.

These divisions are helpful but limited. They allow Jesus to be a real human being. They also remind us that we have an ongoing relationship with Jesus, either directly or through God or the Spirit, even though he was executed two thousand years ago. Unfortunately, many interpreters acknowledge these distinctions only to dismiss the historical Jesus as irrelevant to Christian faith. As a result, Jesus, the Christ, or God can be almost anything to anyone at any time.

The distinction (pre-Easter, post-Easter) is more promising when used by someone like Marcus Borg, who allows the historical Jesus to shape his understanding of Christian faith. We still must confront a fundamental problem, however. What do we do when Jesus' images and understandings of God conflict radically with the New Testament writer's portrayals or claims concerning Jesus, Christ, and God? What do we do when their Christ of faith undermines many of Jesus' intentions and teachings? How are we to reconcile profound differences such as when Jesus tells a parable about vulnerable workers and a ruthless landowner and Matthew's version reverses Jesus' intent so that the workers are chastised and the brutal landowner becomes a God figure? What do we do when Jesus exposes the domination system and contrasts it with the king-dom of God and Matthew compares the domination system to the king-dom of heaven? What do we do when the historical Jesus tells us not to judge others and the Gospel writers portray Christ as a brutal end-time judge? How do we make sense out of Jesus' break with John the Baptist when the Gospel writers place the words of the Baptist onto Jesus' lips? How do we approach fundamental conflicts within scripture such as Jesus' rejection of apocalyptic expectations, including the violence of God, and the Gospel writers and Paul's elevation and use of apocalyptic imagery and expectations as their interpretive keys by which to define the meaning of Jesus' life, death, and resurrection?

I will probe these and other contradictions later. The point here is that we cannot privilege the Christ of faith over the Jesus of history because doing so means ignoring differences between Jesus and later Christian claims about him. These differences include fundamental clashes between Jesus' images of God and those that guided the New Testament writers, who often embraced views of God specifically rejected by Jesus and who allowed those views to infect their interpretations of Jesus and their confessional statements about the Christ. I believe the historical Jesus offers Christians the best example of what God is like. Jesus helps us discern God from not God and helps guide our religious experiences. Jesus' life and faith can help us critically appraise scriptural claims about God, Jesus, and the Christ. My faith in Jesus as a revelation of God leads me to privilege Jesus over the Gospel writers when disputes arise within the New Testament.

CHALLENGING SCRIPTURE

Messy monotheism requires us to change our perspective and our approach to understanding God, Jesus, and scripture. Uncritical accept-ance of Jewish monotheism distorts discussions concerning scriptural authority. It reinforces the view that an objective reality (God) existed long ago and simply communicated God's self, God's commandments, and God's nature to the Jewish people, who wrote down the truth about this God in the pages of the Bible. Christians completed this work in their New Testament. The many pathological images of God and gods found within the Bible contrast sharply with the example of Jesus' life and faith. This fundamental clash in biblical testimony requires us to challenge and rede-fine scriptural authority. Indeed, in a world threatened by violence, the integrity of Christian faith and the well-being of the world depend on it.

Scriptural authority is a troubling issue for all monotheistic religions. Muslims claim that Allah, through the angel Gabriel, dictated the Koran word for word to the prophet Muhammad. The Koran is understood by many Muslims to be God's ultimate truth and final words to humanity. Prophecy ends with Muhammad because God has nothing more to say. If you are Muslim (one who submits to Allah), you memorize and recite the Koran more than you debate its meaning.

Many Christians and Jews treat the Bible less rigidly than Muslims treat the Koran. The Bible is considered sacred, but debating its origins and meaning is generally considered acceptable. The Bible, much like the Koran, however, is often portrayed as the written repository of the one and only true God's self-disclosure. Despite differences, Islam, Judaism, and Christianity all live with the danger of giving too much authority to their sacred scriptures. Attributing every word of the Koran directly to Allah or claiming divine authorship of the Old and New Testaments leave little latitude for scriptural challenges, new revelations, and new interpretations, which are desperately needed if the world is to pull back from the deadly precipice of violent destruction rooted in our distorted images of a violent God. The biblical writers are often treated as if they absorbed God's image, God's self, and God's essence with the efficiency of sponges absorbing water. It would be more accurate to say that if God's revelation is like water that God hopes will be absorbed into the life of the world, then the biblical writers received this water more like asphalt than sponges. This has always been understood by mystics, who, unfortunately, however, often put the historical Jesus on the sidelines in favor of a purely internal search for God.

Challenges to scriptural authority are not welcome by many within the one-true-God religions because scripture is a critical link between human authority and so-called divine revelation. It is not surprising that the Catholic Church claims both that God is the author of the Old and New Testaments and that the pope is infallible. Challenging scriptural authority can raise questions about the institutional expressions of faith dominated by religious professionals and ultimately, it is feared, erode confidence in the existence of God. The temptation to abandon discernment in favor of uncritical appeals to scriptural authority is fed by fears of secularization. Many individuals within a materialistic, capitalist society are surrounded by an ideology and way of life that express little need for spirit, God, mystery, or faith. Ironically, secularism feeds fundamentalist backlashes within Islam, Judaism, and Christianity, while these fundamentalist movements in turn impel people toward secularism.

Christianity with Jesus is a way for Christians to break this mutually rein-
forcing, destructive cycle.

VIOLENCE AND THE DIVINE

Theological certainty amidst messy monotheism resulted in violence on
page after page of the Bible. The pervasive link between violence and the
divine spills over into history. This is another reason why it is important
to challenge scriptural authority. The "God" we encounter in the Bible is
a product of diverse priestly pens and the fusion or harmonization of
many ancient gods. Competing priests had different ideas about God and
about who and how best to mediate between humans and whatever
divine image guided them. Descendants of Aaron clashed with descendants of Moses, non-Aaronid Levites were shafted by Aaronid priests,
rural Levites became destitute when worship was concentrated in
Jerusalem. Their conflicts spilled over into each version of what became
a "unified Torah" marred by disunity, conflict, different gods, and competing priests.

The pathology of God grew out of the dangerous combination of difference and distortion rooted in deeply held convictions. Violence is the
likely result when priestly factions disagree, when they defend and seek
to please jealous gods while securing their own positions of power. If you
believe, as many of the biblical writers did, that your people get battered
by God for doing things wrong and rewarded for doing things right, then
you want to get it right, not to win theological points, but in the hope of
triggering divine blessings and avoiding future punishments. Violence
often erupted amidst divergent claims of competing priestly factions concerning obedience to jealous Gods.

> The LORD your God you shall follow, him alone you shall fear,
> his commandments you shall keep, his voice you shall obey,
> him you shall serve, and to him you shall hold fast. But those
> prophets or those who divine by dreams shall be put to death
> for having spoken treason against the LORD your God—who
> brought you out of the land of Egypt and redeemed you from
> the house of slavery—to turn you from the way in which the
> LORD your God commanded you to walk. So you shall purge
> the evil from your midst.
>
> If anyone secretly entices you—even if it is your brother,
> your father's son or your mother's son, or your own son or

daughter, or the wife you embrace, or your most intimate friend—saying, "Let us go worship other gods," whom neither you nor your ancestors have known, any of the gods of the peoples that are around you, whether near you or far away from you, from one end of the earth to the other, you must not yield to or heed any such persons. Show them no pity or compassion and do not shield them. But you shall surely kill them; your own hand shall be first against them to execute them, and afterwards the hand of all the people. Stone them to death for trying to turn you away from the LORD your God, who brought you out of the land of Egypt, out of the house of slavery. Then all Israel shall hear and be afraid, and never again do any such wickedness (Deut 13:4–11).

Violence in this and many other passages is defended by ignoring its brutality or by justifying its utility. A liberation reading rationalizes murder without mercy by remembering the Exodus as a story about liberation of slaves and defeat of oppressors and by pitting Israel's God against all the other gods. The author of this text reminds people that they were slaves and that their God, unlike many other gods past or present, undermines rather than solidifies the power of oppressive rulers. Problems arise, however, because this liberation reading is not warranted by the book of Exodus and because of the confusing god-talk within messy monotheism.

The author claims to speak for God. In his own mind he knows exactly what God wants. His clarity leads him to justify violence against all who disagree, as if through divine mandate. This is particularly troubling when we remember how the diverse pens and competing perspectives at the heart of the Hebrew Scriptures present God or competing gods in so many confusing ways that one would be hard-pressed to know what to do or how to behave even if one had the best of intentions. Becoming victims of "divinely sanctioned" violence is the fate of all who are trapped within the confusing world of messy monotheism when some group with power imposes its will while claiming to know or speak for God.

The link between violence and the divine is a widespread problem. It extends well beyond the rivalries between competing priests and gods depicted in the Hebrew Scriptures. Primitive religion may have been born out of the sheer fascination, awe, and fear of violence. Walter Wink believes that violence is "the real religion of America."[5] Violence continues to plague the world's monotheistic religions that uphold sacred scriptures in which God is linked to superior violence. The violence of God is used to justify the claims of followers whose recourse to violence is rationalized as part of faithful service to God and in pursuit of God-sanctioned goals. The just and violent God often becomes an instrument or justifier of human revenge. Lurking behind the reality of superior violence is the idea of redemptive violence, the belief that violence saves.[6]

According to the dominant mythologies that guide our religious and political worldviews, superior violence saves us from our enemies. Redemptive violence, however, can also be said to save God. This is true because few people choose to believe in a God incapable of crushing one's enemies either in this life or the next. We will see later how Jesus shatters the mythology of redemptive violence but how neither the Gospel writers nor most Christians, including many Christian pacifists, are willing to let go of it.

CONCLUSION

The pathology of God forces us to choose: God is a pathological killer because the Bible says so or God is not a pathological killer and therefore the Bible is sometimes wrong about God. In this and the previous chapter, I presented evidence of many gods within Jewish monotheism. God's character evolved and was the product of both human understanding and human distortion. God picked up a lot of pathological traits from human beings and a variety of deities along the way. If portrayals of the biblical God were evolutionary and not always revelatory, then we must discern and distinguish between revelation and distortion. It is my fundamental belief that the historical Jesus can help us. We must pay close attention to how Jesus comes to terms with his tradition and his inherited worldview and to the images of God that Jesus embraced or rejected in word and action.

By challenging the faulty assumption of the one God of Judaism and recognizing that multiple gods and personalities of the gods frame the biblical story, we are free to examine more critically our inherited images of God, the scriptures on which they depend, and our understanding of Jesus. This can help us to see why the biblical writers often portray God as hateful and punishing and why violence is featured so prominently in human affairs, so widely attributed to God's character, and so often justified in relation to divine mandate.

Notes

1. John Dominic Crossan, *Jesus: A Revolutionary Biography* (New York: HarperCollins, 1995), 23.

2. John Shelby Spong, *Why Christianity Must Change or Die* (San Francisco: HarperSanFrancisco, 1998), 94.

3. John Dominic Crossan, *The Birth of Christianity* (San Francisco: HarperSanFrancisco, 1998), 188, emphasis in original.

4. Crossan, *Jesus*, 25.

5. Walter Wink, *Engaging the Powers: Discernment and Resistance in a World of Domination* (Minneapolis: Fortress Press, 1992), 13.

6. Ibid., 13–14.

8   FROM LIBERATION TO EXILE

The Bible often portrays God as wrathful, violent, and capable of genocide. Through divine action or mandate nearly all of humanity is
destroyed in a flood, she-bears maul verbally abusive boys, parents or
community leaders murder disobedient children, battlefield victories are
bartered for human sacrifices, Israelites slaughter women and children in
the aftermath of war, compassionate mothers boil their children for
food, and enemies die in waves of genocidal violence. I name these and
other despicable portraits God's pathology, even though they reflect
human bias and not God's will, word, or actual character. Such portrayals force us to question scriptural authority, take Jesus' life and faith seriously as revelations of God, and probe the world of the biblical writers
for clues about why they saddled God with violent images and despicable characteristics.

I traced the pathology of God to human distortions pulsating at the
heart of "messy monotheism" in chapters 6 and 7. The notion of one
God arrived late within the history of Judaism. Competing claims of different priestly factions and ongoing disagreements and power struggles
concerning God or the gods resulted in both human violence and per-

version of the divine image. This chapter and the next explore God's pathology in a different light. They link biblical portrayals of God's wrathful, violent, and genocidal behavior to crises of faith that grew out of human oppression and images of God's power. More specifically, God's pathology is linked to attempts to explain exile: the chosen people's loss of land or freedom.

FROM MESSY MONOTHEISM TO POWERFUL GOD

It took many centuries for Judaism's one God to emerge as a powerful, composite deity with many characteristics of neighboring gods and religions. As Jewish monotheism evolved and took shape, there was no longer a need for a human fertility goddess such as Anat because Yahweh opened and closed wombs and promised more children than the stars to those who were chosen and faithful. If your worship of God or the gods was prompted by concern or gratitude for agricultural abundance, then you need not worship Baal because Yahweh was at the head of the council of gods and Yahweh was the one who delivered or withheld harvests. If you worshiped wind or thunder, then you might find an acceptable alternative in Yahweh, who created and controlled these and other powerful forces of nature. If you longed for divine intimacy and therefore worshiped El or other personal gods of Egypt or Canaan, then Yahweh could be your God. Just as El wrestled with Jacob and told the patriarchs where to go and whom to marry, Yahweh walked with Adam and Eve in the garden, made them clothes, grieved over their sin, and involved himself in daily life and human history. If, on the other hand, divine intimacy offended your religious sensibilities because it made God seem too close or too humanlike, then you need not dismiss or abandon Yahweh worship because there were priests who grafted opposite characteristics onto Yahweh, including Elohim's cosmic otherness and transcendence. If you needed a militarily powerful God, were awed and led to worship God because of violence, or understood God as superior violence, then you could reject Tiamat, Marduk, and Baal. Yahweh's violence was impressively displayed through genocidal floods, plagues, and military triumphs. Yahweh's violence was powerful, operated within history, and could be appropriated by the faithful against their enemies. Much later in the tradition, under Persian influence, faith was linked to life after death. You need not worship Ahura Mazda, however, because Yahweh held the keys to both life and life after death.

Over many hundreds of years the idea of one God took root. Redactors' pens and priestly writers retrojected this monotheistic view back into earlier strands of tradition while preserving the legacy of many gods that is part of the long history of the Israelites evolving understanding of God. Over time, diverse characteristics of the many gods of Jewish monotheism (including those of neighboring gods and religions) were absorbed into the life and character of the one God.

The key point is that by the time Judaism embraced one God, it had absorbed the power of various deities into the nature and character of Yahweh. The transition from the many gods of messy monotheism to a one God tradition, in other words, inevitably led in the direction of a powerful deity. Yahweh was the creator and sustainer of the world. Yahweh was in control of human and agricultural fertility and history, this life and the afterlife. Yahweh caused empires to rise and fall and controlled their historical actions like a divine puppeteer. Yahweh rewarded and punished personal and national obedience and disobedience within and at the end of history. Yahweh chose Israel but was the God of all the nations. Yahweh was all-powerful (Almighty) and all-knowing (Omniscient).

The designation of God as Almighty and Omniscient may seem comforting, but it created enormous difficulties for people of faith trying to make sense out of God, life, and history. The problem seen through the lens of the biblical writers was how to understand God and God's power in light of historical experiences that moved from exodus and the Promised Land (stories of liberation) to exile and foreign domination (stories of oppression). How do you reconcile God's liberating power with subsequent history in which God's chosen people are often subjugated? How, in other words, do you make sense out of God and faith if your self-understanding is that of a people chosen by and in covenant with a powerful, all-knowing, liberating God and yet throughout history you are often a subject people oppressed and dominated by imperial nations?

RE-REVISITING EXODUS

Two conflictive story lines collide in the Bible with the deadly impact of high-speed locomotives meeting head-on in a nighttime crash. I am referring to the Exodus and the Exile and their opposing experiences of God and history. Post-Exodus oppression left the "chosen people" destitute and dominated and uncertain about themselves and God.

I made a case in chapter 6 that historical abuse, the biblical materials themselves, the ongoing spiral of violence, and the life and example of

Jesus all demand that we not view the Exodus as a story about God's liberation of an oppressed people and defeat of an imperial power. I ask the reader in the present context to put aside my objections to the standard interpretation of the Exodus as liberation. It is important to do so because the biblical writers, including the early authors, the redactors, the prophets, the psalmists, and those who stand behind the New Testament all viewed the Exodus as a story of God's liberating power. The fact that they did so is what made exile, loss of freedom, and foreign domination so traumatic and so difficult to explain or understand.

Whenever and wherever the Exodus story was remembered and retold it was intended to convey and reinforce a worldview similar to this: A liberating God intervened in history on behalf of the chosen people who although oppressed were destined by God for greatness and freedom. With divine power God freed the Israelites and gave or empowered them to take control of a land occupied by others within which to be God's people. God made a covenant with this chosen people promising that faithfulness would result in Israel's blessing all the nations or triumphing over the nations.

This interpretation of the Exodus solidifies and overwhelms every other part of the Bible. It is the central motif, the principle reference point, the single most important theme within scripture. The idealized view of Exodus as liberation becomes the lens through which nearly all other biblical themes must be seen. Apart from the Exodus story we cannot fathom the mixture of pride, pain, expectation, disappointment, fear, hope, anger, despair, or confusion at the center of many texts.

Much of the Bible is a collection of stories in which the biblical writers communicate why liberation gave way to foreign domination and what the people could expect from God in the future. Pain and disappointment can become breeding grounds for pathology. Biblical portrayals of God as wrathful, vengeful, violent, and genocidal flow from a Jewish history in which people struggled for meaning. Some rooted their faith in an actual experience of freedom from Pharaoh. Many others rooted their faith and hope in the memory of that experience.

The memory of the Exodus was credible to the people of God because it was grounded in and reinforced by the experience of independent rule in Judah/Israel. This experience kept memory and hope alive even after the land was lost or occupied as subsequent history unfolded. Memory became the basis of future promise:

> Therefore, the days are surely coming, says the LORD, when
> it shall no longer be said, "As the LORD lives who brought the

people of Israel up out of the land of Egypt," but "As the LORD lives who brought out and led the offspring of the house of Israel out of the land of the north and out of all the lands where he had driven them." Then they shall live in their own land (Jer 23:7–8).

The Exodus mythology may have been forgotten had the people never had an actual experience of freedom in the land. They planted and watered their faith and hope in real soil, which they received, according to the Exodus motifs, as a gift from God. Particularly important was the experience of independent Davidic rule. "David," Richard Elliott Friedman writes, "established an enduring line of kings descended from him. The Davidic dynasty was in fact one of the longest-lasting ruling families of any country in the history of the world." Therefore, Friedman continues, there developed "the powerful endurance of the messiah tradition in Judaism and Christianity—the trust that there would always be a descendent of David at hand in an hour of distress."[1] The memory of the Davidic monarchy was so strong, idealized, and distorted within the tradition that Jesus of Nazareth in Galilee had his geography and pedigree changed by the Gospel writers in order to fit the Davidic tradition concerning messianic expectations. That is why Jesus of Nazareth is said to have been born in Bethlehem in Judah and why he is known as the Son of David.

It is remarkable that Jewish faith and hope were not completely extinguished amidst a lived experience of imperial domination. Richard Horsley notes how little actual freedom there was for the people of Israel throughout much of their history:

> The Jews of Jesus' day were a subject people. Ever since the fall of Jerusalem to the Babylonian armies in 587 B.C.E., Jewish society had been subject to one imperial regime after another. The Babylonians destroyed the original Temple of Solomon, deported the ruling class to Babylon, and thus brought the Davidic dynasty to an end. When the Persians conquered Babylon in 540 B.C.E., they reversed the Babylonian imperial policy by allowing the Judean and other indigenous ruling classes to return to their native countries. Although the Persian empire thus appears relatively benign in our sources, most of which were produced by the governing elite, Judea remained a subject territory. Alexander the Great and his Macedonian armies, who conquered all territory from Greece to Egypt and India in the

330s B.C.E., did not simply bring yet another foreign political rule but imposed a cultural imperialism as well. . . . Indeed, the Jewish aristocracy's attempt to implement a Hellenizing "reform" in 175 B.C.E. touched off the massive popular Maccabean revolt (after 168) that asserted the independence of Judean society once again. Yet the tiny country ruled now semi-independently by the Maccabean or Hasmonean high priest was still part of a larger imperial system. As the Hellenistic empire of the Seleucids declined, the Romans exerted their influence and finally conquered the whole eastern Mediterranean, including Palestine, in 63 B.C.E. Thereafter, whether through the Herodian client kings or the collaborating Jewish priestly aristocracy, the Romans controlled affairs in Jewish society.[2]

The faith tradition continued even after Jewish history soured. Liberation themes survived because the historical memory of God's saving action and freedom in the land persisted despite a long history of foreign domination. Perhaps because "God's chosen people" were often so weak, nearly all explanations for exile presumed that God was strong. Almighty God, the divine puppeteer, controlled all events. This presumption of power, unfortunately, gave rise to images of God based on contemporary understandings of power including vengeance, violence, brutality, domination, and even genocide. In sum, much of God's pathology is traceable to biblical accounts that try to reconcile exile with a liberating God. These stories and God's pathology dominate the Hebrew Scriptures and frame the Jesus story in powerful and compelling ways.

THE CENTRALITY OF THE EXODUS

The idealized version of the Exodus as liberation from oppressive rule is a powerful story that influences much of the Bible. Its central motifs can be summarized as follows. A liberating God heard the cries of an oppressed people, knew their sufferings, and identified with their plight. This powerful God freed the people by defeating their Egyptian oppressors. This God, Yahweh, was concerned about the material needs of the chosen people and promised to bring them out of Egypt and into a land of milk and honey. Yahweh was both powerful and partial. He freed the chosen people and gave or authorized their taking a good land even though powerful Egyptians blocked their way and the Promised Land was inhabited by others. Yahweh, according to these motifs, was in solidarity with oppressed Israelites, deeply concerned about their material needs, ethnically partial, and militarily powerful. These themes were etched into the fabric of life and society through rituals that recounted the Exodus as a story of God's liberating action. Rituals prevented the people from forgetting the stories and their meaning. The Exodus story was linked to the past by stressing that God's defeat of Pharaoh and deliverance into a promised land marked fulfillment of earlier promises to Abraham and Sarah to make them a great nation. More important still, rituals carried the past into the present. The book of Exodus includes these instructions concerning the Passover:

> Then Moses called all the elders of Israel and said to them, "Go, select lambs for your families, and slaughter the passover lamb. Take a bunch of hyssop, dip it in the blood that is in the basin, and touch the lintel and the two doorposts with the blood in the basin. None of you shall go outside the door of your house until morning. For the LORD will pass through to strike down the Egyptians; when he sees the blood on the lintel and on the two doorposts, the LORD will pass over that door and will not allow the destroyer to enter your houses to strike you down. You shall observe this rite as a perpetual ordinance for you and your children. When you come to the land that the LORD will give you, as he has promised, you shall keep this observance. And when your children ask you, "What do you mean by this observance?" you shall say, "It is the passover sacrifice to the LORD, for he passed over the houses of the Israelites in Egypt, when he struck down the Egyptians but spared our houses." And the people bowed down and worshiped (12:21–27).

As past history, the Exodus might have been forgotten or more likely would have lost its power to shape the identity of the community. Rituals kept the story meaningful by transforming the lived experience of people who had a liberating encounter with God in the past, even in the distant past, into the foundational experience for people of faith in all generations. Memorializing the Exodus allowed a past event to inform the present and shape the future. Memories triggered and reinforced images of God as the Powerful One who was and is in solidarity with oppressed Israelites, was and is deeply concerned about their material well-being, was and is ethnically partial, and was and is militarily powerful and capable of delivering them from enemies. Memories that idealized the Exodus and linked past and present kept hope alive amidst exile and foreign domination. They were etched into the fabric of cultic life, especially through the yearly celebration of Passover. For this reason, Passover remained one of the most important Jewish festivals in first-century Palestine. The Gospels portray Passover as a tense time in which the Romans and their Jewish collaborators beefed up security in order to quell possible disturbances. Each also placed the execution of Jesus at or near Passover. Biblical sociologist Richard Horsley describes why the celebration of Passover was potentially explosive:

> The principal festivals of the society . . . included not simply celebrations of the annual natural-agricultural cycle, but celebrations of the principal events through which God had given the people freedom from oppression. Under Roman rule, Palestinian Jewish society, or rather the ruling class, had the authority to govern its internal affairs according to the Torah, adjusted of course to the imperial situation. The society, however, was obviously not independent of foreign oppression. Hence, when the Jews celebrated the festival of Passover in commemoration of liberation from Egypt, the freedom celebrated was necessarily in *fantasy* form, there being no actual freedom. It may not be surprising, therefore, that Passover was a time when the underlying tensions of the imperial situation came to the surface.[3]

Celebrating freedom, even fantasy freedom, in a context of actual oppression was risky. A protest "expressed religiously in the Passover celebration of liberation," Horsley notes, "could erupt into explicit protest by an excited mob, given the slightest provocation. The Jews no longer having actual freedom, the celebration had become the last line of defense of their human dignity."[4]

The Exodus was memorialized throughout the Hebrew Scriptures. The preface to the first commandment reads: "I am the LORD your God, who brought you out of the land of Egypt, out of the house of slavery"(Deut 5:6a). Bizarre restrictions having to do with "holiness" and distinctions between "clean and unclean things" were justified with appeals to the Exodus:

> All creatures that swarm upon the earth are detestable; they shall not be eaten. . . . You shall not make yourselves detestable

with any creature that swarms; you shall not defile yourselves with them, and so become unclean. For I am the LORD your God; sanctify yourselves therefore, and be holy, for I am holy. You shall not defile yourselves with any swarming creature that moves on the earth. For I am the LORD who brought you up from the land of Egypt, to be your God; you shall be holy, for I am holy (Lev 11:41, 43–45).

The sabbatical and jubilee traditions were grounded in the assertion, "I am the LORD your God, who brought you out of the land of Egypt, to give you the land of Canaan, to be your God" (Lev 25:38). Appeals to the Exodus were also used to warn the community to establish foundations of fairness and justice. "You shall have honest balances, honest weights, an honest ephah, and an honest hin: I am the LORD your God, who brought you out of the land of Egypt" (Lev 19:36). The Exodus memory of God's liberating power encouraged the Israelites in warfare and justified genocide against enemies:

When you go out to war against your enemies, and see horses and chariots, an army larger than your own, you shall not be afraid of them; for the LORD your God is with you, who brought you up from the land of Egypt. . . . But as for the towns of these peoples that the LORD your God is giving you as an inheritance, you must not let anything that breathes remain alive. You shall annihilate them—the Hittites and the Amorites, the Canaanites and the Perizzites, the Hivites and the Jebusites—just as the LORD your God has commanded, so that they may not teach you to do all the abhorrent things that they do for their gods, and you thus sin against the LORD your God (Deut 20:1, 16–18).

Notes

1. Richard Elliott Friedman, *Who Wrote the Bible?* (San Francisco: HarperSanFrancisco, 1987), 105–7.

2. Richard Horsley, *Jesus and the Spiral of Violence: Popular Jewish Resistance in Roman Palestine* (Minneapolis: Fortress Press, 1993), 3.

3. Ibid., 34.

4. Ibid., 35.

9 UNDERMINING THE SANITY OF GOD

Imagine the conflict at the depth of your being if your tradition affirmed that you were chosen by a powerful, liberating God, destined for freedom and prosperity, and yet within history one empire after another crushed you, your people, and your nation. Why was this happening? What was God doing? How, in other words, could you explain the shift from exodus to exile? Unimaginable trauma! Unanswerable questions! And yet the contradiction between God's liberating power and the people's oppression would not go away. Exile had to be explained or faith and hope would atrophy and eventually die. The biblical writers idealized the Exodus and enshrined it as a story of liberation and gain, God's favor, landedness and secure identity as God's people. The Exile required opposite themes. Exile was a story of domination and loss, God's punishment, landlessness, and erosion of identity followed by new promises. The conflict between exodus and exile was so stark that those who tried to resolve it were driven nearly insane, and their explanations for exile undermined the sanity of God.

GOD THE CONDUCTOR

The stories of the Exodus and the Exile were held together by common images of God's power. If the clash between exodus (liberation and freedom) and exile (oppression and loss of freedom) is like a train wreck, then God must be understood as the divine conductor. An Almighty God willfully orchestrated the train wreck just as an Almighty God had crushed Pharaoh. Exile was hard for an Exodus people to understand. Priests and prophets tried to explain it in relation to holiness and sin, injustice and idolatry. Later in the tradition, as we will see in the next two chapters, some of their explanations no longer made sense. If we are to understand God's pathology and Jesus' life as a revelation of God, then we must pay particular attention to the explanations for exile penned by priests in the context of their desire for holiness, by prophets in the context of their societal critique, and by apocalyptic seers who expected and announced a violent coming of God to resolve the crisis of evil.

IT IS OUR FAULT

Priests, prophets, and apocalyptic seers all sought to explain God, injustice, and oppression to the people of God. Why had God freed the people from Egypt, promised and delivered them into a good land, only to cause or allow them to be driven from or lose control over their land and their lives? More specifically, they addressed four questions. What did the people of God do to deserve a reversal of the Exodus? What was God's role in their oppression? What could the people of God do differently to avoid God's punishment and regain God's favor? What could the people expect from God in the future?

The priests, prophets, and apocalyptic seers who answered these questions shared Exodus beliefs, including the view that God was just, liberating, powerful, and in control of history. Their explanations for exile assumed God's power and reinforced images of a pathological deity capable of unimaginable violence. Simply stated, the biblical writers saw exodus and exile as just fruits handed out by a God who rewarded obedience and punished disobedience. The idea that obedience resulted in divine favor and disobedience in divine curse was a central theme within scripture. It was written back into the Genesis flood stories in which Noah alone was found righteous and therefore was saved amidst a sea of drowning humanity (Gen 7:1). Promise and warning are central themes in this priestly explanation of rewards and punishments:

If you follow my statutes and keep my commandments and observe them faithfully, I will give you your rains in their season, and the land shall yield its produce, and the trees of the field shall yield their fruit. Your threshing shall overtake the vintage, and the vintage shall overtake the sowing; you shall eat your bread to the full, and live securely in your land. And I will grant peace in the land, and you shall lie down, and no one shall make you afraid; I will remove dangerous animals from the land, and no sword shall go through your land. You shall give chase to your enemies, and they shall fall before you by the sword. . . .

But if you will not obey me, and do not observe all these commandments, if you spurn my statutes, and abhor my ordinances, so that you will not observe all my commandments, and you break my covenant, I in turn will do this to you: I will bring terror on you; consumption and fever that waste the eyes and cause life to pine away. You shall sow your seed in vain, for your enemies shall eat it. I will set my face against you, and you shall be struck down by your enemies; your foes shall rule over you, and you shall flee though no one pursues you. And if in spite of this you will not obey me, I will continue to punish you sevenfold for your sins. . . .

. . . I myself will strike you sevenfold for your sins. I will bring the sword against you, executing vengeance for the covenant; and if you withdraw within your cities, I will send pestilence among you, and you shall be delivered into enemy hands. . . .

. . . You shall eat the flesh of your sons, and you shall eat the flesh of your daughters. I will destroy your high places and cut down your incense altars; I will heap your carcasses on the carcasses of your idols. I will abhor you. I will lay your cities waste, will make your sanctuaries desolate, and I will not smell your pleasing odors. I will devastate the land, so that your enemies who come to settle in it shall be appalled at it. And you I will scatter among the nations, and I will unsheathe the sword against you; your land shall be a desolation, and your cities a waste (Lev 26:3–7, 14–18, 24b–25, 29–33).

The promise and threat are clear: If you obey, then all will go well; if you disobey, then you will pay a horrible price. Time after time the biblical writers explained the exile as deserved punishment for human disobedience. The Leviticus text just cited was written *after* the people of God had experienced many of these threatened punishments within their post-Exodus history. Enemies had crushed them. They had been reduced to canni- balism, forced into exile, or subjugated by foreign rulers. The above "prophecy," in other words, was written long after the question, "What did we do to deserve this?" had become a central motif for biblical writ- ers and people of faith trying to make sense of why they had been bat- tered by God. "God will do this to you if . . . " is a "prophecy" written back into the story to bring "the word of God" up to speed with actual historical events.

These prophecies of destruction were hard to reconcile with images of God forged within the Exodus tradition of God's liberating power on behalf of the chosen people. Jeremiah captured the depth of the contra- diction posed by exile: "Who is wise enough to understand this?" he asked. "To whom has the mouth of the LORD spoken, so that they may declare it? Why is the land ruined and laid waste like a wilderness, so that no one passes through?" (9:12). God, according to Jeremiah, answers these questions with words that became standard explanations for exile:

> And the LORD says: Because they have forsaken my law that I set before them, and have not obeyed my voice, or walked in accordance with it, but have stubbornly followed their own hearts and have gone after the Baals, as their ancestors taught them. Therefore thus says the LORD of hosts, the God of Israel: I am feeding this people with wormwood, and giving them poi- sonous water to drink. I will scatter them among nations that neither they nor their ancestors have known; and I will send the sword after them, until I have consumed them (Jer 9:13–16).

Priests and prophets explained that God brutalized the people because of their sin. This could only have added to their grief. They were told that the foreign empires who crushed them were God's servants carrying out God's plans:

> Ah, Assyria, the rod of my anger—
>   the club in their hands is my fury!
> Against a godless nation I send him,
>   and against the people of my wrath I command him,
> to take spoil and seize plunder,
>   and to tread them down like the mire of the streets (Isa 10:5–6).

> So the LORD raised adversaries against them,
>   and stirred up their enemies,

the Arameans on the east and the Philistines on the west,
      and they devoured Israel with open mouth.
For all this his anger has not turned away;
      his hand is stretched out still. . . .
That is why the Lord did not have pity on their young people,
      or compassion on their orphans and widows;
for everyone was godless and an evildoer,
      and every mouth spoke folly.
For all this his anger has not turned away,
      his hand is stretched out still (Isa 9:11–12,17).

In an uneven tit for tat, Isaiah explained God's disfavor for Israel in relation to the people's failure to "defend the orphan [and] plead for the widow" (1:17) and then defended God's use of foreign empires to crush widows and orphans because of the people's sin. Jeremiah, like Isaiah and many other prophets, said God used foreign empires to punish the disobedient people of God (25:8–9). God was crushing the people, and the empires that drove the people into exile were God's servants. Adding insult to injury, the people were told that God not only brutalized them because of their disobedience and sin but that God had promised to do so from the beginning. The victims of current catastrophes were in this way encouraged to blame themselves for their plight because God had warned them what disobedience would bring. They had acted badly and knew better.

These and similar themes were repeated hundreds of times by the prophets. Isaiah framed the destruction of the people by noting their rebellion against God. They, like disobedient children, deserved to be punished. Isaiah's defense of God's punitive violence reminds me of abusive parents or spouses who deny responsibility for violence and blame their victims (1:2b, 4–5a):

I reared children and brought them up,
      but they have rebelled against me. . . .
Ah, sinful nation,
      people laden with iniquity,
offspring who do evil,
      children who deal corruptly,
who have forsaken the LORD,
      who have despised the Holy One of Israel,
      who are utterly estranged!

Why do you seek further beatings?
Why do you continue to rebel?

As in many abusive relationships, violent behavior is followed by promises of change:

For a brief moment I abandoned you,
    but with great compassion I will gather you.
In overflowing wrath for a moment
    I hid my face from you,
but with everlasting love I will have compassion on you,
    says the LORD, your Redeemer (54:7–8).

What did the people of God do to deserve a reversal of the exodus? They spurned God's statutes, abhorred God's ordinances, failed to observe all God's commandments, and broke God's covenant, according to the priestly writer of Leviticus 26. They rebelled against God, says Isaiah. They did not obey God's words and chased after other gods, says Jeremiah. Another explanation for exile echoed hundreds of times by the prophets was that injustice was the cause of God's disfavor. In the same way that God used the criterion of justice to judge the other gods in Psalm 82, God judged the people of God:

How the faithful city
    has become a whore!
    She that was full of justice,
righteousness lodged in her—
    but now murderers! . . .
Your princes are rebels
    and companions of thieves.
Everyone loves a bribe
    and runs after gifts.
They do not defend the orphan,
    and the widow's cause does not come before them (Isa 1:21, 23).

The LORD rises to argue his case;
    he stands to judge the peoples.
The LORD enters into judgment
    with the elders and princes of his people:

It is you who have devoured the vineyard;
>   the spoil of the poor is in your houses.
What do you mean by crushing my people,
>   by grinding the face of the poor? says the Lord GOD of hosts
>   (Isa 3:13–15).

Like a cage full of birds,
>   their houses are full of treachery;
therefore they have become great and rich,
>   they have grown fat and sleek.
They know no limits in deeds of wickedness;
>   they do not judge with justice
the cause of the orphan, to make it prosper,
>   and they do not defend the rights of the needy.
Shall I not punish them for these things?
>   says the LORD,
>   and shall I not bring retribution
>   on a nation such as this? (Jer 5:27–29).

Therefore because you trample on the poor
>   and take from them levies of grain,
you have built houses of hewn stone,
>   but you shall not live in them;
you have planted pleasant vineyards
>   but you shall not drink their wine (Amos 5:11).

As in the Exodus, God's violence was seen as a necessary component of God's justice, only now God's violence was turned against the unjust people of God. The chosen people, Amos says, will plant vineyards "but they shall not drink their wine" (5:11); "in all the vineyards there shall be wailing, for I will pass through the midst of you" (5:17); the rich who drink wine from bowls "shall now be the first to go into exile" (6:7); God is raising up a nation "and they shall oppress you" (6:14); "your sons and your daughters shall fall by the sword and your land shall be parceled out by line"(7:17).

What was God's role in relation to the people's reversal of fortunes? According to the Leviticus text, God brought terror on the people, sent fever to waste their eyes, and caused life to pine away. God turned their land and crops over to their enemies. God was a holy warrior who brought sword against the people, reduced them to vassals ruled by others, punished them sevenfold for their sins, executed vengeance, sent pestilence, forced them to eat the flesh of their sons and daughters, destroyed their places of worship, laid waste their cities, rejected their sacrifices, devastated the land, and scattered the people among the nations. Isaiah and the others agreed, adding with dreaded clarity that the imperial nations destroying the people and undoing exodus promises were servants of God, instruments of divine justice and punishment. Through disobedience, the people of God became the enemies of God. "Therefore says the Sovereign, the LORD of hosts, the Mighty One of Israel: Ah, I will pour out my wrath on my enemies, and avenge myself on my foes" (Isa 1:24).

What could the people of God do differently? How could they avoid further catastrophe, return to God's favor, and trigger God's liberating action on their behalf? At a general level, the answer was stated with stark and misleading simplicity by Isaiah: "If you are willing and obedient, you shall eat the good of the land; but if you refuse and rebel, you shall be devoured by the sword; for the mouth of the LORD has spoken" (1:19–20).

Even if you embrace these vile images of God, you must still deal with the problem of specifics. What constituted sufficient obedience? What was rebellious behavior? Isaiah said, "Zion shall be redeemed by justice" (1:27a). How much justice was enough? Jeremiah said God's punishment resulted not only from injustice but from chasing after other gods. In the context of messy monotheism, what this meant was far from clear. Priestly writers often had different names for God or followed different gods. They assigned incompatible characteristics to God and differed dramatically over what did or did not please God or the gods. For the P writer, all sacrifices had to be done by priests associated with Aaron, and these consecrated priests were "the only intermediaries between humans and God."[1] Jeremiah, representing a different priestly group and whose hero was Moses, disagreed. The P writer used the word *prophet* only once and when doing so referred to Aaron.[2] Jeremiah, a prophet and priest, countered P's claims. He said P's version of Torah "was made for a lie, the lying pen of scribes" (Jer 8:8).[3]

These conflicts reflect other differences as well. Priestly explanations for exile often stressed themes of holiness. "For I am the LORD who brought you up from the land of Egypt, to be your God; you shall be holy, for I am holy" (Lev 12:45). When Aaron's sons, Nadab and Abihu, offered "unholy fire before the LORD" they were killed (Lev 10:1b–2a). The murder of "all who curse father or mother," adulterers, and homosexuals is linked to a priestly desire to purge God's holy land of unholiness. Presumed links between unholiness and God's punishment became a powerful explanation for exile:

> But you shall keep my statutes and my ordinances and commit none of these abominations, either the citizen or the alien who resides among you (for the inhabitants of the land, who were before you, committed all of these abominations, and the land became defiled); otherwise the land will vomit you out for defiling it, as it vomited out the nation that was before you (Lev 18:26–28).

This desire to appease God by ridding the land of unholiness and sin also lay behind the scapegoat ritual of the Day of Atonement. Known as Yom Kippur, the Day of Atonement was one of the most important of all Jewish festivals. It involved two goats. One goat was slaughtered as a "sin offering" (Lev 16:15). The other goat was called a scapegoat because it was allowed to escape into the wilderness after having the sins of the people transferred onto itself. It carried the sins of the people out of the holy land:

> When he [the High Priest] has finished atoning for the holy place and the tent of meeting and the altar [by sprinkling blood from the sacrificial goat], he shall present the live goat. Then Aaron shall lay both his hands on the head of the live goat, and confess over it all the iniquities of the people of Israel, and all their transgressions, all their sins, putting them on the head of the goat, and sending it away into the wilderness by means of someone designated for the task. The goat shall bear on itself all their iniquities to a barren region; and the goat shall be set free in the wilderness (Lev 16:20–22).

The Day of Atonement was a priestly response to exile understood as God's punishment for unholiness. This "annual observance [of Yom Kippur], so important in post-exilic Israel, is never mentioned in the pre-exilic literature."[4] In other words, Yom Kippur was a desperate attempt to appease a punishing God in the context of exile. Many distortions of Jesus are rooted in the Gospel writers' and the later tradition's attempts to make sense out of Jesus' death in the context of the Day of Atonement. Jesus is understood as the sacrificial Lamb of God. The sins of the world are heaped onto Jesus, who stands between a wrathful deity and sinful humanity.

The need for holiness understood as separation from that which is unclean is a theme that dominates priestly explanations for exile. "You shall be holy to me; for I the LORD am holy, and I have separated you from the other peoples to be mine" (Lev 20:26) is a common refrain.

Ezra, the priestly writer who may have been the redactor who gave final shape to the Torah, took this premise to its logical and troublesome conclusion. After the Persian empire allowed the Jewish ruling class to go home, Ezra explained that exile was a consequence of mixed marriages:

> [The officials said] "The people of Israel, the priests, and the Levites have not separated themselves from the peoples of the lands. . . . For they have taken some of their daughters as wives for themselves and for their sons. Thus the holy seed has mixed itself with the peoples of the lands, and in this faithlessness the officials and leaders have led the way. . . .
>
> . . . [I said] "From the days of our ancestors to this day we have been deep in guilt, and for our iniquities we, our kings, and our priests have been handed over to the kings of the lands, to the sword, to captivity, to plundering, and to utter shame, as is now the case" (Ezra 9:1b, 2, 7).

Holiness as separation was a logical outgrowth of the Exodus portrayal of God's ethnically determined solidarity discussed earlier. It became a prominent motif within the Exodus tradition and was used to explain past exile and to frame present and future fears. Ezra forced the people to separate themselves from "the peoples of the lands and from the foreign wives" (10:11) so that "the fierce wrath of our God on this account is averted from us" (10:14b). Jewish writer Regina M. Schwartz notes:

> Ezra wants to erect a virtual fence or a wall around Israel, to deem everything inside holy and everything outside polluted. The demand that those who have intermarried must put away their foreign wives is framed as his effort to purify Israel of its abomination. The images he marshals to describe this contaminated land are leaking bodies of both genders: the holy seed has intermixed with the foreigner, the land is a menstruating woman. Male or female, the body of Israel has been permeable, and now Ezra wants its borders closed. This recourse to the Levitical category of purity is the most xenophobic utterance the Bible will make about drawing the borders of Israel by kinship. Here it is used to turn, not insects or certain sexual practices into abominations, but the foreigner himself who must be expunged and purged for Israel to maintain its purity.[5]

The fear that unholiness triggers God's wrath also led to the codification of things and behaviors into categories of clean and unclean. "You are to distinguish between the holy and the common, and between the unclean and clean" (Lev 10:10). There were clean and unclean foods and animals. Unclean things must, like Israel's "seed," be kept separate. Jesus' interaction with lepers was particularly provocative in the context of these instructions from Leviticus:

> The person who has the leprous disease shall wear torn clothes and let the hair of his head be disheveled; and he shall cover his upper lip and cry out, "Unclean, unclean." He shall remain unclean as long as he has the disease; he is unclean. He shall live alone; his dwelling shall be outside the camp (13:45–46).

Jeremiah and other prophets would have been eager to counter P's image of God as cosmic, transcendent, and incapable of mercy as well as P's solutions to national crises, which centered on holiness through correct worship and sacrifice carried out by P-favored priests linked to Aaron. Although various prophets rejected worship and sacrifice as ways to appease God in their specific historical contexts, it is likely that broader tensions between P solutions and the prophets were expressed in texts such as the following:

> When you come to appear before me,
>   who asked this from your hand?
>   Trample my courts no more;
> bringing offerings is futile;
>   incense is an abomination to me.
> New moon and sabbath and calling of convocation—
>   I cannot endure solemn assemblies with iniquity.
> Your new moons and your appointed festivals
>   my soul hates;
> they have become a burden to me,
>   I am weary of bearing them (Isa 1:12–14).

> I hate, I despise your festivals,
>   and I take no delight in your solemn assemblies.
> Even though you offer me your burnt offerings and grain offerings,
>   I will not accept them;
> and the offerings of well-being of your fatted animals
>   I will not look upon.

Take away from me the noise of your songs;
  I will not listen to the melody of your harps.
But let justice roll down like waters,
  and righteousness like an ever-flowing stream (Amos 5:21–24).

Even if priests and prophets could have agreed about what it meant to leave other gods behind and worship Yahweh exclusively and properly, the imperial context prevented people from doing so. As Richard Elliott Friedman explains:

> When a small kingdom became a vassal to a large empire, the vassal state might place statues of the empire's gods in their temple. It was a symbol of the vassal's acceptance of the empire's hegemony. . . . Periods when Assyria dominated Judah often meant religious conflict in Jerusalem. The king of Judah would honor a pagan god in the Temple, and then Judean prophets would attack him for promoting idolatry. A modern historian would say that the Judean king was accepting Assyria's suzerainty. But the biblical historian, who told history from a religious point of view, would say that the king "did what was bad in the eyes of Yahweh."[6]

We must move away from appeals to "scriptural authority," including crystal clear sounding categories such as "idolatry," and instead try to imagine how awful and confusing this must have been to people trying to make sense out of God in light of historical catastrophes and messy monotheism. If God was Almighty, then God was the willful agent of their destruction, and if God was just, then the people deserved to be destroyed. In the fall of 1998, Hurricane Mitch left thousands dead, millions homeless, and crops destroyed throughout Central America, particularly in Honduras and Nicaragua. In the aftermath, fundamentalist preachers explained the tragedy with reference to Noah. The present flood was God's judgment against sinful people and God's way of showing God's power to a people inadequately fearful of God's wrath.

But what could the defeated people of God expect from God in the future? They received lots of promises. Assurances, in fact, nearly always followed the bloodshed left in the wake of God's punishing violence. All postdestruction promises were rooted in the belief that God was Almighty and in control. Many were connected to a new exodus, a new journey to freedom, defeat of enemies (salvation), and restoration to the land. Isaiah promised that God, who used Assyria to punish Israel, would one day turn on Assyria and restore Israel:

> When the Lord has finished his work on Mount Zion and on Jerusalem, he will punish the arrogant boasting of the king of Assyria and his haughty pride. . . .
>
> > Therefore the Sovereign, the LORD of hosts,
> >   will send wasting sickness among his stout warriors,
> > and under his glory a burning will be kindled,
> >   like the burning of fire. . . .
>
> On that day the remnant of Israel and the survivors of the house of Jacob will no more lean on the one who struck them, but will lean on the LORD, the Holy One of Israel, in truth. A remnant will return, the remnant of Jacob, to the mighty God. For though your people Israel were like the sand of the sea, only a remnant of them will return. Destruction is decreed, overflowing with righteousness (10:12, 16, 20–22).

In this and hundreds of similar passages the people of Israel rooted their hope in a new and violent coming of God. The salvation promised and longed for was defeat of enemies. The violence of God was deadly and circular: God used empires to destroy God's people and send them into exile as punishment for disobedience; God then promised to destroy the empires for their arrogance and abuse of power and to allow a remnant of the people to return to the land. This remnant was sometimes seen as the seedbed from which a marvelous future would sprout. "Then you shall take delight in the LORD, and I will make you ride upon the heights of the earth" (Isa 58:14a).

It is often implied or said that God was God of all peoples and that Israel was to be a blessing to all the nations. This is rarely what the prophets had in mind. Isaiah, for example, assured his people that in the future Israel would triumph over the defeated nations who would serve and enrich a powerful Israel:

> Thus says the Lord GOD:
> I will soon lift up my hand to the nations,
>   and raise my signal to the peoples;
> and they shall bring your sons in their bosom,
>   and your daughters shall be carried on their shoulders.

Kings shall be your foster fathers,
   and their queens your nursing mothers.
With their faces to the ground they shall bow down to you,
   and lick the dust of your feet.
Then you will know that I am the LORD;
 those who wait for me shall not be put to shame.
. . . for I will contend with those who contend with you,
   and I will save your children.
I will make your oppressors eat their own flesh,
   and they shall be drunk with their own blood as with wine.
Then all flesh shall know
   that I am the LORD your Savior,
   and your Redeemer, the Mighty One of Jacob (49:22–23, 25b–26).

Foreigners shall build up your walls,
   and their kings shall minister to you;
for in my wrath I struck you down,
   but in my favor I have had mercy on you.
Your gates shall always be open;
   day and night they shall not be shut,
so that nations shall bring you their wealth,
   with their kings led in procession.
For the nation and kingdom
   that will not serve you shall perish;
   those nations shall be utterly laid waste (60:10–12).

These promises bring us back to the Exodus portrayal of God's superior violence defeating foreign enemies. Hope was grounded in the assurance of sweet victory and sweet revenge. The God who reduced the people to cannibalism, Isaiah promised, would do the same and worse to their enemies. There is nothing in Isaiah's prophecies that would interrupt the spiral of violence, only promises that the oppressed will one day dominate their oppressors: "and the house of Israel will possess the nations as male and female slaves in the LORD's land; they will take captive those who were their captors, and rule over those who oppressed them" (14:1–2). The kings of the nations that once took Israel's leaders into exile would themselves be humiliated, and the wealth of the nations would flow to God's chosen. Israel would enslave the nations. Enemies would bow down and lick the dust from the people's feet! This is not a good foundation for a universal blessing.

CONCLUSION

What did the people of God do to deserve a reversal of the Exodus? They disobeyed. What was God's role in their oppression? God was the almighty architect of their destruction. What could they do differently to avoid God's punishment and regain God's favor? Who knew? Priests and prophets could not agree. More justice would apparently help. Holiness? Proper worship and sacrifice? Atonement rituals? Yes or no depending on who was talking, and allowing for radical differences in meaning. Jeremiah and others told the people to avoid idolatry so that God's wrath could be bottled up. Full compliance with this demand, however, was impossible given the confusion accompanying messy monotheism and in light of the fact that empires brought victorious gods with them when they took control of those whom they had defeated.

People who understood themselves to be pummeled by God because of idolatry may well have asked themselves whether it was better to be guilty of the sin of worshiping other gods and thereby have God crush you for disobedience or to refuse to pay homage to other gods and thereby have the imperial rulers whom God used to reduce you to vassal status crush you for insubordination. Either choice you made, God played the determining role in your destruction. Confusing indeed.

What could the people expect from God in the future? There was a promise of a new "exodus" linked to God's violence and marked by a reversal of fortunes. God's violence, whether the liberating violence of exodus or the punishing violence of exile, was the basis of future hope. When that hope was frustrated throughout many generations it led to cracks in the old theology. Those cracks broke wide open and had to be filled with new explanations and new expectations. Enter the worldview of the apocalyptic seers in which God's pathology reached new heights.

Notes

1. Richard Elliott Friedman, *Who Wrote the Bible?* (San Francisco: HarperSanFrancisco, 1987), 191.

2. Ibid.

3. Ibid., 209.

4. Raymond E. Brown et al., eds., *The Jerome Biblical Commentary* (Englewood Cliffs, N.J.: Prentice-Hall, 1968), 77.

5. Regina M. Schwartz, *The Curse of Cain: The Violent Legacy of Monotheism* (Chicago: University of Chicago Press, 1997), 86.

6. Friedman, *Who Wrote The Bible?*, 90.

10 POWERFUL PROBLEMS

Israel's dominant theology portrayed a well-ordered universe in which freedom was God's reward and exile God's punishment. The people were told to blame themselves for their grief while clinging to promises of a different historical future that would be ushered in by God's liberating violence. This chapter describes how this theology (I refer to it as the old theology) undermined the compassion of God, and it looks at scriptural evidence that some doubted its tidy explanations. Finally, it explores how parts of the book of Daniel embraced the old theology while other parts rejected it in favor of a new apocalyptic theology.

UNDERMINING THE COMPASSION OF GOD

God's credibility is challenged by evil. This is especially true if God is understood to be almighty and all-knowing. Atheism may be an option for moderns, but it was unthinkable for the ancients who made choices among the gods. God controlled all things and so God controlled their destiny. God could not be wrong, so they must have done something wrong.

God could not be blamed for injustice, so they blamed themselves and saw their misery as divine punishment for sin. Priests and prophets offered slightly different reasons for exile, but both agreed that God had orchestrated their loss of land and freedom because of disobedience. "Why do you seek further beatings?" God asked through the prophet Isaiah (1:5).

The "chosen people" were often crushed, and when the people asked, "Why?" the response was that they deserved it. They were not sufficiently holy or just. They chased after other gods. They married foreigners. They broke the covenant. They sacrificed at the wrong places, with the wrong priests, to the wrong gods, or at the wrong time. As God's power became infinite so too did the capacity of the people for error. When the list of acceptable gods narrowed to one almighty deity within the emerging one God tradition, the number of mistakes that triggered God's wrath grew.

Oppression did not kill hope completely, but the price of hope was steep. When priests and prophets explained the people's misery, they favored God's power over God's compassion. As a result, God's pathology deepened while compassion nearly disappeared from the character of God. P's God was never associated with mercy, and within the broader tradition God was rarely compassionate. Those with power to speak for the tradition agreed that a disobedient people did not deserve and would not receive compassion from God. "For this is a people without understanding," the prophet Isaiah wrote, "therefore he that made them will not have compassion on them, he that formed them will show them no favor" (27:11b).

> Who gave up Jacob to the spoiler,
>   and Israel to the robbers?
> Was it not the LORD, against whom we have sinned,
>   in whose ways they would not walk,
>   and whose law they would not obey?
> So he poured upon him the heat of his anger
>   and the fury of war,
> it set him on fire all around, but he did not understand;
>   it burned him, but he did not take it to heart (Isa 42:24–25).

References to compassion did not disappear from the biblical writings, but a lived history of oppression undermined God's mercy. God's compassion was a distant memory, or it became encased within the expectation of future violence:

> But the LORD will have compassion on Jacob and will again choose Israel, and will set them in their own land; and aliens will join them and attach themselves to the house of Jacob. And the nations will take them and bring them to their place, and the house of Israel will possess the nations as male and female slaves in the LORD's land; they will take captive those who were their captors, and rule over those who oppressed them (Isa 14:1–2).

Compassion became militarized within the tradition. It, like salvation, depended on the violence of God. Hope was linked to the promise that God's terrifying judgment against the disobedient people of God was not the final word. God's "liberating" violence would again be made known to the nations as it had been long ago in the Exodus. In short, in the midst of oppression, the people clung to the hope that God would show compassion through saving violence. Compassion and salvation had come to mean the same thing: the chosen people would be favored by God and restored to freedom and their enemies annihilated and foreign nations defeated. History told a different story, and some people grew skeptical.

WHEN OLD ANSWERS FAIL

If I tell my children that I love them and promise to take them to the park, but day after day and year after year I send them out onto mean streets where they are beaten and bruised, then they will someday find it difficult to believe my promises. If I tell them about the good old days when God escorted me personally to the park and guaranteed my safety, but day after day and year after year they have only bad days marred by belligerent bullies, then the old stories will eventually sound empty. If I tell my children that with God's help I will accompany them and crush the bullies who block their path, but day after day and year after year the bullies beat them up, then my promises and the God they point to will lose credibility. If I tell my children that the bullies who beat them up are God's servants delivering deserved punishments because they have not done their homework, and day after day and year after year they do their homework but are still beaten, then my words, my promises, and my references to God will over time make less and less sense.

The biblical writers faced a similar situation. They said oppressive empires were God's servants punishing the people for deserved crimes. At some level, these explanations must have always been suspect. The book of Job lampooned the dominant wisdom that life took place within a well-ordered universe in which an Almighty God ensured that people and nations got what they deserved. It may have been penned in response to the Babylonian captivity. Job "was blameless and upright, one who feared God and turned away from evil" (Job 1:1). Conventional wisdom said he should be blessed, but Job lost everything. He rightfully complained. His friend Eliphaz turned the old theology against Job: "Who that was innocent ever perished? Or where were the upright cut off?" (Job 4:7). Job, Eliphaz said, had no right to complain because Job's plight proved his wrongdoing. He deserved to be punished. It was a well-ordered moral universe after all.

The book of Job challenged the old theology's view that God was almighty and in control of all things and that everything that happened was just and purposeful. A final editor partially sabotaged that challenge by resolving the crisis in favor of God's power. "Where were you when I laid the foundation of the earth?" God asks Job rhetorically (Job 38:4). Job is told to shut up, in other words, because God is more powerful than Job. The criticism of the old story of warranted blessing and curse, however, could not be erased by the bullying tactics of a final editor.

Cracks in the old theology's explanations for exile are also apparent in a number of psalms. The writer of Psalm 44 recalls the Exodus in the context of exile but refuses to accept that the people's awful fate was deserved punishment for disobedience:

> We have heard with our ears, O God,
>   our ancestors have told us
> what deeds you performed in their days,
>   in the days of old:
> you with your hand drove out the nations,
>   but them you planted;
> you afflicted the peoples,
>   but them you set free;
> for not by their own sword did they win the land,
>   nor did their own arm give them victory;
> but your right hand, and your arm,
>   and the light of your countenance,
>   for you delighted in them.
>
> You are my King and my God;
>   you command victories for Jacob.

Through you we push down our foes;
    through your name we tread down our assailants.
For not in my bow do I trust,
    nor can my sword save me.
But you have saved us from our foes,
    and have put to confusion those who hate us.
In God we have boasted continually,
    and we will give thanks to your name forever.

Yet you have rejected us and abased us,
    and have not gone out with our armies.
You made us turn back from the foe,
    and our enemies have gotten spoil.
You have made us like sheep for slaughter,
    and have scattered us among the nations.
You have sold your people for a trifle,
    demanding no high price for them.

You have made us the taunt of our neighbors,
    the derision and scorn of those around us. . . .

All this has come upon us,
    yet we have not forgotten you,
    or been false to your covenant.
Our heart has not turned back,
    nor have our steps departed from your way,
yet you have broken us in the haunt of jackals,
    and covered us with deep darkness. . . .
Because of you we are being killed all day long,
    and accounted as sheep for the slaughter.

Rouse yourself! Why do you sleep, O Lord?
    Awake, do not cast us off forever.
Why do you hide your face?
    Why do you forget our affliction and oppression? (44:1–13,
    17–19, 22–24).

Like the book of Job, Psalm 44 rejects traditional explanations that faithfulness led to blessings and disobedience to curses. God, Psalm 44 says, was once faithful but is no longer. The people remained faithful to the covenant but God turned against them anyway. God was capable of redeeming them but slept while enemies killed them.

Protests such as these prompted stiff responses from the priests who benefited from the old theology's sin-based system. Ezekiel, whose name translates "God is strong," labeled those who raised questions about God in the context of the Babylonian conquest or who compromised their faith due to the imperial situation "idolaters." He blamed "idolaters" for the destruction of Jerusalem that he saw as God's just punishment for their sin:

> Then he cried in my hearing with a loud voice, saying, "Draw near, you executioners of the city, each with his destroying weapon in his hand." . . . The LORD called to the man clothed in linen . . . and said to him, "Go through the city, through Jerusalem, and put a mark on the foreheads of those who sigh and groan over all the abominations that are committed in it." To the others he said in my hearing, "Pass through the city after him, and kill; your eye shall not spare and you shall show no pity. Cut down old men, young men and young women, little children and women, but touch no one who has the mark. And begin at my sanctuary." So they began with the elders who were in front of the house. Then he said to them, "Defile the house, and fill the courts with the slain. Go!" So they went out and killed in the city. While they were killing, and I was left alone, I fell prostate on my face and cried out, "Ah Lord GOD! will you destroy all who remain of Israel as you pour out your wrath upon Jerusalem?" He said to me, "The guilt of the house of Israel and Judah is exceedingly great; the land is full of bloodshed and the city full of perversity; for they say, 'The LORD has forsaken the land, and the LORD does not see.' As for me, my eye will not spare, nor will I have pity, but I will bring down their deeds upon their heads" (9:1, 3b–10).

Despite such threats, there were ruptures in the old theology. The idea that oppression was divine punishment for disobedience and liberation the fruit of fidelity was undermined in the apocalyptic book of Daniel. Not, however, before Daniel no longer made sense to Daniel.

DANIEL VERSUS DANIEL

The book of Daniel in its present form is an edited work that reflects issues and crises that faced Judah in different historical periods centuries apart. Many scholars agree that the first six chapters contain important stories about an ancient notable named Daniel, perhaps a real person or perhaps an ideal character assigned desirable traits. The last six chapters contain apocalyptic visions. It is possible that the book represents the work of one author who crafted materials and stories from the sixth and seventh centuries B.C.E. as a way of addressing an urgent and immediate crisis in the second century B.C.E. It is also possible that within Daniel we find the ideas of two or more authors. There is no scholarly consensus concerning authorship.[1]

In the following discussion I refer to apocalyptic Daniel and nonapocalyptic Daniel. This is not intended to indicate a secure number of authors. It is meant to identify two different streams of thought found within the book. A good deal of material in nonapocalyptic Daniel is consistent with the old theology's emphasis on deserved rewards and punishments. Apocalyptic Daniel breaks with the old theology in an effort to make sense out of God and historical injustices during a period of intense repression. The book of Daniel as a whole conflates stories of faithfulness spanning many centuries in response to different abusive empires. Nonapocalyptic Daniel describes events and stories from the time after Jerusalem was destroyed and the Jewish leaders exiled by the Babylonian empire around 587 B.C.E. It was meant to inspire hope and resistance. Material from this nonapocalyptic stream is a bastion of the old theology, and it repeated many standard explanations for the people's miserable plight.

Apocalyptic Daniel, in my view, was a response to the failure of the earlier tradition to address the people's terrible, present predicament. The writer, writers, or editor behind apocalyptic Daniel addressed the situation of persecuted Jews at the time of tyrannical Syrian rule under the monarch Antiochus IV Epiphanes between 167 and 164 B.C.E. In its final edited form, Daniel is a call to resist and endure in the midst of imperial arrogance and abusive power: "but the people who are loyal to their God shall stand firm and take action" (11:32b). Both apocalyptic and nonapocalyptic Daniel shared this anti-imperial sentiment. At the heart of the book, as Daniel Berrigan notes in his poetic commentary, is the assurance that empires will be judged by God and that faithful people then and now must resist imperial pretensions and power:

[We must] underscore again the message of the book of Daniel. As suggested heretofore, two themes are stressed. One: the kingdoms of earth (the superpowers of that time and our own), persecutors and killers of the faithful—these are unmasked; more, they are declared redundant to God's grand design. They will have an end. The end is judgment. . . . And two: in . . . the time of terror and of the tormentor, the saints are summoned to stand firm in faith and endurance.[2]

These unifying themes, however, can mask important differences between apocalyptic and nonapocalyptic Daniel. For reasons to be discussed below, apocalyptic Daniel rejected much of the old theology even though it was featured prominently within the tradition and within the nonapocalyptic stream of Daniel itself. This old theology explained the people's suffering as divinely sanctioned punishment for sin. In order to keep hope alive and inspire resistance, a writer or writers introduced apocalyptic theology into the tradition. What interests me here is not the nuances of authorship but why within the book of Daniel we find apocalyptic thought that breaks with the old theology. This discussion paves the way for my subsequent examination of the content of the alternative apocalyptic worldview that offered people new explanations for oppression and reasons for hope during the reign of Antiochus.

Apocalyptic Daniel, like the writer of the book of Revelation, used symbolic language and visionary tales to shed light on earthly realities. The chosen people's long history of imperial domination, according to apocalyptic Daniel's vision of four beasts (7:2–8), peaked during the time of Antiochus. Each beast symbolized a specific, oppressive empire. The first was like a lion and signified Babylon. The second was like a bear and represented the Medean empire. This beast was told, "Arise and devour many bodies!" The third beast was like a leopard and symbolized the Persian empire. The fourth beast represented the oppressive rule of the Seleucid empire.[3]

The fourth beast, according to apocalyptic Daniel's vision, was "terrifying and dreadful and exceedingly strong. It had great iron teeth and was devouring, breaking in pieces, and stamping what was left with its feet. It was different from all the beasts that preceded it, and it had ten horns" (7:7). The Seleucid empire was considered worse than those that preceded it because Antiochus ordered the Jews to stop practicing their religion. He arrogantly appropriated the title Epiphanes ("god manifest") for himself, and he was determined to turn the Jewish Temple into a worship center for Zeus. He imposed his will through violence, and he persecuted faithful Jews who resisted his decrees. Some members of the Jewish high priestly establishment cooperated with Antiochus's "reforms" that threatened to destroy the Jewish religion. Berrigan writes:

> A tyrant who passes belief, he moved and removed high priests, looted the temple treasury, ordered savage reprisals against the helpless population of Jerusalem, and erected as a sign of his authority the dreaded Akra (a citadel for foreign troops, a refuse for apostates, and a conspicuous symbol of oppression) within the shadow of the temple. In addition to all this, as opposition to his policies gained in strength, he proscribed the torah and the sacrifices, outlawed the traditional customs, and persecuted to death those who defied his measures. In this program of enforced Hellenization, everything that bore the mark of traditional Judaism was uprooted. But the crowning act of blasphemy, the challenge to God, occurred in 167 BCE, when Antiochus set up the "abomination of desolation" in the temple and ordered the offering of sacrifices to Zeus (Dan 11:31).[4]

Apocalyptic and nonapocalyptic Daniel, like prophets and priests before them, tried to inspire hope and to explain the terrible calamity engulfing their people. The book of Daniel contains competing explanations of why the people of God were being crushed, including references to the old theology that understood exile and loss of freedom as God's just punishment for sin:

> I prayed to the LORD my God and made confession, saying, "Ah, Lord, great and awesome God, keeping covenant and steadfast love with those who love you and keep your commandments, we have sinned and done wrong, acted wickedly and rebelled, turning aside from your commandments and ordinances. We have not listened to your servants the prophets, who spoke in your name to our kings, our princes, and our ancestors, and to all the people of the land.
>
> "Righteousness is on your side, O Lord, but open shame, as at this day, falls on us, the people of Judah, the inhabitants of Jerusalem, and all Israel, those who are near and those who are far away, in all the lands to which you have driven them, because of the treachery that they have committed against you.

Open shame, O LORD, falls on us, our kings, our officials, and our ancestors, because we have sinned against you. To the Lord our God belong mercy and forgiveness, for we have rebelled against him, and have not obeyed the voice of the LORD our God by following his laws, which he set before us by his servants the prophets.

"All Israel has transgressed your law and turned aside, refusing to obey your voice. So the curse and the oath written in the law of Moses, the servant of God, have been poured out upon us, because we have sinned against you. He has confirmed his words, which he spoke against us and against our rulers, by bringing upon us a calamity so great that what has been done against Jerusalem has never before been done under the whole heaven. Just as it is written in the law of Moses, all this calamity has come upon us. We did not entreat the favor of the LORD our God, turning from our iniquities and reflecting on his fidelity. So the LORD kept watch over this calamity until he brought it upon us. Indeed, the LORD our God is right in all that he has done; for we have disobeyed his voice.

"And now, O Lord our God, who brought your people out of the land of Egypt with a mighty hand and made your name renowned even to this day—we have sinned, we have done wickedly. O Lord, in view of all your righteous acts, let your anger and wrath, we pray, turn away from your city Jerusalem, your holy mountain; because of our sins and the iniquities of our ancestors, Jerusalem and your people have become a disgrace among all our neighbors." (9:4–16)

These verses may have been inserted by an editor, but they reflect accurately and compellingly the widespread view that the people were suffering as a consequence of individual or collective failings.[5] Parts of the book of Daniel, like many other Hebrew Scripture texts, say the people were being punished by God. The verses just quoted also capture the common sentiment in the old theology and in nonapocalyptic Daniel that God was almighty and in control. The catastrophe, therefore, was deserved. It was God's doing. "So the LORD kept watch over this calamity until he brought it upon us" (9:14a). Nonapocalyptic Daniel said elsewhere that "the Most High God has sovereignty over the kingdom of mortals, and sets over it whomever he will" (5:21b). This meant oppressive rulers were instruments of God's just punishment. They did God's work and reflected God's will. "Indeed, the LORD our God is right in all that he has done; for we have disobeyed his voice" (9:14b). This was a very confusing message to people being killed by an oppressive ruler. It was especially perplexing because nonapocalyptic Daniel also claimed that God weighed the actions of earthly rulers on the scales of justice and said they would be deposed if found wanting (5:27). To Jews living and dying under oppressive rule, it must have seemed that God's scales were broken. Adding to the confusion, Antiochus sat on the throne, presumably as a servant of God, and used the power of his office to prohibit Jews from worshiping the God who allowed him to rule. The Jews, therefore, were called on to resist God's servant. What is more, the book of Daniel encouraged resistance by recounting stories in which faithful Jews who stood firm against arrogant empires received divine protection.

Shadrach, Meshach, and Abednego rejected the decree of the Babylonian king to "fall down and worship the golden statue that King Nebuchadnezzar has set up" (Dan 3:4–6). They were cast into and survived a fiery furnace that had been "heated up seven times more than was customary" (v. 19). The "fire had not had any power over the bodies of those men" (v. 27) because they were "servants of the Most High God" (v. 26).

Apocalyptic Daniel or a final editor included these stories because Shadrach, Meshach, and Abednego modeled appropriate resistance for his contemporaries facing Antiochus's decrees. In another divine protection account, Daniel refused an imperial order prohibiting prayer to his God. He emerged unharmed after being thrown into a den of lions: "So Daniel was taken up out of the den, and no kind of harm was found on him, because he had trusted in his God" (6:23b).

Trust God and stand firm and you will be okay, nonapocalyptic Daniel told the people. The "good news" of God's protection despite a fiery furnace and den of lions would have been comforting if only they had been true. Unfortunately, at the time in which the writer or writers behind apocalyptic Daniel wrote, Antiochus was firmly in control and the actual bodies of those resisting his oppressive rule were falling like flies. Without validation in the people's experience, it must have been hard for those being crushed, with no end to oppression in sight, to believe or take nonapocalyptic Daniel's "good news" seriously.

The stories of the fiery furnace and the den of lions were meant to reassure a persecuted people. When coupled with the "we deserve it" story lines that dominated the tradition, including nonapocalyptic Daniel, however, they would likely have prompted cynicism rather than resistance among the people suffering under Antiochus. The prominent story lines in nonapocalyptic Daniel, therefore, left the writer or writers behind the apocalyptic tradition of later Daniel in a vulnerable position. The old theology did not make sense.

What happened when hope in God's future acts of saving violence failed to materialize and when old explanations for oppression lost their power to sustain faith and hope? What to do when freedom never or almost never came? What to say when God seemed to be without compassion because the chosen people were almost never free? What alternative basis of hope to offer after expectations of God's liberating violence were frustrated within history? How to respond to the crisis of faith that arose as Antiochus killed the most faithful of the faithful? What promises to make concerning God and history? These or similar questions confronted the writer or writers who introduced apocalypticism to the Jewish tradition within the book of Daniel. Apocalyptic Daniel's answers broke sharply with the old theology and with explanations offered by nonapocalyptic Daniel.

LOSING CREDIBILITY

The theological assumptions at the heart of nonapocalyptic Daniel did little more than proclaim their own absurdity. The chosen people were being crushed by another empire, this one seemingly worse than the others that preceded it (7:2–7). Faced with the inevitable "Why?" questions, the book repeated standard explanations (9:5): the people deserved to be crushed ("we have sinned and done wrong, acted wickedly and rebelled"). God has "sovereignty over the kingdom of mortals, and sets over it whomever he will" (5:21). God, therefore, had orchestrated their destruction (9:14). Nonapocalyptic Daniel contained reassuring stories that highlighted God's power, including reference to the Exodus (9:15) and to a fiery furnace and den of lions in which God protected the faithful from harm (3:27; 6:23). These stories that were meant to reassure may have undermined faith because divine protection and God's power were not in evidence.

Like other texts in the Hebrew Scriptures, the book of Daniel tried to hold together a schizophrenic view concerning oppressive empires. Imperial rulers were portrayed both as God's servants and God's enemies. They executed divine judgment against sinful Israel and they in turn would receive God's wrath. Both apocalyptic and nonapocalyptic Daniel promised that despite present catastrophes the future would be different. The vision of the four beasts (empires) featured prominently within apocalyptic Daniel included promises that the "Ancient One" would judge the arrogance of the beast and destroy it (7:9–11). This is similar to the old theology's promise of a reckoning between God and foreign king once the king was no longer God's servant of destruction (Isa 10:12).

Apocalyptic Daniel included another restatement of the old theology: It revived a prophecy made by an overly indulging priestly advocate of royal power during King David's rule that a descendant of David would rule Jerusalem forever (1 Kings 11:36; 2 Kings 8:19). In apocalyptic Daniel's vision, the Ancient One's judgment and destruction of the beast was followed by a similar prophecy of permanent kingship:

> As I watched in the night visions,
>   I saw one like a human being
>   coming with the clouds of heaven.
>   And he came to the Ancient One
>   and was presented before him.
>   To him was given dominion
>   and glory and kingship,
>   that all peoples, nations, and languages
>   should serve him.
>   His dominion is an everlasting dominion
>   that shall not pass away,
>   and his kingship is one
>   that shall never be destroyed (7:13–14).

Within the New Testament, Daniel's generic "human being" became a full-fledged apocalyptic figure, the Son of Man, which was associated with Jesus and which associated Jesus with a violent judgment or end time. In light of Antiochus's oppressive rule, both Daniel's credibility and the people's patience with the old or slightly revised story lines must have run thin. To this point, neither nonapocalyptic Daniel nor apocalyptic Daniel had offered anything new or remotely credible to a people faced with an unprecedented crisis. Their dead words could not keep hope alive without significant modifications.

AN EMPIRE WORSE THAN THE OTHERS

The Seleucid empire (the fourth beast), according to apocalyptic Daniel, "was different from all the beasts that preceded it" (7:7). It was the depth of crisis and the failure of the old explanations and promises to inspire hope and resistance that led apocalyptic Daniel to offer alternative explanations and promises concerning God and history. The people were being crushed and the old theology was broken. It could not easily be fixed. Antiochus could not credibly be portrayed as God's servant, the Davidic line had disappeared and the promise of a future everlasting kingship must have seemed empty, and the tales of God's protection for the faithful amidst fiery furnace and lion's den were fanciful in light of Antiochus's actual deadly repression. *The Interpreter's Bible* notes that within the book of Daniel, "God's demand for obedience does not promise immediate reward or an immediate safety,"[6] but that is exactly what nonapocalytic Daniel promised through stories of people emerging unharmed from fiery furnace and lion's den.

The idea that blessing or curse was based on faithfulness, an idea challenged previously in the account of Job, was also no longer credible. Why? Because during Antiochus's rule the most faithful of the faithful were killed for resisting imperial decrees. The people being slaughtered were those who obeyed not those who disobeyed, those who clung to God not those who embraced Zeus, those who upheld the traditions not those who abandoned important rituals and practices, those who resisted not those who collaborated. The old theology's claim that people who were killed deserved to die because of sin or disobedience was indefensible.

The writer or writers behind Daniel wanted to inspire resistance to Antiochus's oppressive rule, but the old dead story lines of the inherited tradition must have led to resignation and ridicule. Toward the end of the book, therefore, an apocalyptic seer offered new explanations for historical domination, new promises of vindication, and new expectations of God's saving, violent action.

NEW EXPLANATIONS

If faith and hope were to survive Antiochus's brutal policies, then apocalyptic Daniel had to offer new explanations for what was happening to the people and credible insights into what God was doing. Apocalyptic Daniel broke new ground in three ways. The first innovation was in the realm of cosmology. There was, according to apocalyptic Daniel, a struggle going on in heaven between the forces of good and the forces of evil. The angels of God were doing battle with the angels of the empires (Daniel 10). This warfare in heaven directly mirrored and influenced earthly events. God would eventually triumph against the forces of evil in heaven, but until then the people could not expect justice on earth.

Evil empires would dominate history for a time but the people could live, risk death, and die with the assurance that oppressive rule would not last forever.

Apocalyptic Daniel's cosmology responded to oppressive human violence by projecting violence into heaven. The violence of God demonstrated in the defeat of Pharaoh, in genocidal violence against enemies, and in the crushing punishment of God's people was linked to a cosmic struggle between the forces of good and evil. Apocalyptic Daniel's cosmology universalized and deepened the ties between God and violence. It also offered God a way out or beyond the classical explanation that God controlled all things and therefore was the agent responsible for crushing the people. Apocalyptic Daniel suggested that God wanted justice for the people and in the end time guaranteed it, but that God and God's angels were preoccupied with heavenly battles that must first be fought and won. The angel told Daniel, "Now I must return to fight against the prince of Persia, and when I am through with him, the prince of Greece will come" (10:20b). The chosen people who had been dominated within history by Persian kings and Greek rulers were told that God's angels were at war in heaven with the angels of these nations.

Apocalyptic Daniel also broke new ground when he shifted the promise of salvation and a new future from within history to the end of history. History, as we have seen, rarely conformed to the promises of God. Both the Exodus and independent Davidic rule were distant memories. Real freedom disappeared with exile. After centuries of foreign domination and without a new exodus, old promises of salvation understood as defeat of historical enemies rang hollow. Apocalyptic Daniel resolved the problem of oppressive history by shifting God's promises to the end time. An angel came to Daniel to help him "understand what is to happen to your people at the end of days" (10:14) and then returned to the heavenly struggle.

The people were left behind with the promise of a future violent coming of God. Apocalyptic Daniel suggested, in contrast to the old theology, that God's intervention would end history rather than restore Israel to historical prominence (8:17; 10:14; 11:35; 12:13). This left the people to cope with real history in which Antiochus was still supreme and they were persecuted and dying. Apocalyptic Daniel, like the prophets who came before him, insisted that arrogant empires would not have the final word. Unlike the prophets, however, apocalyptic Daniel suggested that empires would dominate history until the end comes. Empires were powerful, too powerful in fact, for human beings to do much about. In a vision that transparently represented the actual experience of the people, he wrote:

> This is what he said: "As for the fourth beast,
>> here shall be a fourth kingdom on earth
>>> that shall be different from all the other kingdoms;
>> it shall devour the whole earth,
>>> and trample it down, and break it to pieces. . . .
>> He shall speak words against the Most High,
>>> shall wear out the holy ones of the Most High,
>>> and shall attempt to change the sacred seasons and the law;
>> and they shall be given into his power
>>> for a time, two times, and half a time.
>> Then the court shall sit in judgment,
>>> and his dominion shall be taken away,
>>> to be consumed and totally destroyed (7:23, 25–26).

Apocalyptic Daniel anticipated a new violent coming of God but offered little hope within history. He asserted that "no one could rescue the ram from its [the fourth beast's] power" (8:7). Many of his contemporaries disagreed. They joined the Maccabean revolutionaries who fought a guerrilla war against Antiochus's army. Apocalyptic Daniel seemed to advocate nonviolent resistance and urged the people to wait for God's redemptive violence. When he says that the fourth beast "shall be broken" but "not by human hands" (8:25), it could well be his critical commentary on the Jewish Maccabean revolt. Daniel implored the people to "Understand, O mortal, that the vision is for the time of the end" (8:17), a time of unprecedented violence and anguish (12:1).

Apocalyptic Daniel's third innovation was to make resurrection a central theme. Judaism assimilated the idea of resurrection from Zoroastrianism in the context of Persian influence and rule. Resurrection took center stage in the Jewish tradition for the first time, however, in the writings of apocalyptic Daniel during a time in which Antiochus was slaughtering the people. Empires have always seen death as the ultimate deterrent. The promise of vindication of life over death can be a powerful motivator. Apocalyptic Daniel emphasized resurrection in order to inspire people to imitate faithful Jews who were being killed while resisting Antiochus. He rejected and offered an alternative to non-apocalyptic Daniel's divine protection stories of safety amidst lion's den and fiery furnace. Resurrection meant divine vindication, not protection. He encouraged the people to remain loyal to God, stand firm, and take action (11:32) in light of the promise of God's decisive violent intervention at the end of time. Resurrection involved just rewards and punishments:

> At that time Michael, the great prince, the protector of your people, shall arise. There shall be a time of anguish, such as has never occurred since nations first came into existence. But at that time your people shall be delivered, everyone who is found written in the book. Many of those who sleep in the dust of the earth shall awake, some to everlasting life, and some to shame and everlasting contempt. Those who are wise shall shine like the brightness of the sky, and those who lead many to right-eousness, like the stars forever and ever (12:1–3).

The promise of resurrection encouraged hope and resistance. It was also a way of reestablishing God's credibility and reaffirming God's integrity. History was oppressive, but God would vindicate the lives and deaths of the faithful and punish evil people at the end of history. How long till the end? The book of Daniel said "a time, two times, and half a time" (12:7), whatever that meant. It also ended with these words: "Happy are those who persevere and attain the thousand three hundred thirty-five days. But you, go your way, and rest; you shall rise for your reward at the end of the days" (12:12–13).

The biblical writers said that God chose an oppressed people and liberated them. Over time the chosen people lost their land and their freedom. Davidic rule ended. A powerful empire eliminated Israel and a series of oppressive empires dominated Judah. Priests and prophets explained the movement from exodus to exile as God's punishment for disobedience, and they promised that faithfulness would restore God's favor and result in salvation, understood as defeat of enemies and restoration to freedom in the land. Centuries passed and freedom seldom if ever came. Abusive empires crushed the chosen people until the old theology no longer made sense to many.

During the tyrannical reign of Antiochus, apocalyptic seers revisited and then went beyond the old story lines. The apocalyptic seer or seers behind the new theology responded to unprecedented repression and a deepening crisis of faith stemming from Antiochus's deadly decrees. Apocalyptic Daniel offered alternative explanations for the people's plight and alternative reasons for hope. God and God's angels were preoccupied with a war in heaven between the forces of good and evil. When this battle in heaven was won, God would violently intervene on earth at the end of human history. The righteous, including those who died while resisting imperial oppression, would be rewarded. Those who were evil would be punished. God's redemptive violence remained the basis of hope, but apocalyptic Daniel shifted its locus into heaven and emphasized that God's judgment would be at the end time.

What, according to the apocalyptic worldview, did the people of God do to deserve a reversal of the Exodus? Much of Daniel repeated the old theology and said they sinned. Apocalyptic Daniel suggested that arrogant empires crushed the people because God was fighting a battle against the forces of evil in heaven and this battle had to be won before earthly empires could be defeated. What was God's role in their oppression? Much of the book repeated standard themes and showed God as the divine controller of all things and thus responsible for the people's plight. God used foreign empires to punish the people for their individual or collective failings. Apocalyptic Daniel portrayed God violently fighting the forces of evil in heaven. Battles between angels mirrored earthly struggles. Heavenly victories would eventually lead to an earthly triumph at the end of history.

What could the people of God do differently to avoid God's punishment and regain God's favor? Much of the book suggested the standard fare of obedience, proper ritual, and rejection of sin. Apocalyptic Daniel, however, encouraged the people to be loyal to God, stand firm against imperial arrogance, take action, and wait for the appointed end time. Prepare, resist, and wait with the knowledge that only the violent intervention of God could ultimately defeat evil empires at the end of history.

Finally, what could the people expect from God in the future? The people were reassured that God was in control. Despite evidence to the contrary, God would eventually triumph. Evil forces would be defeated in heaven and heavenly victories would profoundly impact earthly realities. This was true, according to apocalyptic Daniel, both because struggles in heaven directly parallel those on earth and because God's defeat of evil in heaven would be followed by God's violent intervention on earth to crush arrogant empires, punish evildoers, and vindicate the righteous at the end of history. Those who were faithful even unto death would have their lives validated by God through a resurrection of the dead. Those who had embraced evil would rise and be punished. Like Job's friend Eliphaz, apocalyptic Daniel insisted that God was overseeing a well-ordered universe. Unlike Eliphaz, however, apocalyptic

Daniel proclaimed that good would be rewarded and evil punished at the end of rather than within history.

THREE CHOICES

What happened to biblical expectations of God when oppression deepened, promises were not kept, and old stories lost their interpretive power? Let me highlight three possible answers. First, people could have clung to the old theology, including its traditional images of God, well-entrenched explanations for oppression, and classical promises of a glorious future of defeated enemies and triumphant independent rule. Some, including the nonapocalyptic Daniel, did so despite all the contrary evidence. Eventually many, apocalyptic Daniel among them, could not.

A second option was apocalypticism. Pioneered by seers like Daniel, embraced by John the Baptist and the Apostle Paul, featured prominently within the Gospels and culminating with the book of Revelation, the apocalyptic worldview filled a void left by a faltering tradition that no longer made sense to many people as history spun out of control. Apocalypticism, like the old theology that preceded it, embraced a powerful God, although the apocalyptic worldview developed images of God's power in relation to a cosmic struggle between the forces of good and evil. Apocalypticism deepened God's pathology while shifting the expectation of God's violent triumph to the end of history.

It is hard to reconcile apocalypticism with an Almighty God. If God were all-powerful, then why would God have so much trouble defeating the forces of evil both in heaven and on earth? Almighty God could presumably zap the forces of evil in the wink of an eye. Apocalyptic Daniel undermines any effort to resolve the problem of evil by seeing it as the consequence of human freedom. According to Daniel, evil is rampant and God is fighting the good fight in heaven as best God can. This small crack in the human tendency to project absolute power onto God has been ignored or denied throughout history by Christian interpreters and within creedal statements. It remained an unexplored contradiction within apocalypticism itself until Jesus.

Before discussing a third option, we should note that the apocalyptic worldview in many ways came to dominate the tradition, including expectations of God at the time of Jesus, Gospel interpretations of Jesus, and Paul's understanding of the Christ. Even more surprising, apocalypticism today dominates the theology of many nonviolent Christian activists for whom the book of Daniel models appropriate resistance to empire. Daniel Berrigan, by way of example, embraces apocalypticism and calls Daniel a "perennial blessing."[7] Berrigan, a friend and mentor, in my view often ignores, embraces, or wiggles around the oppressive violence of God that cascades from the pens of the prophets and from the book of Daniel. An example of this is found in his commentary on Daniel concerning heavenly warfare:

> An apocalyptic note is struck. Gabriel and Michael, we are told, are angelic warriors engaged in heavenly warfare. We have seen it before. According to the celestial imagery evoked here (and in the Book of Revelation), no earthly war can be purely earthbound. The clash of arms penetrates the heavenly court; God is the prey—the God of peace, and God's peaceable disciples. Scripture harps on the truth.[8]

This idealized reading clashes sharply with the pervasive biblical images of the pathologically violent god(s) we have encountered throughout. Neither the old theological traditions, which explained exodus (liberation) and exile (loss) as just rewards and punishments, nor the new apocalyptic theology offered much evidence of either a "God of peace" or of "God's peaceable disciples." And if "scripture harps on the truth," then it would seem to repeat a chorus in which God's violence is the necessary instrument of God's justice and the promise of God's future violence is what reinforces faithful resistance to empire.

I noted earlier that Christians should be concerned about justice, based on its centrality in biblical accounts. The key issue is whether, according to Jesus, God's violence and human violence "sanctioned by God" are the necessary means to justice. A similar problem is posed by the arrogance and abusive power of empires. The question is not whether abusive empires have the last word or whether they should be resisted. The question posed by Jesus is whether we should root our resistance to imperial arrogance and power in violent images and expectations of God or elsewhere. Embracing God's violence results in an enduring and escalating spiral of violence within the biblical story, within the Godhead, within history, and within our own hearts. I find apocalyptic theology an implausible place to ground one's commitment to nonviolence. The dangers of doing so, it seems to me, are laid brutally bare by the fact that both many nonviolent Christian activists and many hate-filled, racist, and violent militia movements ground and defend their actions in the apocalyptic worldview.

Apocalypticism is an alternative to the old theology, but it is problematic. Daniel's cosmology extends God's pathological violence into heaven, and it awaits a future consummating act of God's violence to end history (or, according to some interpretations, to impose justice within history). Apocalyptic Daniel offered God escape hatches from full responsibility for oppression, but it did so by deepening ties between God and violence both in heaven and on earth. It sought to foster hope and resistance among historically oppressed people by reaffirming God's ultimate sovereignty over empires but ironically did so by shifting the locus of hope away from history.

Apocalypticism's blunt distinctions between good and evil are occasionally verifiable but often problematic. They spawn hatred between peoples and fuel the spiral of violence already prevalent within scripture. Joseph utilized food as a weapon on behalf of the pharaoh. As a result, all Egyptians ended up penniless, landless, and enslaved (Gen 47). Resentments flowered. The powerful Israelites suffered when a new pharaoh took control. Hatreds exploded, and as always violence thrived and survived numerous reversals. The Israelites, according to the biblical script, groaned amidst their oppression and with God's help fought back and won. In the aftermath of Pharaoh's defeat, lands were stolen, and "divinely sanctioned" genocide carried out. Elijah won a contest with the priests of Baal and then executed them (1 Kings 18:35–40). Israelites, unable to sing the Lord's song in captivity, anticipated the happy day when they would smash the heads of their captor's children against the rocks (Ps 137:9). Isaiah announced that God would one day come "with vengeance," "save" the people, and "spare no one" (35:4; 47:3). With God's help, Isaiah promised, the oppressed would become oppressors. Kings who took Jewish leaders into exile would themselves be humiliated and the wealth of the nations given over to Israel. "With their faces to the ground they shall bow down to you, and lick the dust of your feet" (49:23). Daniel walked away from the lion's den, and immediately "those who had accused Daniel were brought and thrown into the den of lions—they, their children, and their wives. Before they reached the bottom of the den the lions overpowered them and broke all their bones in pieces" (Dan 6:24).

In this context of a never-ending spiral of violence, apocalyptic expectations of God's final justice made God an instrument of human revenge. Compassion and salvation were militarized, that is, understood as the crushing defeat of enemies. God became the ultimate avenger of wrongs at the end of history rather than within it because the imperial situation made it difficult for humans to carry out the desired punishments.

Apocalypticism feeds on repressed violence. Many nonviolent protesters, myself included, have used the promise of God's future violence to substitute for our own. We can be nonviolent in our tactics because our actions are backed up by God's violence. When nonviolence is rooted in the violence of God, however, it never really penetrates our hearts. Violence infects our words, our spirits, and our actions. In this regard, Berrigan heralds Daniel's theology, anticipating "the sweet revenge of the underdog."[9] In the same spirit, he writes, "Judgment is a theme. And the mighty condemn it, even as they undergo its rigors in nightmares of fear and dread. The lowly, on the contrary, hail its onset with joy; come liberation, come vindication."[10] The spiral of violence rests securely within such divisions and expectations. The betrayal of Jesus lurks in its shadow along with our nonviolent pretenses.

Before moving on to our third choice, we return to Daniel. How are we to make sense of apocalyptic Daniel's revision of his inherited tradition? Conventional interpretive wisdom says that when the old story lines failed, God spoke a new word. God, according to this view, offered new and divinely inspired explanations for historical oppression, made new promises of vindication, and revised but reinforced expectations of redemptive violence. Such views are safeguarded through uncritical appeals to the "authority of scripture," which too often assign divine intent to fundamental human distortions.

I propose an alternative to this "if it's in the Bible, it must be true" approach to scripture. There are two guiding principles. First, we must see the writer or writers behind Daniel as human beings who tried to make sense out of God and history during a time of intense oppression and pain. Their efforts were creative and valuable both to their people and to us. Apocalyptic Daniel's theology is an important resource for our ongoing faith journeys in which we, like Daniel, try to make sense out of God and oppressive history. The book of Daniel, however, is not "God's word," and Daniel does not speak for God. Apocalyptic Daniel seems to have distorted God in many ways.

Second, when it comes to assessing biblical claims about what God is or is not like, I privilege Jesus over the book of Daniel and other voices within the tradition. I insist, in other words, that Christians allow the historical Jesus to guide our approach to life, faith, and biblical images of God. One practical consequence of doing so is to examine Jesus in relation to the apocalyptic tradition. Do Jesus' images of God and expectations of history conform to or break with apocalyptic Daniel's imagery and expectations?

The historical Jesus offers a third answer to the question we have been exploring. What happened to biblical expectations of God when oppression deepened, promises were not kept, and old stories lost their interpretive power? In confronting this question, Jesus fundamentally challenged many of the images of God on which both the faltering old theology and its apocalyptic alternatives were founded. Jesus undermined rather than deepened the relationship between God and violence, and he broke open the cracks concerning human projection of absolute power onto God. As a first-century Palestinian Jew, Jesus apparently embraced the apocalyptic worldview and then, for reasons to be explored later, abandoned it. The Gospel writers and Paul largely betrayed Jesus in favor of the apocalypse. So too have most Christians, including many nonviolent Christian activists.

Notes

1. Arthur Jeffrey and Gerald Kennedy, "The Book of Daniel," in *The Interpreter's Bible*, vol. 6 (Nashville: Abingdon Press, 1956), 346, 360. Jeffrey and Kennedy indicate that throughout the twelve chapters in the book of Daniel, "there are so many little points indicative of a single author that we must conclude that the writer of the visions, living during the latter days of Antiochus Epiphanes, prefaced his visions by a series of stories which would lead up to them." They note that "there is no compelling reason" for assuming "dual authorship." *The Anchor Bible* commentary, in sharp contrast, refers often to the "authors" behind the book of Daniel, and presumes several writers, including an "editor-compiler" who shaped its final form. See Louis F. Hartman and Alexander A. Di Lella, *The Book of Daniel*, Anchor Bible (New York: Doubleday, 1978), 8, 13.

2. Daniel Berrigan, *Daniel: Under the Siege of the Divine* (Farmington, Pa.: Plough Publishing, 1998), 111.

3. Richard Horsley, *Jesus and the Spiral of Violence: Popular Jewish Resistance in Roman Palestine* (Minneapolis: Fortress Press, 1993), 7.

4. Berrigan, *Daniel*, 122.

5. Jeffrey and Kennedy, "Book of Daniel," 351.

6. Ibid., 358.

7. Berrigan, *Daniel*, ix. Daniel Berrigan is a friend, a mentor, and a Christian nonviolent activist whom I respect deeply. It was his faithful resistance during the Vietnam War that reawakened my faith. Berrigan, through his writings and witness, made Jesus and Christianity come alive for me. I embrace his nonviolent witness but challenge his reliance on the apocalyptic tradition as a basis for nonviolence for reasons to be discussed in future chapters.

8. Ibid., 180.

9. Ibid., 31.

10. Ibid., xi.

11 JESUS: JEWISH AND HUMAN

If the Hebrew Scriptures and Christian New Testament both reveal and distort God, then we must use some criteria by which to discern between revelation and distortion. My conviction is that Jesus' life and faith are the best criteria Christians have for doing so. The historical Jesus can help us make sense out of the Bible, God, scriptural interpretations of Jesus and the Christ, our own religious experience, and faithful discipleship. If our religious experience of God, Jesus, or the Christ can lead us to participate in racist militia groups, join Hitler's youth movement, justify apartheid, tolerate injustice, adopt the values of the dominant culture, accept violence, allow ROTC on the campuses of Christian colleges and universities, root nonviolence in violent expectations of God, become soldiers, or embrace a quietistic faith, then our experiences alone are insufficient. If our Christian rituals and sacraments do the same, then they too cry out for revision and reinterpretation based on the life and faith of Jesus. If Jesus is to be our guide, however, then we must meet him as a Jewish man in first-century Palestine.

JESUS THE JEW: BEYOND IDEALIZATION AND DENIAL

Vile and violent portrayals overwhelm positive images of God within the Bible. I presented diverse yet troubling portraits of God in order to ground a discussion of Jesus and to counter two problems common to many Christian interpreters. The first is the tendency to deny or downplay the Jewishness of Jesus. Jesus appears within much of Christianity as the first Christian. He does not wrestle with his Jewish tradition; he is divorced from it. The second problem is idealization of the Jewish tradition. Jesus is placed in a Jewish context based on idealized readings and sanitized renditions of selective texts. This tendency is especially acute among progressive interpreters who, like myself, understand Jesus in the context of justice traditions found in the Hebrew Scriptures.

Progressive interpreters glorify the Exodus, jubilee, sabbatical, and prophetic traditions, censor the pathological violence of God, and ignore the disturbing ethnocentrism that is central to many of these texts. Others, including many nonviolent activists, idealize the apocalyptic tradition because of its clear call to resist empire. Calls to resistance central to the apocalyptic books of Daniel and Revelation are embraced, but apocalypticism's simplistic dividing wall between good and evil and its overwhelming despair concerning history are ignored. The violence of God is either minimized or seen as foundational to God's efforts to insure justice. Nonviolent tactics are rooted in expectations of a violent God. Idealized treatments of liberation and apocalyptic themes draw lofty conclusions from skewed readings of selective texts. The pathology of God is ignored or sidestepped. It resurfaces repeatedly, however, in our own hearts and in the life of the world, where the spiral of violence reigns supreme.

I suspect that both idealization and denial of Jesus' Jewish roots reflect unspoken disgust with many pathological images of God. As mentioned earlier, if we behaved like God does in the Bible or did what God tells us to do, then we could justifiably be judged insane and be put away. Some interpreters, like the abusive pastor who delivered the despicable children's sermon recounted earlier, embrace vile images of God and hold them over parishioner's heads like a club. Many others, however, do not directly defend a God who orders us to murder disobedient children, sanctions or commits genocide, and reduces people to cannibalism. They refuse, however, to challenge the God who is repeatedly associated with such actions or the "sacred scriptures" that describe them. This is akin to maintaining silence about a sexually abusive father because he puts bread and butter on the table. Consciously or unconsciously, many people of faith censor God's despicable behavior even when the pathology that is left out overwhelms the texts from which justice messages are gleaned.

Idealization and denial are different problems, but they end up in a similarly bad place. We are right to be confused, upset, or disgusted with many of the horrible characteristics and behaviors attributed to God by the writers of the Bible. We are wrong to legitimate them as we do each Sunday when we end a Bible reading with high-sounding phrases such as "This is the word of the Lord." We are right to pay attention to our discomfort in reading our children biblical stories overflowing with God's violence. We are wrong to sanitize those stories rather than confront them. Our books, songs, and art depict beautiful rainbows, quaint arks with animals, and walls falling down, all with little or no emphasis on the genocide at the heart of many of these tales. We are right to pay attention to fundamental conflicts between our experiences of God and some of the biblical portraits of a violent, punitive deity. We are wrong to deny these conflicts or proof-text our way around them. We are right to try to make sense out of Jesus in the context of his Jewish tradition. We are wrong to build false bridges between Hebrew scriptural texts and Jesus, wrong to proof-text our way past troubling contradictions between Jesus and his Jewish tradition and between Jesus and Christian claims about the Christ.

We must deal with the Bible's despicable portraits of God head on, not only because integrity requires it, but because many of the images we find so disgusting were rejected by Jesus and then resurfaced to infect New Testament interpretations of his life, death, and resurrection. The historical Jesus can help us only if we meet him as a Jew in first-century Palestine. This means allowing Jesus to be Jewish without idealizing his tradition. We can assume that Jesus, like people in all cultures including our own, was deeply socialized into his tradition. The tradition itself was diverse and conflictive, and Jesus wrestled with it in the context of Roman-dominated first-century Palestine.

Jesus would have heard many stories drawn from both the Hebrew Scriptures and oral tradition. They would have shaped his understanding and response to the injustice, poverty, debt, and inequality that characterized his daily life and that of his friends and neighbors throughout Palestine. He would have been surrounded by competing images of God and diverse and incompatible claims about what pleased or angered God. He would have heard stories of liberation and oppression and different explanations for historical triumphs and failures. He would have listened to a variety of interpretations concerning the people's present plight under Roman occupation and made his way through competing scenarios concerning future expectations of God and history.

The old theology remained strong in first-century Palestine, and Jesus was exposed to its emphasis on sin and holiness, disobedience and punishment, exile and restoration, warnings of divine retribution and promises of salvation. He was also surrounded by arrogant Roman claims that placed emperor and empire in the context of divine will and the counterclaims of apocalyptic voices announcing an imminent violent coming of God to end history or impose justice and to avenge evildoers. Jesus would have heard about links between God and justice, and he would have been surrounded by expectations of God's violence. All these things were part of Jesus' socialization and his social world as a first-century Jew in Roman-occupied Palestine. We must meet Jesus, in other words, as a socialized Jew who was capable of discernment and who made difficult choices that shaped his life, faith, and action in the context of his evolving understanding of God, history, and his tradition.

We do not often speak of Jesus' faith. Perhaps this is because we have placed the historical Jesus safely at the margins of Christianity. We are too busy proclaiming our faith in Jesus to notice the faith of Jesus. Maybe we have internalized the Gospel of John's robotic Jesus who is always in control. Or perhaps it makes us uncomfortable to think that Jesus had a faith life and journey akin to our own, including troubling questions, crisis points, and doubts. His evolving understanding of God, including changing his mind about the nature of God's power and expected violence, is evident in his conduct and his proclamation of the "kingdom of God." The Gospels offer competing, incompatible, and irreconcilable portraits of Jesus. We have no good choice but to choose between them.

LETTING JESUS BE HUMAN

Traditional theology says Jesus was both fully human and fully divine. His divinity, however, has nearly always eclipsed his humanity. That is why some Christian interpreters claim that the historical Jesus is unimportant or even dangerous to Christian faith. And that is why it is important to go beyond tidy distinctions between the Jesus of history and the Christ of faith, the pre-Easter and post-Easter Jesus. Jesus' divinity has so triumphed over his humanity that we rarely notice how frequently Gospel interpretations of the meaning of his life, death, and resurrection conflict with Jesus' own understanding of God.

We cannot adequately probe Jesus' life as a revelation of God without fully embracing his humanity. Jesus was a first-century Palestinian Jewish man who was socialized within his tradition. He had to make sense out of competing claims and explanations of God and history, exile and empire, holiness and sin, old story lines and new apocalyptic promises. We must respect Jesus' humanity or we will miss important Gospel clues about his faith life, including his emerging understanding of God. We must respect Jesus' humanity or we will miss evidence of his rejection of many of the foundational assumptions of the old theology of deserved blessings and curses, his embrace and later break with John the Baptist's apocalyptic movement, or his differences with other Jewish social movements over expectations of God and history. Without respecting his humanity, we cannot accept that Jesus was sometimes wrong about God or that he changed his mind about important matters of great significance to life and faith.

We should remember in this context our need to critically assess what it means to call Jesus the "Son of God." The reality of "messy monotheism" and the irreconcilable characteristics attributed to God as part of the emerging one God tradition make such language confusing and problematic. Is Jesus the "Son" of a "Father" who is patriarchal, distant, and punishing? Is Jesus the "Son" of a pathological deity that uses brutal empires to crush disobedient people? Is Jesus the "Son" of a vengeful God who rejoices when those judged guilty of sin are reduced to slavery or cannibalism? Is Jesus the "Son" of P's merciless God? Is Jesus the "Son" of a God who is so preoccupied with holiness that he orders parents to murder disobedient children, requires homosexuals to be killed, and dissolves marriages to foreigners in order to keep the chosen people's stolen land clean? Is Jesus the "Son" of the God who orders those who gather sticks on the Sabbath to be stoned by the community? Is Jesus the "Son" of God who is God because of superior violence? Is Jesus the "Son" of a bloodthirsty deity who can only be appeased through the violent sacrifice of God's own offspring? Is Jesus the "Son" of a God who is unable to deliver justice within history but who will send the Christ to be an agent of vengeance against enemies at history's end?

These questions are troubling but unavoidable given traditional language about God the Father and Jesus the Son. In the following pages, I look at Jesus' life and faith as windows through which we see what God is or is not like, or at least what God is or is not like according to Jesus. Different questions arise in this alternative context: Is Jesus' God powerful? Does Jesus' God demonstrate power through superior violence?

What does Jesus' teaching on love of enemies suggest about his under-standing of God? Is Jesus' "Father" a biological parent or a life-giving Spirit that Jesus knows intimately? Why is Jesus often associated with food and healing? Why does he intentionally break various laws? What does Jesus expect from God and history? What is Jesus' understanding of salvation? Why do claims from the pens of the Gospel writers concerning Jesus and the Christ so often conflict with and undermine Jesus' claims about God?

We need to meet Jesus as a human being if we are to answer these and other related questions. We will solve the mystery of Jesus' disappearance and we will discover how finding him can revitalize Christian faith if and when we realize how much we miss when we claim that Jesus is God without affirming that Jesus shows us what God is like!

12 THE SUCCESS OF FAILURE

Jesus was born in Roman-occupied Palestine more than 160 years follow-ing Daniel's introduction of apocalyptic thought. Apocalypticism was a popular worldview, perhaps the dominant worldview, at the time of Jesus. It became the primary lens for New Testament writers who interpreted Jesus' death and resurrection. Each Gospel introduces Jesus in the context of John the Baptist, an apocalyptic prophet. Mark, Matthew, and Luke rely heavily on apocalyptic themes in telling their versions of the Jesus story. Apocalypticism's predominant place within the tradition is confirmed in Paul's writings, which predate the Gospels by twenty to forty years. Paul's interpretation of the Christ is incomprehensible apart from Paul's apoca-lyptic hopes and expectations. Mark, the first Gospel written, begins with Jesus being baptized into an apocalyptic movement, and the New Testament ends with Christ terminating history as an apocalyptic judge in the book of Revelation. Apocalypticism's success within the tradition was due to the failure of both the old theology and apocalypticism itself. Apocalypticism's failure, in other words, insured its success, although this dynamic would have been impossible without a few important modifica-tions that fundamentally distorted Jesus, God, and the Christ.

CRACKS IN THE APOCALYPTIC WORLDVIEW

We do not know how influential apocalyptic Daniel was in his time. He encouraged people to "stand firm and take action" (11:32b). The promise that Antiochus would be defeated but "not by human hands" (8:25) may indicate that Daniel, in contrast to the Maccabees, urged nonviolent resistance. In any case, Jewish resistance to Antiochus was fierce, and the Maccabean revolutionaries defeated the Seleucid empire.[1] Daniel would have welcomed the defeat of Antiochus, but it did not fulfill his expectations. On the one hand, many people stood firm and took action, and Antiochus was ousted. The author of nonapocalyptic Daniel might have felt vindicated by these outcomes. He, like apocalyptic Daniel, had called the people of God to faithful resistance amidst imperial pretensions and repression and had promised that in God's broader plan empires would ultimately fall. If nonapocalyptic Daniel had lived to see the rise and fall of Antiochus, then he might have proclaimed, "Message validated. Mission accomplished."

Apocalyptic Daniel may have seen things differently. People stood firm and took action but it was by human hands that the Seleucid empire fell. Violent revolutionaries won the day, and a disappointing history filled with oppression and violence followed. Daniel's apocalyptic promises of God's final defeat of evil and vindication of the faithful at the end of history were never realized. Discrepancies between apocalyptic expectations and actual events point to serious deficiencies. One attempt to minimize them is to suggest that Daniel's apocalyptic imagery masked his real intent, which was to promise the end of oppressive rule within rather than at the end of history. This loophole, if granted, does not lessen the problems posed by subsequent history that proved disastrous for "God's chosen people."

Daniel's apocalyptic predictions were in error on many counts. First, the end time did not come and history did not conform to expectations. The defeat of Antiochus apparently reinforced the old theology's view that God's power had resulted, as with Pharaoh, in the defeat of a militarily superior foe. The victory, however, was not followed by liberation and independent rule, and in stark contrast to new exodus expectations and prophetic promises, it did not mean peace and prosperity. Historical reality was far removed from the old Davidic promise of everlasting kingship restated by Daniel as a promise of "everlasting dominion" (7:14), and it was equally distant from Isaiah's imperial pretensions of a historical reversal in which Israel would "possess the nations as male and female slaves" (14:2b).

In short, apocalyptic Daniel's new theology was undermined by historical events. Neither evil nor domination had been vanquished as the apocalyptic seer had promised. The Seleucid empire was defeated, but history moved forward and evil persisted. Repression, inequality, and brutal factionalism between competing Jewish priestly groups deepened following the Jewish triumph. Evil was alive and well, but with independent rule it wore a transparently Jewish face.

Another fundamental discrepancy between apocalyptic promise and actual event concerned the fate of empires. Antiochus's defeat seemed to validate the claim that empires do not have the last word. The fulfillment of this promise, however, was more illusionary than real. One empire after another had oppressed Israel/Judah, as Daniel's vision of the four beasts made clear. As the Seleucid empire fell, a new empire centered in Rome was rising. It was not long before the people of God again faced a future of domination within empire. Daniel's view of history seemed utterly pessimistic. The defeat of Antiochus and the Seleucid empire (the fourth beast) was assured, apocalyptic Daniel said, as part of God's plan to end history. Empires were so powerful that Daniel could only imagine their defeat as the consequence of God's violent action. Neither history nor imperial pretensions, however, ended with Antiochus's defeat.

An additional failure of the apocalyptic worldview concerns ongoing priestly conflicts and Daniel's notion of vindication of the faithful. The old theology stressed that people were killed by oppressive rulers as God's punishment for their individual or collective sin. The new theology emerged in a context in which the most faithful of the faithful were being killed while resisting Antiochus. Apocalyptic Daniel sought to inspire faithful resistance by promising God's vindication through resurrection of the dead, understood as God's end-time reckoning in which good and evil would be justly compensated. History, as previously noted, did not end, nor did priestly power struggles and conflicts. Having defeated Antiochus and his supporters among Jewish priestly groups, many of apocalyptic Daniel's most faithful of the faithful turned on each other with a vengeance.

The problem of competing priestly factions killing each other, discussed in the context of messy monotheism, warrants further attention in the present context. Hostility between different priestly groups following Antiochus's defeat drove the Essenes into the desert. The Essenes could not imagine resolving their differences with others within society or within history. They withdrew and waited for a new violent coming of God at which time the present leaders of the Temple would be destroyed.

As history unfolded, so too did their vision. After the Roman triumph, the Essenes anticipated God's judgment against both pagan Rome and the leaders of the Jewish Temple.

Priestly writers often disagreed about God, about what did and did not please God, and about which priestly groups were favored by God. A good deal of "God's violence" is traceable to these power struggles. In spite of their differences, however, priestly writers of the "sacred" texts wrote themselves into "divinely sanctioned" positions of power and privilege. As a result, priests argued over questions of legitimacy, but they occupied a central place within the tradition. They used the power of the pen to stamp their authority with a "divine seal of approval" sanctified by the holy Bible. Independent rule usually meant the triumph of one priestly faction over another, and foreign rule often meant increased power for certain high-ranking priests. Priests were powerful because occupying empires relied upon literate indigenous elites to help administer their affairs over subject peoples. Jesus' conflict with religious authorities and the Temple is rooted in this dynamic.

Imperial governance with the aid of indigenous elites is known as indirect rule. In Israel, priests whose authority was sanctioned by sacred Jewish texts were positioned well to benefit from such arrangements. Richard Horsley explains:

> Whereas the Babylonians had deported the Judean ruling class, the Persians established a priestly aristocracy and, initially, returned the remnants of the Davidic family to power. The high priesthood and an apparatus of "priestly" government centered in the rebuilt Temple soon completely eclipsed the Davidic family as the Persians' client rulers. The two Jewish leaders who played the major role in the reconstitution of Judean society, Ezra and Nehemiah, held their authority and power as officers of the Persian emperor. This double role, however, was also true of the high priesthood once it was securely established. That is, the very representative of the Jewish people and their mediator with God was also the representative of the Persian imperial regime. From the Persian imperial viewpoint it made sense to sponsor both the restoration of "the House of the God who is in Jerusalem" and its attendant priesthood. The populace of Judea thus could focus their loyalty and worship on the God of Israel in Jerusalem— and of course bring their tithes and taxes in due season to the

Temple, i.e., to the high priestly officers, who in turn would render loyalty and tribute to the Persian court. This same imperial arrangement of ruling through the priestly aristocracy remained in effect basically until the destruction of the second Temple [in 70 C.E.], with the exception of the period of rule by Herodian client kings. The Hellenistic empires, Ptolemies and Seleucids, both governed Judean society and apparently collected tribute through the Judean high priesthood.[2]

The priesthood, in other words, functioned as an instrument of imperial governance. Foreign rulers often played priestly factions against each other, recruited cooperative priests, and placed them in positions of power. Far removed from the shifting fortunes of the powerful stood the vast majority of common people who were marginalized and exploited by systems in which a few powerful Jews positioned themselves to benefit from unjust rule. Richard Horsley captures some of the dynamics of priestly power struggles and intrigue that were part of the political landscape:

> The very origins of second Temple Jewish society and religion can be understood in this light. Although Ezra, Nehemiah, and the high priests owed their power to their position as officers of the Persian empire, they and the "Priestly writers" of early postexilic times reconstructed and virtually *established* a religious tradition as a way of legitimating the "restored" Jewish social-political order. The priestly aristocracy's attempt at Hellenizing reforms [during the reign of Antiochus] illustrates how, when they abandoned the sacred cultural traditions— even though they made no change in the actual social structure—they suddenly lost legitimacy in the eyes of the people. The Hasmoneans, who rode the Maccabean rebellion into power . . . immediately restored the traditional high-priestly regime with themselves as the new incumbents. However, the compromises and outright violations of tradition that they made in pretending to restore sacred customs (as well as in reestablishing social-economic stratification) did not sit well with some other priests and intellectuals among their former allies. . . . The Dead Sea Scrolls provide vivid witness that to those who had hoped for a more egalitarian and revitalized social outcome of the revolt [against Antiochus], the

Hasmonean "Wicked Priests" simply reverted to the same old "frozen" stratified social order, while legitimating themselves by a putative restoration of traditions.[3]

There are four points made by Horsley that can help us understand new developments in apocalyptic thought following Daniel, key aspects of Jesus' social critique, and the images of God on which Jesus' domination-free order was founded. First, priestly writers used the power of the pen to legitimize their privileged positions through appeals to "sacred" tradition. This often hurt the people and misrepresented God, something that must be considered when assessing "scriptural authority." Jesus, as we will see, tells a parable specifically aimed at exposing oppressive taxation collected by Pharisees under the threat of "divine" sanction (Luke 18:9–14). Second, imperial rulers gave high priestly groups a stake in oppressive systems. Their collaborative role resulted in the oppression of the people and was a major source of social, cultural, economic, political, and religious conflict throughout biblical history, including in first-century Palestine.

Third, priestly factions excluded during times of independent or indirect rule were often resentful. Frustrations grew out of jealousy that benefits flowed to others and concern that the priestly factions in power violated essential aspects of the tradition. Priestly groups locked out by present power arrangements sought to discredit groups in power and offered alternative religious and social visions. Many of their alternatives, however, were grounded in power struggles that tell us more about human rivalries than they do about God.

Finally, independent rule disappointed many. Contrary to expectations rooted in Daniel's "new theology," there was no triumphant end to human history, no permanent justice, and no ultimate defeat of evil. In opposition to centuries of old theological promises, the defeat of enemies (salvation) did not lead to glorious reversals or a more egalitarian social order. Independence meant little more than oppressive rule with a Jewish face as one high priestly faction consolidated its own privileges through violence, repression, and appeals to "sacred texts." Social stratification deepened.

CONCLUSION

Apocalyptic Daniel's new theology may have helped people overcome resignation and maintain faith when the old theology no longer made sense. His apocalyptic promises, however, were not realized. History did not end with Antiochus's defeat, domination and civil strife continued during independent rule, and although the Seleucid empire weakened, a new empire, this time Roman, emerged. Priestly power struggles followed the defeat of Antiochus. In short, imperial domination of history continued and despair intensified despite apocalyptic promises.

Daniel's apocalyptic theology, like the old theology it adapted or replaced, would have been discredited had it not been for two things. First, apocalypticism was born in the midst of despair. The failure of its promises led to even greater despair that proved to be fertile ground in which the apocalyptic worldview grew rather than was buried. The process by which failure led to success within the tradition went something like this. The apocalyptic worldview was a response to profound historical failures and crises. In the midst of oppression, apocalyptic Daniel promised a new violent coming of God to defeat evil and vindicate the righteous at the end of history. Apocalyptic promises were not fulfilled and historical crises worsened in the historical period following Antiochus's defeat and after the political execution of Jesus. The result in both historical settings was even greater despair and a more profound alienation from history. Desperation and deepening despair that accompanied historical catastrophes and apocalypticism's deficiencies turned out to be conducive to the apocalyptic worldview's adaptation and growth.

A second reason the apocalyptic worldview grew stronger when it could have been discredited is that later interpreters adapted the tradition. Apocalyptic Daniel offered a new theology to fit changing circumstances during a period of intense repression. The gap between Daniel's apocalyptic promises and subsequent history prompted another crisis and a new set of questions. What happened to expectations of God and history after apocalyptic Daniel's promises were not realized? How did the Jesus movement and various other Jewish groups respond when apocalyptic expectations were frustrated, independent rule proved disastrous, and a new empire, this time Roman, emerged on the scene more arrogant and powerful than any that had preceded it?

Notes

1. Richard Horsley, *Jesus and the Spiral of Violence: Popular Jewish Resistance in Roman Palestine* (Minneapolis: Fortress Press, 1993), 67–68.
2. Ibid., 9–10.
3. Ibid., 14–15, emphasis in original.

13   MURDER AND METHOD

Rooting Christianity in the life of Jesus requires particulars concerning person, place, and time. Jesus lived, put faith into practice, and was murdered in Palestine in the first century of the common era (C.E.). In order to make sense out of his faith, his parables and teachings, his actions, his life as a revelation of God, his challenge to Rome and Temple, his violent death, the resurrection claims of his followers, and the apocalyptic lens of New Testament writers, we must know about his social world. Stated somewhat differently, any effort to ground the-ological reflection and Christian faith and action in the life and faith of the historical Jesus depends on a credible and convincing portrait of both Jesus and the domination system of first-century Palestine. By domination system, I mean the institutions, groups, and ideas that powerfully shaped and distorted religious, economic, and political life. Directed by Rome and Temple, this oppressive system was responsible for Jesus' death and for the hunger, poverty, violence, and despair that were part of daily life for the vast majority of his contemporaries. In response to and in the context of this system, Jesus announced and embodied the good news of God.

The thorny question is this: If the New Testament writers reveal and distort Jesus, then how do we decide which texts offer a glimpse of the authentic Jesus and which do not? I begin piecing together a portrait of Jesus in the next three chapters through discussion of his life in the context of the domination system of first-century Palestine. The present chapter looks at Gospel and creedal distortions that obscure deadly dynamics within the domination system of first-century Palestine, including who killed Jesus and why.

WHO KILLED JESUS?

A murder lies at the heart of many mystery novels. There are a crime, crime scene, and victim. There are deceptions and cover-ups, suspects with motives and alibis, and detectives looking for answers. Although characters speak for themselves, a narrator often guides readers throughout. Most mysteries end with the murderer named or captured and the motive for murder explained.

The Gospels are not novels, but the integrity of Christian faith requires that we solve a murder mystery involving who killed Jesus and why. We must sift through clues and examine various suspects, motives, and alibis. Our task is complicated because the crime scene is many centuries old and we have four narrators guiding us and leading us astray. Matthew, Mark, Luke, and John are not eyewitnesses to the events they describe. They tell inconsistent tales about the murder and its meaning. They could be held in contempt because of contradictions in their own testimonies. They also disagree profoundly with each other. They present conflicting motives for murder and engage in cover-ups. They also draw on many incompatible scriptural images and themes in a desperate attempt to make sense out of the brutal execution of Jesus in light of Jewish expectations and history.

The Christian creeds are equally problematic. Creeds reinforce distortions found in Gospel accounts and downplay the oppressive role played by key actors in the domination system. They jump from affirmation of an ahistorical birth to falsification of a real death. They omit Jesus' life and distort his birth and execution. Jesus is crucified, according to the creeds, *under* not *by* Pontius Pilate. This language is like a line in a coroner's report indicating the time of death. It says that Jesus was crucified during the reign of Pilate, a Rome-appointed governor who ruled Judea from 26 to 36 C.E. Functionally, this language distorts and downplays the political execution of Jesus, Pilate's role as executioner, crucifixion as psychological warfare tactic, and Rome's oppressive role in first-century Palestine.

Jesus' crucifixion indicates a profound clash between his vision and lived understanding of God and Roman imperial priorities and claims. From the point of view of a detective, crucifixion is the equivalent of finding Roman fingerprints all over the scene of the crime. Martin Hengel writes:

> Among the Romans it [crucifixion] was inflicted above all on the lower classes, i.e., slaves, violent criminals, and the unruly elements in rebellious provinces, not least in Judaea. . . . The chief reason for its use was its allegedly supreme efficacy as a deterrent; it was, of course, carried out publicly. . . . It was usually associated with other forms of torture, including at least flogging. . . . By the public display of a naked victim at a prominent place—at a crossroads, in the theatre, on high ground, at the place of the crime—crucifixion also represented his uttermost humiliation. . . . Crucifixion was aggravated further by the fact that quite often its victims were never buried. It was a stereotyped picture that the crucified victim served as food for wild beasts and birds of prey. In this way his humiliation was made complete. What it meant for a man in antiquity to be refused burial, and the dishonour which went with it, can hardly be appreciated by modern man.[1]

Creeds that omit Jesus' life, distort his death, and falsify Pilate's role in his execution are symptomatic of profound problems inherent in Christianity without the historical Jesus. The creeds not only elevate the Gospel fiction of Roman innocence to the status of official doctrine, they sever the relationship between Jesus' death and his life as a revelation of God. The birth of Jesus, according to creedal logic, is important only because birth predates death. His death is noteworthy because it is understood as an atoning sacrifice and because it is a chronological necessity or precursor to resurrection. His life matters little. We reinforce the acceptability of Christianity without Jesus every time we ignore his life and recite "born of the Virgin Mary, suffered under Pontius Pilate."

Jesus' absence from Christianity, symbolically represented in the creeds, has real and troubling consequences. Creedal formulations that obscure Rome's role in Jesus' murder, in other words, have more than symbolic meaning. A life not mentioned is by implication unimportant. It is not a coincidence that a creed that ignores Jesus' life and softens imperial Rome's role in his death has given rise throughout history to many expressions of Christian faith that are influenced by and comfortable with stately power.

Christianity became an acceptable religion by a decree of Constantine in 313, and by the end of the fourth century it had become the official religion of the Roman empire. Closer to home, Christianity in the United States is often associated with uncritical patriotism and with national mythologies in which the United States is viewed as a benevolent superpower. I have written elsewhere about U.S. warfare against the poor throughout Central America in which U.S. "low intensity conflict" strategy relied on psychological terror tactics similar in design and intent to Roman crucifixions.[2] The key point here is that creedal distortions concerning Jesus' death powerfully shape and distort the contour and content of Christian faith.

That Jesus is essentially missing from Christianity is illustrated in an exercise I do with students. Many do not look to the life of Jesus for guidance. Most believe in God and think a heavenly future awaits them, but they stand alone when making vital lifestyle, vocational, value, and political choices. Faith seems to have been set aside like a forgotten treasure in the far reaches of a dark attic, and Jesus, for all practical purposes, is missing from their lives. A few students wear WWJD bracelets, but they seem to know little or nothing about Jesus, who remains an abstraction. This separation between life and faith is troubling, although not surprising, given creedal formulations. If Jesus' life does not make it into the creeds wherein we confess our faith, why then should we let his life inform our faith and our life choices?

The in-class exercise centers on the question, "Who killed Jesus and why?" Few students have been asked this or a similar question, and it throws them off balance. Two answers triumph numerically as students summarize ideas from their small group discussions. Their responses are rooted in some combination of church experience, memorization of creedal statements, and general recollection of Gospel texts. The most common response is that "the Jews killed Jesus." Further conversation reveals that many students have forgotten or never learned that Jesus was Jewish or that Christianity began as a Jewish reform movement. Their assumption seems to be that Jesus was a Christian who founded the Church and was killed by "the Jews," a generic category of people stripped of social role, function, or position.

Blaming generic Jews for the murder of Jesus fills in the blank left by creeds that, as mentioned above, functionally absolves Rome of responsibility but leaves the question of who killed Jesus unexplored. Christian creeds say that Jesus was crucified during the reign of, not by, Pilate, and they show little interest in Jesus' life. Given creedal indifference to Jesus' life and the cover-up of his death on behalf of his Roman executioner, why should my students care to know about Jesus or Pilate?

Gospel distortions lead to similar problems. Several hundred years before the creeds were formulated and four to seven decades after the death of Jesus, the Gospel writers shifted blame for Jesus' murder from Rome to the Jews. Students who say "the Jews killed Jesus" do not often know chapter and verse, but they base their answer on scriptural memories and creedal impressions. My students, after years of Christian formation, have internalized dangerous biases rooted in the Gospel writers' propensity to scapegoat the Jews and find favor with the Romans. Matthew is a good example:

> When Pilate saw that he could do nothing, but rather that a riot was beginning, he took some water and washed his hands before the crowd, saying, "I am innocent of this man's blood; see to it yourselves." Then the people as a whole answered, "His blood be on us and on our children!" (27:24–25).

These prejudices reach from Gospel accounts to the Holocaust, underscoring the need to read the Gospels critically. Fortunately, the Gospels are not uniform documents. They contain material from many layers of tradition and offer competing testimonies about who killed Jesus and why. For example, Matthew, Mark, Luke, and John have many stories and images that directly challenge Roman arrogance and power. They also transmit materials intended to present Christianity in ways acceptable or pleasing to Rome. Jesus cannot be reconciled with both positions, though each is found in the Gospels. My point here is to emphasize that contradictions within Gospel stories offer important clues that can help us understand the domination system and the meaning of Jesus' life and death.

The second answer offered by my students, with only slightly less frequency, is that "God killed Jesus." Jesus' death is not understood as a murder or execution because God sent Jesus to die. It is a sacrifice willed or orchestrated by a loving God who has Jesus killed in order to heal the rift between sinful humanity and God. The question of why a loving, compassionate God would need or require such a barbaric sacrifice goes unasked, as Christian doctrine and orthodoxy triumph over reason.

When explaining that "God killed Jesus," students refer to songs, sermons, and scripture. Many recite John 3:16 from memory: "For God so loved the world that he gave his only Son, so that everyone who believes in him may not perish but may have eternal life." The first chapter of John's Gospel introduces Jesus with words attributed to John the Baptist: "Here is the Lamb of God who takes away the sin of the world" (1:29b). The atonement view of Jesus' death, which is at the heart of much Christian theology, centers on the belief that Jesus was sent by God to die so that sinful humans could be reconciled to God.

Jesus' sacrificial death, according to this view, atones for humanity's sin. Just as blood from a perfect, unblemished lamb placed on the doorposts and lintels of Jews in Egypt allowed God to "Passover" the Israelites and kill all Egyptian firstborn, so too the blood of Jesus who was born of a virgin and unblemished by sin allows God to pass over the sins of Christians who are saved by Jesus' blood sacrifice. This sacrificial interpretation of Jesus' death lies at the heart of the Christian Eucharist, and although we wrap this interpretation in the language of love, the unspoken implication is that God's wrath could only be appeased through the blood sacrifice of a divine son. Walter Wink notes that the atonement theory is a stunning reversal of Jesus' experience of a gracious God:

> The God whom Jesus revealed as no longer our rival, no longer threatening and vengeful, but unconditionally loving and forgiving, who needed no satisfaction by blood—this God of infinite mercy was metamorphosed by the church into the image of a wrathful God whose demand for blood atonement leads to God's requiring of his own Son a death on behalf of us all. The nonviolent God of Jesus comes to be depicted as a God of unequaled violence, since God not only allegedly demands the blood of the victim who is closest and most precious to him, but also holds the whole of humanity accountable for a death that God both anticipated and required. Against such an image of God the revolt of atheism is an act of pure religion.[3]

Images of God that drive atonement theories are precisely those pathological portraits of God we encountered in previous chapters. God in the Bible, as we saw, ordered people of faith to execute children who talked back to their parents; sent forth she-bears to maul children who insulted a prophet; rejoiced after reducing God's people to cannibalism as a punishment for sin; ordered the murder of all men, women, and children after battle; drowned nearly all of creation and humanity in a punishing flood; sent imperial armies to slaughter disobedient people; exchanged battlefield victories for human sacrifices; and promised eternal punishment for those who did not feed the hungry. Interpretations of Jesus' bloody execution as an atoning sacrifice for human sin and as a means to reconciliation make sense in the context of these images of God. Regina M. Schwartz explains:

> The entire nation of Israel is punished, overrun in stages by conquerors who exile and murder the Israelites at the instigation of an angry Father. While the anger may seem to abate when man does succeed at becoming God in the New Testament, the price of Christ's deification is horrific suffering and death. And the relish that religious traditions have taken in the passion of Christ suggests that the punishment has not been appeased; rather, it has been focused, contracted from exiling the children of God to the sacrifice of one son—with whom all the faithful identify.[4]

A God who reduces people to cannibalism as a consequence of disobedience is capable of deicide, and in our traditional theology, requires it. Perhaps Abraham misread God's desires when he pulled back from sacrificing Isaac. Then again, a human sacrifice may not have been sufficient. Recall that Augustine defended the historicity of the virgin birth because only the sacrifice of a perfect specimen could please God sufficiently to insure he and others would not end up in hell. The key point is that images of God lie behind the atonement theory, and it is doubtful that the atonement would make any sense to Jesus in light of his image or experience of God. As Wink notes, "the God whom Jesus reveals refrains from all forms of reprisal and demands no victims. God does not endorse holy wars or just wars or religions of violence."[5]

In sum, the creeds treat Jesus as a missing person and exonerate Rome. The Gospels make explicit what the creeds with intimations of Roman innocence leave open: the Jews killed Jesus. Matthew says more. The Jews not only murdered God's Son, they called for God's bloody vengeance upon themselves. This sentiment, when coupled with Christian arrogance and real political power, led to numerous pogroms and a deadly holocaust. Blaming the Jews for Jesus' death, ironically, coexists with the belief that God sent Jesus to die. A loving God killed his son so "God" would no longer go on killing us. Twisted logic indeed! Given creedal and Gospel distortions and in the context of traditional Christian interpretations, it is understandable that my students have had little interest in the historical Jesus or in the role of Jewish leaders and Roman authorities in his execution. It also makes sense that Jesus is important solely because of the resurrection, generally understood theologically as the resuscitation of a corpse that offers confirmation of a successful atoning sacrifice that unlocks the keys to heaven.

At this point in the discussion with students we turn to Mark's Gospel. By the middle of the first chapter there is tension in the air when John the Baptist is arrested. Jesus heals a man with a withered hand on the Sabbath at the beginning of chapter 3. This sets the stage for verse 6: "The Pharisees went out and immediately conspired with the Herodians against him [Jesus], how to destroy him." This verse nudges many of my students from a deep religious slumber. The question, "Who killed Jesus and why?" begins to make sense. Like detectives trying to unravel a whodunit, students ask questions and look for clues that can help them solve a mystery. Why is healing the source of so much conflict? Who are the Pharisees and the Herodians? Why, according to Mark's Gospel, did they conspire to murder Jesus?

Awareness of a conspiracy to murder increases student interest in Jesus' life and life setting, including historical and sociological factors. What was life like for people in Jesus' time? What groups and institutions held power? In what ways and for what reasons did Jesus clash with them? Students begin to see that these and related questions have relevance for understanding Jesus' life, his parables and teachings, his execution, his images of God, and later theological claims concerning his death and resurrection.

Some Christians fear that the search for the Jesus of history will undermine faith. Historical Jesus scholarship, they say, is like an onion whose layers of meaning are peeled away until nothing remains. I can only say that, based on my own faith journey and what I see in my classroom, this is not my experience. A more helpful analogy is that of a beautiful table that is covered with layers and layers of thick, ugly paint. Removing these layers reveals the unique beauty of the original wood. After one provocative question and an hour of discussion, many of my students seem excited about Jesus and Christianity. I do not think it is an exaggeration to say that for some this exercise began to revitalize faith that had grown stale and stagnant. A brief encounter with the historical Jesus became a seed from which renewed faith sprouted and grew.

CONFLICTING TESTIMONIES

Gospel accounts and creedal formulations are riddled with differences and disagreements concerning the murder of Jesus. Traditional Christianity resolves these problems by insisting they do not matter. The Gospels, like the Christian creeds, according to this view, are neither mysteries nor historical documents. They are confessional statements of faith that proclaim the resurrected Jesus to be "Son of God" and "Savior of the world." These lofty titles, however, lose their meaning when divorced from the Jesus of history. "Son of God" language, as noted previously, requires examination of what God is or is not like according to Jesus and what Jesus is or is not like according to our images of God. We must make our best judgments concerning who killed Jesus and why because he was murdered as a consequence of his life and his life was an expression of his faith, which is to say, a lived reflection of his understanding of God. Jesus' violent death, I would add, requires that we also probe what God is or is not like according to those who were prime suspects in his murder. A credible portrait of Jesus, in other words, must include adequate profiles of those key actors in the domination system that wanted Jesus dead, including insight into their political and religious perspectives.

Solving the mystery surrounding the murder of Jesus depends on finding answers to important historical and theological questions: Who else in the first century was called "Savior"? Who claimed to be "Son of God"? What did adversaries of Jesus expect from God and history? We will see that conflicting claims concerning Saviors, competing Sons of God, and different understandings of God and history prove to be prime motives for murder.

The Gospel writers, as mentioned previously, offer contradictory testimony concerning the murder of Jesus. Mark 3:1–6 challenges the views expressed in creedal formulations and Gospel accounts, and it challenges common beliefs that either "the Jews" or God killed Jesus and that the Romans were bit actors on a major stage. However, it also requires good detective work. It contains important evidence and helpful clues that can help us solve a murder mystery. It also houses misleading details that can lead us astray.

> Again he entered the synagogue, and a man was there who had a withered hand. They watched him to see whether he would cure him on the sabbath, so that they might accuse him. And he said to the man who had the withered hand, "Come for-

ward." Then he said to them, "Is it lawful to do good or to do harm on the sabbath, to save life or to kill?" But they were silent. He looked around at them with anger; he was grieved at their hardness of heart and said to the man, "Stretch out your hand." He stretched it out, and his hand was restored. The Pharisees went out and immediately conspired with the Herodians against him, how to destroy him (Mark 3:1–6).

METHOD

The biblical writers both reveal and distort God. The historical Jesus can help us decide between distortion and revelation because his life and faith tell us a good deal about what God is and is not like. This means we need to look at scripture critically, take Jesus seriously, and allow insights from this process of discernment to interact with and guide our own religious experience. It also means we need a credible portrait of Jesus and of the domination system of first-century Palestine. Our challenge is this: If the New Testament writers reveal and distort Jesus, then we must decide which texts offer glimpses of the authentic Jesus and which do not. How can we do so? Let me demonstrate my approach in reference to Mark 3:1–6 cited above. I begin with six assertions.

First, a passage is generally more reliable when its content is consistent with what we know about the Jesus of history and the history of first-century Palestine, likewise a passage is more suspect when it is not so consistent. By more reliable, I mean that a passage consistent with the Jesus of history and the historical time period is more likely to tell us something important both about how Jesus saw the world and about his vision and experience of God. This is true because Jesus exposes the domination system and contrasts it with God's intentions when he uses "kingdom of God" language.

The search for reliable historical markers is not an easy one. Let me offer three simple illustrations of what such a search might mean in practical terms. First, despite confusion rooted in Gospel accounts, it is clear that Jesus is from Nazareth in Galilee. Birth accounts linking him to Bethlehem, therefore, are suspect and require a good deal of unpacking. Second, the Gospel writers shift blame for Jesus' death from the Romans to the Jews. Historically, however, we know crucifixion was a Roman form of capital punishment. This discrepancy between history and Gospel accounts offers important clues that can help us make sense out of Jesus' life and faith, including what he was doing and why he was killed. The key to understanding Jesus and his understanding of God is connected to his conflict with the domination system in first-century Palestine. The fact that Jesus was executed by key actors in the domination system adds credibility to this historical approach. Finally, Jesus, as mentioned above, was from Galilee. Many of his parables reflect conditions in rural Galilee. In an interactive and dynamic way, knowledge of the historical situation in Galilee can help illuminate Jesus' parables, and Jesus' parables can shed light on social conditions in Galilee. Paying careful attention to historical details found within the parables and in sociological studies can help us see whether the Gospel writers were faithful to Jesus and his understanding of God or whether they recast his parables to suit their own purposes in ways that may undermine Jesus' intent.

A second assertion is that a particular passage need not be historical to be valuable. A nonhistorical passage is likely to be most useful, however, when its content is consistent with or illuminates historically verifiable clues and markers. The presumption in favor of reliable history, therefore, can help us approach nonhistorical texts. Two examples can illustrate this point. First, Matthew's account of Herod's massacre of the infants (Matt 2:16) probably is not historical, but the brutality it conveys is consistent with what we know about Herod. "IN A SINGLE VIVID CHAPTER in the Gospel of Matthew," Richard Horsley and Neil Asher Silberman write, "Herod the Great appears as a cruel and despotic ruler, always ready to utilize informers and violence to ensure the security of his rule."[6] Matthew's nonhistorical account of brutality by a client-king of Rome (the killing of the innocents, 2:16–18) alerts us to the fact that Jesus' life and faith will need to be understood in the context of political injustice and Herod's oppressive rule.

The virgin birth offers another example. I do not believe that the virgin birth is historical. I do believe, however, that the radical significance of the claim is comprehensible in a historical context of Roman arrogance and power, including claims of divine pedigree for the emperor (see chapter 14). In a similar way, Mark 3:1–6 is filled with valuable historical clues even though details in the account and perhaps the event itself may not be historical (see below).

A third assertion is that missing vital historical clues and markers in historical and nonhistorical texts can result in serious distortions of Jesus and Christian theology. Historical clues can be missed for very different reasons. Luke Timothy Johnson misses them because he thinks the Jesus of history is unimportant to Christian faith. He does not look for clues and does not find them. The Jesus Seminar sometimes misses them because it focuses too narrowly on the historicity of specific passages. The Seminar's commentary on Mark 3:1–6 illumines weaknesses in a purely historical approach:

> The words ascribed to Jesus in this story were created [by the Markan author] as part of the narrative. Specific injunctions like "Get up here in front of everybody" and "Hold out your hand" would not have been remembered and passed around during the period the Jesus tradition was being shaped and transmitted by word of mouth. The story suggests, however, that Jesus did engage in controversy regarding sabbath observance.[7]

This commentary, apart from the final sentence, although technically correct, reduces a rich passage to nothing. Imbedded in this and similar passages are historical clues that can help us glimpse Jesus' conflict with the domination system and the images and understanding of God that guided him. This points to a need for an alternative approach to Luke Timothy Johnson's indifference to history and to the Jesus Seminar's narrow focus on historicity of individual verses or texts. My approach examines this and other texts in light of their consistency or inconsistency with important issues traceable to the historical Jesus and first-century Palestine. I examine Mark 3:1–6, therefore, in the context of what is known elsewhere about the historical Jesus and first-century Palestine, and I look to it to shed light on the historical Jesus and his understanding of God. The Jesus Seminar's commentary on Mark 3:1–6 does this in a limited way when it notes that the account suggests "that Jesus did engage in controversy regarding sabbath observance." It seems to me, however, that the text suggests much more. It is firmly attested elsewhere, for example, that Jesus was known as a healer; that he came into conflict with Pharisees and other religious officials over Sabbath observance and other matters; that he spoke and acted, at least symbolically, against the Temple; that "Herodian" rule made use of spies and that it was brutal and repressive; that Jesus was considered a threat to the established system; and that he was crucified probably with explicit or tacit approval of both Jewish and Roman authorities.

Mark 3:1–6 raises many issues and concerns that are consistent with the historical Jesus and the historical period in which he lived. It is valuable even though the incident described may or may not be historical and even though, as we will see in the next chapter, it may overstate the role of the Pharisees. Despite historical limitations, in other words, it contains historically significant and verifiable information that we need to probe fully.

In sum, I believe that historical information and markers imbedded in the Gospels are important for our understanding of Jesus, including his life, teachings, actions, and the images of God he embodied. Passages consistent with what we know about the historical Jesus and first-century Palestine are likely to be the most reliable indicators of how Jesus saw the world and how he understood God. Passages can contain valuable historical clues even if they are not themselves historical. Missing them can be costly. Mark 3:1–6 may not be historical, but it is riddled through and through with historically verifiable markers consistent with what we know about Jesus' life and about first-century Palestine. It is, therefore, both historically and theologically significant.

A fourth assertion is that passages consistent with Jesus and the historical period should be probed for their many historical, practical, and theological implications. Mark 3:1–6, by way of example, contains references to historically and theologically significant language and themes such as "hardness of heart," which point us back into history to Pharaoh and to the Exodus. I suggest in chapter 15 that these themes, when grounded in the concerns of the historical Jesus, offer clues about how and why Jesus embraced, rejected, and reinterpreted various aspects of his Jewish tradition.

An opposite conclusion is warranted when the circumstances are different. My fifth assertion is that if theological claims about the Christ or God reveal sharp contradictions with what we know elsewhere about the historical Jesus and social conditions in first-century Palestine, then they are suspect and should give us pause. Mark 3:6, for example, raises serious questions about the atonement theory. God, according to common Christian interpretation, sent Jesus to die in order to heal the rift between God and sinful humanity. The text says that Jesus' execution resulted from murderous collusion between representatives of two groups, identified as Herodians and Pharisees. As detectives, we will need to explore the accuracy of these charges of a conspiracy to murder, and with a dead body on our hands we must take them seriously.

Contradictions invite careful scrutiny. If, for example, the above Markan passage ended with Jesus joining the man with a withered hand to plot the murder of Herodians and Pharisees, then we would challenge it because it clashes sharply with what we know elsewhere about Jesus and events of the time. This example is intentionally absurd. There are many equally absurd examples, however, that we allow the Gospel writers and

Christian theologians to get away with all the time. "Villains" within the domination system are exposed in Jesus' parables only to become God figures when the Gospel writers recast them. Jesus rejects the apocalyptic expectations concerning God only to be portrayed by Gospel writers as a cosmic, violent, apocalyptic judge. The Roman governor Pilate, who is known in non-Gospel writings for brutality, washes his hands in Gospel accounts that deflect blame for Jesus' execution away from Rome onto the Jews. Jesus teaches love of enemies, but Jesus the Christ eventually displaces a militaristic Roman God, defends Roman soldiers, champions holy wars throughout later history, and is reconciled with just war theory.

A final assertion is that treating nonhistorical Gospel claims as historical can distort Jesus, God, and faith. Within their collective pages, the Gospels say that Jesus was born of a virgin, walked on water, turned water into wine, and passed miraculously through walls in postresurrection appearances. Many scholars, pastors, and church members treat these claims as historical, meaning they understand them to have really happened. I do not believe that Jesus walked on water, turned water into wine, or passed miraculously through walls in postresurrection appearances. Nor do I believe that he was born of a virgin. The question arises, Does it matter whether or not the events and happenings depicted in these Gospel stories are accepted as historical?

I think the answer is yes for several reasons. First, believing in these events has become a litmus test for the faithful, and I am sometimes defined as being outside the church because I don't accept such events to have really happened. Second, the focus on miracles as the foundation for belief seems to run counter to Jesus' experience of God as a present transforming power at the center of life. John wrote his miracle-laden Gospel sixty or more years following the murder of Jesus and many decades after Paul's writings that reflect no knowledge of such miracles. By the time of John's writing, many doubts had surfaced concerning Christian claims. Assertions that Jesus fulfilled promises made in the Hebrew Scriptures were rejected by many Jews, Roman imperialism remained entrenched, Jerusalem had been destroyed, and Jesus had not returned to end history or establish justice. John's desperation includes placing a bizarre miracle story, the wedding at Cana, near the beginning of his Gospel (2:1–11). Jesus yells at his mother and then performs a miracle so that wedding guests already plastered on bad wine can continue guzzling one of higher quality. John appropriated this miracle story about Dionysus, the Greek god of wine, and attached it to Jesus. As Rudolf Bultmann notes, "No doubt the story has been borrowed from pagan legends and transferred to

Jesus."[8] John tells us why he did this in verse 11, and he attributes his logic to Jesus: "Jesus did this, the first of his signs, in Cana of Galilee, and revealed his glory; and his disciples believed in him." Uta Ranke-Heinemann writes that John has "transformed Jesus into a sort of Christian wine God."[9] This depiction of Jesus is formalized by the celebration of Epiphany on January 6, the traditional feast day of Dionysus.[10]

John's reliance on miracles as the basis of belief and his story of doubting Thomas (John 20:24–29) are a response to a crisis of faith in his community. The story of doubting Thomas allowed John to respond to such a crisis by retrojecting doubt into past stories and thereby suggesting that Jesus anticipated such a crisis. Saddling Jesus with ancient miracle stories and claiming the historicity of miracles as the basis for faith, however, is a dangerous proposition. Not only do such miracles distort Jesus' view of the divine, but the absence of similar miracles in our own time can undermine the credibility of other Gospel claims and can make belief difficult or impossible for many.

Reliance upon miracles as the basis for belief may also signify a creeping despair concerning God and history. There is a strong tendency within apocalyptic thought to seek resolution of serious historical crises through the advent of a violent intervention of God. The world is out of control, so problems can only be rectified by God's violent action to either impose justice on earth or to end history. In a similar way, expectation and belief rooted in the miraculous can reinforce quietism in the face of deepening social crises. Waiting for the miraculous, like waiting for the apocalyptic violence of God, does not require us to change or to challenge the domination systems of our time. A *Newsweek* magazine poll shows that 84 percent of U.S. citizens believe that God performs miracles. Nearly half believe they have experienced or witnessed one. "Overwhelmingly, the poll showed, those who believe in miracles are Christian."[11] One might legitimately wonder what percentage of those who embrace miracles are deeply involved in incarnating God's love in a world torn apart by violence, poverty, and injustice.

Finally, treating Gospel miracles, including the virgin birth and post-resurrection appearances, as historical often means that other meanings that can be derived from these accounts in the context of the historical Jesus and historical period are lost. The virgin birth, by way of example, has a life of its own within Christian interpretation, but its relationship to an ideological sparring match with Rome over the nature of God, power, and history is generally lost (see chapter 14).

An irony often missed in the sharp attacks against historical Jesus scholarship is that those who challenge its relevance often cling to the historicity of nonhistorical passages because they have made them essential to their belief systems. I prefer the lived life of Jesus as an expression of what God is or is not like to a focus on miracles that can trivialize both God and history. Jesus lived and embodied his faith in God in the context of a deadly domination system. It is to that domination system that we now turn.

Notes

1. Martin Hengel, *Crucifixion in the Ancient World and the Folly of the Message of the Cross* (Philadelphia: Fortress Press, 1977), 87–88.

2. Jack Nelson-Pallmeyer, *War against the Poor: Low Intensity Conflict and Christian Faith* (Maryknoll, N.Y.: Orbis Books, 1989).

3. Walter Wink, *Engaging the Powers: Discernment and Resistance in a World of Domination* (Minneapolis: Fortress Press, 1992), 149.

4. Regina M. Schwartz, *The Curse of Cain: The Violent Legacy of Monotheism* (Chicago: University of Chicago Press, 1997), 115.

5. Wink, *Engaging the Powers*, 149.

6. Richard A. Horsley and Neil Asher Silberman, *The Message and the Kingdom* (New York: Grosset/Putnam, 1997), 16.

7. Robert Funk, Roy W. Hoover, and the Jesus Seminar, *The Five Gospels: The Search for the Authentic Words of Jesus* (New York: Polebridge Press, 1993), 50.

8. Quoted in Uta Ranke-Heinemann, *Putting Away Childish Things* (New York: HarperCollins, 1995), 82.

9. Ibid.

10. Ibid., p. 81.

11. *Star Tribune*, 23 April 2000.

14 JEWISH EXPECTATIONS, OPPORTUNISTS, AND ROMAN POWER

Mark 3:1–6 introduces a religious and social world full of tension and intrigue. The story is set in sacred space (synagogue) during sacred time (Sabbath). There are spies watching and listening and a man with a withered hand hoping. Mark's Jesus asks about saving life or killing on the Sabbath. It is a loaded question that I will return to when I look at Jesus' affirmation of a nonviolent God. Here spies are present, Jesus asks them a pointed question, and they decline to answer. Jesus is angry and grieved because of their hardened hearts, an image rich in meaning. He heals the man's hand in a provocative act of civil disobedience, and the "Pharisees went out and immediately conspired with the Herodians against him, how to destroy him."

The conspirators are named, but they point beyond themselves. In broad strokes, they represent Rome and Temple, client kings and Jewish religious officials. These institutions and groups play important roles in an oppressive system that, according to Jesus, undermines compassion, impoverishes the people, and distorts God, faith, and economic life. A conspiracy to murder invites us to explore the nature and dire consequences of collaborative rule. The present chapter explores King Herod's governance in the context of Roman arrogance and power. It also examines expectations and the actual experience of kingly rule within the Jewish tradition.

ROMAN "SAVIORS"

The defeat of Antiochus was followed by a period of shifting power alignments among world empires and near constant internal strife between competing Jewish priestly factions. Jewish Hasmonean high priests pushed aside other priestly groups and consolidated power under the watchful eye of the weakening Seleucid empire. The Romans took control of the area in 63 B.C.E. They continued to delegate authority to Hasmonean priestly groups. In the decades that followed, however, devastating civil wars erupted within the Jewish homeland and more broadly within the territories that were to become the Roman empire.[1]

The lives and military triumphs of Octavius, a Roman general, and Herod, "the ambitious son of the converted Edomite who had served as chief advisor to the last Hasmonean priest-king Hyrcanus,"[2] intersected in the context of these conflicts. Their arrogance and actions profoundly affected Palestine, Jesus, and the content of the Gospels. Octavius, the heir and adopted son of Julius Caesar, was far more powerful than Herod. Through a series of military triumphs, Octavius brought an end to decades of civil war. After the Roman Senate deified his deceased father in 42 B.C.E., Octavius was by proclamation a son of god. He was heralded as Savior of the world, became the first Emperor of Rome, and was given the title Augustus. A decree honoring Augustus announced "that the birthday of our God signaled the beginning of the Good News for the world because of him." The Roman Senate bestowed divine status on Augustus following his death in 14 C.E.[3]

Rome and early Christianity proclaimed competing gospels, saviors and sons of God, and they differed profoundly over where, how, and through whom divine will intersected with history. The first verse of Mark's Gospel should be read as a direct challenge to Rome: "The beginning of the gospel of Jesus Christ, the Son of God." So too should claims of Jesus' virgin birth. Roman political propaganda gave Octavius and his adoptive father Julius Caesar "a mythological genealogy worthy of the new Roman order," which included "divine ancestry."[4] Virgin birth accounts responded to and countered Roman claims. They were a first-century equivalent to one-upmanship, a sort of "my dog's better than your dog" refrain, only the jousting concerned matters of divine favor that impacted views of God, history, life, death, and ultimate allegiance.

Competing gospels, saviors, sons of God, and divine ancestries offer evidence of an ideological shoving match between the Gospel writers and Rome that finds expression throughout the Gospels and within Paul's letters. Horsley and Silberman describe Christianity's antagonism toward Rome:

> Early Christianity was, in fact, a down-to-earth response to an oppressive ideology of earthly power that had recently swept across continents, disrupted economies, and overturned ancient traditions. . . . No believing Christian could possibly accept any of this Augustan propaganda. For them, Rome was the Beast, the Harlot, the Dragon, Babylon, the Great Satan. They knew that Rome's empire was made possible not by divine order but by the acquisition of vast territories through the deadly violence of the Roman legions and the self-serving acquiescence of their own local aristocracies. They knew that, step by step, the Romans had bullied, invaded, and eventually occupied all the lands around the Mediterranean, arrogantly assigning formerly independent peoples roles as clients or servants in their larger imperial schemes. And as the world's riches flowed into Rome and into the treasuries of a select clique of Roman client kings and protégés, the Augustan promise of universal peace and prosperity for all the empire's subjects proved much easier to make than to keep.[5]

Visible in the Gospels and Paul are remnants of a tradition in which Rome is like an invisible punching bag absorbing blow after blow. Horsley and Silberman overstate their case, however, and understate tensions when they suggest that no "believing Christian could possibly accept any of this Augustan propaganda." New Testament evidence of accommodation with Rome undermines such a sweeping statement. The desire to appease Rome is perhaps most evident in creedal and Gospel accounts that distort Pilate's role in the murder of Jesus. Additionally, the book of Acts often reads as an anti-Jewish and pro-Roman polemic disconnected from real history.

Competing perspectives on faith and empire found within the New Testament are irreconcilable. We must choose between them as we seek to make sense out of Jesus' life as a revelation of God. The roots of accommodation run deep. They are imbedded in the Gospels themselves and reinforced by our own cozy relationships with empire that prevent us from seeing the anti-imperial stream within the Gospels and that blind us to the destructive impact of our own nation's imperial pretensions and actions. Our embrace of imperial Christianity distorts the content and substance of Christian faith sufficiently enough to constitute a betrayal of Jesus.

TWO PILLARS, ONE STREAM

Herod, with the help of Roman soldiers, crushed the rebellion among rival Jewish priests battling for control of the Jewish homeland and deposed the last of the Jewish Hasmonean priest-kings. The Roman Senate declared him king of Judea. The half-Jew Herod preferred the title, "king of the Jews." This self-designation did not presume divine status, but it did imply divine approval. In this awkward space between ruling as a Rome-appointed client king and claiming to be God's representative ruler and "king of the Jews," we glimpse conflictive dynamics at play in the context of collaborative rule in a specifically Jewish context. Envision two pillars on which the domination system rested. The first and most important pillar was Rome. The second consisted of powerful priestly groups associated with the Temple establishment. There was no middle class and these pillars stood squarely on the backs of the poor. People lived on one side or other of a great divide. Crossan describes the social classes:

> The Roman Empire was an agrarian society . . . characterized by an abysmal gulf separating the upper from the lower classes. On one side of that great divide were the Ruler and the Governors, who together made up 1 percent of the population but owned at least half of the land. Also on that same side were three other classes: the Priests, who could own as much as 15 percent of the land; the Retainers, ranging from military generals to expert bureaucrats; and the Merchants, who probably evolved upward from the lower classes but who could end up with considerable wealth and even some political power as well. On the other side were, above all, the Peasants—that vast majority of the population about two-thirds of whose annual crop went to support the upper classes. If they were lucky they lived at subsistence level, barely able to support family, animals,

and social obligations and still have enough for next year's seed supply. If they were not lucky, drought, debt, disease, or death forced them off their own land and into sharecropping, tenant farming, or worse. Next came the Artisans, about 5 percent of the population, below the Peasants in social class because they were usually recruited and replenished from its dispossessed members—the former with origins, occupations, or conditions rendering them outcasts; the latter, maybe as much as 10 percent of the population, ranging from beggars and outlaws to hustlers, day laborers, and slaves. Those Expendables existed, as that terrible title suggests, because, despite mortality and disease, war and famine, agrarian societies usually contained far more of the lower classes than the upper classes found it profitable to employ. Expendables were, in other words, a systemic necessity. If Jesus was a carpenter, therefore, he belonged to the Artisan class, that group pushed into the dangerous space between Peasants and . . . Expendables.[6]

The Rome- and Temple-led system was marked by crushing social inequalities and systemic oppression. Demands for justice could potentially challenge the legitimacy of each pillar of power and undermine the collaborative system as a whole. Herod was a Rome-appointed king who claimed to be king of the Jews. He was privileged but in an unenviable position. Herod faced three irreconcilable demands within a system of collaborative rule in which he was an important but junior partner. First, if Herod the Great failed to please Rome, then he would be Herod the Deposed or Herod the Exiled. Second, Herod had to contend with powerful priestly groups who throughout Jewish history had ruled Palestine on behalf of themselves or others. Many priests who claimed to speak for God and to be guardians of God's land and people resented both Rome and Herod. As a half-Jew, Herod had little credibility in the eyes of many priests and other Jews whom he had to control, co-opt, or appease. Priests given a stake in the system shared Herod's dilemma. Just as Herod ruled by pleasing Rome, priests "practiced religion" and conducted the affairs of the Temple by obliging Herod and satisfying Rome. Religious officials could maintain and oversee political, economic, and religious aspects of the Temple as long as doing so served rather than subverted the domination system. Those excluded often became a thorn in Herod's side.

Third, the justice stream within the tradition included expectations of freedom, economic justice and just kingly rule. These expectations clashed sharply with a domination system that rested squarely on the backs of the poor. Dissenting priests, prophets, and common people called on the justice tradition to justify their protests. At times the water from this stream nearly dried up and what remained lapped quietly and harmlessly like gentle waves at the base of the pillars of power. During turbulent storms, however, and there were many in and around first-century Palestine, they became roaring torrents that battered the foundational assumptions and practices of each.

Jewish Palestine was more than a piece of ground. It was the site of land and rituals and competing expectations and explanations of God's actions and intentions past, present, and future. God, Psalm 82 said, was a God of justice. Parts of the tradition stressed that God's holy land was given to God's chosen people who covenanted with God to keep it holy according to God's sacred laws. This land, according to the prophet Isaiah, was at the center of God's master plan in which Jews would return from exile and all nations and peoples would be subjugated (49:23).

Imperial demands that clashed with these elements in the national mythology shed light on Herod's dilemma. He had to please Rome. He also had to deal with priestly leaders accustomed to power and privileges rooted in "divine mandates" and sacred scripture. He had to struggle with competing priestly factions vying for power to mediate between God and the holy people, to administer God's land, and to interpret the sacred laws. He had to contend with revolutionary historical promises and expectations concerning Israel's place in God's plan. Herod's self-designation, "king of the Jews," implied that his rule reflected the will of God as understood within the Jewish justice tradition. It did not. Imperial realities meant that neither Herod nor anyone else could harmonize differences posed by competing demands. Herod and his priestly partners, therefore, pleased Rome, ignored justice, distorted religion, and oppressed the people.

A PERFECT CLIENT KING

Herod, by Roman standards, was an effective client king. He was ambitious, young, opportunistic, and brutal. He literally and figuratively taxed the people to death in order to please the Romans and to enrich himself. His success is marked by the longevity of his rule, which lasted from 37 to 4 B.C.E. Herod the Great set up "an intensely repressive regime" complete with mercenary soldiers and a secret police that made serious opposition nearly impossible.[7] Mark's reference to "Herodian" spies plotting to murder Jesus, although it refers to the time of Herod's son Antipas, is credible in this context.

Herod tried to walk through a minefield of contradictions posed by collaborative rule. His guiding principles seemed to be to please Rome and co-opt the Temple. He built a large city for non-Jews and named it Caesarea. (Naming a city after a contemporary Roman emperor was a first century equivalent to brownnosing.) Herod developed a reputation for being a big spender throughout the pagan world.[8] The Jewish historian Josephus describes some of Herod's development and cultural projects. Built with revenues exacted through oppressive taxation, all would have mightily offended many Jews:

> For in the first place he established athletic contests . . . in honor of Caesar and he built a theatre in Jerusalem, and after that a very large amphitheater in the plain, both being spectacularly lavish but foreign to Jewish customs. . . . All around the theatre were inscriptions concerning Caesar and trophies of the nations which he had won in war, all of them made for Herod of pure gold and silver. . . . Foreigners were astonished at the expense . . . but to the natives it meant an open break with the customs held in honor by them. For it seemed glaring impiety to throw men to wild beasts for the pleasure of other men as spectators.[9]

Herod's problem was that he had both to serve Rome and pacify the Jews. He often offended and oppressed the Jews in order to maintain his good standing with the imperial family and in his role as patron of pagan projects and shrines. "There was, of course, a price to be paid for this new pharaoh's extravagant spending," Horsley and Silberman note. "To support his building projects, lavish court life, and gifts to the imperial family, Herod laid a heavy burden of taxation on his subjects."[10] Herod tried to shore up his claim to be "king of the Jews" by marrying a Hasmonean princess. This was a rather transparent political ploy given the fact that he had deposed a Hasmonean priest-king upon taking power. He abandoned all pretenses and executed his Hasmonean wife and their two sons in 7 B.C.E. out of paranoia and concern for who would rule after him.[11] Herod also appointed his own high priests.[12]

Herod's opportunistic view of religion was also evident in his efforts to rebuild and co-opt the Jewish Temple. The size and splendor of the

Temple rebuilt by Herod would have pleased many Jews. It reinforced priestly power and created employment both through its reconstruction and its role as cultic ritual center. More conflictive was the fact that it confused and conflated Jewish and Augustan images and expectations:

> Posing as a new Solomon, Herod rebuilt and embellished the Jerusalem Temple on a scale of grandeur and opulence that made it one of the wonders of the ancient world. In its time, with its magnificent monumental entrances, royal colonnade built with towering Corinthian columns, spacious courtyards, gates, and central sanctuary structure, Herod's Temple made the previous Jerusalem temples seem like pitifully rustic shrines. Herod's true genius lay in skillfully combining Israel's messianic legacy with Rome's ideology of empire. His patron, Augustus Caesar, in reconstructing temples of Rome in the name of religious revival, had invented a new decorative grammar of Corinthian columns, enthusiastic geometric ornamentation, and lush floral decoration to symbolize the dawn of a new era of abundance and fertility under the peace and security of the Roman Empire. Can there be any doubt from the elaborate floral and geometric decoration of Herod's Temple described by Josephus and observed on fragments recovered in recent years by archaeologists around the Temple Mount that the same message was being issued in Jerusalem? Can there be any doubt that the golden vines with huge golden grape clusters that adorned the facade of the sanctuary—or the soaring golden eagle affixed to the main gate of the Temple enclosure—were symbols of the divinely ordained abundance and order of the Augustan Age?[13]

No amount of imperial window dressing or religious co-optation could fully obscure the fact that Herod's rule intensified oppression, inequality, and poverty within Jewish Palestine. The Roman conquest and Herod's ambition meant growing demand for taxes and tribute and a shrinking land base from which to exact them. This was disastrous for the Jewish peasantry. Herod intensified economic exploitation to support his elaborate regime. He also engaged in "extensive building projects and made a name for himself in the Empire for his astounding munificence to the imperial family and to Hellenistic cultural causes such as athletic games, the whole funded by taxing his people."[14]

KING OF THE JEWS?

Herod rebuilt the Temple and claimed to be king of the Jews. He had no commitment to the justice of God, however, which at least on paper was what God expected of kings and what many Jews hoped for from their rulers. Herod's miserable rule was disappointing and unfortunately, all too typical. A little background is instructive.

The Hebrew Scriptures offer diverse portraits of leaders that include competing hopes and claims concerning the conduct of kings and priests. There were deep suspicions of centralized rule and intense egal-itarian impulses among those who were part of the loose tribal confed-eracy that constituted Israel prior to the monarchy.[15] Kings, pharaohs, and emperors ruled other nations. Israel, according to this part of the tradi-tion, was ruled by Yahweh. The judge, Gideon, refused an offer to be king on the grounds that "the LORD will rule over you" (Judg 8:23). The book of 1 Samuel warns against kingship, saying that kings would use the people's sons as cannon fodder in self-serving wars, would enrich themselves at the people's expense, would steal their produce, and would enslave them (1 Sam 8:10–18).

Human kingship was rejected based on the idea that God ruled the people. At its best, the idea of God's direct rule can be understood as a theological statement with profound political implications. God's ulti-mate sovereignty is to be respected and embodied in the priorities and character of earthly rulers and systems. The "kingdom of God" lan-guage used by Jesus, for example, points to a sharp conflict between the domination system in first-century Palestine and Jesus' understanding of God's intent. Jesus says the "kingdom of God" is present on earth whenever life accurately reflects the will and sovereignty of God. It is the way life and society would be if a compassionate God were in charge or imitated instead of Roman governors, client kings, and the Temple establishment. More specifically, because Jesus' life was inter-twined with the destitute, the indebted, and the outcasts, the "kingdom of God" is what their world would be like if they undermined the key institutions of the domination system and incarnated God's character in actions of daily living.

God's direct rule was and is impossible, which makes all theocracies past, present, and future dangerous. The biblical writers could not agree on what God was or was not like, including what did or did not please God. As a result, sacred and authoritative texts were riddled with conflicting and incompatible images and characteristics of God. God appeared often within sacred texts as a pathological killer capable of unfathomable violence. Despicable portraits of God enabled humans to justify numerous atrocities in God's name and in service to God's will. The key point is that because God could not and cannot rule directly, it is always left to humans to govern. In biblical times, kings, priestly supporters, or high priestly rulers made the case that their rule reflected divine will and intent. They did so even when their actions were oppressive and self-serving, as the prophets and Jesus reminded them repeatedly. A prayer of the psalmist expressed the hopes of the people:

> Give the king your justice, O God,
>   and your righteousness to a king's son.
> May he judge your people with righteousness,
>   and your poor with justice.
> May the mountains yield prosperity for the people,
>   and the hills, in righteousness.
> May he defend the cause of the poor of the people,
>   give deliverance to the needy,
>   and crush the oppressor (Ps 72:1–4).

The prophet Jeremiah, however, expressed the reality:

> Woe to him who builds his house by unrighteousness,
>   and his upper rooms by injustice;
> who makes his neighbors work for nothing,
>   and does not give them their wages;
> who says, "I will build myself a spacious house
>   with large upper rooms,"
> and who cuts out windows for it,
>   paneling it with cedar,
>   and painting it with vermilion.
> Are you a king
>   because you compete in cedar?
> Did not your father eat and drink
>   and do justice and righteousness?
>   Then it was well with him.
> He judged the cause of the poor and needy;
>   then it was well.
> Is not this to know me?
>   says the LORD.

But your eyes and heart
   are only on your dishonest gain,
for shedding innocent blood,
   and for practicing oppression and violence (Jer 22:13–17).

The Bible is rightly praised because it rarely covers over the flaws of its protagonists and because prophets challenge powerful people. Moses was a murderer (Exod 2:12). David committed adultery with Bathsheba, orchestrated the murder of her husband, married her, and was called on the carpet by the prophet Nathan (2 Sam 11–12). Such honesty often leads to the conclusion that God works through flawed human beings. This is undoubtedly true. Unfortunately, we rarely state the logical corollary: Flawed human beings wrote the Bible, and their perspectives often do not reflect God's character or will.

Emphasizing how God works through flawed human beings can also obscure the human tendency to idealize the past. Bad times often prompt longings for "the good old days" based on highly selective memories. This impulse is evident in biblical writings that idealize David's rule and that shaped and distorted both Jewish expectations of God's future action and Gospel portraits of Jesus. Jesus of Nazareth was said to have been born in Bethlehem in order to meet expectations of a Davidic messiah. Similar expectations result in the messianic title "Son of David" being assigned to Jesus, even though it is indefensible when expectation and reality meet and collapse at a Roman crucifixion. David's actual role may have conflicted sharply with "divine rule," and distorted historical memory may have elevated his status, but discrepancies were even more pronounced with his successor. Solomon, known for his wisdom, would be remembered more accurately for womanizing (1 Kings 11) and priestly-sanctioned oppressive rule:

King Solomon was king over all Israel, and these were his high officials: Azariah son of Zadok was the priest; Elihoreph and Ahijah sons of Shisha were secretaries; Jehoshaphat son of Ahilud was recorder; Benaiah son of Jehoiada was in command of the army; Zadok and Abiathar were priests; Azariah son of Nathan was over the officials; Zabud son of Nathan was priest and king's friend; Ahishar was in charge of the palace; and Adoniram son of Abda was in charge of the forced labor. . . .

King Solomon conscripted forced labor out of all Israel; the levy numbered thirty thousand men. He sent them to the

Lebanon, ten thousand a month in shifts; they would be a month in the Lebanon and two months at home; Adoniram was in charge of the forced labor. Solomon also had seventy thousand laborers and eighty thousand stonecutters in the hill country, besides Solomon's three thousand three hundred supervisors who were over the work, having charge of the people who did the work. At the king's command, they quarried out great, costly stones in order to lay the foundation of the house with dressed stones (1 Kings 4:1–6; 5:13–17).

This passage can help shed light on Herod's rule, the domination system in first-century Palestine, and Jesus' conflict with Roman and Jewish authorities. First, it offers an earlier example of how oppressive kingly rule was sanctioned by priestly authorities. Priestly power was entrenched and often hereditary. The above passage mentions that Zadok and his sons were priests. As Richard Horsley notes, "the office of high priest itself became a virtual dynasty in control of the same Zadokite family from the sixth to the second century."[16] This dynasty was interrupted by the rise of Hasmonean priests connected to the successful Maccabean revolt against Antiochus's oppressive rule. This new priestly line was altered but acknowledged by Herod when he appointed his own high priests and married a Hasmonean princess (whom he later murdered). High priestly representatives often abused their power. The Talmud records the following passage:

Woe unto me because of the house of Baithos; woe unto me for their lances! Woe unto me because of the house of Hanin (Ananus). . . . Woe unto me because of the house of Ishmael b. Phiabi, woe unto me because of their fists. For they are high priests and their sons are treasurers, and their sons-in-law are Temple overseers, and their servants smite the people with sticks! (Pes. 57a).[17]

Oppressive high priestly rule was often a consequence of the imperial situation. It had a life of its own, however, was the fruit of historical opportunity, and was shored up by references to sacred scriptures and Jewish tradition. It became an entrenched part of despotic rule before, during, and after the time of Jesus. The priestly leaders who returned to Israel after the Persians defeated the Babylonian empire ran roughshod over the Jews who had been left behind. During the time of Daniel, some priestly groups supported Antiochus's reforms. Others resisted. The Hasmoneans who eventually took power maintained a highly stratified order, waged war against other priestly groups, and legitimated their own rule and privileges.

Second, the 1 Kings passage tells us that Solomon, who supposedly ruled as God's representative, used forced labor to build both his own opulent palace and God's dwelling place, the Temple. Kings and priests reconciled a God of justice with the king's palatial home and style of life built with the sweat and blood of oppressed workers. They also presented God as one who desired and was pleased to dwell in a Temple constructed by such means. With a new king came hope, often illusionary, of a fresh start and better treatment. After Solomon died, the people in the northern part of the kingdom appealed to his son Rehoboam to lessen their burden: "Your father made our yoke heavy. Now therefore lighten the hard service of your father and his heavy yoke that he placed on us, and we will serve you" (1 Kings 12:4). Rehoboam denied their request: "My little finger is thicker than my father's loins. Now, whereas my father laid on you a heavy yoke, I will add to your yoke. My father disciplined you with whips, but I will discipline you with scorpions" (12:10b–11). We will see that events following the death of Herod parallel those recounted above.

Returning to Herod the Great, he claimed to be "king of the Jews" but chose Roman sovereignty over God's justice. He embraced foreign culture, ruled through repression and terror, and pleased the Romans beyond even their own expectations. All this was made possible through ruthless exploitation of the people, especially the peasantry. Herod built temples for Augustus, appointed his own high priests, and married and later killed a Hasmonean princess. Common people were never truly represented by high priestly groups vying for privileges that stemmed from direct or collaborative rule, but, not surprisingly, Herod's appointees served them no better.

The reconstruction of Jerusalem's Temple seemed equally calculated and misguided. The restored Temple, like Solomon's only on a far grander scale, was paid for with the sweat, blood, and taxes of impoverished peasants and workers. Was the glorious Temple a commanding symbol of political, economic, and religious power and promise? Or a forceful example of oppression clothed in religious garb? The answer is probably both.

Over the centuries since the destruction of Solomon's Temple by the Babylonians, the rural population of Judea, and later of

Galilee as well, had gone back and forth in its allegiance to the Temple—ranging from what seems to have been wholehearted identification at times of external threat (as during the Maccabean rebellion) to widespread passive resistance and evasion of the growing burden of tithes, offerings, and taxes that were required of them. Its official representatives and most energetic supporters were to be found all over the country—in the families of the twenty-four priestly "divisions," most of whom served in Jerusalem for only short periods, and in the "scribes and the Pharisees" mentioned often in the gospel, who apparently served in the villages as experts in the Law and religious functionaries. Their presence among the rural population would have been conspicuous, especially at the times of firstfruits and harvest, when they supervised the collection of offerings and tithes. And despite their assurances that the Temple and its elaborate sacrificial cult were meant for the benefit of all Israel, the real sacrifices seemed to be those made by the already overtaxed and hard-pressed peasantry.[18]

The Temple was a source of schizophrenia for many Jews. This was especially true for impoverished Jews who internalized mythologies of national destiny and greatness rooted in both God's promises and Temple ideologies that obscured the Temple's role in their oppression.

CONCLUSION

Roman arrogance and power were at the heart of the domination system in first-century Palestine. Rome established the repressive parameters of collaborative rule. Herod served Rome well. His death at or shortly before the birth of Jesus posed challenges to Rome, and it profoundly shaped the social setting in which Jesus lived and announced the alternative "kingdom of God."

Notes

1. Richard Horsley, *Jesus and the Spiral of Violence: Popular Jewish Resistance in Roman Palestine* (Minneapolis: Fortress Press, 1993), 10.

2. Richard A. Horsley and Neil Asher Silberman, *The Message and the Kingdom* (New York: Grosset/Putnam, 1997), 15.

3. John Dominic Crossan, *Jesus: A Revolutionary Biography* (New York: Harper Collins, 1995), 1–2.

4. Ibid., 3.

5. Horsley and Silberman, *The Message and the Kingdom*, 10–11.

6. Crossan, *Jesus*, 25–26.

7. Horsley, *Jesus and the Spiral*, 10–11.

8. Horsley and Silberman, *The Message and the Kingdom*, 17.

9. Josephus as quoted in Horsley and Silberman, *The Message and the Kingdom*, 72.

10. Ibid.

11. John Dominic Crossan, *The Birth of Christianity* (San Francisco: HarperSanFrancisco, 1998), 232.

12. Horsley, *Jesus and the Spiral*, 11.

13. Horsley and Silberman, *The Message and the Kingdom*, 17–18.

14. Horsley, *Jesus and the Spiral*, 13.

15. Norman K. Gottwald, *The Tribes of Yahweh* (Maryknoll, N.Y.: Orbis Books, 1979).

16. Horsley, *Jesus and the Spiral*, 10.

17. Quoted in Horsley, *Jesus and the Spiral*, 47.

18. Horsley and Silberman, *The Message and the Kingdom*, 75.

MY THREE SONS, PILATE, AND MESSIANIC PRETENDERS

Although few Jews lamented Herod's death, his passing posed problems for the Romans, who had appreciated and rewarded his repressive governance. This chapter examines Roman rule following the death of Herod. It frames the portrait of Jesus painted in subsequent chapters.

MY THREE SONS

The Romans continued a system of indirect rule after the death of Herod. They appointed his sons, with lesser titles, to rule over a divided Palestine. Antipas was given authority over Galilee and Perea and the title *tetrarch,* or section ruler. Archelaus received more important territory and a more impressive title, that of *ethnarch,* or people ruler. He controlled the middle and southern areas of the country including Samaria, Judea (which included Jerusalem and the Temple), and Idumea. Philip received territories further north and east and was given the title *tetrarch.*[1]

Antipas ruled effectively from the perspective of the Romans. Archelaus did not. Herod the Great had kept a lid on social turmoil through violence and cunning that characterized his repressive rule. His death led to massive rebellions in all areas of Palestine as the people's pent-up fury exploded into protests. Signs of problems to come surfaced shortly before Herod's death. A group of nonviolent protesters under the leadership of two respected Pharisaic teachers pulled down a statue of Rome's golden eagle from the Temple portal. The golden eagle symbolized both Roman arrogance and the Temple's subservient position. Its removal was a provocative act carried out by protesters who may have mistakenly assumed Herod's passing. Herod, sick but not dead, ordered the nonviolent protesters burned alive. After Herod died, the people, as was the case following the death of Solomon, appealed to the dead ruler's son to lessen their oppressive burdens. They demanded that Archelaus reduce the yearly tribute, repeal Herod's special taxes, release political prisoners, and punish those responsible for the brutal murder of the distinguished teachers and students involved in the golden eagle protest.[2] The demands apparently were made during the Passover celebration in which thousands of Jews visited the city.

The weight of the grievances and Archelaus's disappointing response may have triggered dangerous Passover memories of liberation while highlighting realities of subjugation. Archelaus, fearing a revolt and eager to please the Romans, who demanded stability as a condition of rule, sent in troops to control leaders and quell the protest. When some of his soldiers were killed, Archelaus sent his whole army to regain control and to punish. They killed more than three thousand Jews, many of whom were carrying out their traditional Passover sacrifices.[3]

Archelaus might have saved his position as client king had the protests ended there. They did not and he did not. Three legions of Roman troops stationed in Syria were sent to crush a revolt that extended from Jerusalem to every major section of the countryside in Galilee, Perea, and Judea. In each area of resistance, popular movements acclaimed their own "kings" to rule. In the end, however, these popular kings or messianic claimants were no match for well-equipped Roman legions.[4] In the aftermath of the failed revolt, Rome reestablished direct rule in the territories previously controlled by Archelaus under the authority of a Roman governor who was expected to maintain order and keep taxes and tribute flowing more efficiently than the inept Archelaus. The most famous of these governors was Pilate, whose oppressive rule is well attested outside the Gospels and downplayed within.

POPULAR KINGS AND MESSIAHS

Before looking at Pilate and Herod Antipas, let us take a brief detour into the theological mindset of the messianic movements and popular kings that arose following Herod's death. I described earlier how apocalyptic Daniel responded to intense imperial oppression and cracks in the old story lines that emphasized deserved blessings and curses. Historical catastrophes were understood within apocalypticism as temporary setbacks in a cosmic struggle between good and evil rather than as God's just punishments for disobedience. God was waging a war in heaven, victory was coming soon, the faithful would be vindicated, and evildoers would be punished as God intervened on earth to end injustice or to end history. Apocalypticism blurred the line between justice and revenge, and it deepened ties between God and pathological violence. Historical enemies would be punished by divine wrath as part of a final judgment.

Apocalyptic promises may have encouraged resistance to Antiochus, but it was guerrilla warfare that led to victory. Subsequent history, however, took another bad turn. Evil was not vanquished. Injustice was not defeated. History did not end. Priestly factions did not stop fighting each other. Although the geopolitical ground shifted, oppressive empires did not go away. Apocalyptic promises proved unreliable. Failure insured success, however, because deepening despair fed apocalyptic impulses like gasoline feeds a fire.

Civil strife and ongoing injustice following Antiochus's defeat ultimately reinforced apocalyptic expectations but not before taking a detour. The road to John the Baptist's apocalyptic movement that announced a new and decisive violent coming of God twisted and turned over rocky historical terrain. Apocalypticism may have inspired resistance to Antiochus, but his defeat at the hands of the Maccabees rekindled the old theology's emphasis on God the holy warrior and on salvation as defeat of enemies. According to Marcus Borg, the victories of the Maccabees provided "empirical verification for the claim of the Book of Judith that Yahweh gives victory to the chosen people, [and] demonstrated that resistance was reasonable, even when it seemed foolish on more pragmatic grounds."[5]

Successful revolt against Antiochus, at least for some, validated the view that Yahweh had joined with the people to defeat a militarily superior foe. This interpretation of events centered on God's redemptive violence, which was featured centrally in many psalms and many prophetic utterances. It offered hope to those battling powerful enemies at any time, including during the period of Roman occupation. Memories of God's saving violence cast a long shadow over events following Herod's death. Freedom fighters drew inspiration from Jewish history, including Antiochus's defeat, Saul's popular kingship, and David's military successes, in which Israel's own military strength was understood to have been blessed by God and supplemented by God's power. Violent uprisings led by messianic leaders and the appointment of "popular kings" through-out Palestine following Herod's death would have fit this pattern, at least during the initial period marked by successful revolt. The "messianic claimants who *fought* for freedom in the rebellions following Herod's death," Crossan notes, "invoked the ancient models of Saul and David."[6]

Tensions between memory and reality arose during the period of inde-pendent rule, however, because other recent historical events did not conform to the reformation of the old story lines. Repression and social stratification continued, and disappointment deepened as another empire, this time Roman, controlled Palestine through the brutal client king Herod. Domination systems were resilient and wore many faces. Historical nightmares, which clashed sharply with temporary victories and memories of God's redemptive violence, would have influenced pop-ular hopes and expectations concerning kings, messiahs, and God's plan for the people of Israel.

Richard Horsley and Neil Asher Silberman describe how in "the decades immediately preceding the birth of Jesus a wide variety of mes-sianic visions grew more fervent and vivid among the People of Israel." As in the case of apocalypticism, these visions were shaped by historical failures. Because "the members of the royal house of Judah and the later Hasmonean kings had proved themselves utterly powerless to live up to the responsibilities of their office and defend the people of Israel against the relentless advance of foreign empires a radically new vision of the character of Israel's true messiah arose."[7] Historical failures, in this case and for a time, led away from apocalypticism. They revived and refined visions of an idealized earthly ruler. This is why messianic movements keenly interested in David arose following Herod's death. The new vision, according to Horsley and Silberman, centered on "the arrival of a messianic figure, a new son of David, who would finally lead Israel to regain its former glory and establish the Kingdom of God."[8]

Recall that apocalyptic thought was born in the midst of historical catastrophe. It was reinforced by the failure of Daniel's vision to be real-ized within history, by continuing injustices during independent Hasmonean governance, by the emergence of the Roman empire and oppressive client king rule. Recall also that Antiochus's defeat revived aspects of the old theology that were dashed by subsequent historical events. This gave rise to messianic expectations that diverged from the apocalyptic worldview and centered on the coming of a new David who would establish God's kingdom. In this context, the rise and initial success of "sons of David" in rebellions throughout Palestine following Herod's death would have spawned intense expectations. Isaiah's vision of Israel's triumph over the nations was about to be completed by God.

We cannot fully imagine the agony of another crushing defeat in which Roman legions slaughtered Jews, burned cities, and lined roads with crosses on which decaying corpses became food for birds and wild animals. The destruction of popular kings and messianic claimants who fought against Rome and its client regimes following Herod's death would have had devastating consequences beyond the carnage of war. It marked another failure of historical promise and theological vision. It is likely once again that bad news was good news for apocalypticism. Rome's triumph set the stage for John the Baptist's historically pessimistic apocalyptic movement. It also helps explain why the Gospel writers adapted and then relied heavily on apocalyptic language and themes to explain the death of Jesus, the death of yet another messiah.

Historical catastrophes in first-century Palestine created conditions ripe for a groundswell of apocalyptic expectations and interpretations of events. The Gospel writers were caught up in this groundswell for a variety of reasons. I name three here. First, Jesus was crucified. Apocalypticism offered a lens to make sense of his death. Second, between three and four decades after Jesus' murder and shortly before the Gospels were written, the Jewish Temple and Jerusalem itself were destroyed in the Roman-Jewish war of 66–70. Apocalypticism offered a framework in which the destruction of Temple and city could be understood as divine punishment for Jews rejecting Jesus. Finally, by the time the Gospels were written, many Jews had rejected Jewish Christian claims that Jesus fulfilled God's promises as laid out in the Hebrew Scriptures. Apocalypticism served as ideological window dressing for growing Christian hatred and desired revenge. These points require elaboration.

The crucifixion of Jesus sent literate Jewish followers back to their sacred traditions in an effort to find clues for why he had been killed. Searching sacred scriptures for meaning in the aftermath of a painful tragedy is certainly understandable, but the results of such a search were not always fruitful then or now. It was impossible to convince many Jews that Jesus or anyone else who had been brutally crucified was the "son of David" or "son of God" whose death fulfilled the tradition.

One common explanation for Jesus' violent death used by the Gospel writers was to present him as the apocalypse personified. Daniel's "human one" was linked to Jesus, who was understood as a specific apocalyptic figure, the Son of Man, who would return soon as cosmic judge.

Remember that apocalyptic Daniel reconciled God with brutal but temporary historical setbacks. He promised an imminent victory through the violent coming of God that would destroy evil and vindicate the faithful. Understanding crucifixion as a temporary setback or as an unexpected instrument in God's divine plan, promoting the resurrection as the beginning of the end (Jesus is seen as the first fruit of a general resurrection), and portraying Jesus as "Son of Man" and cosmic judge placed Jesus' execution within an apocalyptic framework. It had the additional advantage of responding to the desire for revenge that arose from the intense pain of rejection felt by many Jewish Christians when many Jews rebuffed their claims.

Those who repudiated Jewish Christian interpretation of Jesus did not fare well in Gospel accounts. They were blamed for the murder of Jesus, and their rejection of Jesus was used to explain Rome's destruction of Jerusalem and the Temple. It was only a small step to make God's punishment permanent. Those who rejected Jesus would face the same harsh fate as all enemies of God: they would fry. The transformation, or better said, *deformation,* of Jesus is astounding. The nonviolent Jewish Jesus who taught love of enemies, revealed a nonviolent God, and inspired alternatives to the domination system within history became God's murderous apocalyptic accomplice who would return soon to violently judge and crush enemies and all evildoers at the end of history.

PILATE

The failure of Herod's son Archelaus to rule effectively resulted in his dismissal. Rome subsequently set up direct rule in Judea with a Roman governor in charge of affairs in the territories previously assigned to Archelaus. Pilate, who ruled from 26 to 36 C.E., was known outside of Gospel sources for his insensitivity to Jewish customs and his brutality. There was a massive nonviolent Jewish protest against Pilate's introduction of imperial images on the shields of Roman soldiers. In this case, apparently a rare one, Pilate backed down. When Jews nonviolently protested the use of Temple funds to pay for construction of an aqueduct, however, Pilate ordered them slaughtered.[9] Oppressive Pilate comes off nicely in Gospel accounts and later Christian tradition. Uta Ranke-Heinemann offers an honest, damning assessment of Gospel distortions:

> Over the years from 70 to 95, we can watch the process from Mark to Matthew and Luke (the later two are dependent on

Mark), all the way to John, the last of the four Gospels. The bottom line is that Pilate is increasingly excused, while the guilt of the Jews is depicted in ever more glaring colors. . . . Three times Luke has Pilate stress the fact that he finds no guilt in Jesus, that he wants to let Jesus "go free." . . . The Pilate described by the Gospels is not a historical figure. That picture is a malicious anti-Judaic legend. . . . By washing his hands, Pilate exposes the fact that they [the Jews] are a pack of murderers, unconcerned with justice but keen to satisfy their hatred. In so doing, he lays the foundation for the long and bloody history of the persecution of the Jews as the murderers of Christ. This story stretches all the way to Auschwitz.[10]

Ranke-Heinemann notes that these distortions are reinforced in the Christian creeds that downplay Pilate's role as executioner. She then concludes:

Thus the Christian judgment of Pilate grew more and more favorable from Gospel to Gospel. Bad as the development of the legend of Pilate has been for the Jews, Pilate later came off very well with the Christians. In the period after the New Testament, he continued his Christian career. Pious apocryphal writings were composed in his name, for example, a letter to Emperor Claudius and correspondence with Herod. His wife acquired even greater prestige, since in Matthew's Gospel she had sent word to him, "Have nothing to do with that righteous man, for I have suffered much over him today in a dream" (Matt. 27:19). Origen (d. 253) says she converted to Christianity. . . . In the so-called Paradosis, the "tradition" of Pilate (5th century), which describes how Pilate, too, came to believe in Christ and was beheaded for his faith by order of the emperor, we even learn her name: Prokla in Greek, Procula in Latin. . . . And to bring this tale to a happy ending, both Pilate and his wife were honored as saints . . . in the Ethiopian calendar.[11]

The move from executioner to saint marks a remarkable turnaround. Putting aside revisionist Christian history, we can say that when Roman leaders were intensely dissatisfied with Archelaus's failure to govern, they reestablished direct rule over his territories. Pilate, the best known of these rulers, was effective from the perspective of the Romans, including his disposal of a subversive named Jesus. Pilate, like the "Herodians" named by Mark, had both motive and means and most likely a policy in place that would have made trial and formal conviction unnecessary. Despite the portrayals in the Gospels, it may well be that there was an arrest and execution without a trial.[12]

HEROD ANTIPAS

Antipas, like his father, was ambitious and wanted to be king over all of Palestine. Herod the Great, however, changed his will shortly before his death to name Archelaus as heir to the throne. The good news for Antipas was that Augustus defied Herod's will. The bad news was that he gave Antipas a lower title than Archelaus and control over the less prestigious territories of Galilee and Perea. Even after Antipas proved himself more reliable than Archelaus during the uprisings following their father's death, Augustus granted authority to rule Judea, Samaria, and Idumea to a Roman governor rather than expand the area under Antipas's rule. Despite differences, it is clear that the Romans approved of Antipas's rule, which lasted until 36 C.E.

We cannot make sense out of Jesus without understanding the nature of Antipas's rule in Galilee. Rural Galilee and its dependent relationship to urban centers is the setting for many of Jesus' parables and the primary place where he communicated his understanding of God and history. I will take a closer look at Jesus' parables later. Here I intend to sketch some important features of life in Galilee from the time of the rebellion against Herod the Great and during Antipas's rule that would have impacted Jesus in important ways.

Near the time of Jesus' birth and four miles from his hometown of Nazareth in Galilee, armed Jews taking part in the widespread rebellion following the death of Herod the Great took control of the arsenal in the royal palace at Sepphoris. Their victory was short-lived. The Roman general Varus successfully hunted down the leaders of the rebellion and crucified two thousand people. The grisly scene of human remains nailed to crosses lining the roadways was part of Rome's psychological warfare, a deterrent to future protesters. Varus then burned the city to the ground.[13]

This rebellion and its aftermath may have impacted Jesus' expectations of God and history and the nature and trajectory of his movement. Memories of Sepphoris may have spurred Jesus' interest in John the Baptist. I believe Jesus was a follower of John the Baptist and participant in John's apocalyptic movement but that he broke with John over experiences and expectations of God and history. Baptized into John's movement, Jesus anticipated an imminent violent coming of God that would fulfill Daniel's promised end-time defeat of evil and vindication of the faithful. We do not know exactly why Jesus broke with John, but the Gospels offer a good deal of evidence that a break occurred. Among their differences, Jesus eventually rejected the violence of God expected by John. Jesus, as we will see when examining the parables, was more interested in exposing, discrediting, and building alternatives to the oppressive system than he was in apocalyptic prophecies and expectations of the end time.

The crushing defeat of Jews throughout Palestine, including and especially the destruction of Sepphoris in Galilee, was significant in other ways as well. Antipas rebuilt Sepphoris and populated it with non-Jews.[14] Within the domination system of the time, cities inevitably meant exploitation of the surrounding peasants on whose labor and taxes the well-being of urban dwellers and the opulent lifestyles of elites depended. Citing the work of Gerhard Lenski, Crossan notes that peasant "is an interactive term for farmers who are exploited and oppressed—a definition presuming that somewhere there must be exploiters and oppressors."[15] In short, the rich in Palestine lived well because the peasants lived poorly.

Following the death of Augustus in 14 C.E., Antipas mimicked several actions of his father. He married his half brother Philip's wife, a Hasmonean princess. John the Baptist challenged the marriage as part of a broader attack against Antipas's illegitimate rule. Antipas also repeated his father's imperial brownnosing and built a second capital in Galilee, which he named Tiberias, after the new emperor. This meant that Galilee now had two urban centers located about twenty miles from each other that were constructed about twenty years apart. This was disastrous for Jewish peasants. Roman urbanization, as Crossan notes, "dislocated the traditional peasant way of life and pushed individuals from poverty to destitution, from small landowner into tenant farmer, from tenant farmer into day-laborer, and from day-laborer into beggar or bandit."[16] The existence of Sepphoris alone, according to Jonathan Reed, would have put serious pressure on the food supply of Galilee. Feeding Tiberias would have seriously added to those strains. "In terms of food alone," Reed says, "the agricultural practices of Galilee were completely realigned and stretched with the foundation of these two cities. The picture of numerous self-sufficient farms or hamlets in Galilee radically changed. The entire agricultural focus," he adds, "turned to feeding Sepphoris and Tiberias."[17]

The economic exploitation of peasants in Galilee during Antipas's rule is the setting for Jesus' alternative "kingdom" movement. Peasant troubles

were far deeper than the problem of greater taxation of agricultural produce upon which the food supply and wealth of Sepphoris and Tiberias
depended. Antipas's development program in the context of Roman
demands meant a shift from traditional to commercialized agriculture.
Peasants were always vulnerable within oppressive systems. Within traditional agriculture that marked life in Palestine, peasants had lived on the
land for generations but lost much of its produce in the form of taxes and
tithes. Taxes were demanded by imperial decree, and the tithes that secured
the economic fortunes and political power of temple elites were ordered by
God. That, at least, is what priestly writers had written into the Torah.

Jesus' "kingdom movement" responded to Roman commercialization
as well as to the system of double taxation involving Rome and Temple.
Commercialization meant that the land itself, and not just produce from
the land, was valuable and desired. Land became a commodity to be
owned. This view of land clashed sharply with traditional Jewish understanding that the land belonged to God and that it was given as a gift to
the people of God, to be managed and cared for according to God's justice. One common means of taking ancestral land from those who
wanted to keep it was to foster indebtedness among impoverished peasants, foreclose on debts, and take title.

Land was not the only area of the economy commercialized during
Antipas's rule. Horsley and Silberman describe the following trends in
fishing:

> Although scenes of fishing on the waters of the Sea of Galilee
> in the time of Jesus are often bucolically portrayed in illus-
> trated Bibles and Sunday-school textbooks, with images of
> solitary fishermen standing in their rowboats and peacefully
> casting their nets upon the waters, the pace and purposes of
> fishing on the Sea of Galilee may have taken on quite a differ-
> ent aspect by the time of Antipas. For thousands of years, fish-
> ing on the lake had been a highly localized, seasonal occupation,
> conducted by the farmers of the region in the relatively quiet
> period between sowing and harvest. Long-distance trade in
> fish was out of the question. After only a few hours out of the
> water, the catch—unless it was immediately cooked and eaten—
> would have begun to go bad. Yet all that began to change in
> the Hellenistic and Roman periods, when techniques were
> developed for salting and pickling fish on something approach-
> ing an industrial scale. And with the production process came

a vast and growing market: urban populations throughout the Roman empire grew to love the spicy, smelly fish sauces called garum and stews of salted fishheads and chopped pieces called salsamentum. . . . By Antipas's time, Magdala had become such a famous center of this industry that it was commonly referred to as Tarichaeae, or the "Town of Salt-Fish." And anyone who thinks that fishermen on the Sea of Galilee in the time of Jesus were just picturesque peasants in rowboats does not appreciate the sheer weight of fish flesh that had to be hauled in every day and transported to Magdala's processing centers to be salted, pressed, fermented, and refined. . . . This was an industry that apparently brought great wealth to some and great misery to others. . . . Yet the production of salted fish was only one entrepreneurial venture. . . . Like most other client kings and local rulers of the time, Antipas had to rely on two basic methods to make the landscape more productive: intensified tax collection and more frequent use of conscripted peasant labor to carry out public works projects and to develop his privately held lands.[18]

In this context, Gospel references to Mary Magdalene are something akin to identifying her as "Mary of the sweatshops," and Jesus' invitation to fisherman to become disciples takes on a radical edge.

CONCLUSION

When Mark includes "Herodians" in his description of a conspiracy to murder Jesus, he invites us to pay attention to how Rome ruled. In a section on Mark's Gospel in his book *Living Jesus*, Luke Timothy Johnson, who warns that historical Jesus scholarship is misguided and dangerous, has less than one sentence on the Herodians: "Mark in 3:6 mentions the Herodians (about whom we otherwise know nothing)."[19] Johnson rejects Mark's invitation to probe important markers essential for an adequate portrait of Jesus. He thereby loses sight of vital historical clues that can help us make sense out of Christian faith in light of Jesus' images of God and Jesus' expectations of God and history.

Client kings such as Herod the Great and his son Antipas were oppressive and effective. Another son, Archelaus, was brutal and ineffective and was replaced by a Roman governor as Rome reestablished direct rule over parts of Palestine. The most famous governor was Pilate, whose role in the Gospels is sufficiently distorted to conceal the nature of the conflict between Rome and the Jesus movement and to muddy the waters concerning his murder.

There were other changes following the death of Herod the Great. Most important, priestly groups connected to the Temple played an expanded role in the domination system of first-century Palestine. The system left the vast majority of people hungry, poor, illiterate, and with little hope. We need to know how various social groups as well as impoverished people made sense out of their situation, history, and God. We also need to know how key beneficiaries of the domination system justified that system, their own privileges, and the people's unfortunate plight. This points us to the Temple and to groups such as the Pharisees, mentioned early in Mark's Gospel as coconspirators in the plot to murder Jesus.

Notes

1. John Dominic Crossan, *The Birth of Christianity* (San Francisco: HarperSanFrancisco, 1998), 232.

2. Richard Horsley, *Jesus and the Spiral of Violence: Popular Jewish Resistance in Roman Palestine* (Minneapolis: Fortress Press, 1993), 50, 71–77.

3. Ibid., 51.

4. Ibid., 43–44, 50–54.

5. Marcus Borg, *Conflict, Holiness, and Politics in the Teachings of Jesus* (New York: Edwin Mellen Press, 1984), 55.

6. John Dominic Crossan, *Jesus: A Revolutionary Biography* (New York: HarperCollins, 1995), 40, emphasis in original.

7. Richard A. Horsley and Neil Asher Silberman, *The Message and the Kingdom* (New York: Grosset/Putnam, 1997), 15.

8. Ibid., 14–15.

9. Horsley, *Jesus and the Spiral*, 105–6.

10. Uta Ranke-Heinemann, *Putting Away Childish Things* (San Francisco: HarperSanFrancisco, 1995), 109–10.

11. Ibid., 111–12.

12. Crossan, *Jesus*, 152.

13. Horsley, *Jesus and the Spiral*, 43–44.

14. Horsley and Silberman, *The Message and the Kingdom*, 24.

15. Crossan, *The Birth of Christianity*, 216.

16. Ibid., 223.

17. Quoted in Crossan, *Birth of Christianity*, 221.

18. Horsley and Silberman, *The Message and the Kingdom*, 25–26.

19. Luke Timothy Johnson, *Living Jesus: Learning the Heart of the Gospel* (San Francisco: HarperSanFrancisco, 1999), 130–31.

16 RELIGIOUS COMPLICITY

Mark's reference to Herodians plotting to murder Jesus pointed to the role of client kings in the domination system. His inclusion of Pharisees calls attention to Jewish religious groups in first century Palestine. This chapter examines Jesus' conflict with Temple authorities and religious functionaries who played important roles in the oppressive system.

ROME AND TEMPLE

The domination system in Palestine produced opulence and power for a tiny elite and poverty and despair for the overwhelming majority. Elite consumption was made possible by wealth drained from the countryside through ruthless exploitation. The system was controlled by imperial Rome, backed by oppressive military power, and guided by "religious" authority centered in the Jewish Temple. The word *religious* is placed in quotes because there was no separation between religion and politics, and the Temple was an institution of enormous political, economic, and religious consequence in first-century Palestine.

The key players in the domination system were arrogant, powerful, and cruel, not because they were inherently evil, but because oppression was a systemic necessity. At the pinnacle stood the Roman Empire and under it those who ruled on its behalf. Rome's power touched all aspects of life. Its arrogance included religious claims concerning the blessings of the gods and the divinity of the emperor. Its brutality featured massacres and crucifixions of potential and actual rebels as part of a strategy of psychological warfare, intimidation, and control. Its propaganda and ideological persuasion included promotion of the emperor cult and Rome's "gospel" of peace through military conquest. Its support for Greek cultural activities, including athletic games, diverted attention from fundamental problems much like professional sports do today. Its power over client kings, governors, and high priests insured political control.

For all the wonders of Roman power, the system could not function smoothly in Palestine without cooperation and co-optation of the Jewish Temple. This meant that while Roman governors and client kings exercised ultimate authority over the Temple, they could not ignore Jewish priestly leaders. This dilemma meant Jewish elites were given a stake in the system. The priests who benefited from collaborative rule influenced society directly and through retainers such as the scribes and Pharisees. Recent archeological evidence demonstrates that collaborative rule brought significant benefits to high priestly groups:

> Ever since the vast expansion of the Temple structures and institutions, these high-priestly families and families of priestly officers in charge of the Temple's treasury, workshops, storerooms, and supply facilities had amassed considerable fortunes, passing down their particular responsibilities and privileges— and wealth—from fathers to sons. Unlike the members of the twenty-four priestly courses who lived throughout the country, *these* priestly officials were permanent residents of the Holy City, and the impressive archaeological remains of their Jerusalem residences show how elegant their lifestyle had become. In spacious structures unhesitatingly dubbed "mansions" by the archaeologists who uncovered them in the 1970s, we can get a glimpse of a lavish life in mosaic-floored reception rooms and dining rooms with elaborate painted and carved stucco wall decoration and with a wealth of fine tableware, glassware, carved stone tabletops and other interior furnishings, and elegant peristyles. . . . Their wealth and prominence

in Judean society has been further underlined by the elaborate family tombs which they built on the outskirts of the city. . . . Beyond the fascinating recovered relics, however, lies a more sobering historical reality. For it is quite clear that the continued wealth of the high-priestly families and their political fortunes were dependent on the Roman authorities. Piety and right-eousness had long since ceased being the main criteria for a High Priest's successful term in office; ever since the deposition of Archelaus, the High Priests had been the *de facto* representa-tives of the Judean people to the Roman authorities and they were saddled with the responsibility of maintaining order in Jerusalem. Roman officials could—and did—appoint them and depose them at will.[1]

In addition to wealth and power, Rome offered Jewish leaders religious tolerance with tight political strings in exchange for their help in collect-ing tribute and taxes and maintaining order. The Jews celebrated Passover and other freedom rituals, but they could not be free. Even crit-ics of Temple abuses, including the Pharisees, focused on aspects of the Torah that stressed personal piety, proper sacrifices, and rituals, while ignoring matters of justice. They kept the Sabbath holy but failed to effectively respond to the cycles of indebtedness, land loss, and destitu-tion that broke the backs and spirits of the poor.

Temple leaders were not evil. They were dependent partners in an imperial system, and their power grew considerably following the replacement of Archelaus. Ultimate authority rested with the Roman governor who resided in Caesarea, but, as Richard Horsley notes, "domestic Jewish affairs were left to the priestly aristocracy" which "also dominated the Sanhedrin or high council throughout the period."[2] Judea became for all practical purposes a "dependent temple state . . ."[3] High priestly rulers stood between the people and Rome while claiming to stand between the people and God. This is something akin to having one foot planted on solid ground and the other in quicksand.

The power of religious leaders depended on Rome's blessing system-wide. The high priest and high priestly families pleased Rome or were replaced. Midlevel functionaries such as scribes and Pharisees had less power. This meant less attention from Roman officials, but it did not mean real freedom. As in any patronage system, they depended on those above them in the pecking order. Patronage meant different layers of dependency and different consequences for insubordination.

Differences and resentments were part of the unequal partnership between Temple officials and Rome. Some found rhetorical expression. Others boiled over into actual protests. There were lines that could not be crossed, as Antiochus discovered when he tried to turn the Jewish Temple into a worship center for Zeus. When the Roman emperor Gaius ordered a statue of Zeus with his own features erected in the Jerusalem Temple, it spawned massive nonviolent protests including an agricultural strike. Pilate's introduction of images of Caesar on the standards of Roman soldiers led to similar protests because it violated Jewish prohibitions against engraved images.[4] Popular protests sprang from the outrage of common people bent on holding the line against Roman encroachments. Reluctant leaders waffled.

Jesus was in conflict with religious authorities because empires always distort religion and Judaism in Roman-dominated first-century Palestine was no exception. Horsley describes the system:

> The Temple was clearly the basis of an economic system in which the agricultural producers supported the priests, particularly the priestly aristocracy who administered the system and were its chief beneficiaries. Besides its religious basis, the tithes and offerings ostensibly being given to God, the system had the political backing of the empire, Caesar having decreed shortly after Rome took control of Palestine that the tithes would be brought to the high priests. . . . [The Temple] stood at the center of power in Jewish society in every respect, and it stood at the vortex of the imperial relationship between Rome and the Palestinian people. Besides the sacrifices called for in the Torah, sacrifices were offered also in honor of Rome and the emperor, and failure to perform them was tantamount to rebellion. The Temple was thus functioning as an instrument of imperial legitimization and control of a subjected people.[5]

As junior partners in an oppressive system, Jewish officials had little choice but to please or appease Rome or else face brutal consequences for insubordination. Temple leaders made concessions to the Romans and benefited nicely from the bargain. Midlevel functionaries such as the scribes and Pharisees were compromised in relation to both Rome and Temple because threats of removal or other unpleasant sanctions hung over their heads like guillotines. One reason Rome preferred indirect rule was that resentments stemming from an oppressive system could be deflected onto others.

A powerful symbol of dependent status is that the high priest, the most important official within Judaism, was a political appointee of the Roman empire. "The Roman administration of Judea," Crossan writes, "depended . . . on the cooperation of the native Jewish aristocracy and especially on the collaboration of the Temple's High Priest, whom the Romans deposed and replaced with a regularity calculated to keep such collaboration if not fervent at least secure."[6] Rome also held the sacred vestments worn when the high priest entered the Holy of Holies, the most sacred space within the Temple, on the Day of Atonement, the holiest day of the year. Set on imperial footings, Judaism sank deep into the muck of oppression. Authentic God and faith nearly disappeared along with compassion and the justice of God.

The imperial situation meant collaborating Jews were incapable of upholding a justice tradition. This was true for high priests, aristocratic families, and midlevel retainers alike. None could truly defend widows and orphans, break cycles of indebtedness, insure rights to and fair distribution of God's land, or rule in light of the sovereignty of God as parts of the Torah and other aspects of the tradition demanded. Why? Because satisfying Rome and securing their own positions of power depended on faithful exploitation of the people. Pleasing Rome, defending their own privileges, and in some cases plain survival, necessarily led to exploitation of the people and to distortion of God, Temple, and Torah.

Only part of the blame for oppressive rule can be laid at the feet of the Romans, however. During times of independent rule, Jewish elites often oppressed the people and distorted God and scripture in pursuit of wealth, power and other privileges: "The LORD enters into judgment with the elders and princes of his people: It is you who have devoured the vineyard; the spoil of the poor is in your houses. What do you mean by crushing my people, by grinding the face of the poor? says the Lord GOD of hosts" (Isa 3:14–15). Priestly groups, as noted earlier, often did not agree about God or what did or did not please God, and they often fought each other bitterly. Prophets declared the people's suffering to be a just consequence of disobedience at the hands of a God who would not tolerate idolatry or injustice. Common people, like Jesus and those with whom he associated, were nearly always the victims of such interpretations and disputes. The book of Isaiah contains a passage typical of many others that Jesus would likely have greeted both with profound sympathy in light of its concern for the poor and with deep concern over its misleading explanations for oppression and its troubling images of God:

> So the LORD cut off from Israel head and tail,
>   palm branch and reed in one day—
> elders and dignitaries are the head,
>   and prophets who teach lies are the tail;
> for those who led this people led them astray,
>   and those who were led by them were left in confusion.
> That is why the Lord did not have pity on their young people,
>   or compassion on their orphans and widows;
> for everyone was godless and an evildoer,
>   and every mouth spoke folly.
> For all this his anger has not turned away,
>   his hand is stretched out still (Isa 9:14–17).

This passage illustrates that the temptation to shift attention and blame for oppression and suffering away from the domination system and onto God and the victims of that system extended even to the prophetic justice tradition. The Jewish leaders of the people both during Isaiah's time and in first-century Palestine undoubtedly led the people down disastrous paths. They pursued their own interests, confused the people, and in many ways were responsible for the people's suffering. Jesus, unlike Isaiah, however, refused to link God's punishing violence to the people's miserable plight that in Isaiah's vision extended all the way to God's lack of compassion for widows and orphans.

Jesus, as we will see throughout much of the rest of this book, focused attention squarely on the domination system as the opposite of God's intended domination-free, compassion-filled order. He embraced justice concerns rooted in the Exodus story, Isaiah, and other prophetic texts that challenged unjust rulers and their supporters among the priests and prophets. He undermined the expectation of God's liberating violence that was rooted in the Exodus, however, and the notion of God's punishing violence that is featured centrally in much of the Hebrew Scriptures. E. P. Sanders notes Jesus' disinterest in the prominent Jewish theme of repentance as a means to avoid God's punishing violence:

> There is not a significant body of reliable sayings material which *explicitly* attributes to Jesus a call for *national* repentance. . . . There is no firm tradition which shows that he issued a call

for the national repentance in view of the coming end, as did John the Baptist. . . . It seems that he did not make thematic that Israel should repent and mend their ways so as to escape punishment at the judgment.[7]

Jesus lays little stress on repentance because his focus is on dynamics at play in the oppressive system and because his images of God break with expectations of a punishing deity. This point is missed by Sanders but not by Crossan:

> *If* you believe that imperial oppression was divine punishment for Jewish sin, you would have to call for Jewish repentance prior to God's deliverance. If you did *not*, then you would *not*. The data supports the interpretation that Jesus did *not* think imperial oppression was a divine punishment. It was simply an injustice that the Jews and God would have to resist as best they could. Jesus, and probably most peasants, knew exactly where the fault lay, and they did not blame on Jewish sin what came rather from Roman greed.[8]

Crossan's insight is critical but one corrective is needed. The injustice was rooted in a domination system that included Roman greed but was not limited to it. The deadly plot that followed an illegal Sabbath healing revealed how out of control the domination system had become, including its "religious" component. It was a system subservient to Roman needs *and* priestly privileges. The Temple was supposed to be God's dwelling place, but it had become a clearinghouse for Roman influence, tribute, and taxes. Temple leaders collaborated with Rome's rule to their mutual benefit. Priestly elites and those under their employ, including the Pharisees, collected taxes on behalf of Rome as well as the taxes or tithes prescribed within the Torah on which their own wealth and power depended.

Roman and Jewish elites thrived under this system of double taxation. The people, especially vulnerable peasants, languished in poverty. Jeremiah said that the Temple had become a "den of robbers" (Jer 7:11) because of persistent injustice, a perspective shared by Jesus (Mark 11:17; Matt 21:13; Luke 19:46). As Crossan notes, "a den of robbers is not where robbers rob others but where they run for safety when they have robbed others elsewhere."[9] According to Jesus and Jeremiah, the Temple leaders and those under their employ were thieves, and the Temple itself was their safe haven. It had become a reservoir where religious leaders stored the fruits of systemic injustice.

Many interpreters, including Richard Horsley, offer Jesus' symbolic attack against the Temple as proof of his embrace of apocalyptic expectations of God and history. This seems both unnecessary and misguided. It is clear that Jesus opposed the Temple because he rejected many aspects of the Temple that served the domination system. He rejected the view that the Temple was God's dwelling place as well as national mythologies trumpeting visions of Israel's triumph over the nations. The Temple's oppressive role—economic, political, social, and religious—is sufficient to account for Jesus' prophetic critique.

The Gospel writers had many reasons to interpret Jesus, including his Temple action, in an apocalyptic light. There is, however, nothing necessarily apocalyptic about Jesus' views or actions concerning the Temple. In fact, Jesus' persistent and unrelenting focus on the domination system (and as we will see, alternatives to it) speaks against an apocalyptic interpretation. If Jesus were expecting, announcing, and promoting an imminent violent coming of God to rectify historical injustices or to end history, then his movement would be merely an extension of John the Baptist's. It is difficult to reconcile Jesus' constant effort to expose the inner workings of the domination system and to discredit and create meaningful alternatives to it with apocalyptic expectations. A God of justice would not be at home in the Temple or use it to fulfill an illusionary glorious plan of national triumph and redemption when the Temple itself was built on the backs of the poor and served the destructive domination system as a faithful partner.

Foreign domination and the imperial situation made justice difficult if not impossible for the Jewish people. The psalmist's question asked during captivity in Babylon (Ps 137:4) had to be restated consciously or unconsciously many times in the context of captivity *within* the Jewish homeland: "How can we sing the Lord's song when our land, God's land, is occupied by foreigners who rule with the help of client kings and our own priests?" There was much confusion, many competing claims, and no easy answers.

CO-CONSPIRATORS

Jesus healed a man with a withered hand on the Sabbath. The domination system's response, according to Mark, was swift: "The Pharisees went out and immediately conspired with the Herodians against him, how to destroy him (Mark 3:6). The Markan inclusion of Herodians in such a plot is highly credible in light of the discussion of client king rule in the previous chapter. The mention of Pharisees as coconspirators raises important issues, including whether or not the Gospels are accurate when they portray Jesus and the Pharisees in frequent conflict.

There is a great deal of scholarly debate and no consensus about these matters. Two insights guide many scholars. First, the Pharisees who became client rulers on behalf of Rome following the Jewish Revolt (66–70 C.E.) were less powerful during the time of Jesus. It is very unlikely that they ruled the Temple. Richard Horsley says that in the first century, the Pharisees "appear to have been reduced basically to brotherhoods devoted to rigorous study and practice of the (Mosaic) Torah." He presents the Pharisees as midlevel functionaries in the imperial system with limited power and some measure of independence.[10] Second, Jewish Christian communities were in conflict with Pharisees at the time the Gospels were written. The likelihood that the Pharisees were midlevel functionaries during the time of Jesus and the fact that Pharisaic communities were competitors with early Christian communities leads some scholars to conclude that Jesus was not in conflict with the Pharisees. Others suggest that the Gospels greatly overstate the conflict between Jesus and the Pharisees. According to these views, problems between Jewish Christians and the Pharisees were retrojected back into the Jesus story.

Let me clarify my own position in the context of the passage in Mark 3. First, Mark's charge that Pharisees were centrally involved in a murder conspiracy surrounding Jesus seems unlikely. The Pharisees, by most accounts, simply were not that influential. Pilate? Yes. The Herodians? Yes. Temple leaders? Yes. The Pharisees? Probably not. Second, I believe Jesus did have serious conflicts with the Pharisees. I do not think Mark invented this conflict between Jesus and the Pharisees, although he may have embellished it. Stated somewhat differently, even if the Pharisees were not involved in the conspiracy to murder Jesus and even if they were in conflict with Mark's community, this does not rule out the possibility that Jesus clashed with the Pharisees. We need to explore this conflict in the context of specific issues. Finally, Mark's inclusion of the Pharisees in a murderous plot to eliminate Jesus points more generally in the direction of the Temple establishment's role in the domination system. Given the Gospel writer's conflict with Pharisees at the time they wrote, it is likely that Mark's linkage of Herodians and Pharisees may exaggerate the role of one of his community's key adversaries. Mark overstates *their* power and influence, but he points rightly to *the* power and influence of religious authorities and institutions in the domination system of first-century Palestine during the time of Jesus.

Amidst any ambiguity in scholarship, the crucial point is that Mark's naming of the Pharisees in his account of a murderous plot tells us that religion in first-century Palestine played an important and oppressive political role within the domination system. The conspiracy to murder Jesus that involved Herodians and religious officials is highly credible given the analysis provided above. Other questions remain or must be probed more fully, however. What did Jesus say and do that led representatives of the established order to kill him? And even if they did not participate in a murderous conspiracy, why did Jesus and the Pharisees clash? If Jesus opposed the domination system but rejected expectations of God's apocalyptic intervention as the means to do something about it, then what did he expect of himself, others, and God?

I explore answers to these and other questions in the next several chapters. Here let me say simply that early on in Mark's Gospel it is clear that Jesus was killed, not as an atoning sacrifice, but as a consequence of his life and faith that conflicted sharply with a domination system controlled by Rome and Temple.

Notes

1. Richard A. Horsley and Neil Asher Silberman, *The Message and the Kingdom* (New York: Grosset/Putnam, 1997), 78–79, emphasis in original.

2. Richard Horsley, *Jesus and the Spiral of Violence: Popular Jewish Resistance in Roman Palestine* (Minneapolis: Fortress Press, 1993), 11.

3. William R. Herzog II, *Parables as Subversive Speech: Jesus as Pedagogue of the Oppressed* (Louisville, Ky.: Westminster/John Knox Press, 1994), 55.

4. Horsley, *Jesus and the Spiral of Violence*, 100–101.

5. Ibid., 286–87.

6. John Dominic Crossan, *Jesus: A Revolutionary Biography* (New York: HarperCollins, 1995), 136.

7. Quoted in John Dominic Crossan, *The Birth of Christianity* (San Francisco: HarperSanFrancisco, 1998), 339, emphasis in original.

8. Crossan, *Birth of Christianity*, 339, emphasis in original.

9. Ibid., 205.

10. Horsley, *Jesus and the Spiral of Violence*, 17–18.

SUBVERSIVE HEALING, COMPETING TORAHS, AND THE POWER TO EXCLUDE

Mark 3:1–6, as discussed previously, contains historically verifiable markers consistent with what we know from other sources and passages about Jesus and first-century Palestine. Client king rule was oppressive. Jesus was a healer who was in conflict with religious officials over Sabbath observance. Jesus clashed with the Temple and its established leaders and functionaries. The present chapter examines these markers with an eye on the nature of the conflict between Jesus and religious officials within first-century Palestine.

SUBVERSIVE HEALING

I return to Mark 3:1–6 in order to explore broader theological insights concerning Jesus' faith and understandings and expectations of God. The reference to the "hardness of heart" (3:5) of Jesus' adversaries is striking. It points back to the Exodus story, to Pharaoh's heart and oppressive rule. Recall that the book of Exodus opened with a description of a new pharaoh coming to power who did not know Joseph. Joseph had used food as a weapon in service to a prior pharaoh. As a result, all Egyptians lost their money, cattle, land, and freedom. A new pharaoh turned the tables on the Israelites. They who had benefited from Joseph's cozy relationship with imperial power were now enslaved. When the Israelites demanded liberation, Pharaoh, whose heart was hardened, forced them to work under even harsher conditions and refused their demand for freedom.

The book of Exodus and the Markan account explain hardness of heart very differently. The Markan passage contrasts Jesus' compassionate act of healing with the murderous intentions of Herodians and Pharisees aligned to the domination system. In the book of Exodus, however, it is God who hardens Pharaoh's heart in order to create an opportunity to prove that God is God through superior violence. Jesus, in this and many other places, challenges the widespread view that linked God to superior violence. His focus is clearly on the domination system, which he associated with oppressive actions that reflected the opposite of God's intent.

Let me note four striking features in the Markan text that link hardness of heart to systems of domination. First, the oppressive situation of Jesus' contemporaries is similar to the pathetic plight of the Egyptians during Joseph's abusive alliance with Pharaoh and of the Israelites after the reversal in which they are enslaved by a new pharaoh. In each case, an abusive system left people oppressed, sick, disheartened, impoverished, landless, and without freedom. Second, the Markan text, unlike the Exodus account, offers no hint that hardness of heart is linked to God's will or God's violence. The problem of hardness of heart is placed squarely in the lap of the domination system where it belongs. Rather than being an opportunity to prove God's credentials through superior violence, hardness of heart, according to Jesus, is a consequence of obedience to an oppressive system rooted in violence. Jesus puts attention on the violence of the domination system in his own time, and he invites his people and us to revisit the meaning of the Exodus story. Pharaoh, in this reading, had a hard heart because he was a servant of a heartless system. Hardened hearts are not acts of God but products of systems that make compassion impossible. Pharisees and Herodians have hard hearts because oppressive systems undermine human compassion and the compassion of God.

The Exodus story understood as a manifestation of God's superior violence had captivated the imaginations of the people throughout centuries of oppression. They awaited a new, violent coming of God, as part of either the old theology's promise of God's saving violence to defeat historical enemies or the newer apocalyptic theology's promise of God's violence to end history or impose justice and to destroy evil and vindicate the faithful. Jesus' constant focus on the domination system suggests an alternative view of God and history. The people had become captive to false expectations of God's liberating, punishing, or apocalyptic violence. This was true because, according to Jesus, the domination system was not going to disappear in a flash of God's redemptive violence. The people needed to confront the system directly by imitating the compassion of God. This necessarily required them to understand how the domination system worked, to abandon illusions of God's liberating violence, to refuse to internalize their oppression, and to live according to the intentions of a compassionate God. Jesus' attention to detail in relation to these concerns, evident in his teaching in relation to the spiral of violence (chapter 18), speaks forcefully against an apocalyptic reading of Jesus or the Christ.

A third such feature in the Markan passage is a recurring theme in the life and message of Jesus, namely, that salvation means healing and restoration to the community and not the crushing defeat of enemies. Kathleen Norris writes in *Amazing Grace* that "the Hebrew word for salvation means literally 'to make wide'" and that "the Hebrew words usually come from a military context and refer to victory over evil or rescue from danger in this life." She also notes that salvation "in the gospels . . . is often physical healing that people seek from Jesus" and that when Jesus "says to them that their faith has saved them, it is the Greek word for 'made you well' that is employed."[1] What she does not say is that these understandings of salvation are incompatible and that time after time in the Hebrew Scriptures the promise "to make wide" involves expectations of the crushing defeat of enemies based on God's superior violence. Jesus' link between salvation and healing also has an etymological foundation. The root verb *salvar* means "to heal," which is also evident in the word *salve*. The idea that healing is linked to restoration to community can also be traced etymologically. Within the tradition, holiness was understood as separation from that which defiles. It can also mean wholeness. For Jesus, salvation and holiness were linked to healing and wholeness including restoration to community.

The domination system hurt both victims and victimizers. This may explain why Jesus was said to be both angry and grieved by his adversary's hardness of heart, and why, as we will see in later chapters, all people were invited into the domination-free order. The system left victims sick, destitute, and ostracized and left beneficiaries bereft of compassion. Jesus made much the same point when he highlighted how economic ties to oppressive systems made compassion difficult if not impossible. Jesus looked upon a rich man, loved him, and told him to sell what he had, give the proceeds to the poor, and come follow. The economic perks of the domination system held the man captive, and he refused the invitation. "When he heard this, he was shocked and went away grieving, for he had many possessions" (Luke 10:22).

Jesus also stressed that religious convictions central to the domination system, including preoccupation with purity and holiness, were obstacles to wholeness, community, and compassion. Luke records the parable of the compassionate Samaritan, in which a priest and Levite see a man beaten by the road and cross over to the other side (10:30–37). They do so presumably not out of indifference alone but because of fears connected to purity regulations, defilement, and preoccupation with holiness. Marcus Borg writes of this parable:

> The hearers would have understood the legal dilemma facing the two clerics, which centered around the possibility of incurring ritual defilement through proximity to a corpse. If the wounded victim were dead (and since he was "half dead," one could not tell without approaching closely), the situation posed three risks of defilement (which would also occur if the man, though alive, died in the presence of the cleric): by coming within four cubits of the corpse; by casting one's shadow over the corpse; or, if an overhanging rock overshadowed the corpse, by stepping within that shadow. On the other hand, if the priest were certain that the person was a neighbor (a Jew), he had an obligation to help; but such certainty required close examination, which was precisely what the danger of defilement precluded. In a situation of doubt, preference was to be given to fulfilling that law which could be fulfilled with certainty (in this case avoiding defilement) and the priest was thereby entitled to travel on. Yet there was legal justification for a priest to risk defilement, but only with the concomitant risk of the inconvenience and cost of subsequent purification and temporary loss of the right to receive tithe. . . . [T]he ethics of the time gave no decisive guidance; either course of action was justifiable as a fulfillment of God's law, though stopping did entail risks. Such was the dilemma facing the clerics. . . . Manifestly, that which explained and justified their action was the quest for a holy community, understood as separation from that which defiles. The

parable concluded by eliciting the judgment that the [heretical half-breed] Samaritan, not the priest or Levite, actually became a neighbor to the wounded man. Hence the parable judged negatively the action of the priest and Levite, despite their legal rectitude. Jesus claimed that their action, motivated by and consistent with the Pharisaic dynamic of holiness, really amounted to a failure to be a neighbor.[2]

This parable challenges preoccupation with holiness in a variety of ways. First, the heretical, hated, half-breed and therefore unholy Samaritan was the hero of the story. Samaritans were disliked in part because they intermarried during a period of captivity and so had not kept Israel's "seed" pure and holy. Second, the despised Samaritan was an instrument of salvation (healing) because he took the steps necessary to restore the wounded man's health just as Jesus had helped the man with a withered hand. The Samaritan's behavior also contrasted sharply with the actions of the priest and Levite, who in crossing to the other side bypassed an opportunity for healing (salvation) and with those of the Pharisees in Mark's account who were offended by healing (salvation) and plotted to murder Jesus. Third, the healing action of the Samaritan marks a startling reversal of expectations for those who awaited salvation from oppression through a violent action of God that would defeat enemies. Sufficient holiness was considered by some to be a necessary precondition to trigger God's redemptive violence. In this case, salvation, expressed as healing and wholeness, came not as a result of God's violence against enemies but through the compassionate actions of one's enemy. Fourth, Jesus linked the legal but problematic conduct of the priests and Levites to inconveniences and concerns rooted in purity and holiness regulations. These issues were not trivial. A high priest defiled by a corpse was banned from the priesthood for life. The absence of compassion, Jesus implied, was not always or often due to trivial matters. It was a systemic necessity.

Jesus said that compassion required a break with the conventional wisdom of the domination system. For the victims of the system this meant abandoning the false promises of God's redemptive violence. It also meant exposing and demystifying the mechanisms of domination and refusing to internalize the worldview of the oppressive system itself, including its nasty claims about the poor. For the beneficiaries, it meant shattering political, economic, and religious ties to systems that made compassion impossible. Changing course is the essence of conversion. It is not something you do to trigger God's intervention into unjust history but is a response to the existing presence of God. It is, in other words, invitational rather than apocalyptic. For Jesus, the reason to change course is not to avoid God's punishing violence or to prepare the way for God's redemptive violence. Change course because the violence of the oppressive system destroys life. Change course because God's alternative is present and available. Change course because that is the only way the domination system can be challenged or replaced. Change course because abundant life depends on it.

Jesus' grief over hardness of heart and the conspiratorial plot to kill him were set in a holy place (synagogue) at a holy time (Sabbath). This leads to many questions concerning Jesus' conflict with others over images of God and his relationship to various streams within the Jewish tradition. Why was healing so controversial? How did Jesus and his adversaries differ over images of God, their understanding of holiness, and the Sabbath?

COMPETING TORAHS

Hardness of heart and conspiratorial plots in the context of holy place and holy time point to competing Sabbath traditions and conflicting perspectives on holiness within the Torah. Jesus' reference to hardness of heart invited his people to revisit the meaning of exodus. His parable about a compassionate Samaritan illustrated how conventional preoccupations with purity and holiness blocked compassion. His illegal Sabbath healing called attention to long-neglected sabbatical provisions involving social justice that had been lost amidst holiness and purity concerns.

Paula Fredriksen criticizes Marcus Borg for misunderstanding purity and holiness in Jewish thought. Borg, she says, yanks Jesus out of his own culture. She accuses him of conflating "the purity code with morality" and "purity, morality, class and gender." She says that a "Jesus who rejects his own religious culture turns out to be a 20th century person in ancient garb—a modern secular liberal offended by impurity's sharp lines."[3] It seems to me, however, that Fredriksen consistently yanks issues of purity and holiness out of their necessary political context. Jesus' approach to Sabbath was every bit as Jewish as that of his adversaries. Each party stressed different streams within the conflictive tradition. Jesus is linked to sabbatical legislation calling for periodic breaking of the cycles of poverty through debt forgiveness, freedom for slaves, and the redistribution of land. In this part of the tradition, God's holiness is an expression of God's justice.

Others saw holiness differently and believed that the absence of holiness had dire political consequences. The Exile, for example, was understood as the threatened or realized consequence of not being holy. God's land was holy land. If the people of God were not sufficiently holy, then God would vomit them out of the land and allow their enemies to devour them. Jewish writer Regina M. Schwartz notes:

> A stubborn emphasis on oneness asserts itself in preoccupations with purity. Whether as singleness (this God against the others) or totality (this is all the God there is), monotheism abhors, reviles, rejects, and ejects whatever it defines as outside its compass. . . . "Be Holy for I am Holy" is how that divine command is often translated. "Holiness," then, is literally set-apartness, and that which is set apart is also spoken of as pure or clean. Classifying land as either clean or unclean is pivotal to this system. Leviticus asserts that the land must be kept undefiled or else its inhabitants will be ejected, "vomited" out of the land. The purity of the land is determined by its people following all the law.[4]

Some within the tradition stressed that one important way to demonstrate fidelity is to be clean, pure, and holy. They connected holiness and purity to the promise of God's saving violence to defeat enemies and restore God's people to the land. If impurity leads God to vomit people out of the land, then perhaps God will reward purity and holiness with defeat of enemies. Finally, in the imperial context, holiness became a means of maintaining Jewish identity amidst foreign nations or cultures. The identity of a threatened people is often shored up through the establishment of recognizable boundaries. Circumcision, hand washing, rules surrounding table fellowship, purity regulations, tightly controlled mechanisms for healing or forgiveness, and other rituals are signs of and means to cultural cohesion. Those who challenge them are dangerous.

If one believed that God vomited the chosen people out of the land or allowed empire after empire to occupy and defile it because the people were not holy enough, then one might be persuaded that it was in their interest and that of the nation to kill "a man who lies with a male as with a woman," adulterers, and disobedient children (Lev 20:9–10, 13). The same can be said if holiness might trigger God's aid and help them defeat enemies and get their land back. If unholy behavior put the people of God and the nation in jeopardy by undermining cultural solidarity, then it might also be prudent to keep the Sabbath day holy by stoning a man to death for gathering sticks during sacred time (Num 15:32–36). Murdering Jesus, who performed illegal Sabbath healings, would be both justified and expedient.

Jesus may well have grieved at the hardness of heart of his adversaries because their images of God and their explanation for the people's misery contrasted so sharply with his own. Deep fears and harsh threats associated with a punishing God fed the desire for purity and holiness. Schwartz's political reading of purity and holiness, as well as my own, diverges sharply from Fredriksen's apolitical view that purity "enables proximity to holiness."[5] The fact that holiness concerns are so often linked with terrifying images of God may explain why Jesus only once refers to God as holy. Just as Jesus empathizes with the social critique of the prophets while rejecting their punishing visions and expectations of God, he also rejects the Pharisaic assumption that insufficient holiness triggers God's judgment and its predictable corollary that sufficient holiness can jump-start God's redemptive violence. Jesus embodies God's compassion and speaks often of God as compassionate and merciful.

THE POWER TO EXCLUDE

Rome backed up demands for obedience, taxes, and tribute with military force. Temple elites and their functionaries used violence when necessary but generally relied on other means. They appealed to God and their God-given authority to sanction noncompliant Jews. Borg describes religious sanctions employed by the Pharisees:

> The policy of the Pharisees, simply because more is known about it, is especially instructive. Though the Romans could enforce payment of taxes levied by them with police power, the Pharisees had no police power to enforce the payment of Jewish taxes. Their . . . major sanction was social and religious ostracism. The most offensive of the non-observant, "the sinners," were declared to have lost all civil and religious rights; they were deprived of the right to sit on local councils and lost their place as children of Abraham in the life of the age to come. They became "as Gentiles," having forfeited their status as members of the holy people of God.[6]

The Romans expected client kings and high priestly groups to maintain order. This was difficult because the imperial situation was inherently unstable. Intolerable oppression inevitably spawned a variety of protests that the system met with escalating violence. Religious leaders sometimes joined or led popular protests. More often than not, however, they used their power as the guardians of the sacred order to impose discipline. They, like Roman rulers, claimed rights of divine sanction to justify their privileged positions and power. Both Roman and Temple leaders used violence and intimidation to insure stability. Jewish Temple leaders, however, controlled the mechanisms of forgiveness and used them like sharp swords. They called on sacred traditions to justify their own privileges and to explain away the people's suffering. Horsley and Silberman describe religious taxes that were collected forcibly, if necessary, by Pharisees and other religious functionaries:

> [In addition to the royal taxes, the] villagers of Galilee (like all other members of the People of Israel) were instructed to set aside a significant portion of their produce for priestly tithes, first-fruits offerings, and various other sacred donations for the Temple in Jerusalem. By the first century, every Israelite male was required to make an annual contribution of a half-shekel to the Temple (and for villagers, that coin could be obtained only through the exchange of crops or agricultural products—in addition to the ten percent already required for the annual tithe). And even in seasons when drought or blight severely limited the harvest, the tax collectors and priestly representatives still turned up at the local threshing floors and olive presses to make sure that every family contributed their due. Penalties for nonpayment could be severe and violent when the farmers of a particular village or region did not willingly yield up the lion's share of their harvest to satisfy the demands of the official representatives of the Jerusalem Temple and Herodian state.[7]

The Pharisees were among the "official representatives" that collected taxes and tithes. This highlights another potential area of dispute with Jesus. Physical intimidation was only one of a number of sanctions to encourage compliance. As noted above, the Pharisees and others could define a person as clean or unclean, pure or impure, holy or unholy, in or outside the community. They drew especially on Torah provisions that stressed sin, holiness, sacrifice, priestly roles, Temple tithes, and taxes. They ostracized impoverished Jews unable to pay their tithes while they ignored other parts of the Torah that addressed the issues of debt, land, and justice that were at the heart of the peasants' noncompliance.

The absence of justice and the widespread emphasis on sin, purity, and holiness within the tradition were signs of the not so subtle influence of the imperial situation on the substance of faith. Rome was generally tolerant of religion but utterly intolerant of freedom. Richard Horsley refers to this posture as "repressive tolerance."[8] Rome accepted the rights of Jews to carry out religious rituals but repressed any efforts toward real freedom. It undoubtedly appreciated a religious emphasis on sin and holiness that downplayed or explained away fundamental injustices rooted in the oppressive system. "Repressive tolerance," like shock therapy, sent a signal, in the form of conditioning violence. It effectively encouraged certain behaviors and discouraged others. The Pharisees and other religious leaders learned consciously or unconsciously to avoid the interface between God and justice. They found creative ways of bypassing Torah provisions concerning land, debt, and interest.

One disastrous, though perhaps well-intentioned, reform linked to the Pharisees had to deal with circumventing debt forgiveness. The sabbatical provisions of the Torah called for forgiveness of debt every seven years. In violation of the spirit of Torah, many Jews were reluctant to loan money as the seventh year approached because they would lose their capital. The Pharisees created a legal device that allowed creditors to avoid canceling debts on the seventh year. This concession to the domination system, which may have clashed sharply with Jesus' efforts to discredit it, took away sabbatical protections that were designed to prevent permanent indebtedness. The result was a deepening debt that led to loss of land and destitution. "Ironically," as Horsley notes, "the very measure taken by Pharisees to alleviate the pressure on the peasantry worked over the long run to exacerbate the problem of indebtedness and loss of land by the former freeholding peasant families."[9] More broadly, the imperial situation conditioned the Pharisees to focus religion on personal sin, piety, and purity:

> The Romans allowed the exercise of Jewish religion so long as it took no form other than mere cultic celebration, personal belief, and the reinforcement of local social order. The minute it became more collective in its expression and had political implications, the Romans intervened with renewed physical repression. The presence of the Roman troops on the Temple porticoes provides a vivid example of this enforced limitation

of Jewish religious celebration. This repressive tolerance was not without its effects on Palestinian Jews. For example, blocked in their social-political exercise of the Torah, the Pharisees focused on personal piety and purity in their brotherhoods. Another result was to reinforce the focus on sin as the cause of individual and collective suffering. This in turn reinforced the importance of the sacrifices necessary to atone for sin—which, of course, were controlled by the ruling priestly aristocracy. Given the actual structure of the imperial situation, therefore, the Roman toleration of the limited exercise of Jewish religious traditions became a repressive reinforcement of the basic structural violence and oppression.[10]

Controversy surrounding Jesus' healing is understandable in this context. Jesus linked sickness, suffering, violence, land dispossession, and the absence of compassion to the domination system. Religious officials saw sickness as a consequence of sin and suffering as God's punishment for inappropriate behavior including violations of holiness. They had many reasons to focus on personal piety and sacrifices. They controlled the mechanisms of forgiveness, including the redemptive media of the sacrificial system. The focus on sin, personal holiness, and piety gave them the means and the mandate to tax, to ostracize, and to forgive. They benefited from the domination system and they did not want to violate their compact with the Romans or their client rulers. The system offered them tightly controlled religious freedom so long as they collected tribute and taxes and helped maintain order. Jesus' illegal and unauthorized healing bypassed institutional channels. Illegal healings undermined traditional authority. Healing itself was an expression of the compassion and character of God that challenged classical explanations for oppression and threatened the whole system.

CONCLUSION

The domination system made life miserable for the people of Israel. Client kings such as Herod and his sons exploited the people to enrich themselves and to deliver the tribute, taxes, and stability Rome demanded. Archelaus's fate also demonstrated the consequences of failing to please Rome, a message that would not have been lost on Antipas in Galilee, Pilate in Judea, and the religious officials throughout Palestine. Rome gave Temple authorities a stake in the system so long as the demands of Temple and Torah did not threaten the system itself. Some of these authorities lived in luxurious mansions in Jerusalem. Jesus exposed the fragile nature of "repressive tolerance" by exposing violence at the hidden heart of collaborative rule, violence that came to light in a conspiracy to murder Jesus hatched by Herodians and "Pharisees" following an illegal Sabbath healing.

The Temple's collaborative role in the context of Roman imperial rule was a major cause of the people's oppression. Jesus linked sickness and suffering to hardness of heart, which is central to all systems of domination. He used the compassion of God to measure claims of God's sovereignty and as a yardstick to challenge and judge the religious and political pretensions of the system's architects, servants, and overseers. In the next chapter, I offer additional evidence that Jesus' images of God and his expectations of history clashed sharply with Roman imperial claims and with the Temple establishment's use and abuse of God and sacred scripture.

Notes

1. Kathleen Norris, *Amazing Grace* (New York: Riverhead Books, 1998), 20.

2. Marcus Borg, *Conflict, Holiness, and Politics in the Teachings of Jesus* (New York: Edwin Mellen Press, 1984), 104–5.

3. Paula Fredriksen, "Did Jesus Oppose the Purity Laws?" *Bible Review* (June 1995), 22, 45.

4. Regina M. Schwartz, *The Curse of Cain: The Violent Legacy of Monotheism* (Chicago: University of Chicago Press, 1997), 63.

5. Fredriksen, "Did Jesus Oppose," 45.

6. Borg, *Conflict, Holiness, and Politics*, 69.

7. Richard A. Horsley and Neil Asher Silberman, *The Message and the Kingdom* (New York: Grosset/Putnam, 1997), 28.

8. Richard Horsley, *Jesus and the Spiral of Violence: Popular Jewish Resistance in Roman Palestine* (Minneapolis: Fortress Press, 1993), 45.

9. Ibid.

10. Ibid.

18 JESUS, VIOLENCE, GOD, AND HISTORY

The bitter fruit and predictable harvest of the domination system in first-century Palestine was violence. Violence was rooted in poverty and economic dislocation, in desperate rebellion and the repressive counterviolence of Roman soldiers and client kings, in fractured communities and disappearing hope, in religious abuse and widespread images and expectations of God. Scriptural accounts offer compelling evidence that Jesus challenged many forms of violence without using violence. Why Jesus acted nonviolently is the subject of the present chapter.

EXPECTATIONS OF GOD AND HISTORY

It is impossible to know with certainty what Jesus expected from God and history. At times words attributed to Jesus are nearly identical to those of John the Baptist (e.g., Matt 3:10; 7:19; 25:30, 46). In such cases, Jesus appears to be an apocalyptic prophet expressing confidence in God's avenging violence. At other times, Jesus clearly breaks with John's apocalyptic images including expectations of divine wrath, fire, and brimstone (Matt 5:43–45). Within scripture, Jesus' words, actions, and images of God clash sharply with those of the Baptist and contradict Jesus himself. The Gospel writers, in other words, pit Jesus against Jesus.

I could use scripture to argue that Jesus was or was not apocalyptic, that he did or did not expect the world to end soon, that he embraced or rejected violent images of God. Scripture presents incompatible portraits of Jesus, Christ, and God that pose difficult dilemmas and decisions upon us. There is significant scriptural evidence that Jesus rejected promises of God's saving violence. If true, then this would have posed radical questions to people then and now. If promises of redemptive violence were illusionary, then how could injustice be challenged? How were people to live if John the Baptist and other advocates of apocalypticism were wrong and the domination system was not going to disappear in the flash of God's punishing violence? What were God and God's power like? How did the domination system cloak itself? How could it be exposed? Could people resist and build alternatives to domination without feeding a vicious spiral of violence in which the poor got crushed in spite of the justice of their cause? What was abundant life? How could poor people experience it when they had almost nothing? Why were the rich unable to grasp its meaning?

NONVIOLENT JESUS—VIOLENT GOD?

No one can say for sure that Jesus was nonviolent, nor can anyone prove he broke with expectations of a violent God including popular promises of God's redemptive or apocalyptic violence. Many scholars agree, however, that Jesus acted nonviolently. This raises two issues. First, although the nonviolence of Jesus is embraced within Christian scholarship, it is rarely considered normative or even relevant to the Christian life. The nonviolence of Jesus, in other words, is acknowledged but ignored when it comes to faith, life, ethics, and action. A second issue is that many people who accept the nonviolence of Jesus embrace the violence of God. Even those who acknowledge that Jesus was nonviolent often reject the suggestion that God is nonviolent. Jesus acted nonviolently, according to this view, because he affirmed, expected, and awaited the actions of a violent God to judge, punish, and make right.

Mennonite pacifist theologian John Howard Yoder writes that far "from constituting an embarrassment for those who follow Jesus' nonviolence, Hebrew holy war is the historical foundation of the same."[1] This is similar to nonviolent activist Daniel Berrigan, who in his commentary on Daniel, eagerly awaits God's judgment and "the sweet revenge of the underdog."[2] Berrigan draws heavily on the prophets and the apocalyptic books of Daniel and Revelation as he anticipates the justice of God with its dreadful but deserved punishment of the powerful and long-awaited liberation of the poor. The presumption of Yoder and Berrigan seems to be that we, like Jesus, can be nonviolent because we live with the full assurance of God's just and punishing violence. Anticipating the justice of God, protesters can act nonviolently while trusting in the promise of God's violent retribution against unjust individuals and institutions. Thomas Merton, the contemplative Trappist monk, wrote in a similar spirit:

> We know that the "poor in spirit" are those of whom the prophets spoke, those who in the last days will be the "humble of the earth," that is to say the oppressed who have no human weapons to rely on and who nevertheless resist evil. They are true to the commandments of Yahweh, and who hear the voice that tells them: "Seek justice, seek humility, perhaps you will find shelter on the day of the Lord's wrath" (Soph 2:3). In other words, they seek justice in the power of truth and of God, not by the power of man. Note that Christian meekness, which is essential to true non-violence, has this eschatological quality about it. It refrains from self-assertion and from violent aggression because it sees all things in the light of the great judgment. Hence it does not struggle and fight merely for this or that ephemeral gain. It struggles for the truth and the right which alone will stand in that day when all is to be tried by fire (1 Cor 3:10–15).[3]

These three advocates of Christian nonviolence invite us to resist evil and testify to the truth without using weapons. We are to place our faith in a violent God who will deliver justice, including punishments as part of the "great judgment." I offer one other example, from biblical sociologist Richard Horsley. Horsley roots the nonviolence of Jesus in the apocalyptic violence of God even though he offers, without formal acknowledgement, compelling evidence that Jesus rejected apocalyptic notions of a violent deity. In *Jesus and the Spiral of Violence*, Horsley writes that "there is no evidence that Jesus advocated violence" and "that Jesus, while not necessarily a pacifist, actively opposed violence, both oppressive and repressive, both political-economic and spiritual."[4] He also notes that "Jesus' prophecies and other sayings do not elaborate much on the violent character of God's judgment."[5] Horsley cannot imagine a nonapocalyptic Jesus, although in his interpretation Jesus expects earthly justice and not an end to history:

> Jesus' proclamation and practice of the kingdom of God indeed belonged in the milieu of Jewish apocalypticism. But far from being an expectation of an imminent cosmic catastrophe, it was the conviction that God was now driving Satan from control over personal and historical life, making possible the renewal of the people Israel.[6]

Horsley and I understand Jesus to be a follower of John the Baptist who was baptized into John's movement. However, I break with Horsley on the subject of Jesus and the apocalyptic worldview. He does not address what might have precipitated Jesus' break with John or, more specifically, that the fault line may be precisely along apocalyptic lines. One finds numerous contradictions in *The Message and the Kingdom*, which Horsley coauthored with Neil Asher Silberman. Jesus is apocalyptic. Jesus breaks with apocalyptic expectations. Jesus is like John. Jesus is dramatically different from John. Jesus' vision of the kingdom is an outgrowth of John's vision of the kingdom. Their kingdom visions are incompatible. We must ask in each case, "Which is it?" because both cannot ultimately be true. Horsley draws on but does not choose between incompatible scriptural evidence. He leaves us with stunningly conflictual messages about Jesus, John, and the kingdom:

> John's overarching message was one of apocalyptic expectation and preparation: "Repent for the Kingdom of God is at hand" (Matt. 3:2) . . . .He turned his focus . . . on God's imminent destruction of those wicked nobles and arrogant leaders who would soon receive their just rewards.[7]
>
> The time was approaching when God would intervene directly in human affairs. At some point after his baptism by John, Jesus apparently became active in the anti-Herodian renewal movement. . . . Jesus' understanding of the Kingdom of God would ultimately prove far more influential than that of John the Baptist and far more powerful than that of Herod Antipas. For Jesus did not believe that the Kingdom of God would arrive with fire and brimstone.[8]

> John the Baptist [unlike Jesus] did not perform miraculous healings. His style was that of an ancient prophet warning the People of Israel of the impending threat of God's fiery vengeance, soon to rain down on the earth and incinerate the evil and the unrepentant like so much useless chaff. Jesus was different. Although he, too, seems to have urged his listeners to examine their lives and repent . . . he usually spoke with kindness and good humor, occasionally confronting critics and doubters with provocative parables and amusingly pithy turns-of-phrase. . . . He possessed extraordinary skill as an exorcist and healer.[9]

These quotations reveal profound differences between Jesus and John and offer evidence that Jesus broke with apocalyptic expectations of God and history. While John found comfort in promises of God's vengeful violence, Jesus comforted and healed the sick. No one understood the causes of illness in Jesus' world. It is understandable, therefore, that sickness was often associated with sin and Satan. Jesus, however, redefined the significance of healing and the meaning of salvation. He associated salvation with healing and restoration to community rather than the crushing defeat of enemies.

Horsley and Silberman seem to ignore the implications of their own evidence. Just two pages after noting that "Jesus was different," they make another stunning reversal. The people find "resonance" with "Jesus' words and actions," which leads many "to believe that the Kingdom of God *that John the Baptist had preached about* [emphasis added] was not merely imminent but was *already* present [emphasis in original]."[10] Jesus and John both teach the kingdom of God. The only disparity is that for Jesus the kingdom is already here. Radical differences in "kingdom" expectations are downplayed. More confusion follows:

> [Jesus] would "release the captives, make the blind see, raise up the downtrodden." He would also "heal the sick, resurrect the dead, and announce glad tidings to the poor." For many people in Galilee, Jesus offered that kind of *alternative to John's vision of fire and brimstone. He preached that the evil and unjust would certainly be punished in God's vengeance,* yet Jesus also offered stunning evidence that God's power was already manifest and available to the long-oppressed rural population of the Land of Israel.[11]

Horsley and Silberman acknowledge that it is difficult to reconcile a "grim understanding" of Jesus as an "uncompromising prophet of doom and destruction" and "the joyful, life-affirming message that the former carpenter from Nazareth announced in the people's midst."[12] They do so, however, by insisting that Jesus expected the end of domination and not the end of history and that Jesus proclaimed God's just vengeance against evildoers *and* offered signs of a positive new order to come. Their efforts to reconcile the irreconcilable fall flat because Horsley and Silberman themselves offer compelling evidence that Jesus broke with apocalyptic expectations:

> As the power moved through Jesus to restore the lame, deaf, blind, and demon-possessed, Jesus stressed the close connection between the energy displayed in his healings and the spirit energizing the larger Renewal of Israel. . . . God was certainly controlling events, but He did not need armies or weapons of war to carry out His will. In contrast to those among the People of Israel who eagerly looked forward to an impending celestial battle between the Sons of Light and the Sons of Darkness to bring on the Age of Redemption, or those who advocated direct military action against the Romans and the Herodian mercenary forces (a path that could only result in another bloody repression against the poorly armed, poorly trained bands of guerrillas), Jesus suggested that God was establishing His Kingdom by creating an alternative society.[13]

These conflicting and contradictory images and quotes seem confusing and forced because they *are* confusing and forced. Over and over Horsley and Silberman acknowledge differences between Jesus and John and between Jesus' alternative program and common apocalyptic expectations. They never formally acknowledge a break, and so they explain the nonviolence of Jesus in light of violent expectations of God.

In sum, to one degree or another, Yoder, Merton, Berrigan, and Horsley place Jesus' nonviolence, and in the first three cases their own, in the context of expectations of a violent God's ultimate imposition of justice within or at the end of history. Jesus was nonviolent, according to this view, because he left judgment and revenge in the hands of a violent God.

I believe these and other scholars and activists affirm the nonviolence of Jesus while holding onto the violence of God because of their uncritical approach to scripture. If the Bible says God is a holy warrior, then this image must be reconciled with Jesus no matter how incompatible it is with Jesus. Within this approach, theology becomes the art of making square pegs fit into round holes. I start with the premise that the Bible offers competing claims and is sometimes wrong about God, Jesus, and Christ. The Bible's incompatible and grisly images of God force us to make choices. A God who orders us to kill disobedient children and the holy warrior God are so at odds with Jesus that either Jesus is completely off base concerning his experience of God or the ideas themselves must be seen as the deadly fruit of human projection. Walter Wink writes:

> The violence of the Old Testament has always been a scandal to Christianity. The church has usually ducked the issue, either by allegorizing the Old Testament or by rejecting it. Biblical scholar Raymund Schwager points out that there are six hundred passages of explicit violence in the Hebrew Bible, one thousand verses where God's own violent actions of punishment are described, a hundred passages where Yahweh expressly commands others to kill people, and several stories where God irrationally kills or tries to kill for no apparent reason (for example, Exod. 4:24–26). Violence, Schwager concludes, is easily the most often mentioned activity in the Hebrew Bible. . . . In the Hebrew Bible, God's alleged punishments are usually carried out by human beings attacking each other. This indicates, says Schwager, that the actual initiative for killing does not originate with God, but is projected onto God by those who desire revenge.[14]

Wink contrasts these human projections with Jesus' revelation of a non-violent God:

> The God whom Jesus reveals refrains from all forms of reprisal. God does not endorse holy wars or just wars. God does not sanction religions of violence. . . . To be true God's offspring requires the unconditional renunciation of violence. The reign of God means the elimination of every form of violence between individuals and nations. This is a realm and a possibility of which those imprisoned by their trust in violence cannot even conceive.[15]

Walter Wink, a friend and my former New Testament professor at Union Theological Seminary, has probably done more than anyone to illuminate and draw out the practical implications of Jesus' nonviolence (see chapter 24). Like Yoder and others who root the nonviolence of Jesus in the violence of God, however, Wink too falls victim to scriptural authority issues but in a different way. Rather than running with the powerful insight that the Bible is often wrong about God because of human projection, Wink insists that false human projections and erroneous portrayals of God's violence were part of God's plan. "Yahweh's followers projected their own jealousy on God and made God as jealous as they. But something new emerges nonetheless: Yahweh openly insists on this jealousy, which begins to reveal Yahweh's unique relationship to Israel as one of love."[16] He continues:

> The violence of the Bible is the necessary precondition for the gradual perception of the meaning of violence. . . . The violence of Scripture, so embarrassing to us today, became the means by which sacred violence was revealed for what it is: a lie perpetrated against the victims in the name of God. God was working through violence to expose violence for what it is and to reveal the divine nature as nonviolent.[17]

God, according to Wink's interpretation, was not jealous, but after humans projected their own jealousy onto God, God became jealous in order to reveal God's love. In a similar way, God who is nonviolent used human projections of a violent God for good. Working through violence, God exposed a "scapegoat mechanism" that is at the heart of all violence. Wink, drawing on the work of Rene Girard, describes the scapegoat mechanism as part of a "sacrificial system . . . in which a smaller amount of violence is perpetrated against a single victim in order to prevent a greater amount of evil from engulfing a society."[18] When the community unites around a sacrificial death, it lessens the amount of violence within the community. The authorities who killed Jesus, according to this logic, executed Jesus as a scapegoat to unite the community through a ritual of sacred violence. Something went wrong because Jesus was innocent and the people identified with him and, through him, with all the victims of violence. It was God's intention throughout the scriptures, according to Wink, "to reveal the scapegoating mechanism." "From Genesis to Revelation," Wink writes, "the victims cry for justice and deliverance from the world of violence, where they are made scapegoats. In the cross these cries find vindication."[19]

I find Wink's placement of the theory of scapegoating at the center of God's intent throughout scripture in conflict with his vital insight that

Jesus reveals a nonviolent God. Without going into more detail than my own argument requires, let me note two important differences I have with Wink's analysis summarized above. First, Jesus' execution at the hands of Roman authorities and Temple leaders does not fit the pattern of the scapegoat mechanism. Scapegoating involves a community uniting around violence against a sacrificial victim in order to reduce violence. Caiaphas wanted to silence Jesus because Jesus' activities invited Roman retaliation against client rulers charged with maintaining order (John 11:50). He wanted Jesus dead because Jesus was a subversive who could have united the people in opposing and offering alternatives to the domination system. Jesus' death, however, was meant to demoralize rather than unify the people. Like all torture and acts of state-sponsored terror, the death of Jesus was not meant to bring the people together through an act of sacred violence but to rob them of hope. The execution of Jesus let an oppressed populace know that the domination system would not tolerate an alternative future. Jesus' death was no more a scapegoating death than was Gandhi's, King's, or Oscar Romero's. In each case a political murder was followed by escalating violence, deepening demoralization, and crisis.

Second, Wink insists that the cross both exposes and *defeats* the powers. I agree that the cross exposes the deadly system as unjust and oppressive, but I believe that the powers that lie behind oppressive policies and systems are alive and well. God did not triumph over the powers because of the crucifixion. The domination system's execution of one who revealed the character of God shows its power even as it sabotages the system's credibility. The cross exposes the system's pretenses and its brutality. We should also exercise care when speaking about implications of the resurrection. Neither the crucifixion nor the resurrection of Jesus ends abusive power. The crucifixion exposes the powers. The resurrection of Jesus counters the system's ultimate sanction that is death. This frees us to challenge evil and injustice, but it should not lead us to proclaim evil's demise, as Burton Cooper cautions:

> The resurrection of Christ is sometimes invoked as the Christian answer to evil. The thought that the resurrection of Christ heralds our own resurrection, and that the raising of the faithful from death to eternal life provides, in itself, sufficient justification for the few, short years of earthly suffering from pain, injustice, and death. Sadly, there are difficulties in this response that are not unlike those found in the apocalyptic

answer. It forces us to weigh unbearable horror now against unspeakable joy later. But how does a later joy justify an earlier horror? And it leaves evil on earth largely untouched. It neither transforms nor redeems evil; it simply moves life to a plane where evil has no sway.[20]

Returning to Wink and the meaning of the cross, the distinction between exposure and defeat has profound implications for our images of God and our understanding of Jesus' death. Wink notes that Jesus revealed an unconditionally loving God: "Jesus simply declared people forgiven, confident that he spoke the mind of God (Mark 2:1–12)."[21] A compassionate God is, in my view, incompatible with all atonement theories. Wink, however, tries to revamp rather than discard them. He seems unwilling to confront fully the implications of human projections onto God because they raise uncomfortable questions about scriptural authority. By interpreting Jesus in light of the scapegoat mechanism and insisting that violence and jealousy are human projections but used by God for good, Wink creates a dilemma concerning why Jesus died. He rejects the theory of blood atonement but tries to revamp the theory itself:

> The God whom Jesus revealed as no longer vengeful, but unconditionally loving, who needed no satisfaction by blood—this God of mercy was changed by the church into a wrathful God whose demand for blood atonement leads to God's requiring his own Son's death on behalf of us all. The nonviolent God of Jesus becomes a God of unequaled violence, since God not only allegedly demands the blood of the victim who is most precious to him, but holds humanity accountable for a death that God both anticipates and requires.[22]

Atonement theories grow out of vile and violent portraits of God. They should be placed on the scrap heap of distorted history and theology. Wink, however, offers a "Christus Victor theory of atonement" as an alternative to the blood theory. It insists that through the cross, "what Christ has overcome is precisely the Powers themselves." "God triumphed over the Powers through Jesus' nonviolent self-sacrifice on the cross" and God used Jesus' "arraignment, trial, crucifixion, and death" in order to strip "the scapegoating mechanism of its sacred aura."[23] Citing the work of Schwager, Wink notes that a redemptive act of God was necessary not to appease God but to deliver humans from their hatred of God.[24]

If the death of Jesus does not fit the category of the scapegoat mechanism and if the crucifixion of Jesus exposed rather than defeated the domination system, then Wink's effort to bypass a direct confrontation with scriptural authority falls apart. My alternative states openly that the Bible both reveals and distorts God. This opens up the possibility of discerning within scripture a nonviolent Jesus revealing a nonviolent God. Jesus was not sent by God to die in order to appease a violent deity, nor did he defeat the Powers by dying on the cross. His death was not an atoning sacrifice or a way of bringing a scapegoat mechanism to light. It was a political murder meant to sow terror and to undermine hope. His violent death exposes the domination system as oppressive and violent. His resurrection challenges the ultimate power of the system and invites us to be people of God here and now where oppressive systems remain powerful and must be challenged. Jesus teaches us how to live and shows us the risks of living God's compassion in an unjust world.

If we accept that the Gospels offer incompatible portraits of Jesus, then we must sift through diverse images in search of meaning. Jesus' life and faith can help us discern between revelation and distortion. This approach to scripture requires theology to deal with contradictions rather than the smashing of square pegs into round holes. It helps us wrestle with incompatible portraits of Jesus concerning violence, expectations of God, and history.

NONVIOLENT JESUS—NONVIOLENT GOD?

There are a growing number of scholars and activists who, like myself, understand the nonviolence of Jesus to be a revelation of a nonviolent God. Walter Wink writes of "the nonviolent God of Jesus" who is of "infinite mercy." "To be this God's offspring," he says, "requires the unconditional and unilateral renunciation of violence. The reign of God means the complete and definitive elimination of every form of violence between individuals and nations."[25] In *The Nonviolent Coming of God*, activist James Douglass writes that "in response to his people's oppression," Jesus embodied "a nonviolent revolution initiated by God in Jesus" similar to "Gandhi's 'constructive program' in India." This "nonviolent coming of God in Jesus, in Israel, and in all of Humanity was Jesus' experience of God . . ."[26]

John Dominic Crossan says that Jesus was eschatological in an ethical sense, meaning that he rejected and countered the values, institutions, and priorities of the oppressive system but that he broke with expectations of God's apocalyptic violence. In *The Birth of Christianity* he writes:

> As long as apocalypticism involves a God who uses force and violence to end force and violence, they [apocalypticism and ethicism] cannot be combined; one has to choose between them. . . . Ethicism, short for ethical eschatology, is ethical radicalism with a divine mandate based on the character of God. What makes it *radical* or *eschatological* ethics is . . . the fact that it is nonviolent resistance to structural violence. It is absolute faith in a nonviolent God and the attempt to live and act in union with such a God. . . . Ethical eschatology is . . . nonviolent resistance to systemic violence. An attendant issue here is the difference between divine revenge and divine justice. Revenge and justice lie close together in our human hearts and are projected thence, in equally close conjunction, onto our God. It seems to me, however, that Jesus distinguished the kingdom-of-God movement from the baptism movement on precisely that point. It may well have been the absence of an avenging God before, during, or after John the Baptist's own execution that convinced Jesus of a different type of God—the nonviolent God of a nonviolent kingdom, a God of nonviolent *resistance* to structural as well as individual evil.[27]

That the nonviolence of Jesus reflects his rejection of apocalyptic images and his embrace of a nonviolent God is reinforced by some interpretations of Q. Q is material found within both Matthew and Luke that is absent from Mark. It is presumed to be part of a lost but common source. Q scholars identify two or three layers of Q (Q1, Q2, and Q3). Q1 contains many sayings of Jesus. Crossan believes that a "Common Sayings Tradition" linked to Jesus is found within Q1 and within the *Gospel of Thomas*, which, like Q, has different layers that can be identified as early or late.

According to Crossan, Q1 is the earliest part of the tradition and the violence of God is absent from Q1. Q2 contains apocalyptic images and sanctions. In a similar way, the *Gospel of Thomas* in its final form places early Jesus sayings material paralleled in Q1 in a Gnostic context. Gnosticism, in sharp contrast to the earthy Jesus, looks at the world negatively and seeks redemption in insight or knowledge. Later editors who stand behind Q2 and the *Gospel of Thomas*, according to Crossan, added an apocalyptic edge or a Gnostic framework to the original sayings material, which undermined Jesus' original message and intent. Crossan believes Q1 is as close as we get to the actual words and mindset of Jesus. It is free of apocalyptic imagery and sanctions. Early Q seeks to persuade but without threats of recrimination. The second stratum of Q (Q2) is apocalyptic. Q2, according to Crossan, is "characterized by recrimination rather than persuasion, polemics rather than preaching."[28] Q1 tells you to share your goods with the poor because doing so reflects the character of God. Q2 tells you to share and if you don't then you'll be punished by God. According to Crossan, "the original Common Sayings Tradition contained neither Gnosticism nor apocalypticism but required redactional adaptation toward either or both of those eschatologies."[29] In other words, Jesus' original sayings were not apocalyptic and the apocalyptic edge, including threats of divine retribution, was added later by others.

WHERE I STAND

No one can argue definitively that Jesus reflected and embodied the will of a nonviolent God. The Gospels offer conflictive rather than definitive testimony, and the Gospel writers themselves, like many Christian interpreters, adopt apocalyptic images when explaining the meaning of Jesus' life and death. We must take conflictive evidence concerning Jesus, God, and violence and do our best to explain incompatible portrayals rather than impose an artificial harmony. Did Jesus act nonviolently? The Gospels overwhelmingly answer Yes. Did Jesus root his nonviolence in the nonviolence of God? The Gospels say Yes and No. We must decide and be honest about why we choose one answer over another.

I must also be honest about my concerns and presuppositions. From Littleton to Kosovo and everywhere in between, I see the world fracturing as a result of violence. The pervasive reality of violence pulls and tempts me, and I suspect many others, in two contradictory directions. Violence seems to be the language of the world, and efforts to rein it in or respond to evil effectively with nonviolent means and methods seem absurd. In a world with so much violence, nonviolence may be for idealists and idiots. On the other hand, violence condemns itself. What is absurd, by this way of thinking, is not nonviolence but the fact that anyone, anywhere could believe in the utility of violence despite centuries of barbarous futility. It is equally absurd to associate violence with the character of God when so much senseless violence carried out by Christians,

Muslims, Hindus, Jews, and others is justified in the name of God and through appeals to God's will.

This debate lives inside me, but I cannot resolve it on tactical grounds alone. As a Christian, I try to follow Jesus, who for me reveals the character of God. My commitment to nonviolence, therefore, includes but is more than a tactical decision. It is a matter of faith, rooted in my experience of Jesus as a revelation of a nonviolent God who responds to and breaks with the spiral of violence then and now. Concern about pervasive violence leads me into scripture. The Jesus I encounter there and the God revealed through his faith and actions push me to deepen my commitment to nonviolent social change.

I also find it theologically, morally, and practically untenable to root the nonviolence of Jesus or my own nonviolent commitments in the violence of God. Whether you believe that Jesus is God, that Jesus reveals God, or that Jesus became God following the resurrection, it is difficult to hold together a nonviolent Jesus with a violent God. Doing so allows us to project our own unresolved violence onto God, internalize it, and repress hatred of people and institutions with whom we disagree.

As long as we promote violent images of God, then the nonviolence of Jesus will be rejected or ignored by the vast majority of Christians. Jesus' nonviolence will continue to be disconnected from the content of Christian faith, life, ethics, and action. Without roots in the nonviolent character of God, Jesus' nonviolence will be dismissed as a part of an "interim ethic" no longer relevant to people in the twenty-first century, or linked to his status and mission as a "paschal lamb" slaughtered by God as part of an atoning sacrifice, or superseded by God's violence. Not surprisingly, very few Christians who embrace the violence of God follow the nonviolence of Jesus.

I embrace the nonviolence of Jesus as a revelation of a nonviolent God. Critics will say that I have simply created a Jesus to my own liking. Perhaps. Let me note six things I can say with confidence. First, all Christians should reexamine images of Jesus, Christ, and God to see if and how we have distorted faith by conforming these images to our desires. Many Christians, I would argue, have created or stressed images of Jesus, Christ, and God that sanctify violence and have ignored other images that would lead them to take nonviolence seriously.

Second, my sincere goal is to be faithful to God and to the life and faith of Jesus as a revelation of God, not to create a Jesus to suit my own interests. If I have created a Jesus to my own liking, then I find it interesting that the Jesus I have "made in my own image" is very hard for me to live with or to follow. The nonviolent portraits of Jesus and God that make sense to me in the context of a violence-obsessed world, my experience of faith, and my understanding of scripture shake my life at its very foundations. They disturb me, inspire me, and require me to live differently. I confess that I try to do so and that I often fail.

Third, violence was the defining feature of the domination system in first-century Palestine. It permeated all aspects of life, from the lack of daily food to Roman crucifixions, from explanations of personal and national catastrophes to images of God that framed historical memories and future expectations of God and history. Our portraits of Jesus must be painted within this backdrop of pervasive violence.

Fourth, violence remains the dominant feature of life today. Any portrayals of Jesus and God and any expressions of Christian faith that ignore the pervasiveness of violence both past and present are likely to be distorted and unhelpful.

Fifth, the Bible contains conflictive and incompatible images of Jesus, Christ, and God. Our portraits of God and Jesus emerge from and are reinforced by biblical images and stories. Both Gandhi and the pastor who terrorized children from the pulpit with images of a vengeful deity drew inspiration from biblical texts. We must choose between contradictory evidence and be as honest as we can about why we embrace certain images and stories and how we make sense out of those we reject.

Finally, although nobody can prove that Jesus' life and faith reveal a nonviolent, gracious God, it is possible to make a strong biblical case that this is true. No one can prove that Jesus was nonviolent and that his nonviolence was rooted in his experience of a nonviolent God, but no one can prove the opposite either, although once again a strong biblical case can be made. Gospel evidence is conflictive as is the judgment of scholars.

In the next several chapters, I make a case that Jesus profoundly challenged the domination system, that he did so nonviolently, and that he rooted his life, actions, and teachings in his commitment to and his experience of a nonviolent, gracious God. Jesus' life is best understood as a faithful response to a loving God in the context of a spiral of violence that overwhelmed people in first-century Palestine and that threatens us today.

Notes

1. John Howard Yoder, *For the Nations* (Grand Rapids: Wm. B. Eerdmans Publishing Co., 1997), 85.

2. Daniel Berrigan, *Daniel: Under the Siege of the Divine* (Farmington, Pa.: Plough Publishing, 1998), 31.

3. Thomas Merton, *Faith and Violence: Christian Teaching and Christian Practice* (Notre Dame, Ind.: University of Notre Dame Press, 1968), 17.

4. Richard Horsley, *Jesus and the Spiral of Violence: Popular Jewish Resistance in Roman Palestine* (Minneapolis: Fortress Press, 1993), 318–19.

5. Ibid., 322.

6. Ibid., 160.

7. Richard A. Horsley and Neil Asher Silberman, *The Message and the Kingdom* (New York: Grosset/Putnam, 1997), 32.

8. Ibid., 42.

9. Ibid., 48.

10. Ibid., 50.

11. Ibid., 51, emphasis added.

12. Ibid., 53.

13. Ibid., 54.

14. Walter Wink, *The Powers That Be: Theology for a New Millennium* (New York: Galilee Doubleday, 1998), 84–85.

15. Ibid., 89.

16. Ibid., 85.

17. Ibid., 85–86.

18. Ibid., 83–84.

19. Ibid., 86.

20. Burton Cooper, *Why God?* (Atlanta: John Knox Press, 1983), 122.

21. Wink, *The Powers That Be*, 88.

22. Ibid., 88–89.

23. Ibid., 90, 87, and 86.

24. Ibid., 92.

25. Ibid., 89.

26. James W. Douglass, *The Nonviolent Coming of God* (Maryknoll, N.Y.: Orbis Books, 1991), 56.

27. John Dominic Crossan, *The Birth of Christianity* (San Francisco: Harper San Francisco, 1998), 287, emphasis in original.

28. Ibid., 251.

29. Ibid., 255.

19 THE MANY FACES OF VIOLENCE

The domination system in first-century Palestine spawned and deepened violence on many fronts. The first part of this chapter introduces the spiral of violence, a concept that emerged within Latin American liberation theology and that has great relevance for our understanding of Jesus. This chapter and the next two look at how the parables of Jesus expose and counter different expressions of violence that live at the heart of the domination system.

LIBERATION THEOLOGY AND THE SPIRAL OF VIOLENCE

Latin American liberation theology emerged in the 1960s in response to social systems marked by injustice, inequality, and violence. Land and other productive resources were controlled by a tiny elite who relied on repressive military forces, paramilitary groups, and a compliant church to maintain unjust privileges. The misery of hungry majorities contrasted sharply with the lifestyles and power of the opulent few. Liberation theology stresses God's desire for justice and the Christian responsibility to work for justice. It affirms the dignity of the human person and the need for political and economic priorities and systems to reflect and foster dignified living. It says that God sides with the oppressed in struggles for justice and that therefore the church must exercise a preferential option for the poor. It roots sin in both individual conduct and in the structures of society. It sees the crucifixion of Jesus as a consequence of his faith, which led him to confront oppressive groups and institutions in first-century Palestine. It affirms the resurrection as a validation of that life, which Christians are to emulate and follow.

Liberation theology expresses divine and human solidarity with the poor. It also encourages poor people themselves to live out their faith by working to improve their lives and communities and to build just societies. Christians influenced by the method and content of liberation theology gather together in small groups to analyze local and national problems, study scripture, reflect on the meaning of faith, and plan and carry out appropriate actions.[1] As liberation theology inspired social change movements throughout the 1970s and 1980s, its followers experienced intense repression. U.S. foreign policy targeted liberation theology as its principal enemy in Latin America. The "Committee of Santa Fe" released a report in 1980 that became a blueprint for U.S. policy in the region. It specifically targeted liberation theology:

> U.S. foreign policy must begin to counter . . . liberation theology as it is utilized in Latin America by the "liberation theology" clergy. . . . Unfortunately, Marxist-Leninist forces have utilized the church as a political weapon against private property and productive capitalism by infiltrating the religious community with ideas that are less Christian than communist.[2]

"Countering" liberation theology was a bloody affair. The well-known murders of Archbishop Romero, four U.S. church women, and the Jesuit priests in El Salvador are all traceable to U.S. foreign policy and to the U.S. Army School of the Americas (SOA), a military training facility presently located at Fort Benning, Georgia. The SOA has an ugly reputation. A Los Angeles Times editorial noted that "it is hard to think of a coup or human rights outrage that has occurred in [Latin America] in the past 40 years in which alumni of the School of the Americas were not involved."[3] The Cleveland Plain Dealer said that the "SOA's best known products have shared a distressing tendency to show up as dictators or as leaders or members of death squads. They have been agents of oppression."[4] And the New York Times has editorialized in favor of closing the SOA, noting that closure would "announce that America will no longer train and encourage Latin American thugs."[5] The School of the Americas' official web site acknowledged the U.S. role in attacking progressive religious workers in Latin America, denigrated its domestic critics, and justified death or dismissal of both by linking them to Marxism: "Many of the [SOA's] critics," the web site stated, "supported Marxism—Liberation Theology—in Latin America—which was defeated with the assistance of the U.S. Army."[6] In an effort to quell protests, the SOA changed its name without reforming the foreign policy that gave rise to the atrocities associated with the school.[7]

Ironically, in the context of violence against its followers, critics accused liberation theology of embracing or fomenting violence. This attack was based on a slim foundation. Within what could be called "revolutionary situations," some members of base communities joined or aided armed revolutionary movements. It was far more common, however, for Christians influenced by liberation theology to participate in or lead nonviolent social change groups among women, peasants, students, and workers. Supporters of liberation theology stressed that violence was nearly always destructive but that it was a pervasive feature of life that must be countered in comprehensive ways.

Liberation theology speaks of a "spiral of violence" with three key dimensions or spokes.[8] Violence #1 is characterized by oppression, hunger, and poverty. Children who die of hunger or who are stunted by malnutrition are victims of violence. So too are people whose ill health, illiteracy, and death are linked to economic inequalities or concentrated landownership that directly or indirectly prevent them from receiving medical care, from attending school, or from being adequately nourished. This expansive definition links violence to social injustice and moves beyond traditional meanings that focus too narrowly on guns and warfare. Liberation theology speaks of institutionalized violence and social sin in order to highlight that violence #1 is rooted in the structures of an unjust society.

Violence #2, the second spoke in the spiral, is characterized by rebellion. People living and dying amidst poverty and squalor, social injustice and oppression, sometimes strike out violently against those they hold responsible for their misery. Violence #2, therefore, is a response to and predictable outcome of violence #1. People who protest against violence #1 often do so nonviolently. They demonstrate, write letters, join unions, strike, vote, and boycott. Peaceful protests are often met with repressive violence (violence #3), and the absence of redress through nonviolent means can lead to rebellion (#2) that is often the result of desperation and not design. Rebellion, in other words, marks an escalation in conflict after peaceful protests seem to have failed. It is often considered an option of "last resort" after other methods of protest have been ignored, rejected, or violently crushed.

Violence #3, according to liberation theology, is the repressive violence used by elite forces against those who rebel. This includes the lethal violence of military forces aligned with the State and economic elites, and the terror and torture practices of paramilitary groups and death squads associated with them. Most rebellions are violently suppressed because the resources and lethal violence of the state and its allies are generally far superior to that of protesters and insurgents. State violence and terror (#3) can successfully, though sometimes only temporarily, crush violent rebellions (#2), but in doing so they often deepen the violence of hunger, poverty, oppression, and social inequality (#1). As social injustices worsen new protests arise, and without substantive changes another round of rebellion and repression follows. The spiral of violence intensifies.

Liberation theology decries violence, but it rightly names and condemns violence in all its forms. The spiral of violence challenges churches profoundly. Historically, many churches and traditional theologies bolstered economic elites and supported the repressive apparatus of the state. Consistent with a broader theological challenge to reassess Jesus, faith, and God in the context of structural injustice, liberation theology insists that if the church is to oppose violence then it must work to break the spiral of violence. This means concentrating its energies on addressing violence #1, that is, on overcoming the systemic causes of hunger, poverty, and oppression. This must include an honest assessment of whether church theology, dogma, and practices encourage liberation or injustice. At the same time, the church must sever its political alliances with elites and discredit the repressive violence of the State (#3) that reinforces unjust systems (violence #1).

THE SPIRAL OF VIOLENCE IN FIRST-CENTURY PALESTINE

Richard Horsley has examined the social setting of Jesus in the context of the spiral of violence.[9] Drawing on liberation theology, Horsley's work, and my own experience, I prefer to examine Jesus as a revelation of God in the context of a spiral of violence with five rather than three spokes: Violence #1: hunger, poverty, and oppression; violence #2: rebellion; violence #3: state terror/repression; violence #4: dysfunctional/deflective violence; and violence #5: spiritual violence/violent images of god. The first three categories of violence are the same as those introduced above. The two additional spokes require some explanation.

By dysfunctional/deflective violence I mean violence used against others that does not challenge systems or address the causes of hunger, poverty, or oppression. Rebellion is usually motivated and accompanied by political goals. Violence in the context of rebellion is often understood as a necessary means to bring about greater social justice. Dysfunctional/deflective violence, by way of contrast, is rarely motivated by justice or linked to political goals. It often involves poor people striking out at other poor people because they are nearby and not because they are understood to be power brokers in an unjust system. Dysfunctional/deflective violence increases as poverty feeds despair and as communities break down. A contemporary example would be the high incidence of murder and crime that characterizes many impoverished neighborhoods.

Dysfunctional/deflective violence shifts people's anger away from individuals or institutions that exercise power within an unjust system and onto others. It leaves powerful systems in place and powerful people unnamed. It thrives in an environment in which people internalize the worldview of the oppressive system. Dysfunctional/deflective violence makes life miserable for many and feeds a spiral of community hostility and breakdown.

By spiritual violence (#5), I mean images of God that explain human misery as God's will or that project human desire for vengeance onto God within or at the end of history. Many of the pathological portraits and actions attributed to God by the biblical writers reflect spiritual violence. God uses floods and she-bears to punish. God commands genocide against peoples in Canaan and orders the murder of disobedient children. These and other violent images and actions of God can encourage hatred of self and others. Telling people that they are reduced to cannibalism because of their sin or that Babylon and Rome are God's servants delivering deserved punishments are other examples of spiritual violence. So too are promises that God will crush the people's enemies directly or enable "the people of God" to do so. Contemporary examples of spiritual violence include explanations that Hurricane Mitch and AIDS are God's response to sin, threats of hell and damnation used to condition behavior, and any and all efforts to justify human violence and holy warfare through appeals to the divine.

SUBVERSIVE PARABLES

William Herzog's penetrating treatment of the parables places Jesus amidst
the spiral of violence in first-century Palestine. In parable after parable Jesus
confronts oppression, hunger, and poverty (violence #1), which are the
tragic fruits of the domination system that he seeks to expose, undermine,
and replace. Herzog pays close attention to real history as he examines Jesus
and the parables. In doing so, he challenges premature spiritualization and
he reinforces my view that *Jesus' life* needs to be understood as a revelation
of God. The parables, traditionally understood to reveal universal spiritual
wisdom, speak first and foremost to historical injustices:

> The parables were not earthly stories with heavenly meanings
> but earthy stories with heavy meanings, weighted down by an
> awareness of the workings of exploitation in the world of its
> hearers. The focus of the parables was not on a vision of the
> glory of the reign of God, but on the gory details of how
> oppression served the interests of a ruling class.[10]

Herzog's questions shift the ground of traditional interpretation:

> What if the parables of Jesus were neither theological nor
> moral stories but political and economic ones? What if the con-
> cern of the parables was not the reign of God but the reigning
> systems of oppression that dominated Palestine in the time of
> Jesus? What if the scenes they presented were not stories about
> how God works in the world but codifications about how
> exploitation worked in Palestine. . . . What if the parables are
> exposing exploitation rather than revealing justification?[11]

Interpreting the parables of Jesus within the context of historical violence
and injustice makes sense in light of Jesus' crucifixion. "The great difficulty
with so many of the contemporary models imposed on Jesus," Herzog
notes, "is that they fail to explain his crucifixion."[12] Adequate interpretation
of the parables must account for the fact that Jesus was brutally killed in a
Roman-style execution. Our understanding of the parables, in other words,
must be consistent with and shed light on Jesus' murder. Herzog continues:

> If he [Jesus] had been the kind of teacher popularly portrayed
> in the North American church, a master of the inner life, teach-

ing the importance of spirituality and a private relationship with God, he would have been supported by the Romans as part of their rural pacification program. That was exactly the kind of religion that the Romans wanted peasants to have. Any beliefs that encouraged magic, passivity before fate, and withdrawal from the world of politics and economics into a spiritual or inner realm would have met with official approval. Had Jesus' parables indulged in apocalyptic speculation or threatened the end of the world, he would have been watched but left alone. . . . Had he anticipated narrativity and metaphoricity he would have been remarkable but not crucified. Narrativity and metaphoricity were not capital crimes in the Roman Empire, and the one thing that can be known with certainty was that he was executed as an enemy of the state and the Temple. . . . If parabling was a part of Jesus' public activity that was followed with suspicion and eventually deemed actionable, then his parables must have dealt with dangerous issues, which always means political and economic issues, since the preservation of power and the extraction of tribute from the peasants dominated the concerns of the ruling elites of the ancient world. Any teaching that exposed exploitation and demystified the forms of legitimation used to sanctify oppression would have been considered a threat.[13]

Herzog demonstrates that Jesus exposed violence and exploitation at the heart of the domination system only to have the Gospel writers undermine his meaning. We see this reversal generally when Matthew introduces the parables with the phrase, "the kingdom of heaven is like . . ." or "the kingdom of heaven can be compared to. . . ." Matthew, in other words, says listen to a parable and you will learn about heavenly things, whereas Jesus' says listen and you will better understand earthly oppression as an affront to human beings and to God. This reversal of meaning and intent between Matthew and Jesus is illustrated clearly in the parable of the laborers in the vineyard (20:1–16), in which Jesus focuses attention on an exploitative vineyard owner who becomes a "gracious" God figure in Matthew's account. The characters and story line in this parable seem straightforward. A large landowner who is wealthy enough to have a steward to manage his vineyard is in need of workers to harvest his grapes. He goes out and hires laborers early in the morning and agrees to pay them "the usual daily wage." He hires workers again at 9 A.M., at noon, at 3 P.M., and at 5 P.M., saying he will pay them "whatever is right." At the end of the day he pays the workers the same amount but in reverse order. Those who had worked since six in the morning get paid little and last. They "grumbled against the landowner" because they had worked all day in the scorching heat only to receive the same wages as those who were hired at five in the afternoon. Citing his right "to do what I choose with what belongs to me," the vineyard owner dismisses their complaints.

Matthew interprets this parable by assigning meaning through metaphors. "Matthew," Herzog writes, "invested key elements of the parable with theological values." The vineyard is a metaphor for Israel or the church, the daily wage (denarius) is a metaphor for salvation, the first-hired workers represent the Jewish people, the last hired are the Gentiles or recent converts. Most importantly for Matthew, this parable introduces what "the reign of heaven is like" with the "lord of the vineyard" portrayed as a gracious God figure who offers salvation to all.[14] Like Matthew, Herzog notes, nearly all interpreters have ignored the details of the parable:

> Following Matthew's lead, they have all assumed that the owner of the vineyard is a God figure. The meaning of the parable can be found by figuring out how to justify the owner's concluding words and vilify the workers. However pervasive the sense of unfairness at the end of the parable might have been, interpreters ignored the workers' voices so that the action of the owner could be construed as an example of God's gracious, generous goodness.[15]

Herzog's alternative reading is based on the commonsense but now radical assumption that if Jesus told a parable about a vineyard, a vineyard owner, and workers, he was actually talking about a vineyard, a vineyard owner, and workers. "The characters who appear in the parable," Herzog writes, "are not abstract theological types but belong to identifiable social classes or groups in advanced agrarian societies. To understand the parable, it is necessary to know who appears in the social script."[16] Jesus places a vineyard and vineyard owner at the center of a parable that he tells to impoverished rural people. It would have raised important issues and triggered numerous thoughts, feelings, and images drawn from their life experience in the domination system. Wealthy landowners commonly converted land to vineyards because grapes could be processed into wine, an exportable commodity. They did so after displacing vulnerable peasants from the land that had provided their sustenance and grounded their faith. The burden of Roman taxes and Temple tithes, increased debt loads and added stresses linked to the commercialization of agriculture and urban development noted in prior chapters combined to push many peasants from poverty into destitution, from landed to landless, from vulnerable to desperately unemployed.

Jesus, who announced "good news to the poor," apparently had great sympathy for laborers such as those depicted in the parable who, as Luise Schottroff notes, "are evidently in such a weak position that they go off to work without any clear agreement on wages."[17] Jesus portrays them as victims of a calculating vineyard owner who engages in tactical humiliation by singling out one worker to serve as an example to the others: "Take what belongs to you and go" (20:14a). The vineyard owner, Herzog notes, "picks out their leader and makes an example out of him." "The spokesperson has been banned, shunned, blackballed, or blacklisted; he will not likely find work in that neighborhood again."[18] Jesus' concern for the oppressed workers (violence #1) contrasts sharply with Matthew's chastisement of these same workers who, according to his interpretation, unfairly challenge the authority of a gracious God.

PARABLES AND PURPOSE

Many parables posed but did not resolve pressing issues and problems. They were conversation starters meant to encourage understanding and discussion about life and death issues connected to the domination system. The mechanisms of exploitative economics, violence, and disastrous collaborative rule had to be understood in order to be changed. Once again the Gospel writers, in this case both Matthew and Mark (3:11–12), miss the boat. Matthew places these words on the lips of Jesus to explain why he speaks in parables:

> The reason I speak to them in parables is that "seeing they do not perceive, and hearing they do not listen, nor do they understand." With them indeed is fulfilled the prophecy of Isaiah that says:

> "You will indeed listen, but never understand,
>   and you will indeed look, but never perceive.
> For this people's heart has grown dull,
>   and their ears are hard of hearing,

> and they have shut their eyes;
>   so that they might not look with their eyes,
>   and listen with their ears,
> and understand with their heart and turn—
> and I would heal them." (13:13–15).

This reversal of Jesus' intent is as stark as turning an exploitative vineyard owner with sufficient power to hire displaced peasants at any time of day, pay them destitution wages, and humiliate those who complain, into a God figure. Matthew's Jesus speaks to the people in parables in order to confuse them. He does not want the people to understand him so that a prophecy many hundred years old can be fulfilled. Just as God is said to have hardened Pharaoh's heart in order to create an opportunity to offer superior violence as proof of God, Jesus is said to have deliberately engaged in incomprehensible speech.

I have argued throughout that the Bible reveals and distorts God and Jesus and so we have no choice but to read scripture critically. If passages in which God orders us to kill disobedient children, reduces people to cannibalism as punishment for sin, sends she-bears to maul boys who insult a prophet, and this one in which Jesus speaks in parables so that the people will not understand him, do not convince us of the need to critically approach scripture, then nothing is likely to do so.

The key point here is that Gospel distortions of Jesus profoundly undermine his challenges to the domination system and misrepresent his views of God. When Gospel writers turn oppressive vineyard owners into God-figures, they lead us astray. Fundamental discrepancies such as these point out the absurdity of clinging uncritically to the "authority of scripture," as if doing so in itself resolves serious problems. They also highlight problems in seeking to resolve Gospel contradictions by distinguishing between the Jesus of history and Christ of faith, the pre-Easter and post-Easter Jesus. They demonstrate why the Jesus of history must be at the heart of all Christian faith. We must be willing to reassess theological interpretations imbedded in the texts themselves and in subsequent interpretations. We must reenter these texts to look for crucial historical clues that can help us make sense out of Jesus, his understanding of both God and society, and how and why the Gospel writers, and modern interpreters, often distort his message and meaning. The best light in which we can place Matthew is to say that while trying to account for the rejection of Jesus he fundamentally misrepresented the purpose of parabolic speech. Matthew distorted both the content and methodology of the parables of Jesus, and in doing so, he profoundly misrepresented Jesus' images of God.

Herzog identifies questions that forced him back into the text to search for meaning beyond that assigned by Gospel writers and later interpreters and to look for clues pointing to authentic Jesus and original meaning and context:

> Why would Jesus formulate his parables in such a way that their characters and events undercut the theology usually assigned to them? How could a scene in which a rich landowner exploits day laborers express the generosity of God and the unfathomable nature of God's grace? The cognitive dissonance between the social scene and the theology ascribed to it was just too great. This indicated that the use and purpose of some of the parables might need to be reexamined, a task that implied a similar reconsideration of the public activity of Jesus. Second, what social construction of reality was being presented in the parables? If they were typifications of everyday life, then whose life did they represent? What did they reveal about the larger social, political, cultural, and economic systems within which Jesus spoke and the crowd heard?[19]

In sharp contrast to Matthew's portrayal of parables as deceptive speech meant to conceal, we have Jesus' parables as subversive speech meant to remove scales from the eyes of those who heard them. It is likely that parables were meant to stimulate lively discussion and debate:

> Jesus' parables codify systems of oppression in order to unveil them and make them visible to those victimized by them. To disclose the source of exploitation, Jesus introduces a highly visible elite; to depict collusion between retainers and elites, Jesus introduces the steward. In the absence of the householder [vineyard owner], the steward would have received the displaced anger of the workers at the end of the parable. As it is, Jesus can design a confrontation between two social groups who might never have encountered each other, the elites and the expendables. . . .
>
> It is probably impossible to reconstruct the lively conversation that the encoded parable generated, but the landowner's final remarks likely would have met with initial approval from

the peasants and villages who had, after all, internalized the oppressor's world.[20]

Jesus used parables to create space to discuss and comprehend systemic injustice and to reassess the character of God. The parable of the laborers in the vineyard addresses directly or indirectly several spokes in the spiral of violence. The social setting of the parable frames the domination system in miniature when it depicts and exposes oppressive relationships and structures at the heart of the domination system that result in hunger and poverty (violence #1). It also points to dysfunctional deflective violence (#4). Internalization of the worldview of the beneficiaries of domination made solidarity impossible and it contributed to the fracturing of communities. As Herzog notes:

> In addition to bringing together the social extremes of agrarian society, the elite and the expendables, Jesus arranged their meeting at the one of the few moments in the economic cycle in which the elites were dependent on the lowliest of laborers. To ensure a timely harvest, the landowner needed their labor. Yet the lack of cohesion so evident among the day laborers allowed the landowner to conquer them by dividing them. This is why the owner spoke to "one of them." The banishment of that one served to intimidate the others and put them in their place. . . . In so doing, he smothered the truth that he was dependent on them and, as a result, that they could have power but only a power that grew out of their solidarity. Divided, they would fall one by one before the withering hostility and judgment of the elite.[21]

Families and communities often imploded as Roman taxes, Temple tithes, indebtedness, loss of land, and limited employment accelerated insecurities and tensions.

> [Because] any active expression of resentment against the dominant system or society is blocked by institutionalized repressive measures, subject peoples tend to vent their frustration in attacks against one another. Feeling steadily under attack from the larger system, individuals, families, and villages become suspicious and defensive with regard to one another as well as outsiders.[22]

When Jesus tells a parable about a compassionate Samaritan (Luke 10:25–37), he intends to challenge hostilities that keep people divided, fuel dysfunctional deflective violence, and leave oppressive systems intact.

Jesus tells the parable of the friend at midnight (Luke 11:5–8) against this backdrop of dysfunctional/deflective violence that includes community strain, increased poverty, and the erosion of hospitality. Each was a predictable yet disastrous consequence of an oppressive system tightening its grip on the lives and hopes of impoverished peasants. After some grumbling and excuse making, "the villagers rise to the occasion and provide hospitality for their unexpected guest."[23]

The desperate position of displaced peasants depicted in the parable of the laborers in the vineyard points to the violence of the domination system in other ways as well. Some displaced peasants resorted to banditry (violence #4) in a desperate effort to survive. Others revolted (violence #2), and as we will see in the next chapter, faced brutal repression (violence #3). Many others saw little reason for hope apart from God's future violence (violence #5).

CONCLUSION

Pervasive violence was the defining feature of life in first-century Palestine. The social situation depicted in the parable of the laborers in the vineyard unmasks the spiral of violence at the heart of the domination system. If a parable started conversations about the nature of domination, then it should not surprise us that other parables facilitated further discussion concerning the spiral of violence, the domination system, religious legitimacy of oppression, and alternatives rooted in other images of faith, economics, community, and God.

Notes

1. For background on liberation theology, see Gustavo Gutierrez, *A Theology of Liberation* (Maryknoll, N.Y.: Orbis Books, 1973); Phillip Berryman, *Liberation Theology* (Philadelphia: Temple University Press, 1987); Leonardo Boff and Clodovis Boff, *Introducing Liberation Theology* (Maryknoll, N.Y.: Orbis Books, 1987).

2. For more information on U.S.-sponsored repression of progressive religious groups, see Jack Nelson-Pallmeyer, *War against the Poor: Low-Intensity Conflict and Christian Faith* (Maryknoll, N.Y.: Orbis Books, 1989), 15.

3. Editorial by Frank del Olmo, *Los Angeles Times*, 3 April 1995.

4. *Cleveland Plain Dealer*, 20 July 1995.

5. *New York Times*, 24 March 1995.

6. "U.S. Army School of the Americas Frequently Asked Questions."

7. James Hodge and Linda Cooper, "School of the Americas Reforms Merely Cosmetic, Critics Say," *National Catholic Reporter*, 2 June 2000. The school was to be called the Defense Institute for Hemispheric Security Cooperation but was later changed to the Western Hemisphere Institute for Security Cooperation. SOA critic Congressman Joseph Moakley said that name and other cosmetic changes are like putting "perfume on a toxic dump."

8. Helder Camara, *Spiral of Violence* (London: Sheed & Ward, 1971).

9. Richard Horsley, *Jesus and the Spiral of Violence: Popular Jewish Resistance in Roman Palestine* (Minneapolis: Fortress Press, 1993).

10. William R. Herzog II, *Parables as Subversive Speech: Jesus as Pedagogue of the Oppressed* (Louisville, Ky.: Westminster/John Knox Press, 1994), 3.

11. Ibid., 7.

12. Ibid., 27.

13. Ibid.

14. Ibid., 80.

15. Ibid., 82.

16. Ibid., 84.

17. Ibid., 86.

18. Ibid., 92, 93.

19. Ibid., 50.

20. Ibid., 87, 95.

21. Ibid., 95–96.

22. Ibid., 255.

23. Ibid., 207.

20 VIOLENCE, TOLL COLLECTORS, AND TENANTS

The present chapter continues the discussion of Jesus' nonviolent challenge to the spiral of violence at the heart of the Rome- and Temple-dominated system. It looks primarily at two parables and addresses several spokes in the spiral of violence. The parable of the Pharisee and the tax collector (Luke 18:9–14) exposes the Temple as an institution of violence (#1) while the parable of the wicked tenants addresses the temptation of oppressed people to engage in violent rebellion (#2) and the deadly consequences of doing so (#3).

VIOLENCE AND THE TEMPLE

Rome's bottom-line demands for those who ruled on its behalf included stability and faithful collection of tribute and taxes. These demands applied to all rulers, including Roman citizens such as Pilate, Jewish client kings such as Herod and his sons, and Temple leaders. Under the weight of these demands, *all* collaborative rulers functioned as instruments of oppressive Roman policy. "Roman imperium, imperial province, client kingdom, and temple hegemony had much in common" so that "changes in political rulers had little effect on peasants, artisans, and other rural poor."[1] The governing system was flexible, but the inevitable result was exploitation because injustice was the common denominator of both direct and indirect rule. The failure of Archelaus following the death of Herod the Great, however, increased the abusive power of Temple elites:

> The removal of the house of Herod from Judaea meant that the Romans had to rely on the high priestly families of Jerusalem and their elite collaborators to maintain internal order and to collect the tribute assigned to them. In effect, this move converted the province of Judaea into a dependent temple state.[2]

This is the context for Jesus' conflict with the Temple, Temple elites, and midlevel functionaries in the religious system. Like other Jews, Jesus wrestled with God and with a diverse religious tradition in a specific historical context marked by colonial injustice. When we allow Jesus to have a faith life and to live in a particular social setting, we hear the parables in a new way. We can probe Jesus' life, looking for points of continuity, disagreement, and rupture with his tradition. "Jesus was shaped by the Torah and the readings of the Torah prevalent in his time," Herzog writes. "While he developed his own reading of Torah as an instrument for spelling out the justice of the reign of God, he also learned *to read his colonial context*, which was dominated by Roman overlords."[3] Jesus' parables reveal how he "read his colonial context," including how he understood the "reign" or "kingdom" of God. When he read the signs of the times, however, he met more than Roman overlords. He saw vineyard owners and others benefiting from the commercialization of land at the expense of the people. He met large landholders finding ways around Torah restrictions on interest in order to rob peasants of their produce, foster indebtedness, foreclose, and take title to their land. In Herzog's reading of Jesus' parable of the talents (Matt 25:14–30; Luke 19:11–27), for example, the "hero of the parable is the third servant. By digging a hole and burying the aristocrat's talent in the ground, he has taken it out of circulation. It cannot be used," Herzog writes, "to dispossess more peasants from their lands through its dispersion in the form of usurious loans."[4]

In reading his "colonial context," Jesus also came face-to-face with Temple leaders and functionaries who benefited from abusive Roman rule and justified their actions with appeals to sacred texts and traditions. If the parables of Jesus address the domination system, then it should not surprise us that some expose directly or indirectly the collaborative role played by the Temple, Temple elites, and midlevel functionaries such as the Pharisees. Parables shed light on the complex faith tradition that includes both the justice of God and the injustice of an oppressively complicit Temple. Jesus exposes and counters the domination system, including its "religious" aspect, because it is an obstacle to and, in many ways, opposite of God's intended compassionate order. The domination system, shored up with appeals to God, undermines abundant life willed by, hoped for, and expressive of the character of a loving, nonviolent God. Herzog summarizes key insights from Gerhard and Jean Lenski concerning domination and religious legitimacy:

> Just as the cities became the centers of the political and financial bureaucracies . . . they also became the centers of holy places, whose priests justified the emergent order and tended the temples that embodied that order's traditional legitimation. The role of the priestly retainers was to produce an ideology that either could motivate cultivators to turn over their surplus to the rulers or, failing that, would justify the coercion of those cultivators and their subsequent oppression by the ruling class.[5]

Within the Jewish tradition there were Sabbath and jubilee provisions meant to institutionalize justice, including access to land, forgiveness of debts, and restrictions on interest. This justice stream could be called on to break the links between the sacred order and oppression. At the same time, however, there was a long history of abusive power centered in the Temple. Priests wrote their own privileges into sacred texts, and priestly groups served as independent or collaborative rulers who oppressed the people. Herzog places the parable of the Pharisee and the tax collector (Luke 18:9–14) in this context of abusive religion. "To understand the parable," he writes, "one must know who appears in its social script and the significance of their location."[6]

The characters and basic story line seem straightforward. Two men, a Pharisee and a tax collector, go to the Temple to pray. The Pharisee stands by himself and gives thanks to God that he is not a thief, a rogue, an adulterer, or a tax collector. He fasts and he tithes. The tax collector stands far off and, in sharp contrast to the Pharisee, beats his breast and pleads to God for mercy. Jesus announces that the tax collector and not the Pharisee went home justified. Luke introduces his interpretation by noting that Jesus "told this parable to some who trusted in themselves that they were righteous and regarded others with contempt" (v. 9), and he closes the parable by having Jesus cast the reversal (the tax collector and not the Pharisee is justified) in terms of humility. Humility leads to justification, self-righteousness to exclusion. Most commentators follow Luke's lead and read the parable "as a contrast between two types of piety, the arrogant self-righteousness of the Pharisee and the humble dependence on God's mercy of the toll collector."[7] Within this reading, "Pharisees represent a type of self-confident righteousness that claims merit for itself even as it despises and condemns others, while toll collectors represent humble, repentant sinners who call on the mercy of God."[8]

The problem with this traditional reading, Herzog notes, "is that it seems more deeply indebted to sixteenth-century Reformation theology than to the practices and beliefs that animated Judaism during the first century."[9] Herzog's reading is grounded in Temple dynamics concerning debt, tax collection, destitution, moral stigmatization, and the power to forgive. The parable offers clues as to "why Jesus was stigmatized as a friend of toll collectors and sinners and why he was eventually crucified by Jerusalem elites with the assistance of Roman provincial officials." This parable, Herzog notes, "was designed to enable peasants to demystify the Temple and the role of the redemptive media and more specifically, the name-calling of Pharisaic rule-enforcers and moral entrepreneurs, so that the peasants could name oppression as a prelude to renaming their world."[10]

To understand the relevance of these conclusions for unpacking the spiral of violence we need to return to the characters and location of the social script provided by Jesus in the parable. Herzog clarifies that the "tax" collector named in the parable is actually a toll collector. Tax collectors were state officials who would have been directly supervised by Roman prefects and procurators in Judea and by Antipas in Galilee. Toll collectors, on the other hand, were low-level functionaries. They were "subsistence-level wage employees used by the toll contractors" who "rarely realized any benefit or profit from their work." Like the vulnerable workers in the parable of the laborers in the vineyard they "had no bargaining power and could easily be replaced by others as desperate for work as they were." They were "hated by nearly everyone else because of the way they were used to cheat and defraud the public." The toll collector "was a convenient target for the Pharisee's assault, for he was poor, socially vulnerable, virtually powerless and without honor, a pariah figure considered an 'extortioner,' a 'swindler,' and an adulterer of God's law."[11]

Jesus places a hated toll collector at the center of this parable. Toll collectors were visible, easy targets for displaced rage (dysfunctional/deflective violence) even though they were as vulnerable and exploited as many displaced or impoverished peasants. Many of those who despised toll collectors apparently had little or no understanding of the Temple's collaborative role in overseeing the whole system that met Roman demands and bankrolled the privileges of Temple elites. They were not likely to have had much awareness of how the oppressive system was built into privileged readings of the Torah:

> Toll collectors, who actually staffed the booths and cheated the public on behalf of the chief toll collectors or toll farmers whom they served, were visible and socially vulnerable. On them fell the full force of popular resentment toward the whole oppressive system in which they were but minor functionaries. Roman taxation was not the sole burden in the land. Temple taxation was equally oppressive, although it was mystified and represented in the form of religious obligation.[12]

Unlike Matthew, who chastised the laborers Jesus defended, Luke portrays Jesus in sympathy with the vulnerable toll collector. In framing the parable around issues of piety and humility, however, and by disconnecting the parable from the domination system it seeks to challenge, Luke distorts Jesus' meaning almost as profoundly as Matthew. Herzog's interpretation illumines three key points. First, Jesus' parable would better be named "the parable of two toll collectors." The irony at the heart of the parable is that the Pharisee who stands piously before God in opposition to the despised and lowly toll collector is himself a toll collector. His prayer "masks the fact that he and the toll collector belong to parallel systems of tributary exaction."[13] The Pharisee legitimates and collects oppressive tithes and taxes and chastises those who cannot pay. There is further irony in the fact that the toll collector who is the object of his venomous diatribe is universally hated because as a low-level functionary in an oppressive system he cheats the people on behalf of others. The Pharisee in the story, on the other hand, was probably well respected and admired. This is true even though the toll collector is a bit actor on a vast Roman stage whereas the Pharisee, according to Herzog, "is a functionary in a larger institutionalized expression of oppression." The Pharisee depersonalizes and dehumanizes the toll collector. His "outburst identifies the Pharisee as a deviance-processing agent who participates in the systematic, institutionalized violence originating from the Temple, the kind of violence that violates the personhood of the toll collector."[14]

Pharisees fasted and tithed. They rooted their piety, including payment and collection of Temple tithes and taxes and their condemnation of others, in recognized interpretations of Torah. This connection to Torah is Herzog's second key insight. Jesus exposes the Temple's oppressive role in taxation and traces the roots of that oppressive role to the Torah itself. "God" had commanded the people to pay tithes as payment for debts owed to Yahweh. "In second Temple times," Richard Horsley writes, "the income of the priestly aristocracy, and the basis of their wealth and power, was provided by the tithes and offerings given to 'god who is in Jerusalem.'"[15]

Herzog's third key insight concerns debt and forgiveness. Jesus exposes the Pharisee as a toll collector who works on behalf of an oppressive Temple that legitimated itself and the payment of tithes through appeals to the Torah. Jesus also points out that it is to the Temple that those who fail to meet obligations must go to be humiliated and seek forgiveness. As Herzog notes:

> The setting of the parable in the Temple precincts is important because the Temple was the primary place where the redemptive media of Palestine were institutionalized. . . . Together with the Torah, which provided ideological support for the role of the Temple and spelled out the nature of obligation to it, the Temple dominated the life of the people of the land, whether they lived in Galilee or Judaea.[16]

Linking tithes to redemptive media reinforced images of God linked to spiritual violence and enhanced the power of Temple officials:

> In Galilee and Judaea, the bringing of tithes to the Temple was one important way in which the people acknowledged their debt to Yahweh, who brought them out of slavery in Egypt and gave them a land flowing with milk and honey. It was also a way of ensuring good crops for the following year, because any laxity toward Yahweh could produce dire consequences. Conversely, not to render to God what is God's left one stigmatized and forever indebted. Whatever fate befell a debtor in this context was little more that the just retribution of God for failing to participate in the redemptive media.[17]

In this parable, Jesus addresses the spiral of violence in a variety of ways. He calls forth sympathy for a hated toll collector who himself is powerless, vulnerable, and the recipient of dysfunctional/deflective violence. He exposes the Pharisee and Temple as part of an oppressive tax system (violence #1) rooted in interpretation of Torah (violence #5), and he addresses spiritual violence further when he challenges the Temple's status and power to be instruments of God's judgment or forgiveness. The hypocrisy condemned is not a matter of personal piety but systemic injustice. As Herzog notes:

> Of course, this system worked to the benefit of priestly and nonpriestly elites in Jerusalem as well. The tithes rendered to the Temple supported the elite priestly families, and the second tithe, which was supposed to be spent in Jerusalem, enriched the other elite families of the city. Even if the people of the land had to impoverish themselves to pay their tribute, they were expected to accept the price. In consequence of this system, common peasants lived in squalor while they paid their Temple tribute to support the conspicuous consumption of urban elites in Jerusalem, and if they refused, then they were vilified and stigmatized.[18]

This sheds light on the earlier discussion concerning purity and holiness and why Jesus clashed with the Temple and with Pharisees. It also illuminates other aspects of the spiral of violence. The peasants paid their Roman taxes under threat of military force (#3). They could, according to Herzog, "avoid Temple tribute, which could not be compelled, although in doing so they faced social ostracism, shunning, and vilification by Temple authorities"[19] who claimed to speak for God and who rooted their threats in violent images and expectations of God (spiritual violence). As we saw above, payment of a debt presumably owed to Yahweh provided the means for a privileged few to live opulently. It also led to indebtedness and eventual loss of land for strapped peasants. Equally troubling, according to Herzog, "the scribal Pharisees made the debt code a function of the purity code. The failure to pay tithes rendered one impure, and once impure, one remained forever in debt, unable to satisfy the demands of the redemptive media."[20] Herzog describes the violence implicit in this system:

> If one recognizes that much of the violence against persons is accomplished covertly through institutions and structures, then it becomes increasingly clear that the Temple, in some important

respects, represented such an institution. The important thing is that what appeared to be a condemnation of the peasant farmers of the land for their laxity in keeping the Torah masked the economic bind that forced them to withhold their tithes for the sake of survival. The demands of the Torah were being formulated in such a way that they created a class of poor peasants who were unable to meet its tithing requirements. Rather than acknowledge the contradictions, scribal retainers mystified it by negatively labeling the peasants and branding them as enemies of the Torah. In this way, the peasants' actual cycle of perpetual indebtedness was seen as a reflection of their Torah laxity. Unable to meet their tithing obligations, they were depicted as unwilling to fulfill the requirements of the redemptive media. Once they had been so labeled, their further exploitation and degradation were made easier; they were no longer the people of God, whose covenant with Yahweh resided in their patrimonial plot of land, but rebellious reprobates, whose refusal to pay their tithes threatened the well-being of the land.[21]

Purity codes defined everything as pure or polluted. Within the framework of a "purity culture" with clear boundaries, "the Pharisee and the toll collector represent one more incompatible pair, the clean and the unclean."[22] This parable of Jesus shattered these and many other boundaries. A parable such as this one would have prompted many questions.

The toll collector had made no restitution and the Pharisee had seemingly done nothing wrong and yet the former not the latter went home justified. On what basis? By whose word? How could God speak outside of official channels? If the toll collector is justified by a mercy as unpredictable and outrageous as this, then who could not be included? And if toll collectors and sinners are justified in the very precincts of the Temple itself, then how is one to evaluate a Temple priesthood and its scribes who declare that nothing of the kind is possible?[23]

REBELLION AND REPRESSION

The domination system pushed some displaced peasants into banditry. It must have forced many others (or at least tempted them) to outright rebellion while feeding messianic hopes or apocalyptic expectations.

Even a cursory look at key social groups at or near the time of Jesus underscores how persuasive arguments in favor of human and/or divine violence must have been. Renewed interest in a Davidic Messiah followed on the heals of the failed Hasmonean dynasty. John the Baptist's apocalyptic movement found fertile ground after popularly appointed kings with messianic pretensions arose and fell during rebellions following the death of Herod the Great. Sometime after Jesus' execution, the Sicarii emerged. These Jewish daggermen went about Jerusalem assassinating Jewish leaders who collaborated with the Romans. The most organized violent rebellion was that of the Zealots who fought the Romans during the Jewish revolt of 66–70.

Jesus would have had to position himself in relation to these or similar movements, expectations, and actions. Tendencies and temptations to violence would have been compelling and logical as already impoverished people and communities lost ground, both literally and figuratively. Jesus' parables address many of these issues, including the likely consequences of violent rebellion and the futility of common messianic expectations. A notable example of the former is the parable of the wicked tenants (Mark 12:1–12), which Herzog insightfully renames "Peasant Revolt and the Spiral of Violence."

Jesus again chooses a vineyard owner to expose deadly dynamics in the domination system, only to have the Gospel writer, in this case Mark, turn the owner into a God-figure. Like Matthew, Mark ignores the social script presented by Jesus in favor of a theological reading that undermines Jesus' intent. The characters and dynamics of the parable are familiar. A man plants a vineyard, builds a watchtower, leases it to tenants, and leaves. At harvest time he sends a slave to collect his share. The workers seize the slave, beat him, and send him away empty-handed. The vineyard owner sends another slave, who is beaten and insulted, and then another, whom the tenants kill. Many others are sent, only to be beaten or killed. Finally, the vineyard owner sends his son to collect his share of the harvest. The workers "seized him, killed him, and threw him out of the vineyard" (v. 8). Jesus then asks and answers an ominous question: "What then will the owner of the vineyard do? He will come and destroy the tenants and give the vineyard to others" (v. 9).

This parable would have been an explosive conversation starter. Mark preempts the discussion. Just as Matthew has Jesus explain that he spoke in parables in order to confuse people in fulfillment of a scriptural passage, Mark explains the parable of the wicked tenants by placing a scriptural quotation on Jesus' lips: "Have you not read this scripture: 'The stone that the builders rejected has become the cornerstone; this was the Lord's doing, and it is amazing in our eyes'?" (v. 10). As Herzog notes, the parable's meaning for Mark and most interpreters is clear:

> The man who planted the vineyard is Yahweh, and the vineyard itself refers to Israel whether as a historical manifestation of God's people or as God's kingdom. . . . The tenants are the leaders of Israel, specifically, the Jerusalem authorities; the servants are the prophets sent by God; and the "beloved son" . . . is Jesus himself, the culminating messenger and servant. . . . "The others" refers to the emerging church as the new vineyard of God whose leaders will become the new tenants of the vineyard.[24]

The preoccupation of the Gospel writers and interpreters who follow their lead is not on what Jesus said and meant when he told the parable in a context of the domination system. They seek rather to explain why Jesus was rejected and to show that his rejection fulfilled God's promises as recorded in the Hebrew Scriptures. Before describing Herzog's alternative reading, I want to take a slight detour. The Gospel writers often interpret events surrounding Jesus or indicate something has happened because it "fulfills scripture." When they do so, alarm bells should sound to alert us that something is likely to be amiss. At the heart of many serious distortions of Jesus and God are Gospel explanations of events based on fulfillment of scripture. I have cited several examples previously. The "virgin" birth account, itself a misreading of the cited text, is explained with the words, "All this took place to fulfill what had been spoken by the Lord through the prophet" (Matt 1:22). Jesus of Nazareth is born in Bethlehem "for so it has been written by the prophet" (Matt 2:5). Jesus spoke in parables to deliberately confuse the people so that with "them indeed is fulfilled the prophecy of Isaiah" (Matt 13:14). Mark casts Jesus' parable about rebellion and its likely consequences as a rejection of Jesus based on a scriptural reference to "the stone that the builders rejected" as part of God's plan (Mark 12:10–11).

These are not helpful or harmless additions by Gospel writers in the transition from "the Jesus of history to the Christ of faith." Their proof texts serve as interpretive lenses that singularly and collectively distort our understanding of Jesus, God, and faith. The "virgin birth" account has had disastrous consequences for women and others in and outside the church. According to Augustine, women are evil and pass sin on through childbirth. God, who is violent and vindictive, can only be appeased with a perfect sacrifice (Jesus born of a virgin). The tale of a Bethlehem birth props up claims that Jesus was a descendent of David, but Jesus tells a parable in which he rejects expectations surrounding Davidic messiahship. The claim that Jesus spoke in parables in order to confuse the people is absurd. It would be laughable except it distorts both the methodology and content of Jesus' message and social critique and helps explain why the Gospel writers' theological readings of the parables conflict so sharply with Jesus' intent. Turning a parable about the spiral of violence into a rejection of Jesus' story based on fulfillment of scripture robs the parable of its transforming power and allows Mark, like Matthew, to portray abusive actors in the domination system as God-figures.

One other example of scriptural fulfillment accounts illustrates why we need critically to assess scripture, including Gospel citations. I discussed earlier that a nonhistorical text can reveal historically relevant information that can help us understand the social setting of first-century Palestine. One such text is Matthew's account of Herod's "massacre of the infants" (2:16). Although there is no evidence that the slaughter of children actually happened, this account offers important clues about Herod's repressive rule that can frame and inform our portrayals of Jesus. Listen carefully, however, to Matthew's explanation for the slaughter: "Then was fulfilled what had been spoken through the prophet Jeremiah: 'A voice was heard in Ramah, wailing and loud lamentation, Rachel weeping for her children; she refused to be consoled, because they are no more'" (2:17–18).

There are two things to note here. First, the scriptural fulfillment strategy of Matthew takes attention away from Herod's oppressive rule. The slaughter fulfills scriptural promises and therefore is attributed to God's will. According to Matthew's circular logic, the children are killed by Herod in order to fulfill an ancient prophecy and because this ancient prophecy has been fulfilled you can trust his interpretation of Jesus. Second, if we go back to the Jeremiah text (31:15) to which Matthew refers, we see God offering words of comfort to Rachel and other exiles in the subsequent verses: "they shall come back from the land of the enemy; there is hope for your future." Why Rachel's children "are no more" and why she needs comforting, however, is because of God's punishing violence:

> I have dealt you the blow of an enemy,
>   the punishment of a merciless foe,
> because your guilt is great,
>   because your sins are so numerous.

Why do you cry out over your hurt?
    Your pain is incurable.
Because your guilt is great,
    because your sins are so numerous,
    I have done these things to you (30:14b–15).

In this bizarre episode of scripture fulfillment, Herod slaughters infants to fulfill a prophecy about Rachel weeping because God killed her children as a just punishment for sin. None of this is remotely similar to the God revealed through Jesus. This is why I find the Gospel writers' reliance and appeal to scriptural fulfillment so troubling. They reinforce many images of God that are clearly at odds with Jesus, and they distort our understanding of Jesus, God, and faith. This brings us back to Mark's interpretation of the parable of the wicked tenants. Mark throws up two red flags. He relies on scriptural fulfillment to explain events, and he turns a vineyard owner ready to crush a violent rebellion into a God-figure. Mark's interpretation of the parable is far from Jesus.

PEASANT REVOLT AND THE SPIRAL OF VIOLENCE

The key to a more adequate interpretation of Jesus' parable is once again to take the radical, commonsense step of taking historical characters and setting seriously. If Jesus told a parable about a vineyard owner, workers, rebellion, and brutal retaliatory violence, then these are the issues he meant to talk about and meant those who heard the parable to ponder. It does not take much imagination to understand why Jesus would tell such a parable in the midst of the spiral of violence gripping first-century Palestine. There were probably few vulnerable peasants who had not considered the possibility of violent rebellion. As Herzog notes, peasants forced from their land and struggling for survival often "had no choice but to rebel. It is one such small rebellion that is codified in this parable."[25]

Vineyard owners expanded their holdings at peasant expense, and the parable begins by describing a familiar scene: a takeover of peasant land is followed by conversion into a vineyard. "The most likely way he would have added the land to his holdings," Herzog writes, "was through foreclosure on loans to free peasants who were unable to pay off the loans because of poor harvests." In contrast to the poverty of the peasants, the vineyard owner in the story must be rich because only "the very wealthy could afford to make the investment required to plant a vineyard, because it would produce no crop during the four years required for the vines to mature."[26]

If parables were conversation starters, then this one would have elicited many feelings and prompted much discussion. Peasants had every reason to resent wealthy landowners who pushed them off their ancestral lands and then converted them into vineyards. The ultimate indignity was that displaced peasants could be hired to work their former lands as tenants raising the new owner's export crop. If their survival was at stake, then rebellion may have seemed the only option. As Jesus told this parable, some who heard it may have experienced a sense of power and joy as the workers did what they themselves wanted to do: carry out what must have seemed just retribution against the vineyard owner's servants. As Herzog notes, "the parable provided its hearers with a vicarious experience of striking back: first, the hearers vicariously beat, brutalized, and killed the hated retainers; then, they attacked the son who would inherit what was once their land."[27]

As the parable unfolds, one senses the exhilaration of the oppressed tenants and those living vicariously through its telling. They who are humiliated, humiliate others. They who are shamed do the shaming. They who are killed or considered disposable do the killing and dispose of the body of the owner's son. They who are the disinherited rightful heirs to the land deny the inheritance of an illegitimate heir. There must have been a feeling of power as oppression gave way to rebellion and the vicarious experience of justified revenge.

Had the parable ended here, Jesus' hearers may have joined together and gone on a rampage against any deserving oppressor. But Jesus' parable includes an ominous question and response: "What then will the owner of the vineyard do? He will come and destroy the tenants and give the vineyard to others" (12:9). The parable as Herzog notes highlights the spiral of violence, illuminates different interpretations of land rooted in conflicting uses and abuses of Torah, underscores the futility of violent rebellion, and leaves one groping for alternative forms of protest and resistance:

> They were peasants pushed over the edge of survival, and they were heirs of Yahweh's allotment of the land whose inheritance had been stolen from them. Their violent outburst was their way of reasserting their honorable status as heirs, not the shameful act of usurpers. Yet the ruling elites portrayed themselves as Yahweh's rightful heirs and the rebellious peasants as

outlaws. Their readings of the Torah justified their acquisitive greed. . . . The parable codified this conflict of interpretations over the meaning of owner, heir, and inheritance, and the strongly held convictions of the characters animated the hearers' enjoyment of the forms of revenge visited on the retainers and the son. But the final word has not yet been spoken. . . . [T]he rebels may have survived for a time, winning a few victories. But eventually and inevitably, the sanctioned power of the state would crush them. . . . Oppression generates violent reactions because it continually feeds the first phase on the spiral of violence. But in a world where elites controlled the means of production of weapons and retained the armies to use them, revolts reproduced the impotence that ignited them and legitimated more intense forms of repression. . . . The parable may codify the futility of armed rebellion, but it does more. . . . [T]he spiral of violence leaves the hearers with a dilemma. How can they reclaim their honorable status as heirs if violent revolts always end in futility? Are there other ways to assert their claims?[28]

Notes

1. William R. Herzog II, *Parables as Subversive Speech: Jesus as Pedagogue of the Oppressed* (Louisville, Ky.: Westminster/John Knox Press, 1994), 55.

2. Ibid.

3. Ibid., 17, emphasis in original.

4. Ibid., 167.

5. Ibid., 58.

6. Ibid., 178.

7. Ibid., 173.

8. Ibid., 175.

9. Ibid., 176.

10. Ibid., 193.

11. Ibid., 187–88.

12. Ibid., 180.

13. Ibid., 191.

14. Ibid.

15. Richard Horsley, *Jesus and the Spiral of Violence: Popular Jewish Resistance in Roman Palestine* (Minneapolis: Fortress Press, 1993), 153.

16. Herzog, *Parables as Subversive Speech*, 178.
17. Ibid., 179.
18. Ibid.
19. Ibid., 181.
20. Ibid., 184.
21. Ibid., 181–82.
22. Ibid., 183.
23. Ibid., 193.
24. Ibid., 101.
25. Ibid., 108.
26. Ibid., 102.
27. Ibid., 109.
28. Ibid., 112–13.

21 NO MESSIAH—APOCALYPSE NEVER

How can the people of God work for justice or resist injustice if violent revolts always end in futility? The present chapter continues Jesus' critique of the spiral of violence. In the parables discussed thus far, Jesus exposes the inner workings of a domination system in which vineyard owners have the power to hire, fire, underpay, and permanently ostracize vulnerable workers. He describes justifiable rebellion only to demonstrate that it inevitably leads to repressive violence. He demystifies the Temple and its functionaries who confuse, economically oppress, and spiritually terrorize the people. He exposes priestly leaders and their junior partners, who collaborate with Rome, ignore justice, and use and abuse Torah to justify their own privileges and to demonize others. He demonstrates how resentment and violence get deflected onto toll collectors and leave oppressive systems intact. He defends hospitality and community solidarity in the face of the oppressive system.

Jesus shatters pretenses, exposes mechanisms of oppression, and demystifies religion. He suggests that nothing new is possible until the violence and oppression of the domination system are understood and challenged and until the myths of redemptive violence, God's and our own, are rejected. This is all helpful, but it leaves us groping. The Gospel writers misrepresent Jesus' parables so profoundly that we have no alternative but to wrestle with all their claims using the few real glimpses of Jesus they offer. There can be no easy embrace of the Christ of faith when the theology behind it so often betrays Jesus' faith and his images and experiences of God.

What are the people of God to do in the midst of an imperial system that is resilient and powerful? What can we expect from God? Before addressing these questions in the next chapter, it is important to see that Jesus rejected two other common expectations concerning God and history, which would have fed a deeper sense of confusion and urgency among those who asked such questions.

NO MESSIAH TO SAVE US

Jews expected, and occasionally announced the arrival of, a messiah in Israel to reestablish Israel's privileged and powerful place among the nations, purge the defiled land of imperialism, and replace the Temple's collaborative priestly rulers. Jesus was not such a figure. The Temptation narrative (Matt 4:1–11; Luke 4:1–12) indicates that Jesus rejected messianic expectations and their implicit and explicit understandings of God and history. There would be no one sent by God to miraculously do away with hunger, inspire proper belief and practices by performing miracles at the Temple, or rule in place of oppressive empires.

Jesus' rejection of messianic pretensions and promises is one likely reading of the parable of the unmerciful servant (Matt 18:23–35). Herzog offers two possible interpretations of this parable. One sees it as a codification of "the futility of one popular form of the messianic hope"[1] and the other as a window through which to see the relationship between rulers and retainers. Remembering that parables were conversation starters, and noting that each of these parables is consistent with Jesus' concerns, it is possible that both address the spiral of violence.

The parable depicts a king who forgives the enormous debt of one of his slaves who cannot pay and begs for forgiveness. This slave leaves the king and encounters someone who owes him a substantial but far smaller debt than the one the king just canceled to his benefit. Rather than reciprocate the king's generosity, he treats the debtor harshly: "Seizing him by the throat, he said, 'Pay what you owe'" (v. 28). He, in stark contrast to the king, refuses the debtor's plea for mercy and has the debtor thrown into prison. When the king hears of it he is outraged and turns the slave "over to be tortured until he would pay his entire debt" (v. 34).

Matthew uses the parable to reinforce the idea of mutual forgiveness within the community of the faithful, and he places the parable at the end of a discourse on community discipline.[2] As is characteristic of Matthew, he reinforces the desired conduct by linking disobedience to harsh sanctions. As such, Matthew identifies the king in the parable as a God-figure, which means he embraces an image of God who conspires with torturers. The problem with Matthew's reading is that it is difficult to reconcile a parable about forgiveness with an unforgiving God who sends a servant to the torturer's chamber.

Herzog's readings conflict sharply with Matthew. Herzog emphasizes historical setting and details as he looks for clues concerning Jesus' intent and meaning. In one reading, he sets the parable "in the court of a ruler" who is likely to be a client king of Rome. "The primary conflict in the parable is between the ruler and an important retainer in his court." Herzog focuses on a retainer rather than a slave because a slave would never owe the huge amount of money named in the parable, nor would anyone be indebted to a slave in the way depicted. The situation and role of the "slave" in the parable identify him as a retainer. Rulers needed retainers to extract wealth from the peasantry and others. "The resources of the state were his possession to plunder" but no "ruler could exercise power alone."[3]

In this reading, a valuable, but always vulnerable, retainer errs and begs for mercy from an oppressive ruler. Because the retainer is "literate and nearly indispensable,"[4] the prudent ruler, after threatening to cast him into destitution, forgives his indiscretion and debt. The retainer is sent back out on the road to shrewdly multiply wealth on the ruler's behalf. He had just survived the most fearful moment in his life. The king had nearly sold him, his wife and children, and all his possessions, which would have left him destitute. Back on the road, the retainer encounters a debtor. The brutality with which he treats him, however, unnecessarily threatens the broad system of patron and client relationships that were held together by a veil of decency. "By his actions, the bureaucrat has shamed the king, violated his honor in some fundamental way." One indiscretion was pardonable. Two are not. The king acts swiftly. The retainer "is abandoned to the torturers."[5]

In Herzog's first reading of the parable of the unmerciful servant, Jesus demystifies exploitation by offering a glimpse into the world of rulers and retainers who oppress peasants. The role of retainers, as I mentioned previously, was also the subject of the parable of the talents (Matt 25:14–30; Luke 19:11–27), which Herzog calls "The Vulnerability of the Whistle-blower." It describes a retainer who pays a high price after digging a hole and burying a talent rather than allowing usurious loans to dispossess more peasants.[6] "You wicked and lazy slave! You knew, did you, that I reap where I did not sow, and gather where I did not scatter?" (Matt 25:26) the master says accusingly. "As for this worthless slave," he continues, "throw him into the outer darkness, where there will be weeping and gnashing of teeth" (v. 30).

Matthew again transforms a brutal master into a God-figure, but the point I want to emphasize here is that in both the parable of the unmerciful servant and this one, Jesus exposes the world of retainers and rulers. The story of a vulnerable whistle-blower exposes a key aspect of the domination system (the world of rulers and retainers), and it raises important issues concerning deflective dysfunctional violence, including obstacles to and the need for solidarity.

> What would happen if retainers identified with the peasants rather than the aristocracy? What would it mean for them to realize that their interests really do not lie with the aristocracy that exploits them . . . ? What would happen if retainers refused to carry out their assigned tasks? To the hearers [peasants] . . . how would you react to a whistle-blower? Would a former retainer find a welcome in a peasant village? Or would the former hostilities suffocate even the possibility of a latter-day coalition? Do the people of the land realize the role played by retainers? Do they understand how their bitter animosity toward them plays into the hands of the ruling elite? Can peasants and rural poor folks realize how their interests can be tied to the very class of people whom they despise?[7]

The "kingdom movement" led by Jesus during his lifetime and inspired by him following his death and resurrection invited people out of the oppressive system and into a new community. There needs to be a place for people who leave the domination system to land on their feet.

In Herzog's second reading of the parable, Jesus directly challenges false messianic expectations and promises held by oppressed people who long for, need, and deserve justice. Messianic movements appointed popular kings throughout Palestine following the death of Herod. Rebellions were triggered by oppressive rule, including excessive taxes, increased

debt, repression, and loss of both land and freedom. Supporters hoped
that these movements would enforce jubilee and sabbatical provisions
and promises. There would be relief from oppressive taxation and reversal of land loss.

> The opening scene of the parable depicts a messianic moment,
> not in spiritualized terms but in an earthy economic image of
> a king canceling debt. . . . If the largest amount of debt imagi-
> nable has been canceled, then the messianic king has arrived
> and the messianic age has begun. It is the fulfillment of sabbat-
> ical and jubilee hopes condensed into a moment.[8]

In this reading, the king is a messianic figure who announces forgiveness of debt only to have the messianic moment unravel. His long-hoped-
for action turns sour because the domination system includes an
entrenched, exploitative bureaucracy. "It is the failure of the servant to
take his cue from the king's action that leads to disaster," Herzog notes.[9]
The calamity also reflects a problem, borne out by centuries of experience, that "messiahs" can betray the people.

> No sooner has the new age of debt forgiveness been inaugu-
> rated than it is canceled by the cutthroat tactics of a typical pow-
> erful bureaucrat. In light of the servant's subsequent action, the
> king looks like a fool or, worse yet, like a weak and gullible ruler
> without power over the behavior of his subjects. Backed into a
> corner, the king reverts with a vengeance to business as usual,
> delivering the courtier to the torturers. . . . Whether expressed
> in the traditions of popular kingship or in other forms of mes-
> sianic hope, the reliance on a future king to rescue the people
> from debt and bondage harbored a fatal, unnoticed contra-
> diction. Kingship was an institution embedded in a bureau-
> cratic system.[10]

Just as tenants got a temporary rush from the vicarious experience of
justified revenge, only to be brought back to reality by Jesus' ominous
question and answer ("What then will the owner of the vineyard do? He
will come and destroy the tenants and give the vineyard to others") so it
is with the hearers of this parable. Jubilation over the arrival of the messianic moment dies fast. Kingship in Israel rarely if ever lived up to the
hopes of the psalmist for justice and righteousness (Ps 72:1–4). Even

David, the most idealized of all the kings, was often arbitrary, violent, self-serving, and unjust. The Hasmonean dynasty that ruled after the defeat of Antiochus maintained and even deepened many aspects of oppressive rule. The subsequent rise of Rome led some to embrace apocalyptic expectations, while others revamped expectations of a Davidic Messiah. Excitement may have reached fever pitch when messianic movements arose following the death of Herod the Great. These hopes were dashed after a wave of Roman violence. Just as the exhilaration of violent rebellion against an unjust vineyard owner gave way to Jesus' sobering reminder of the brutal counterviolence to follow, these messianic movements and their popular kings were crushed.

In the context of the spiral of violence, Jesus rejected promises and expectations that a popular king or messiah would emerge to solve pressing problems rooted in a well-entrenched, highly bureaucratized domination system. The bureaucracy was an instrument of institutionalized violence involving kings and priests, retainers, scribes, and other midlevel functionaries. It had to be exposed, but so too did the false messianic promises and pretensions that masked but could never overcome despair. False messianic promises and expectations, Jesus suggested, stifle authentic hope. It is a great and tragic irony that with the aid of Gospel distortions Christianity turned Jesus into a largely otherworldly Messiah when Jesus' own life, faith, and experience of God led him to reject messianic promises and pretensions.

APOCALYPSE NEVER

"Okay," hearers of Jesus' parables might have said, "maybe this messiah stuff is overrated. Daniel and John the Baptist were right after all. History is so out of control that our hope rests not with a messiah but squarely on the apocalyptic shoulders of a violent God whose direct intervention will destroy evil, end history, or do away with injustice." To which Jesus may have responded, "Let me break it to you this way. . . ."

The apocalyptic worldview was a response to historical catastrophes. Intense suffering, injustice, and pain could no longer be explained credibly as God's punishment for sin. New interpretations were offered concerning what God was doing, why people suffered, and why Israel was overrun by yet another empire. Apocalyptic Daniel said that imperial powers crushed the people because God was engaged in a violent cosmic struggle and had not yet defeated the forces of evil in heaven. History was temporarily out of control, but a new violent coming of God would make things right. Hope was rooted in the promise that judgment and restitution were near. Apocalyptic thought was always ambiguous about whether this violent coming of God meant the end of history or God's imposition of justice on earth. Apocalyptic Daniel implies the former, but both readings are possible. He had encouraged resistance to Antiochus's brutal rule by promising a universal resurrection in which those who died without giving up the faith or succumbing to imperial demands would be vindicated: "You shall rise for your reward at the end of the days" (12:13). Daniel also satisfied the longing for revenge by insisting that the evil ones would arise "to shame and everlasting contempt" (12:2).

Apocalypticism was fed by the failure of its own vision. Despite messianic and apocalyptic promises, neither the world nor the world of injustice ended. Israel, at the time of Jesus, remained an oppressed colony in a sea of Roman imperialism. Rome's triumph over messianic claimants and popular kings apparently refueled apocalyptic hopes and set the stage for John the Baptist's movement. His image of God and his expectations of what was coming were horrifying:

> Even now the ax is lying at the root of the trees; every tree therefore that does not bear good fruit is cut down and thrown into the fire. . . . His winnowing fork is in his hand, and he will clear his threshing floor and will gather his wheat into the granary; but the chaff he will burn with unquenchable fire (Matt 3:10, 12).

The prevalence of apocalyptic thought within the New Testament necessarily means that any focus on the life and faith of Jesus must address his relationship to the apocalyptic tradition. I have argued that Jesus was baptized into John's movement and that Jesus later broke with John over images of God and expectations of history. Bad news, however, is always good news for apocalypticism, and Jesus' crucifixion led the Gospel writers and Paul to rely heavily on apocalyptic language and themes to explain the death of Jesus. Apocalyptic impulses were also fed by the destruction of the Jewish Temple, which occurred before the Gospels were written. By the time Matthew, Mark, Luke, and John were compiled, many Jews had rejected Jewish Christian claims that Jesus fulfilled God's promises as laid out in the Hebrew Scriptures. Apocalypticism said God destroyed Jerusalem and the Temple because the Jews rejected Jesus, and it served as ideological cover for growing hatred and revenge.

PAUL: APOCALYPSE NOW

In the present context of assessing Jesus' rejection of and the tradition's reliance on apocalyptic thought, I would be remiss not to address briefly the apostle Paul. "Paul," Neil Elliott writes, "has been appropriated by the powerful to perpetuate their own privileges."[11] The apostle has been used to shore up patriarchy, slavery, repression or discrimination against homosexuals, murderous anti-Semitism, apartheid, and tyrannical governments. As Elliott notes, "The canonical Paul was . . . intricately involved in the network of prejudices and policies that coerced conformity and submission: a dependable spokesman for an Establishment that remained overwhelmingly conservative, oppressively straight and male, and impenitently prone to war."[12]

Elliott sets out "to reduce the distortion of Paul," indicating that "Paul is not responsible for many of the things said in his name today."[13] Paul has in many ways gotten a bum rap. Just as there is a great deal of "not God" in biblical discourse about God, and much "not Jesus" in Gospel portrayals and New Testament accounts of Jesus, there is a good deal of "not Paul" attributed to Paul. Elliott documents persuasively that the passages most often used to shore up Paul's oppressive vision, images, and practices were not written by Paul. These "not Paul" passages are then used by interpreters as the lens to "understand," that is, distort authentic Paul.

> Many of the passages from the Pauline writings that have played so notorious a role in history, that have served most readily to legitimize structures of injustice, occur in . . . *letters not written by Paul himself.* Other individuals wrote them, seeking to capitalize on the apostle's authority to advance their own policies and prejudices. Still other passages are interpolations by such individuals into the genuine letters of Paul.[14]

Within the last several years there has been an avalanche of Pauline scholarship that dramatically shifts the lens used to interpret Paul. Many scholars no longer understand Paul as the promoter of a universal, spiritualized religion aligned with conservative political, economic, and social forces. Paul's primary conflict is understood to be with Roman arrogance and power rather than with "the Jews." Paul, like Jesus, was Jewish. He belonged to and promoted a Jewish Christian faction that, in opposition to James and the Jerusalem church, said it was acceptable for Gentiles to join the Jewish Christian faith without adopting Jewish religious and cultural practices such as circumcision and purity rituals concerning food and hand-washing.

Although problems concerning these issues were real and deep, recent scholarship and archaeological evidence suggest that a far deeper conflict divided Christianity from Rome. Paul established his alternative Christian communities precisely where the Roman emperor cult and imperial patronage system were strongest. Christian communities, in other words, were established in direct opposition with and as fledgling alternatives to the Roman imperial system. As Richard Horsley writes, the fact that Roman "political-religious and social-economic" power was expressed through the emperor cult and the imperial patronage system requires "a significant shift in our understanding of the background and significance of many of the most basic Pauline terms and symbols, that is, over against Roman imperial religio-politics, not over against 'Judaism.'"[15] A recent book on Revelation reinforces this view. It argues persuasively that the key issue for many Christian communities was how to step out of empire, reject the domination system, and embrace radical alternatives.[16]

The "liberated Paul" brought to light by Elliott and the anti-imperial Paul evident in recent scholarship offer us better tools to assess Paul's interpretation of the Christ in light of the historical Jesus. The Gospel writers often betray Jesus by turning oppressive vineyard owners and rulers into God-figures. If we look at Jesus' life as a revelation of God, then what can we say about Paul? What did Paul get right and wrong in light of Jesus' understanding of God, faith, and history?

Let me make three observations. First, the anti-imperial reading of Paul noted above is consistent with the stream within the Gospels that presents Jesus in opposition to Roman arrogance and power. New Testament accounts offer a good deal of evidence of an ideological sparring match with Rome over the nature of God, power, and history. Despite efforts to soften conflicts with Rome, including shifting blame for the crucifixion onto the Jews, there are indications of a fundamental clash, including competing Gods, competing Gospels, competing miraculous birth accounts, and competing claims about who is ultimate sovereign over history. Second, Paul's emphasis on building alternative communities involving common meals, God's presence, economic sharing, inclusivity, hospitality, and healing are consistent with authentic Jesus (see chapter 22). Third, the important values and priorities that Paul shares with Jesus are largely undermined by Paul's apocalyptic vision. Jesus' rejection of the apocalyptic tradition was both attested to and undermined by the Gospel writers. It was also ignored by Paul. Their apocalyptic views overshadowed and in many ways negated Jesus' understanding of God. Paul never met Jesus, and like the Christian creeds, he shows little interest in Jesus' life. His worldview and images of Christ are dominated by a visionary encounter with the resurrected Jesus that led him to embrace apocalyptic expectations. As Horsley and Silberman note, Paul had "a private mystical revelation that completely transformed his outlook on both the future and the present state of the world."[17]

Paul's fundamental betrayal of Jesus is his embrace of apocalyptic images and expectations of God and history that Jesus firmly rejected. Paul believed with absolute certainty that in his lifetime, as a consequence of God's plan and his own work, the world would end—indeed, that it was in the process of ending. The end time was set in motion by the resurrection of Jesus, which Paul understood as an apocalyptic event. The resurrection of Jesus was the inaugural event in a general resurrection that would soon be completed as apocalyptic promises were fulfilled.

Several insights guided Paul as he prepared for, testified to, and awaited the consummation of history to be accomplished with his help and in his lifetime. Paul considered Rome to be of no consequence, with one exception to be noted later. Rome's arrogant claims and real power counted for nothing. The anti-imperial thrust in Paul is rooted in his conviction, which he held absolutely, that the apocalyptic end that was coming, indeed that was already in motion, meant the end of Rome. Rome was already nothing because of God's resurrection of Jesus, and Rome's nothingness, visible already to those with eyes to see, would soon be apparent to all. God, not Rome, was in control, and the general resurrection and Jesus' second coming were imminent. As Horsley and Silberman note, Paul "came to believe that the security concerns of the Jews of Damascus were soon to become completely irrelevant when Jesus returned to earth as Israel's messiah, completing the establishment of the Kingdom of God by bringing about the conquest of evil and the vindication of the forces of good."[18] Paul's mystical encounter with Jesus convinced him that God's apocalyptic plans were unfolding before his eyes:

> Like their co-religionists in Galilee and Judea, many Jews of the diaspora shared a vibrant apocalyptic tradition of messiahs, heavenly councils, angelic hosts, and divine timetables, through which they envisioned that God would bring final defeat of evil and the triumph of the forces of good. Their hopes had often been disappointed as the sudden appearance of comets and other celestial omens in the heavens, or news

reports from the East of tumults and miracles, proved to be just passing sensations. Yet now, in the waning days of the reign of Tiberius, a new flurry of excitement arose. . . . In describing the events that had taken place just a year or two before in Jerusalem . . . [prophets and teachers of the Renewal Movement] proclaimed that those events were unmistakable proof that God had at last begun to intervene on behalf of the righteous men and women of Israel. . . . Told and retold throughout the diaspora, they convinced many people that God had demonstrably taken the first step in bringing about the *general* resurrection of Israel's righteous martyrs and freedom fighters that was expected to occur at the End of Days.[19]

Paul and the others who rooted their faith and hope in the imminent apocalypse were wrong. This is true whether apocalyptic promises anticipated the end of history or the end of oppression. The "End of Days" did not come, the general resurrection did not happen, justice did not prevail, and Roman imperial power remained entrenched. Although some would say that Christianity eventually triumphed over the Roman empire, becoming its official religion and outlasting it, an opposite case can be made. When Christianity got cozy with empire, it marked the complete disassociation of the religion from the values, images of God, and expectations of history that inspired Jesus.

Paul was guided by another expectation that proved equally mistaken and had far-reaching consequences. Paul's vision was driven by his belief that the resurrection of Jesus and the apocalyptic events it set in motion meant that Isaiah's prophecies concerning Israel's restoration were being fulfilled. At times the book of Isaiah projected a restored Israel as a beacon from which all the nations would be blessed (25:6; 60:3). More often, however, it said Israel's salvation meant the crushing defeat of the nations: "Nations shall bring you their wealth, with their kings led in procession. For the nation and kingdom that will not serve you shall perish; those nations shall be utterly laid waste" (60:11–12).

There is something inherently troubling and dangerous when *one* people claims to be uniquely chosen by the *one* God. This is what the Jewish writer Regina M. Schwartz means when she writes about the "violent legacy of monotheism."[20] Claiming divine mandate, even as blessing to others, gives way often and easily to imperial pretensions and desires for revenge. The problem of *exclusive* identity and *exclusive* God masquerading as *universal* blessing was present in the very beginning of the tradition. God tells Abraham, "I will make of you a great nation, and I will bless you, and make your name great, so that you will be a blessing. I will bless those who bless you, and the one who curses you I will curse; and in you all the families of the earth shall be blessed" (Gen 12:2–3). Selective blessings and curses backed up by divine power do not bode well for universal harmony. This is especially true when a few verses later we hear that at "that time the Canaanites were in the land. Then the LORD appeared to Abram, and said, 'To your offspring I will give this land'" (vv. 6–7). Land thievery is not a realistic foundation for a universal blessing, although it can ignite a spiral of violence.

Paul grafted elements of Isaiah's expectations onto his own apocalyptic vision. Paul understood Israel's restoration to be central to God's plan to save faithful people in all nations: "For my house shall be called a house of prayer for all peoples. Thus says the Lord GOD, who gathers the outcasts of Israel, I will gather others to them besides those already gathered" (Isa 56:7b–8). In Elliott's insightful treatment, the book of Romans addresses the problem of Christian arrogance far more than that of Jewish legalism. Paul's main concern, Elliott argues, is that many Gentile Christians ignored the importance of Israel to God's plan of salvation.

Taking this a step further, we can say that Paul believed fulfillment of God's apocalyptic promises, already set in motion by the resurrection of Jesus, hinged on two things. Israel had to be restored or at least show signs of restoration because salvation still included and even depended on the people of Israel. "You who remind the LORD, take no rest, and give him no rest until he establishes Jerusalem and makes it renowned throughout the earth" (Isa 62:6b–7). At the same time, the apocalyptic Gospel had to reach all the nations because God was extending the promise of salvation to all people willing to embrace it. Israel had to do well, in other words, and the news of the imminent apocalyptic completion of history had to be spread to the ends of the earth.

Paul, never short on vision or ego, saw himself as instrumental to these endeavors. He worked tirelessly to establish the objective conditions on which fulfillment of God's apocalyptic promises depended. One sometimes senses that Paul believed *everything* depended on him. He faced two immediate problems. First, the church in Jerusalem was in the midst of a serious crisis. Paul responded by organizing a major effort to share economic resources with the struggling church in Jerusalem:

> In villages throughout Galatia, in the workers' quarters of Philippi and Thessalonica, in Ephesus and the towns of the

province of Asia, scattered communities now acted in concert. Every Sunday, as Christian brothers and sisters gathered to sing hymns of faith and thanksgiving to God, the clink of coins could also be heard. By gathering a great fortune from the members' often humble donations of coins, family heirlooms, and personal bangles and bracelets that might otherwise be rendered to the pagan gods or to Caesar, the "saints" of Paul's movement had undertaken a grand act of economic defiance to be delivered at Jerusalem which would capture attention of Jews and Gentiles the world over, both symbolizing and bringing on the Kingdom of God.[21]

No one can doubt Paul's sincerity in wanting to help the church in Jerusalem, but his motives went well beyond immediate material needs. "In the spring of 55 C.E.," according to Horsley and Silberman, "Paul . . . became convinced that the delivery of the collection to Jerusalem—under his leadership—would trigger a sequence of events culminating in the dawning of the Kingdom of God."[22] Paul delivered the collection to the church in Jerusalem, in other words, believing he and it would move the apocalyptic promises of God forward.

Paul was wrong. His offering was apparently rejected by leaders of the Jerusalem church.[23] Not only that, Paul's presence and the collection itself called unwanted attention to the Jerusalem church and its leaders. As Horsley and Silberman note, the "arrival in Jerusalem of Paul at the head of a Gentile delegation would . . . have been a highly provocative act in the explosive political atmosphere of the city."[24] Paul had come to Jerusalem to help usher in the desired apocalyptic end. He instead precipitated a cataclysmic series of events that resulted in his own imprisonment, persecution of the Jerusalem church, and the martyrdom of its leader, James the brother of Jesus:

In these very days, he believed, the Holy Spirit had called the righteous sons of Japhet to send offerings to Zion—just as Isaiah had foretold would occur at the end of days. Surely the wicked would soon feel the pain of God's vengeance, and the righteous of all nations would inherit the Kingdom of God. The reaction to this heterodox preaching was expectable. Paul was quickly arrested by Roman guards and hustled off to prison. . . . Paul's arrest in the Temple compound initiated a sequence of events that would determine the future character of his own assemblies and, indirectly, result in the virtual destruction of the Jerusalem community. . . . [I]t seems clear that Paul not only *did not* convert the people of Jerusalem to his gospel through the delivery of the collection, but he attracted the unwelcome attention of the high-priestly administration and the Romans toward both the Jerusalem community of the Jesus Movement and himself [and James who was brutally martyred].[25]

Paul's plan to spread the gospel to the ends of the earth did not turn out well either. Paul apparently decided that he needed the inconsequential Romans after all, or at least access to their roads, between now and the end time. "Be subject to the governing authorities," Paul said in Romans 13 as he made a pact with the devil. A friend to tyrants and dictators throughout history, this passage, as Horsley and Silberman note, suggests "temporary resignation to the rule of the powers-that-be."[26] The pact was to be for an interim period of short duration, giving Paul time to preach the good news to the ends of the earth. God's apocalyptic promises, which Paul clearly understood to include the fall of Rome, would be fulfilled through use of Roman roads and a temporary alliance. The sweet irony was too good to be true. Paul did not get far. He was imprisoned and probably executed in Rome. The legacy of his apocalyptic worldview, a worldview that Jesus rejected, lives on, however, as do the eerie shadows of his pact with empire. Both profoundly influenced the content of Christian faith in ways that betrayed and would have been unrecognizable to Jesus.

APOCALYPSE NEVER

The case that Jesus broke with apocalyptic expectations and promises seems to me a strong one. Jesus was clearly different from John the Baptist. Few scholars dispute that a break between John and Jesus occurred, and the most compelling explanation for that break is found in relation to expectations of God and history. Many scholars acknowledge that Jesus acted nonviolently. Some scholars believe apocalyptic images are absent from early Q and reappear later in the tradition. Eminent scholars such as Walter Wink and John Dominic Crossan affirm that Jesus' nonviolence reflects his understanding of a nonviolent God.

There are also many good reasons why Jesus may have rejected violence and violent images of God. He came from Nazareth, a town four miles from Sepphoris, a city destroyed by the Romans as they put down revolts following Herod's death. Jesus would have heard about the thousands of Jews crucified in the aftermath of revolt and he would have heard stories and seen the rise and fall of various messiahs. If Jesus believed in the inevitability and prompt disposition of God's violence in either its apocalyptic or messianic forms, then he would have led a guerrilla struggle or stayed with John as they awaited God's decisive action. And if the Baptist's apocalyptic vision reflected the reality of God, then why had God not intervened to save John? John's arrest and execution would have reinforced Jesus' break with John and apocalypticism, which apparently occurred while both men were alive.

The parables offer further evidence of Jesus' break with apocalyptic images of God and expectations of history. Although Luke Timothy Johnson claims that the "parables have existential rather than historical truth, for they depict the mystery of call and response to the Messiah who now lives,"[27] Herzog has helped recover their subversive character for then and now. Many parables set out to help peasants understand and change their reality by exposing and positing alternatives to the domination system. It is hard to reconcile Jesus' parables with expectations that God is about to intervene decisively either to end history or impose justice. Jesus rejected both messianic pretensions and apocalyptic promises that look for easy solutions but are never forthcoming. "Had Jesus' parables indulged in apocalyptic speculation or threatened the end of the world," Herzog writes, "he would have been watched but left alone."[28] And as Robert Funk states, of "the twenty-odd parables that are probably authentically from Jesus, the strange thing is that not one says anything about the end of the world or the apocalyptic trauma that is supposed to accompany that event."[29]

It seems reasonable that Jesus exposed and posed alternatives to the domination system precisely because he did not anticipate its imminent demise. Discrediting and building alternatives to the system are incompatible with apocalyptic or messianic fantasies of imminent destruction or God-imposed justice. When Jesus took apocalyptic and messianic expectations of God and history off the table, he left the people something of an empty menu from which to choose how they were to act and what could be expected of God. Okay, Jesus. No messianic pretensions. No apocalyptic fantasies. What now?

Notes

1. William R. Herzog II, *Parables as Subversive Speech: Jesus as Pedagogue of the Oppressed* (Louisville, Ky.: Westminster/John Knox Press, 1994), 131.

2. Ibid., 133.

3. Ibid., 135–36.

4. Ibid., 142.

5. Ibid., 146.

6. Ibid., 150,167.

7. Ibid., 167–68.

8. Ibid., 147.

9. Ibid.

10. Ibid.

11. Neil Elliott, *Liberating Paul: The Justice of God and the Politics of the Apostle* (Maryknoll, N.Y.: Orbis Books, 1994), xi.

12. Ibid., 17.

13. Ibid., 20.

14. Ibid., 21, emphasis in original.

15. Richard Horsley, ed., *Paul and Empire: Religion and Power in Roman Imperial Society* (Harrisburg, Pa.: Trinity Press International, 1997), 3.

16. Wes Howard-Brooke and Anthony Gwyther, *Unveiling Empire: Reading Revelation Then and Now* (Maryknoll, N.Y.: Orbis Books, 1999).

17. Richard A. Horsley and Neil Asher Silberman, *The Message and the Kingdom* (New York: Grosset/Putnam, 1997), 123.

18. Ibid.

19. Ibid., 115.

20. Regina M. Schwartz, *The Curse of Cain: The Violent Legacy of Monotheism* (Chicago: University of Chicago Press, 1997).

21. Horsley and Silberman, *The Message and the Kingdom*, 184–85.

22. Ibid., 186.

23. Ibid., 193.

24. Ibid., 194.

25. Ibid., 195–96, emphasis in original.

26. Ibid., 191.

27. Luke Timothy Johnson, *The Real Jesus: The Misguided Quest for the Historical Jesus and the Truth of the Traditional Gospels* (San Francisco: HarperSanFrancisco, 1996), 146.

28. Herzog, *Parables as Subversive Speech*, 27.

29. Robert Funk, *Honest to Jesus* (San Francisco: HarperSanFrancisco, 1996), 69.

IMAGES OF ABUNDANCE
AND LOVE OF ENEMIES

The parables of Jesus suggest that the domination system is not going to disappear in a flash of God's redemptive violence either within or at the end of history and that it is not going to be replaced through the coming of a messiah either. Rome and Temple, client king and Roman governor, priestly elite and legitimating Torah, direct rule or dependent Temple state, tactics of divide and conquer, and displaced anger and illusionary promises of God's redeeming violence hold it together like glue. Domination systems are not inevitable, permanent, or outside the parameters of God's concern. They are, however, resilient and strong. Jesus exposes and demystifies the system, illumines the spiral of violence, sheds light on Temple abuses, and unmasks the mechanisms of domination. Jesus invites his people and us to challenge and create alternatives to domination.

The people who pondered Jesus' parables would have asked, "What now?" More specifically, if domination systems are strong and violent rebellions fail to bring them down, then what are we to do? Bury our heads in the sand? Do nothing? Allow oppressors to exploit or kill us or our neighbors? Accept the injustice of unrepentant evil? If a messiah is not going to save us and if God's apocalyptic promises are as empty as the arrogant imperial claims they were meant to counter, then do we abandon hope and the idea of justice altogether? If God's redemptive violence will not help us overcome evil, then what can we expect from God? Without messianic pretensions or apocalyptic fantasies, where are we?

Jesus' subsequent words and actions would by necessity have responded to a crisis that now included not only the oppression and spiral of violence at the heart of the domination system but *a faith crisis* left in the wake of shattered expectations concerning messianic pretensions and apocalyptic fantasies. We may share both a common sense of confusion and a crisis of faith with our first-century counterparts. The biblical writers project so much pathological violence onto God as to leave us no alternative but to challenge scriptural authority. The Gospel writers betray Jesus when they recast oppressive actors in the domination system as God-figures in the retelling of Jesus' parables, and their accounts contain irreconcilable portraits of Jesus and God. To complicate matters further, much of the Christian tradition elevates Paul to a status far superior to Jesus. Many Christians allow Paul to determine their understanding of the character of God and the meaning of Jesus' death and resurrection based on his mystical encounter with the Christ. They do so even though Paul largely ignored the life of Jesus in favor of his own apocalyptic views. Paul's anti-imperial thrust and his emphasis on alternative communities are consistent with Jesus, but he was flat-out wrong about many things. None of this instills confidence in the integrity of scripture, and one temptation is to throw up our hands in despair and abandon faith altogether.

Our faith crisis, like that of our first-century counterparts, may intensify because Jesus took messianic and apocalyptic expectations off the table. What can we expect from God? What does God expect from us? How are people of faith to resist injustice if violent revolts fail and domination systems remain strong? What options do we have beyond rebellion or resignation, fight or flight? Are there other ways to live and die that can break the spiral of violence? If God does not function as a violent revolutionary aide or apocalyptic judge insuring victories against oppressive foes in or at the end of history, then what is God like, according to Jesus? Will God's violence insure justice in other ways, or do we need to abandon images of a violent God altogether? What is God's power like? Do Jesus' choices concerning how to confront the spiral of violence shed light on his images and understanding of God?

Those asking such questions are like butterflies flying into a stiff wind, like birds facing a tornado. Holding up the possibility and necessity of nonviolence, including affirmation of a nonviolent God, would have been as scandalous in Jesus' time as our own. It is like swimming in turbulent waters, against strong currents of actual violence and violent images of God that threaten to destroy all who venture near. It is here, however, amidst violent winds and turbulent streams that we meet Jesus face-to-face, revealing and following a nonviolent God.

Having shelved apocalyptic and messianic fantasies, the question before us in the next several chapters is "What now?" It is my belief that Jesus responded to this question with his whole life and being. The Gospels, however, give us only a few glimpses of what Jesus said and did. These glimpses offer insight into Jesus' vision and experience of God. They are for me powerful and life-transforming. The answers Jesus offered, for one reason or another, however, must have been considered inadequate. Paul ignored Jesus when he shaped his interpretation of Christ in light of a visionary experience and his own apocalyptic expectations. If early Q preserved evidence of a nonapocalyptic Jesus, then violent images and sanctions attributed to Jesus and to God were added within a matter of a few years. By the time the Gospels were compiled, we find only a skeleton of Jesus amidst a great body of apocalyptic images and logic in which God's redemptive violence is embraced as the key to justice within or at the end of history. In the next several chapters, I try to put some flesh on the bones of the remaining skeleton based on glimpses of Jesus' images of God still visible within scripture.

ABUNDANCE NOT SCARCITY

Jesus looked at the world and God differently than many of his contemporaries and most of us. I am referring to more than the fact that Jesus looked at an esteemed Pharisee and saw a tax collector ripping off the people; or that he saw toll collectors that others loved to hate in a sympathetic light; or that he looked upon the magnificent temple supposedly befitting the grandeur of God and saw exploitation; or that he saw and unmasked the oppressive situation facing peasants, peered into their hearts, drew them into the vicarious experience of justified rebellion, and then brought them back to the reality of retaliatory violence; or that he saw the most powerful empire on earth as spiritually bankrupt and in opposition to God. I am more amazed that Jesus looked at and called people out of this world of oppression because within the parameters of his sight he saw abundant life rooted in the abundance of God's love.

Jesus exposed and called others to challenge the violence and exploitation of the domination system. He looked injustice straight in the eye and named it for what it was—an offense to God's intentions for humanity and creation. He walked hand-in-hand with the destitute and the marginalized and challenged the system responsible for their poverty. Jesus looked at the world with a no-holds-barred honesty and saw abundance not scarcity. And the source of the abundance he saw and experienced was God, the Spirit imbedded in all life, surrounding us at all times and in all places. Jesus looked at God and saw and experienced abundant love, not a limited good available to some but not to others. Regina M. Schwartz compellingly names the relationship between violence and perceptions of scarcity concerning goods and God that dominated the world in which monotheism evolved:

> When everything is in short supply, it must all be competed for—land, prosperity, power, favor, even identity itself. In many biblical narratives, the one God is not imagined as infinitely giving, but as strangely withholding. Everyone does not receive divine blessings. Some are cursed—with dearth and with death—as though there were a cosmic shortage of prosperity. And it is here, in this tragic principle of scarcity, that I find the biblical legacy to culture so troubling. . . . Scarcity is encoded in the Bible as a principle of Oneness (one land, one people, one nation) and in monotheistic thinking (one Deity), it becomes a demand of exclusive allegiance that threatens with the violence of exclusion.[1]

Jesus experiences the domination system in first-century Palestine as the polar opposite of God's intended "kingdom." It is a world that is permeated by assumptions of scarcity and the violence of exclusion. The "haves" in terms of wealth and power violently exclude the "have nots." The have nots eagerly project violence onto God as they await the promised reversal or attribute divine will to the violence of their own hands. The world is defined by "religious haves" who mediate between God and the "religious have nots" who will not be in good standing until the religious haves say so. The religious haves are insiders who hold the power to define who is or is not holy, acceptable, or just in the eyes of the community and God. They determine what steps the religious have nots must take in order to be in good standing with a God of limited blessing and unlimited punishing power.

Jesus sees, names, and counters the mechanisms of oppression that keep the domination system strong. What is most amazing, however, is that even *in this world* he sees the possibility and actual evidence of life lived as intended by God. Jesus discerns a world of plenty already in place in which there is abundance and not scarcity of resources and God's love. There is no scarcity of divine blessing and no shortage of prosperity, no cosmic deficiency of God's grace. Jesus sees and experiences a God infinitely giving:

> That's why I tell you: Don't fret about your life—what you're going to eat and drink—or about your body—what you're going to wear. There is more to living than food and clothing, isn't there? Take a look at the birds of the sky: they don't plant or harvest, or gather into barns. Yet your heavenly Father feeds them. You're worth more than they, aren't you? Can any of you add one hour to life by fretting about it? Why worry about clothes? Notice how the wild lilies grow: they don't slave and they never spin. Yet let me tell you, even Solomon at the height of his glory was never decked out like one of them. If God dresses up the grass in the field, which is here today and tomorrow is thrown into an oven, won't God care for you even more, you who don't take anything for granted? (Mt. 6:25–30).[2]

The Buddhist concept of mindfulness articulated by peacemaker Thich Nhat Hanh expresses the essence of Jesus' vision:

> In Buddhism our effort is to practice mindfulness in each moment—to know what is going on within and all around us. . . . When we are mindful touching deeply the present moment, we can see and listen deeply and the fruits are always understanding, acceptance, love, and the desire to relieve suffering and bring joy.[3]

Thich Nhat Hanh believes that "mindfulness is much like the Holy Spirit." It allows "you to see the nature of reality, and this insight liberates you from suffering and confusion. Peace is already there to some extent: the problem is whether we know how to touch it."[4]

Jesus, mindful of the heart of God, sees, experiences, and trusts the abundance of God, and he asks others to imitate behavior rooted in abundance rather than scarcity. The "Lord's prayer" asks for food sufficient for the day (Matt 6:11). Jesus invites us to imitate the generosity of God. "Give to everyone who begs from you" (Matt 5:42). The feeding of the five thousand is a story in which scarcity and hoarding give way to sharing and unexpected abundance (Matt 14:13–21). Jesus has compassion on a large hungry crowd that the disciples want to send away: "Jesus said to them, 'They need not go away; you give them something to eat.'" The disciples presume scarcity: "We have nothing here but five loaves and two fish." Jesus takes what they have, offers a blessing to God, and distributes the food to the crowd. In the end, "all ate and were filled; and they took up what was left over of the broken pieces, twelve baskets full." Assumptions of abundance replace those of scarcity. Jesus laments the conduct of a wealthy landowner who pulls down his barns and builds larger ones to store grain that belongs this day to God (Luke 12:13–21), and he tells a parable of a great dinner to which all are invited "and there is still room" (Luke 14:15–24). Matthew is notorious for adding threats and sanctions to Jesus' words and for presenting God as violent and punishing in direct opposition to Jesus. Remove Matthew's pathology from the Great Judgment story (25:31–46; I will suggest an alternative judgment story in the next chapter) and you have a powerful plea for individuals and nations to feed the hungry, clothe the naked, and visit the imprisoned because doing so reflects the very heart of God.

Jesus consistently exposes and then counters injustice in the domination system. He sees through the eyes of God's intended abundance. There must have been more than a few peasants whose communities were fracturing under the weight of Roman commercialization and taxes and oppressive temple tithes who thought Jesus needed to have his eyes checked. Herzog interprets the parable of the friend at midnight (Luke 11:5–8) in a context in which pressures to pull back from community responsibilities and the moral norms of sharing and reciprocity were great. Jesus places each hearer of the parable at the center of the story. "Suppose one of you has a friend, and you go to him at midnight." You ask him for three loaves of bread because a friend of yours has arrived unexpectedly and you have nothing to set before him. What do you do if your friend refuses to give you the bread and offers up lame excuses? You persist until he gives you what you need, if not because of friendship then because of your insistence.

Luke treats the parable as a statement about God and the need for persistent prayer, but it addresses real issues of hospitality, community, and peasant survival. "To Palestinian peasants rooted in the values of village life," Herzog writes, "it would have been simply inconceivable that a neighbor who had been awakened to help fulfill the obligations of hospitality would try to excuse himself from helping by offering flimsy rationalizations." Hospitality was a village obligation and peasants survived by sharing risks and helping each other. "If a village neighbor asked for help," Herzog writes, "one always agreed to help because, by doing so, one obligated the neighbor to reciprocate when the situation was reversed. When any family's subsistence was in jeopardy, it could stake a claim to the resources of the village."[5] As the domination system squeezed peasant communities, these claims became more urgent even as they became harder to meet:

> These trends most likely had their effects on village life by increasing stress on each family and thereby the strains between families. As goods became more limited, the scarcity challenged the value of hospitality. . . . Every occasion of hospitality threatened to drive the peasant over the edge of survival. Yet in the village depicted in the parable, the villagers rise to the occasion and provide hospitality for their unexpected guest. "Where are the values of the reign of heaven to be found?" Jesus asks. The answer lies in the extravagant hospitality of the village and in the code of honor that sustains it.[6]

Jesus experiences God as infinitely hospitable and he invites us to imitate the hospitality of God. Abundant life is found in community hospitality reflected in shared risks and resources. It finds expression when we refuse to let perceived or real scarcity be a basis for violence or indifference.

Scarcity was also a theological category. Regina Schwartz notes the fatal competition for God's limited blessing at the heart of the Hebrew Scriptures.[7] In the case of Cain and Abel, rejection of one gift results in murder in a context of limited blessing, competition, scarcity, and images of a wrathful and arbitrary deity that one tried to appease with sacrifices. The theme of brothers competing for scarce blessings continues as the biblical story unfolds. Joseph is sold into slavery because "when his brothers saw that their father loved him more than all his brothers, they hated him, and could not speak peaceably to him" (Gen 37:4). Sandwiched between the rivalries of Cain and Abel and Joseph and his brothers is the story of Esau and Jacob in which "that uncomfortable rule of scarcity appears again. There is not enough divine favor, not enough blessing, for both Jacob and Esau."[8] And so Jacob, with the aid of his mother, steals the blessing rightfully belonging to Esau. When Esau complains, his father Isaac explains that he had only one blessing to give and it has been taken away by his brother who received it deceitfully (Gen 27:35). The result is pent-up violence: "Esau hated Jacob because of the blessing with which his father had blessed him, and Esau said to himself, 'The days of mourning for my father are approaching; then I will kill my brother Jacob'" (Gen 27:41). The scarcity of blessing has important consequences within the biblical story and beyond. As Schwartz notes:

> In the Bible, these brothers are the eponymous ancestors of peoples: peoples whose enmity grows and is nurtured for centuries, peoples who define themselves and their prosperity in that close atmosphere of scarcity, peoples who conceive of the Other as cursed and murderous outcasts.[9]

The violent legacy of Cain and Abel, Esau and Jacob, and Joseph and his brothers lives on in our world today. It finds expression in Kosovo, Bosnia, Northern Ireland, Rwanda, in denial of health care to millions of U.S. citizens, in the globalization of the economy where people and nations are written off as disposable, and wherever and whenever ethnic, religious, or economic divisions feed a spiral of violence and hatred. "We are the descendants of Cain," Schwartz writes, "because we too live in a world where some are cast out, a world in which whatever law of scarcity made that ancient story describe only one sacrifice acceptable—a scarcity of goods, land, labor, or whatever—still prevails to dictate the terms of a ferocious and fatal competition."[10]

In the context of a violent and deadly rivalry rooted in perceived scarcity of both goods and God, Jesus' parable of the prodigal son (Luke 15:11–32) should be understood as a dramatic reversal of expectations and a dramatic reconceptualization of God. A father agrees to his younger son's request for his inheritance, which he quickly squanders in irresponsible living. After falling into destitution and longing to eat the food of swine the younger son decides to return home and beg his father for mercy so that he might live as a hired hand. As soon as his father sees him, however, and before the younger son can ask for mercy, the father "was filled with compassion; he ran and put his arms around him and kissed him" (v. 20).

Without acknowledging his son's apology, the father sends word that the fatted calf is to be slaughtered so that the son's return can be celebrated. The oldest son then enters the story. He is furious because from his perspective the wayward son is being treated far better than he deserves and better than the faithful oldest son himself. The oldest son, in a manner similar to the stories of scarcity and violence surrounding Cain/Abel, Jacob/Esau, Joseph/Joseph's brothers, operates with the presumption of scarcity. He is in competition with his brother for inheritance, acceptance, and blessing. His view of the world is clearly foreign to the ways of the father. The younger son receives the undeserved compassion of the father simply because that is the way the father is and the way the father sees the world.

Jesus depicts God as the source of unlimited and undeserved compassion, and the world as a place of plenty. If taken seriously, these images would do much to end the spiral of violence rooted in scarcity, competition, and longed-for reversals associated with the redemptive violence of God. There is, according to Jesus, plenty of blessing, goods, and compassion for everyone, and it is available without any need to ask for forgiveness. Jesus experiences God as infinitely giving and forgiving and invites us to imitate the unlimited forgiveness of God (Matt 18:22).

If we take Jesus' images of God seriously, then there is no need for a sacrificial system of any kind—no need for priests to mediate between sinful humans and God, no need for sacrifices to restore good standing, and certainly no need for the ultimate atoning sacrifice of "God's son," in which Jesus saves the world and bears our sins in order to appease a wrathful deity who would otherwise turn punishing violence upon us. Jesus' vision of the unlimited and undeserved graciousness of God troubles not only the oldest son but many of us as well because it offends our basic sensibilities concerning justice and it challenges our very human tendency to project our own desire for revenge onto God.

LOVE OF ENEMIES

Images of abundance rather than scarcity are not the only shocking reversals of expectations expressed through the words and actions of Jesus. More startling still are words from Jesus found in Matthew and Luke, such as this passage:

> You have heard that it was said, "You shall love your neighbor and hate your enemy." But I say to you, Love your enemies and

> pray for those who persecute you, so that you may be children
> of your Father in heaven; for he makes his sun rise on the evil
> and on the good, and sends rain on the righteous and on the
> unrighteous (Matt 5:43–45).

I put aside until chapter 24 the question of what loving enemies meant
in the context of the oppressive domination system of first-century
Palestine. I stress here that these are among the most radical and most
unexpected verses in the Bible. Love of neighbor was well attested within
the Hebrew Scriptures and a common expectation of faithful Jews, yet
nowhere in the Hebrew Scriptures does it specifically advocate hatred of
enemies:

> Until the discoveries in Qumran, no one could make sense of
> this line from the Sermon on the Mount. The Old Testament
> does tell us to love our neighbor (Lev 19:18), but nowhere are
> we told to hate our enemies. It remained unclear where this
> was "said," or where the Jews might have "heard" it. Since the
> excavations at Qumran, it's clear whom Jesus means: Hatred of
> the enemy was a basic tenet of the Qumran community.[11]

Recall that the Qumran community probably formed as the Essenes
fled to the desert following the successful Maccabean revolt, which
replaced oppressive Seleucid rule with oppressive Jewish rule.
Hasmonean priests replaced those from the priestly line of Zadok, who
had held the office of high priest for centuries. As Crossan notes, the
Essenes "abandoned what they considered to be the polluted Temple and
invalid high priesthood of the Hasmonean dynasty . . . [and] in the second half of the second century B.C.E., they built their sectarian settlement
in the desert and lived in ritual purity and apocalyptic expectation of the
imminent coming of God."[12]

The compound of the Essenes was destroyed in 68 C.E. by the Romans
but not before the community hid its library, which revealed how central
"hatred of enemies" was to its theology and ideology. The *Rule of the
Community* stated that the "man of understanding" is expected to "hate
all that He [God] has despised." Members of the community were to
"love all the sons of light,/ each according to his lot in the Council of
God;/ and . . . hate all the sons of darkness,/ each according to his fault
in the Vengeance of God." "These are the norms of conduct for the man
of understanding in these times, concerning what he must love and how

he must hate. Everlasting hatred for all men of the pit because of their spirit of hoarding."[13] According to Uta Ranke-Heinemann:

> This hatred will break out in the approaching eschatological war. The end of the world, which the Qumran sect expected to come soon, would be preceded by a war of revenge and retribution, the war of the "sons of light" (the Qumran community) against the "sons of darkness." This war is described in detail in the *War Scroll* (1QM). . . . It will go on for forty years. In the first twenty years, all the foreign nations will be conquered; in the following twenty, all other Jews.[14]

Ranke-Heinemann points out another profound difference between Jesus and the Essenes that flows from their different expectations of God and history:

> The priestly or military retinue of Qumran's messianic lords is quite different from the people who followed Jesus. "The blind, cripples, the lame, and the deaf" were not admitted into the Qumran community. . . . Handicapped people would naturally be a hindrance in the approaching final struggle. The *War Scroll* makes it clear that such people are not suited for the final struggle: "And all those that strip the dead, and plunder, and purify the earth and keep watch over the weapons and prepare the provisions, they shall all be from twenty-five to thirty years old. And no lame man, nor blind, nor crippled, nor having in his flesh some incurable blemish, nor smitten with any impurity in his flesh, none of these shall go with them into battle." . . . Jesus, by contrast, did not exclude these military rejects, because he wasn't summoning people to war or to hatred but to love of one's enemy.[15]

Jesus' counsel to love enemies would have offended many of his contemporaries beyond the Essenes who embraced hatred of enemies as part of their foundational creed. Although no specific passage can be cited, hatred of enemies is implied on page after page of the Hebrew Scriptures. The national theology and mythology centered on an interpretation of the Exodus in which God is God because of superior violence directed against the enemies of the chosen people. Exile is explained as God's punishing violence against the chosen people now become enemies of God through sin. And the overwhelming definition of salvation is the crushing defeat of enemies either within or at the end of history.

Both the weather and the defeat of enemies are conditional blessings within the parameters of the covenant. God is understood in relation to the scarcity of blessing and within the confines of violent and jealous monotheism laid out in Leviticus 26:

> If you follow my statutes and keep my commandments and observe them faithfully, I will give you your rains in their season, and the land shall yield its produce, and the trees of the field shall yield their fruit. . . . You shall give chase to your enemies, and they shall fall before you by the sword. . . . But if you will not obey me, and do not observe all these commandments . . . I in turn will do this to you: I will bring terror on you. . . . You shall sow your seed in vain, for your enemies shall eat it. I will set my face against you, and you shall be struck down by your enemies (vv. 3–4, 7, 14, 16–17).

Faith is always in some measure about imitating God. The actions of people of faith necessarily reflect what we think God is like or how we experience God. It is hard to imagine a more compelling contrast in terms of expectations and images of God than those expressed in Leviticus and the verses we are considering from Jesus in the Sermon on the Mount. The conception of God that guides the author of the Leviticus passage is of a punishing deity whose "justice" depends on God's vengeful violence against Israel's enemies or against Israel itself when the people of God become disobedient. Even rain and sunshine are conditional blessings and become weapons in God's hands. Jesus, on the other hand, experiences and presents God as infinitely giving and infinitely loving and he invites us to imitate the generosity of God. God, like the father in the prodigal parable, is compassionate. We are, Jesus says, to love enemies because God loves enemies. Rain and sunshine are not conditional blessings or objects of rewards and punishments. They are God's good gifts to all, the evil and the good, the righteous and the unrighteous.

Jesus says clearly both *that* we are to love enemies and *why* we are to do so. His directive to love enemies is rooted in his experience of a loving God. It is not linked to fear of God's punishing violence; it is an invitation to imitate a loving God. This is stated clearly in the final verse in this section, which the NRSV translates: "Be perfect, therefore, as your heavenly Father is perfect" (Matt 5:48). Kathleen Norris indicates why this plea is troubling for many of us:

> Perfectionism is one of the scariest words I know. It is a marked characteristic of contemporary American culture, a serious psychological affliction that makes people too timid to take necessary risks and causes them to suffer when, although they've done the best they can, their efforts fall short of some imaginary, and usually unattainable standard. . . . The word that has been translated as "perfect" does not mean to set forth an impossible goal. . . . It is taken from a Latin word meaning complete, entire, full-grown. . . . To "be perfect," in the sense that Jesus means it, is to make room for growth, for the changes that bring us to maturity, to ripeness. . . . Perfection, in a Christian sense, means becoming mature enough to give ourselves to others.[16]

This definition keeps us in the realm of the possible and focuses our attention on giving ourselves to others. I prefer the Jesus Seminar's translation of the concluding verse in Matthew, however, which avoids any misgivings we might have about being perfect: "To sum up, you are to be unstinting in your generosity in the way your heavenly Father's generosity is unstinting."[17] The NRSV translates a similar verse in Luke, "Be merciful, just as your Father is merciful" (6:36). Again I prefer the Jesus Seminar's translation, which fits the overall sense of the text and reads simply, "Be compassionate in the way your Father is compassionate."[18]

The reason God loves enemies and asks us to love and pray for them is not because they ask for forgiveness. God loves and asks us to love enemies because God is infinitely loving and beckons us to imitate and be instruments of that love. God does not send rain and sunshine because we ask for them or because our good conduct makes us deserving or because we beg forgiveness for wrongdoing. The rain and sunshine are part of the earth's mysterious treasure of gifts that flow from the Spirit at the heart of all life. God "sends" rain and sunshine on the evil and good because God's Spirit by its very nature is compassion.

As was the case in the prodigal parable, this passage encourages us to purge faith of all sacrificial notions. We do not need to ask God for forgiveness but only to give thanks that the Spirit's loving embrace invites us to new life everywhere and always. Our experience of an infinitely loving God should prompt thanksgiving and compassionate actions rather than petitions for pardon. When we ask God for forgiveness, it implies that God is a theistic being ready to strike with punishing violence at any moment due to our transgressions. When we celebrate Jesus' death as an atoning sacrifice, it suggests that only Jesus stands between a vengeful God and human destruction, between a violent, punishing deity and sinful humans who become the enemies of God by virtue of our sin. When we turn rain and sunshine into weapons, it suggests that the environmental crisis is a punishment from God instead of the consequence of human abuse. When we give thanks to God because we experience the gracious presence of the Spirit, then we acknowledge the true character of God and can move on to live in the fullness of and imitate the loving presence we call God.

Jesus' images of God also undermine expectations that ultimate justice will be *imposed* by a powerful, violent God. The God revealed through Jesus is not vengeful, violent, judging, or punishing because all of these attributes are foreign to God's nature. Jesus' God, quite simply, is not powerful, at least not in the ways human beings have associated power with violence and then projected that power onto God. The nonviolent power of God is not coercive because God's power is invitational and is not backed by punishing sanctions. God, according to Jesus, is the all-encompassing Spirit that embraces us everywhere and always. This Spirit calls us to new life here and now. When we are mindful of the Holy Spirit, as Thich Nhat Hanh notes, "the fruits are always understanding, acceptance, love, and the desire to relieve suffering and bring joy."[19] As Stephen Mitchell notes in *The Gospel according to Jesus*, "inside the Kingdom of God there is only acceptance."[20] The Spirit is infinitely giving, loving, compassionate, and forgiving. We cannot imagine or accept such a gracious God, and so violence spirals out of control, and the abundant life of the "invitational kingdom" exists in the shadows of our lives just beyond our reach.

Notes

1. Regina M. Schwartz, *The Curse of Cain: The Violent Legacy of Monotheism* (Chicago: University of Chicago Press, 1997), 3.

2. Robert W. Funk, Roy W. Hoover, and the Jesus Seminar, *The Five Gospels: The Search for the Authentic Words of Jesus* (New York: Scribner, 1993), 151–52.

3. Thich Nhat Hanh, *Living Buddha, Living Christ* (New York: Riverhead Books, 1995), 14.

4. Ibid., 14, 16.

5. William R. Herzog II, *Parables as Subversive Speech: Jesus as Pedagogue of the Oppressed* (Louisville, Ky.: Westminster/John Knox Press, 1994), 198, 205.

6. Ibid., 207.

7. Schwartz, *The Curse of Cain*, 2.

8. Ibid., 4.

9. Ibid.

10. Ibid., 3–4.

11. Uta Ranke-Heinemann, *Putting Away Childish Things* (San Francisco: HarperSanFrancisco, 1995), 259.

12. John Dominic Crossan, *Who Killed Jesus? Exposing the Roots of Anti-Semitism in the Gospel Story of the Death of Jesus* (San Francisco: Harper San Francisco, 1996), 165.

13. Quoted in Ranke-Heinemann, *Putting Away Childish Things*, 259.

14. Ranke-Heinemann, *Putting Away Childish Things*, 259.

15. Ibid., 266.

16. Kathleen Norris, *Amazing Grace* (New York: Riverhead Books, 1998), 55–57.

17. Funk et al., *The Five Gospels*, 145.

18. Ibid., 297.

19. Nhat Hanh, *Living Buddha, Living Christ*, 14.

20. Stephen Mitchell, *The Gospel according to Jesus* (New York: HarperPerennial, 1993), 55.

23 REASSESSING GOD'S POWER

Questions about God's power and God's compassion emerge from previous chapters and are discussed here and in chapter 24. If God is infinitely loving and compassionate, then what does this suggest about God's power? Is there a difference between coercive and invitational power? What does it mean to say that God is nonviolent, and what implications does God's nonviolence have for the Christian life? What is abundant life and how do we experience or miss it? What did it mean for people to love enemies in the context of the spiral of violence in first-century Palestine? What would it mean for us? If God loves justice but is not a violent judge, and if God lacks the power to *impose* justice, then what can we expect from God? What does God expect from us? Can we work to establish justice nonviolently, or must we abandon a commitment to justice altogether?

JUDGMENT AND POWER

The idea that God is capable of imposing justice through redemptive violence is widespread and popular. Within the Exodus tradition, the broader

Hebrew Scriptures, and much of the New Testament, and among the vast majority of Christians, including many nonviolent activists, God is God because of superior violence. God's violence is understood and embraced in a variety of ways. Within the framework of *redemptive or messianic violence,* God the holy warrior crushes Pharaoh's soldiers or fights alongside the people. God urges the chosen people into battle, assures victory, or promises a messiah to save them from enemies, bring them out of exile, and restore Israel to world supremacy. The God of *punishing violence* uses empires to chastise the disobedient people of God, sends people into exile, reduces them to cannibalism, or casts them into an eternal fire. The God of *apocalyptic violence,* with Jesus returning as the "Son of Man" or the slaughtered Lamb become slaughterer, defeats evil in heaven and on earth, judges humanity, imposes justice, crushes evil, punishes evildoers, and vindicates the faithful within or at the end of history.

The Gospel writers often associate Jesus and God with violent power, including terrifying punishments. Matthew places threatening words on the lips of Jesus in order to express his own passionate hatred of Jews who rejected claims that Jesus fulfilled messianic promises rooted in the Hebrew Scriptures: "I tell you, many will come from east and west and will eat with Abraham and Isaac and Jacob in the kingdom of heaven, while the heirs of the kingdom will be thrown into the outer darkness, where there will be weeping and gnashing of teeth" (8:11–12). More often, however, Matthew uses Jesus to convey images of God's punishing violence in order to encourage and reinforce proper behavior within the Christian community.

Matthew cannot seem to imagine people choosing abundant life or doing the right thing without warnings of violent judgment. Threats from God that are manifestations of spiritual violence are featured centrally in his Gospel. Matthew ends the judgment of the nations parable with Jesus saying: "Then he [the Son of Man] will answer them, 'Truly I tell you, just as you did not do it [feed the hungry, clothe the naked, visit the imprisoned] to one of the least of these, you did not do it to me.' And these will go away into eternal punishment, but the righteous into eternal life" (25:45–46). Matthew's Jesus consistently uses heavily apocalyptic imagery when warning the people of the judgment soon to come:

> Just as the weeds are collected and burned up with fire, so will it be at the end of the age. The Son of Man will send his angels, and they will collect out of his kingdom all causes of sin and all evildoers, and they will throw them into the fur-

nace of fire, where there will be weeping and gnashing of
teeth (13:40–42).

Matthew also uses an apocalyptic lens to interpret the meaning of Jesus'
life and death in order to serve his own purposes. Some apocalyptic images
may be traceable to Jesus from the time in which he was part of John the
Baptist's movement. In light of Jesus' later break with John and in light of
the images of God discussed in the previous chapter, however, it must be
said that the Gospel writer's reliance on apocalyptic images, as well as our
own, is a betrayal of Jesus and the images of God that guided him.
Matthew is often an unreliable witness to Jesus. He repeatedly turns key
actors in the oppressive domination system into God-figures. These God-
figures, whom Matthew blesses with the authority of Jesus' voice, consistently send people to the torturers or to other terrible punishments: "Then
the king said to the attendants, 'Bind him hand and foot, and throw him
into the outer darkness, where there will be weeping and gnashing of
teeth'" (22:13). Then "the master of that slave will come on a day when he
does not expect him and at an hour that he does not know. He will cut him
in pieces and put him with the hypocrites, where there will be weeping and
gnashing of teeth" (24:50–51). Concerning the slave who buried his talent,
the master instructed, "As for this worthless slave, throw him into the outer
darkness, where there will be weeping and gnashing of teeth'" (25:30).

Jesus' favorite activity, according to Matthew, is to threaten people with
violent punishments using his preferred phrase, "weeping and gnashing
of teeth." These vile images and violent portraits of God linked to
Matthew's Jesus are entirely at odds with the images of God that guided
Jesus in the passages explored in the previous chapter. It is impossible to
reconcile "love of enemies" or the compassionate actions of the father in
the prodigal story with divine threats of "weeping and gnashing of
teeth." Either Jesus was a paranoid schizophrenic or Matthew and the
other Gospel writers lead us astray.

We must choose between competing portraits of Jesus and incompatible images of God. When pastors, priests, nonviolent activists, John
the Baptist, Jesus as a follower of John, or Matthew link God to "weeping and gnashing of teeth," to threats and punishments such as throw-
ing adversaries and enemies into the outer darkness or into the furnace
of fire or cutting them into pieces, they engage in spiritual violence.
Spiritual violence has many expressions, but it nearly always involves
threats of God's punishing violence to motivate people to "do the right
thing." Such threats were central to the Baptist's movement to which

Jesus once belonged. Jesus eventually rejected punishing images of God, and he countered spiritual violence as directly as he did the other spokes in the spiral. He rejected messianic expectations and apocalyptic fantasies rooted in the liberating or punishing violence of God and insisted that God is both nonviolent and compassionate. Matthew records an incident in which Jesus responds to a request for a sign by saying that no sign will be given "except the sign of Jonah" (16:4). Matthew draws a parallel between Jonah spending three days in the belly of a whale and the time associated with Jesus' death and resurrection. The request for a sign, however, implies that Jesus' conversation partners were expecting him to validate their view that the apocalyptic moment was near. His answer rebuffed these expectations, and those who held them were probably as outraged as Jonah was when God did not destroy Nineveh (Jonah 4:1). Jesus' conversation partners want assurance that with God's assistance their enemies will fry. Jesus disappoints them with a story in which God's compassion thwarts the human desire for revenge. Robert Jewett sees Jesus' response as a clear rebuttal to apocalyptic expectations:

> His [Jesus'] attitude toward the end of the world . . . was that apocalyptic warfare should be avoided rather than advocated. He opposed the end-of-time fanatics who were promoting a climactic war with Rome. . . . When asked for the "signs of the times" . . . Jesus replied, "No sign shall be given . . . except the sign of Jonah" (Matt. 16:4). Jonah, you may recall, had yearned for the destruction of Nineveh, but divine compassion averted it. The sign of Jonah is evidence of God's will that the wicked world may be spared from the burning some people are sure it deserves. In place of the apocalyptic schemes favored by ancient and modern fanatics, Jesus advocated a commonsense approach to history. In Matt. 16:1–3 he refers to the regularity of weather as a clue to the signs of the times, and the only regularity visible in his era was the monotonous collapse of apocalyptic schemes after they had brought disaster to those who believed. In his eloquent word to the women of Jerusalem, Jesus warned about the consequences "for yourselves and for your children" if their men followed the course of apocalyptic zeal into the final war against Rome (Luke 23:28–31).[1]

Jesus' rejection of apocalyptic judgment and violence has not led Christianity to purge itself of a punishing God's righteous vengeance.

God's wrathful justice is featured prominently in the end-of-the-world rhetoric of right-wing fundamentalists and the justice discourse of progressive nonviolent activists. When asked about the merit of the book of Revelation for the year 2000, John Dominic Crossan responded:

> Apocalyptic eschatology means that we (a small group, whoever we are) believe that God is going to slaughter everyone else except us. I want you to hear very clearly that apocalyptic eschatology is not just an innocent statement that the end of the world is coming soon and that if the statement's wrong, well, that's all right. Apocalyptic eschatology can corrupt the human imagination profoundly in that it imagines a God whose solution to the problems of the world is slaughter. I call it "divine ethnic cleansing." It's much better than human ethnic cleansing because it really does the job. . . . No I don't think it applies to the year 2000. . . . And I don't think it was the solution to the Roman Empire that Jesus had in mind.[2]

Images of God matter. Jesus invites us to imitate the infinitely loving, infinitely hospitable, infinitely giving, infinitely forgiving, and infinitely compassionate Spirit of God that surrounds us everywhere and invites us always to abundant life. We must choose between these images and other images and expectations of God that promise "weeping and gnashing of teeth." What is amazing is that very few people embrace a God who is infinitely loving. We prefer God's violent power and God's imposed justice to God's compassion. It is difficult for us to believe in the "powerless God" revealed by Jesus, a God who beckons us always to justice and compassion but is not sufficiently coercive to impose either. Human beings prefer to project violence onto God and to turn God into another weapon in their struggle against enemies and evil. Few are willing to embrace the mystery and power surrounding a nonviolent God.

POWER, COMPASSION, AND EVIL

The biblical writers tried to explain a train wreck of monumental proportions. Yahweh, according to the national mythology, had proven to be God through superior violence. A crisis resulted when exodus gave way to exile and the chosen people were crushed by foreign empires. If God was God as a result of superior violence and if God was all-powerful, then there were relatively few ways to make sense out of their plight. One option was to abandon Yahweh and adopt the gods of the empires that conquered them. The superiority of foreign gods could have explained Israel's defeat. This explanation was a road not taken, although interpreters continued to graft characteristics of various deities onto Yahweh. Another explanation for exile would have meant diminishing claims of or redefining God's power. This was a road not taken until Jesus.

The biblical writers found a way out of the crisis of exile without abandoning Yahweh in favor of other victorious gods and without diminishing God's power. They reconciled God's power with the experience of exile by *expanding the parameters of God's violence and power*. They elevated God's status to that of divine puppeteer. Yahweh, who began his career as a powerful territorial deity, became a universally powerful God who pulled the strings that determined the actions of all parties and forces within the universe, including human history. Yahweh's power was manifested in earthquakes and storms and in the defeat of Pharaoh. It was further demonstrated when God used foreign empires to punish the people's disobedience with exile.

This explanation left the people and their religious architects with a troublesome dilemma that pitted God's power against God's compassion. If God was responsible for evil, including their oppression, then God was powerful but not compassionate. Holding onto God's power in the face of injustice by attributing suffering at the hands of foreign empires to God's will undermined God's compassion while feeding hatred of self. Suffering was understood within this logic as deserved punishment meted out by a powerful God against a disobedient people who had displeased God. The people or nation were not holy enough, or just enough, or they worshiped the wrong gods or the right God at the wrong places under direction of the wrong priests. In any case, their suffering, which must have seemed unjust to many despite explanations from competing priests, was in this line of reasoning a consequence of God's justice. The disobedient people and nation deserved to be punished by God, and so God's liberating power (exodus) had given way to God's punishing power (exile). When this explanation did not satisfy many in the context of the actions of the oppressive Seleucid empire, the book of Daniel introduced apocalypticism. Daniel first repeated much of the "deserved punishment" rhetoric and then offered something new. Apocalyptic Daniel held onto God's power by projecting God's violence into heaven where God was valiantly waging war against evil. God wanted justice on earth and in the end would guarantee it through superior violence, but God was preoccupied in heaven.

Other explanations for the train wreck (the movement from exodus to exile) that would have held on to the compassion of God were possible but rejected. They would have meant abandonment of images of an Almighty God of superior violence. If God is compassionate but not almighty, then God's spirit or God as Spirit might constantly urge human beings to be just and fervently wish to see greater justice but be unable to impose it by force. This, as we will see, seems to be Jesus' view of God and the human challenge and predicament in the context of injustice and the pervasive power of oppressive systems of domination. Exile could have been understood as a tragedy that had to be faced, but not as a punishment from God. Imperial violence could have been seen as a scandalous affront to both God's spirit and human dignity, as something to be challenged by people of faith, but not as punishing blows of retribution delivered by God's imperial instruments.

These explanations would have kept God's compassion intact but not without undermining God's omnipotence rooted in superior violence. Belief in a compassionate God in a violent and unjust world, or in a world of earthquakes and hurricanes, requires a reassessment of God's power. Otherwise, if God is almighty and all-knowing and the people of God are oppressed, then God has the knowledge and the power to free them or to avoid their destruction but chooses not to act. God, in this case, is powerful but not compassionate. Omnipotent God or compassionate God? Captivity in Babylon, Roman imperialism in first-century Palestine, Hitler's death camps, Hurricane Mitch, U.S.-sponsored wars against progressive churches in Latin America, debt and death that mark globalization of the economy, genocide in Rwanda, or pervasive evil anywhere and everywhere force us to choose. Elizabeth A. Johnson describes this dilemma:

> Radical suffering afflicts millions of people the world over in intense and oppressive ways. In face of one innocent child, described so graphically by Dostoevsky; in face of the unfathomable degradation of the Jewish holocaust narrated so searingly by Elie Wiesel; in face of the boundless affliction of a freed slave woman explored so hauntingly by Toni Morrison; in face of these and all the singular and communal ills which plague living creatures in history, the idea of the impassible, omnipotent God appears riddled with inadequacies. The idea of God simply cannot remain unaffected by the basic datum of so much suffering and death. Nor can it tolerate the kind of

divine complicity in evil that happens when divine power is conceived as the force that could stop all of this but simply chooses not to, for whatever reason. A God who is not in some way affected by such pain is not really worthy of human love and praise. A God who is simply a spectator at all of this suffering, who even "permits" it, falls short of the modicum of decency expected even at the human level. Such a God is morally intolerable.[3]

Many theologians have chosen another way out of the dilemma of God's power versus God's compassion in a world of injustice. God is said to be all-powerful but chooses not to exercise that power within history in deference to human freedom. The problem with this explanation is that it is far removed from the claims of the biblical writers and even farther removed from Jesus. Those who propagated Israel's national theology in the context of the Exodus understood that God defied human freedom repeatedly, including when Yahweh stepped into a historical battle and defeated Pharaoh's forces or when God used imperial powers to punish Israel. If God defied human freedom throughout biblical history, then why not again and why not now? That was the biblical question. Avoiding the tension between God's power and God's compassion by claiming God's respect for human freedom allows us to cling to images of God's power rejected by Jesus and it prevents us from re-envisioning power in light of Jesus' life and faith as revelations of God.

I noted previously that the P writer never associates God with mercy. P's God expects the people of God to be just and holy, encourages right behavior with promises of blessings and threats, and backs up those threats with punishing violence. P's God can only be satisfied by some combination of right conduct (justice), separateness (holiness), and right worship and sacrifice (ritual) carried out at the proper places (sacred space) by the proper priests (right authority). P's God is the powerful, cosmic, transcendent ruler of the universe, but P's God is not merciful. It is impossible for me to reconcile Jesus with or believe in a compassionless God. If forced to choose between traditional portrayals of God's power and God's compassion, and choose we must, then I choose compassion. Both the extent of suffering and the life of Jesus require it. As a Christian, I am willing to reassess and revision God's power because Jesus as a revelation of God and an embodiment of God's compassion in a suffering world did so and invites us to do so.

VIOLENT JUSTICE?

Our images of God do not make God, but they matter nonetheless. Human beings have projected so much violence onto God as to make God's dominant image that of a pathological killer. As noted previously, "there are six hundred passages of explicit violence in the Hebrew Bible, one thousand verses where God's own violent actions of punishment are described, a hundred passages where Yahweh expressly commands others to kill people, and several stories where God irrationally kills or tries to kill for no apparent reason."[4] It is because violent images of God shape our faith and lives so profoundly that we need to examine them carefully. More to the point here, however, is our need to probe why we do not challenge the ironclad link between violence and power and why we do not face the tension between God's power and God's compassion posed by injustice.

One common approach to these issues is to deny the tension by saying that God is God. God, in other words, can be anything God chooses to be, including both all-powerful and all-compassionate. This seems to be the solution of many Muslims, Christians, and Jews. Islam, Judaism, and Christianity have generally embraced the link between power and violence and have downplayed the tension between God's power and God's compassion. They diminish the tension by ignoring it or by wrapping it up in a shroud of divine mystery or, as noted in the case of many Christians, by claiming an all-powerful God's respect for human freedom. The problem with these "solutions," especially for Christians, is that they cut us off from the central challenge posed by Jesus to his world and our own, namely, the need to revision the meaning and modes of power, including God's power. This is precisely what Jesus invited his people and us to do when he presented God as nonviolent and as infinitely giving, loving, compassionate, hospitable, and forgiving.

People of faith have almost universally resolved contradictions between power and compassion in favor of traditional notions of God's power. Our standard confessions and most people of faith—including theologians and pastors, those of us who fill the pews on Sunday mornings, and the biblical writers themselves—emphasize God's power. Power is understood most often as the capacity to control or dominate "the other," including enemies, nature, history, and even death itself. "I believe in God the Father Almighty" is standard fare.

God Almighty is a popular image for many reasons, including two to be mentioned here. First, the notion of an all-powerful, controlling God is among the most visible, damaging, and enduring legacies of religion born within the cradles of male-dominated societies (patriarchy). It is difficult for men, who are used to being in control, to conceive of God as something other than the powerful controller of all things and the one who legitimates men's power within systems men dominate. That is why patriarchal metaphors for God such as Father, King, Ruler, Lord, and Judge are featured so prominently within scripture (as noted in chapter 2).

A second reason for the popularity of God's power and why images of a violent God overwhelm God's compassion is that many of us want God to be powerful because we feel weak or powerless when faced with death, injustice, or evil. Only a very powerful God seems capable of delivering on the biblical promise of life after death. More immediate and tangible are concerns about historical injustices. Something as terrible and terrifying as the Holocaust raises questions about God's power, God's compassion, and even God's existence. God, we might say, cannot be almighty and allow such a horrible tragedy. God, we might say, cannot be compassionate and allow such a horrible tragedy. God we might say, cannot be both almighty and compassionate and allow such a horrible tragedy. God, we might say, simply cannot be.

It is ironic that as we enter the twenty-first century, many people are abandoning faith for reasons as different as night and day. Some whose lives are marked by affluence and progress no longer need God. Others scarred or traumatized by pervasive evil no longer trust God. It is also true, however, that many who believe in God do so because of God's presumed power. God's power is attractive to people of faith in an insecure world where evil and injustice seem out of control, a world marred by profound cultural changes and economic divisions, a world in which everything, including God, seems up for grabs.

Just as bad news is always good news for apocalypticism so, too, insecurity can be said to be good for fundamentalism. But the desire for a powerful God does not end there. Those of us who are committed to social justice and who continue to believe in God despite all the injustice in the world also lean on a God who is mighty because we want God to be powerful enough to overcome evil and to crush those we see as most responsible for oppression. The result is that many of us choose a slightly different option than those noted above. God, we might say, may choose not to exercise power within history in deference to human freedom, but God is violent and almighty and will destroy evil, crush evildoers, and vindicate the faithful as part of a final judgment in which justice will triumph.

In an unjust world, it is natural that oppressed people and others concerned about justice long for a deity that is both compassionate and powerful. They need a God compassionate enough to be moved by their unfortunate plight and powerful enough to do something about it. They find what they need in traditional interpretations of the Exodus: "I have observed the misery of my people who are in Egypt; I have heard their cry on account of their taskmasters. Indeed, I know their sufferings, and I have come down to deliver them from the Egyptians" (Exod 3:7–8).

Oppressed people need empathy and solidarity but most of all they need God's power, and so over and over within the Hebrew Scriptures God's power overwhelms God's compassion. This is evident in the prophetic promises of historical reversals in which the oppressed will become oppressors (Isa 60:10–12) and in psalm after psalm in which salvation is understood to mean defeat of enemies. The primacy of God's power also explains why God's compassion was militarized within much of the tradition. God demonstrates compassion through superior violence and defeat of enemies (Isa 14:1–2). The promise of apocalypticism is that God's punishing violence will impose justice within or at the end of history. God's powerful violence conveniently becomes both the instrument of human revenge and the means to God's justice. People of faith concerned about or living amidst evil and injustice embrace images of a powerful God projected in psalm after psalm:

> O Lord, you God of vengeance,
>   you God of vengeance, shine forth!
> Rise up, O judge of the earth;
>   give to the proud what they deserve!
> O Lord, how long shall the wicked,
>   how long shall the wicked exult?
>
> They pour out their arrogant words;
>   all the evildoers boast.
> They crush your people, O Lord,
>   and afflict your heritage.
> They kill the widow and the stranger,
>   they murder the orphan,
> and they say, "The Lord does not see;
>   the God of Jacob does not perceive."
> . . . [God] will repay them for their iniquity
>   and wipe them out for their wickedness;
>   the Lord our God will wipe them out (94:1–7, 23).

We often spiritualize violent images of God in psalms that remain popular as daily meditations. I suspect, however, that their attraction reveals both the violence and deep sense of powerlessness lurking in our hearts. The desire for God to be powerful enough to punish enemies and restore justice is understandable. The triumph of God's power over God's compassion is clearly in conflict with Jesus, however, and one expression of that conflict is claiming the violence of God as the foundation for Christian nonviolence. Gandhi said when confronted with injustice we can ignore it, collaborate with it, resist it using violence, or resist it nonviolently. He said that violent resistance was better than ignoring or collaborating with injustice but that nonviolent resistance was the best option and the option most consistent with God. I would say, in a similar way, that nonviolent action rooted in the violence of God is preferable to indifference, collaboration, or violent resistance, but that nonviolence rooted in a nonviolent God is most consistent with Jesus.

Religious progressives committed to nonviolence often explain away God's pathology by placing it in the context of the "liberating violence" of God. The liberation theme itself is often the product of idealized readings of selective texts that exclude or excuse God's pathology by stressing its utility in service to liberation. "Liberating" interpretations of God's violence are motivated by legitimate concerns about profound social injustices, and they may even help to counter feelings of despair. As Martin Luther King Jr. wrote:

> At times we need to know that the Lord is a God of justice. When slumbering giants of injustice emerge in the earth, we need to know that there is a God of power who can cut them down like the grass and leave them withering like the green herb. When our most tireless efforts fail to stop the surging sweep of oppression, we need to know that in this universe is a God whose matchless strength is a fit contrast to the sordid weakness of man.[5]

It is certainly scandalous that many Christians show little or no concern for nonviolence or social justice. It is also a betrayal of Jesus and God, however, for progressive Christians concerned about economic, political, or military oppression to embrace scriptural passages that project violent power onto God sufficient to impose justice and punish the evil and the complacent. This ignores God's pathology, feeds a spiral of violence, and betrays Jesus' alternative vision of God's power.

Many of us want desperately for God to be powerful enough to overwhelm evil and impose justice. This is why many nonviolent activists affirm a nonviolent Jesus and a violent God. Jesus' nonviolent example and assurances of God's redemptive violence do not call us to effective *action* but rather to faithful *witness*. God's justice will be established on earth or as part of a final judgment that is God's business not ours. Our task, according to this line of reasoning, is to nonviolently witness to God's truth and power over against the arrogant claims and abusive power of empire and its servants. In this sense, many nonviolent Christian activists are like Paul. Recall that Paul's apocalyptic expectations led him to believe that the end time was already set in motion by the resurrection of Jesus. All Paul had to do to insure fulfillment of God's plan in his lifetime was to help Jerusalem and preach the gospel to the ends of the earth. In Rom 12:9–21, Paul encourages his brothers and sisters in the faith to extend hospitality, avoid arrogance, live in harmony, and if "it is possible, so far as it depends on you, live peaceably with all" but to "never avenge yourselves, but leave room for the wrath of God; for it is written, 'Vengeance is mine, I will repay, says the Lord.'" In a similar way, activists who root their nonviolence in the violence of God seek to live peacefully and to resist the arrogant claims and policies of empires while trusting confidently in the redeeming violence of God.

Many nonviolent activists are drawn to an anti-imperial reading of the book of Revelation because it reinforces many of these views and expectations. Their rightful disdain for injustice and indifference leads them to embrace texts such as this one:

> Then another angel, a third, followed them, crying with a loud voice, "Those who worship the beast [empire] and its image, and receive a mark on their foreheads or on their hands, they will also drink the wine of God's wrath, poured unmixed into the cup of his anger, and they will be tormented with fire and sulfur in the presence of the holy angels and in the presence of the Lamb. And the smoke of their torment goes up forever and ever. There is no rest day or night for those who worship the beast and its image and for anyone who receives the mark of its name."
>
> Here is a call for the endurance of the saints, those who keep the commandments of God and hold fast to the faith of Jesus (Rev 14:9–12).

Wes Howard-Brooke and Anthony Gwyther argue persuasively that the book of Revelation is an anti-imperial text calling Christians to live in opposition to empire. Their book *Unveiling Empire* is alternative and antidote to distorted readings that present Revelation as a coded text that reveals the timing of the end of the world and Jesus' second coming. However, this book makes a strong case that the violence of God is foundational to Christian nonviolence. I disagree. I believe that the violent images and sanctions of God that Howard-Brooke and Gwyther take from Revelation and embrace in their own analysis to justify nonviolent resistance to empire are entirely at odds with Jesus. Opposing and building alternatives to empire are, in my view, entirely consistent with Jesus. Nonviolent resistance to empire rooted in the violence of God is not.

Those who root nonviolence in the apocalyptic tradition hold on to promises of God's violent power as a lifeline against evil. In a chapter entitled, "'Vengeance Is Mine!' Says the Lord," Howard-Brooke and Gwyther write approvingly of the kind of punishing images of God that guided the pastor who delivered the abusive children's sermon noted earlier:

> Fire-and-brimstone rhetoric often filled people with fear and guilt, leading them to feel bad both about themselves and about God. However, dropping of all homiletic references to God's "wrath" or judgment results in an incomplete Christian message, for the voices of the souls under the altar [those killed by imperial violence] continue to cry out, "How long?" When will there be justice? In other words, will evil ever be banished from our midst, or will we always be faced with the tragic choice of whether to be a part of empire's violence as perpetrators or as victims? . . . What premillennialists take seriously that mainline church members should remember is the *necessity of God's judgment against unrepentant evil*. Plagues *were* ineffective as a road to repentance. But the task of the bowl plagues [in which much of humanity dies as a result of God's punishing violence] is not repentance but *justice* in response to the cry of those under the altar. They reveal the tragic fact that some people seem unwilling to repent; they are just as committed to the worship of empire's Beasts as the two witnesses and the countless multitude in the heavenly choir are to the worship of the One on the throne and the Lamb. How long will unrepentant evil be allowed to wreak havoc? This is the question that the bowl plagues address. . . . [T]he purpose of all this violence

is the establishment of justice. As the heavenly choir proclaimed upon blowing of the seventh trumpet, "The nations raged, but your wrath has come, and the time for judging the dead, for rewarding your slaves, the prophets and holy ones and all who fear your name, both small and great, and for destroying those who destroy the earth. . . ." The punishment befits the crime: those who shed blood must now drink blood.[6]

A case is made based on this and similar apocalyptic texts that Jesus was nonviolent and we can be nonviolent because we live with the complete assurance of God's violence. I will argue in the final chapter that this is exactly the opposite of the dilemma posed by Jesus. Jesus reveals a nonviolent God, a God incapable of violently ousting the Romans, of violently imposing justice, of violently stopping genocide in Rwanda or Nazi Germany, of violently derailing the U.S.-backed militaries in Latin America. We cannot root nonviolence in the violence of God, according to Jesus, because God is not violent and God's power is not coercive. The question Christians live with, therefore, is this: If God is nonviolent in a violent world, then how are we to live? If God's power cannot impose justice or do away with unrepentant evil within or at the end of history, then how are we to respond to injustice and to unrepentant evil?

The problem for Christians is not that we associate God with power but is the kind of power we project onto God. We rarely allow Jesus close enough to force a revisioning of God's power or our own. God's power was and is traditionally understood as superior violence and salvation as defeat of enemies. One consequence of the image of an Almighty God, the association of God's might with superior violence, and the linkage between salvation and defeat of enemies is that people of many faiths believe that violence (usually divinely sanctioned) saves. Redemptive violence is a central theme in the Bible, and its pervasive logic dominates modern life. It is the central message of most cartoons, TV dramas, and films, and it has come to dominate church theology and ethics including approaches to war and peace.

The link between God, superior violence, and defeat of enemies helps explain why God's power is claimed and prized by both religious despots and religious revolutionaries. Just as the rich tend to view wealth as a gift from God, despots or "benevolent superpowers" see earthly power as proof of divine blessing. Religious revolutionaries or those wanting to be in solidarity with the oppressed, on the other hand, appropriate God's violent power in their fight against oppressive systems.

Nonviolent activists, to their credit, resist injustice. By ignoring God's pathology or casting it in a liberation framework, however, or by laying claim to God's violence in the course of a final judgment as the foundation of their nonviolent actions, they undermine the credibility of nonviolence and insure that few people will take it seriously. God's violent power is appropriated by everyone until human violence threatens all.

Walter Wink is right when he says that violence "is the ethos of our times" and the "spirituality of the modern world." Violence is "accorded the status of a religion, demanding from its devotees an absolute obedience to death." And he is also right when he says that the "roots of this devotion to violence are deep" and that violence, not Christianity, "is the real religion of America."[7] As bold as these statements are, however, they dramatically understate the problem. Violence today is God, the one and only God at the center of all monotheistic religions. Proclaiming God Almighty and restricting God to One whose power is understood as superior violence means that in monotheistic faiths, *violence is God because violence saves God* in the sense of establishing and maintaining God's credibility. Most people refuse to believe in a God incapable of crushing enemies or establishing justice in this life or at a final judgment. All monotheistic religions will contribute to the destruction of the world as we know it unless and until they affirm the nonviolence of God.

The phrases "O God of vengeance, shine forth," "O LORD how long?" and "Our God will wipe them out" from Psalm 94 capture the sense that injustice puts God on trial, that God's violence is expected, and that without God's effective violent deliverance a faith crisis would deepen. Psalm after psalm makes it clear that God's credibility hinges on effective violence because it is God's redemptive violence that establishes and maintains God's credentials to be God:

> But God will shoot his arrow at them;
>   they will be wounded suddenly.
> Because of their tongue he will bring them to ruin;
>   all who see them will shake with horror.
> Then everyone will fear;
>   they will tell what God has brought about,
>   and ponder what he has done (Ps 64:7–9).

> Make a joyful noise to God, all the earth;
>   sing the glory of his name;
>   give to him glorious praise.

> Say to God, "How awesome are your deeds!
> Because of your great power, your enemies cringe before you"
> (Ps 66:1–3).

Various priests, prophets, and apocalyptic seers offered competing explanations or ways out of the dilemma posed by God's liberating power (exodus) and the people of God's oppression (exile). Unfortunately, experiences and contradictions rooted in the discrepancy between God's liberating power and the people's oppression became fertile ground in which the biblical writers planted and watered the seeds of God's pathology. We have been watering them ever since despite Jesus' efforts to turn off the spigot.

The idea of one powerful God capable of destroying enemies was normative for Jews in first-century Palestine. Although some powerful Jews collaborated, many of Jesus' contemporaries, like Jesus himself, opposed Roman occupation. For the most part, conflicts arose between competing Jewish factions, not over God's ability to violently crush historical enemies within or at the end of history, but over what actions by the Jewish people would prompt God to act on their behalf. Few doubted God's capacity for redemptive violence, in other words, but different groups offered competing views on when it would happen, why the nation was dominated by another foreign power, and what the people of God had to do to trigger God's favor.

Jesus entered this fray with some rather shocking ideas about God, God's power, resistance, abundant life, and the alternative "kingdom." Jesus and the renewal movement with which he was associated encouraged his contemporaries and encourages us to reassess traditional definitions of power, including common expectations of the nature and character of God. If we take Jesus' life seriously as a revelation of God, then we must grapple with issues of God's violence, the relationship between justice and violence, and human violence or nonviolence rooted in divine mandates. Jesus offers a way out of God's pathology and a way into nonviolent resistance to oppression.

Notes

1. Robert Jewett, *Jesus against the Rapture* (Philadelphia: Westminster Press, 1979), 11.

2. John Dominic Crossan, "Jesus and the Kingdom: Itinerants and Householders in Earliest Christianity," in Marcus Borg, ed., *Jesus at 2000* (Boulder, Colo.: Westview Press, 1997), 51–52.

3. Elizabeth A. Johnson, *She Who Is: The Mystery of God in Feminist Theological Discourse* (New York: Crossroad, 1992), 249.

4. Walter Wink, *The Powers That Be: Theology for a New Millennium* (New York: Doubleday, 1998), 84.

5. Martin Luther King, Jr., *Strength to Love* (Philadelphia: Fortress Press, 1963), 20.

6. Wes Howard-Brooke and Anthony Gwyther, *Unveiling Empire: Reading Revelation Then and Now* (Maryknoll, N.Y.: Orbis Books, 1999), 152, emphasis in original.

7. Walter Wink, *Engaging the Powers: Discernment and Resistance in a World of Domination* (Minneapolis: Fortress Press, 1992), 13.

24 ABUNDANT LIFE, INVITATIONAL JUDGMENT, AND GOD'S NONVIOLENT POWER

In this chapter I seek to redefine power and images of God in light of Jesus' embrace of nonviolent action rooted in the character of a non-violent God. Jesus rejected not only the domination system but also messianic and apocalyptic hopes that God's violent power or divinely sanctioned human violence were the keys to justice, liberation, and the demise of oppressive systems. His alternative conceptions of God and power were visible in his life and teaching, which emphasize abundant life, invitational judgment, noncoercive power, the practice of nonviolence, and a modest "kingdom."

SUBVERSIVE WEEDS AND OTHER SURPRISES

> [Jesus] also said, "With what can we compare the kingdom of God, or what parable will we use for it? It is like a mustard seed, which, when sown upon the ground, is the smallest of all the seeds on earth; yet when it is sown it grows up and becomes the greatest of all shrubs, and puts forth large branches, so that the birds of the air can make nests in its shade" (Mark 4:30–32).

The kingdom of God is like the tiniest of seeds. This shocking metaphor clashes sharply with expectations. Conventional wisdom said the arrival of God's reign would be dramatic, even cataclysmic. Third Isaiah had promised that God was "about to create new heavens and a new earth" (65:17). "For the LORD will come in fire, and his chariots like the whirl-wind, to pay back his anger in fury"(66:15). All the wealth of the nations would flow to Israel "like an everflowing stream" (66:12), and all the nations and all the kings would see Israel's vindication and glory (62:2).

The Gospel writers did not appreciate Jesus' humor and the rejection of apocalyptic pretensions it implied. Like most of Jesus' contempo-raries, they found the tiny mustard seed an inadequate metaphor for the glorious kingdom, and so they sought to rescue the image by revising it. The Jesus Seminar's commentary is helpful:

> The mustard seed is proverbial for its smallness. The mustard plant is actually an annual shrub or weed, yet in Matthew and Luke it becomes a tree, while in Mark it becomes the biggest of all garden plants. Only in Thomas does it remain simply "a large plant." The mustard seed is an unlikely figure of speech for God's domain in Jesus' original parable. His listeners would probably have expected God's domain to be compared to something great, not something small and insignificant. As the tradition was passed on it fell under the influence of two fig-ures: that of the mighty cedar of Lebanon as a metaphor for a towering empire (Ezekiel 17:22–23); and that of the apocalyp-tic tree of Dan 4:12, 20–22. In Daniel, the crown of the tree reaches to heaven and its branches cover the earth; under it dwell the beasts of the field and in its branches nest the birds of the sky. These well-known figures undoubtedly influenced the transmission and reshaping of the original parable. In his use of this metaphor, Jesus is understating the image for comic effect: the mighty cedar is now an ordinary garden weed. This is par-ody. For Jesus, God's domain was a modest affair, not a new world empire. It was pervasive but unrecognized, rather than noisy and arresting.[1]

Mustard seed as metaphor for the kingdom flew in the face of theo-logical, historical, and mythological expectations. Its use in direct oppo-sition to the tree imagery in Daniel is another indication that Jesus broke with apocalyptic expectations. The book of Revelation's embellishment of Daniel's tree image should alert us that Daniel and Revelation are likely to have much in common with each other (including calls to non-violence backed up by the violence of God), but each may be far removed from Jesus' expectations of God and history.

Much of the Jewish tradition could never have embraced the mustard seed as metaphor for the reign of God. God's promise to Abraham was that Israel would be a great nation with inhabitants more numerous than the stars. God, according to national Exodus theology, was God because of superior violence used on behalf of the chosen people. God crushed Pharaoh's army and freed the people. God the holy warrior fought along-side the chosen people when they took control of the Promised Land through genocide. David, God's faithful servant, conquered other nations, consolidated power, and ruled over a powerful kingdom, prompting promises of everlasting kingship. In the context of exile, God was under-stood to have used empires to crush the disobedient people, but Almighty God promised salvation and would one day turn God's power against arrogant empires.

In the rhythm of biblical history, bad times were nearly always fol-lowed by big promises of good times. In the context of exile and foreign occupation, therefore, there were deep longings and expectations for a "new heaven and a new earth," a renewed kingdom, a David-like messiah to come and save the people, or a harsh apocalyptic judge to impose jus-tice and crush evil. God, Isaiah said repeatedly, would defeat all the nations and send their wealth to Israel as foreign kings processed as cap-tives into God's holy city. John the Baptist promised that evildoers were about to burn in the unquenchable fire of God's wrath. The Essenes awaited the final battle between the forces of light and the forces of dark-ness. You can guess where they placed themselves and who they expected to win.

Jesus countered these inflated expectations and illusionary hopes with parables, metaphors, and actions that challenged messianic and apoca-lyptic expectations. Having taken these big items off the table, he replaced them with simple images of daily food, of healings and whole-ness, of visions of extended families, and with humor. Jesus said to his highly expectant people, "With what can we compare the kingdom of God, or what parable will we use for it? It is like a mustard seed."

The crowd must have gone wild as Jesus laid a goose egg. Talk about a letdown. Most of us, like many of Jesus' contemporaries, when faced with evil and the power and resiliency of domination systems, bring out our giant-sized imaginations. Our hope hanging by a thread, we cling to promises of God's redemptive or apocalyptic violence. We wait for God to hand over some new weapon in the divine arsenal, only to be given a packet containing a single seed. When we complain that we do not have time for the seed to grow into a mighty cedar, Jesus tells us that our packet contains a mustard seed.

Most of us throw the seed away. We cling to illusionary messianic promises and apocalyptic fantasies that have failed to materialize over thousands of years rather than accepting the seed, planting it, nurturing it, and seeing how it grows. We continue to idealize scriptural passages in our telling and retelling of biblical stories about God's redemptive, punishing violence. God's violence is placed in service to justice and the struggle against unrepentant evil as God's pathology is shielded beneath a canopy of liberation themes. We repeat these tales even though they leave the spiral of violence intact and bring us to the brink of destruction. We may be dissatisfied with the old story lines, but under our breath we can be heard to mutter, "A mustard seed? What gives?"

The Gospel writers did not like the metaphor of the mustard seed either. That is why they stress its growth into a tree. They reverse Jesus' intent by trying to turn something small into something big. They also miss other radical implications intended by Jesus, as Crossan notes:

> The mustard plant is dangerous even when domesticated in the garden, and is deadly when growing wild in the grain fields. And those nesting birds, which may strike us as charming, represented to ancient farmers a permanent danger to the seed and the grain. The point, in other words, is not just that the mustard plant starts as a proverbially small seed and grows into a shrub of three, four, or even more feet in height. It is that it tends to take over where it is not wanted, that it tends to get out of control and that it tends to attract birds within cultivated areas, where they are not particularly desired. And that, said Jesus, was what the Kingdom was like. Like a pungent shrub with dangerous take-over properties.[2]

Jesus invites us to work for justice, reject violence, and embrace a call to be subversive weeds. To accept this vocation, however, we must stop projecting violence onto God. God, according to Jesus, will never violently impose justice, not within history and not as part of an end-time judgment. Why? Because God is nonviolent. We must stop waiting for God to do what Jesus says God is incapable of doing: impose justice through violence. The alternative to violence is to embrace nonviolence, sow mustard seeds, live as communities of subversive weeds, and imitate the nonviolent compassion of God. This is where abundant life is to be found.

The mustard seed was not the only surprising metaphor used by Jesus. Equally shocking was his association of the kingdom of God with children in a society in which a child "was quite literally a nobody unless its father accepted it as a member of the family rather than exposing it in the gutter or rubbish dump to die of abandonment or be taken up by another and reared as a slave."[3] Another provocative message was Jesus' claim that abundant life, like the kingdom itself, was the province of the poor. As Crossan notes, it is a "stark and startling conjunction" to link "blessed poverty and divine Kingdom," especially when the Greek word translated as "poor" means destitute.[4]

Jesus must have seemed demented in the eyes of many when he rejected national mythologies of greatness and compared the kingdom of God to a small seed, a subversive weed, a "worthless" child, and to those who were destitute. His mental health index would have dropped further when he advocated love of enemies and prayer for persecutors when there were so many legitimate targets to hate. Some might have agreed to refrain from using violence against enemies because they trusted in the vengeance of God. Jesus' understanding of judgment by invitation would only have deepened people's sense that something was desperately wrong with this man who claimed to live in the Spirit of God.

JUDGMENT BY INVITATION

Then Jesus said to him, "Someone gave a great dinner and invited many. At the time for the dinner he sent his slave to say to those who had been invited, 'Come; for everything is ready now.' But they all alike began to make excuses. The first said to him, 'I have bought a piece of land, and I must go out and see it; please accept my regrets.' Another said, 'I have bought five yoke of oxen, and I am going to try them out; please accept my regrets.' Another said, 'I have just been married, and therefore I cannot come.' So the slave returned and reported this to his master. Then the owner of the house became angry and said to his slave, 'Go out at once into the streets and lanes of the town and bring in the poor, the crippled, the blind, and the lame.' And the slave said, 'Sir, what you ordered has been done, and

there is still room.' Then the master said to the slave, 'Go out
into the roads and the lanes, and compel people to come in, so
that my house may be filled. For I tell you, none of those who
were invited will taste my dinner'" (Luke 14:16–24).

This story reflects a notion of God's judgment remarkably different
from those cited in the previous chapter. Recall Matthew's Jesus threatening people with eternal fire and weeping and gnashing of teeth and
Revelation's description of those who will "drink the wine of God's
wrath, poured unmixed into the cup of his anger" so as to be "tormented
with fire and sulfur in the presence of the holy angels and in the presence
of the Lamb." In sharp contrast to these images, this Lukan passage
moves markedly in the direction of a noncoercive vision of God's power.
There is no threat of being thrown into "outer darkness," no punishment
involving "weeping and gnashing of teeth," and no projected "torment
with fire and sulfur." There is an open invitation to dinner that includes
everybody. Not everyone accepts the invitation, but exclusion from dinner is the choice of those who are preoccupied with other things.

God invites rich people to the dinner. Most are too busy to come. God
then invites those specifically excluded from the Qumran community
because they would be inadequate fighters in the coming final confrontation with the forces of darkness: "the poor, the crippled, the blind,
and the lame." God is so determined that people come to dinner that servants are instructed to "compel people to come in." This is a far cry from
compelling people to live in outer darkness or excluding them from the
community because of sin, nonpayment of tithes, lack of holiness, or
other matters of ritual purity.

The Jesus Seminar sees verse 24 as a Lukan addition: "Luke excludes
the Pharisees, who reject the invitation to the (messianic) banquet."[5]
Even if we include this verse as part of Jesus' original story, then the only
sanction is that some invited guests "will not taste" the dinner because
they reject the invitation. They miss abundant life because they are preoccupied with other things of their own choosing. In other words, Jesus
invites all to live and experience abundant life here and now in the presence of God's invitational Spirit, but our choices determine whether or
not abundant life is experienced.

It would be hard to imagine more striking differences concerning the
nature of God's judgment as portrayed in this Lukan account and those
noted earlier in Matthew. Matthew's version of this parable (22:1–14)
reveals how free the Gospel writers were to use and distort Jesus to their

own purposes. Matthew treats this parable as an allegory about salvation. His purposes are to explain why God destroyed the Jews and Jerusalem in 70 C.E. and to threaten disobedient members of his Christian community. In Matthew's version, a king (God) prepares a feast for his son (Jesus) and invites guests (the people of Israel) to a banquet (salvation). The guests ignore the invitation in favor of other things, and they kill some of the king's slaves. The king is furious and sends armies to kill the people and burn their city. He then invites others (foreigners/Gentiles) to the banquet. Some of the new invitees are good and others are bad. The king notices an attendee improperly attired (one who is bad). He has him bound hand and foot and thrown into the outer darkness where there will be "weeping and gnashing of teeth." Matthew warns those who are part of the Christian community but not toeing the line that they can be thrown out. If you are bad but remain within, then you will still be purged because a vengeful God will get you in the end! None of this remotely resembles Jesus.

Judgment, according to the Lukan version of Jesus' parable, is not something a powerful, punishing God does to individuals or nations who make mistakes. It is self-exclusion. If we miss the beckoning of the Spirit and make bad choices, then we miss abundant life. I call this *invitational judgment* because abundant life and whether others have a decent life depends on acceptance or rejection of an invitation that is open to all and available always. Invitational judgment does not mean that people who suffer have made bad choices. This is not a story about karma or getting what we deserve. My bad choices can hurt others and vice versa. I can choose to join with others to shape a tax system that concentrates wealth and power and hurts the poor. We have done this in the United States, so that the wealth of the richest one percent is equal to that of the bottom 95 percent. In doing so, we not only miss out on Jesus' invitation to abundant life found in generosity, equity, and sharing, we deny others access to resources needed for meaningful life. The important thing about invitational judgment, and this is hard for many of us to accept, is that God's power cannot force us to live justly or punish us for being unjust. Our acceptance or refusal of the invitation to abundant life has consequences for ourselves and others, but God's invitational power excludes the punishing sanctions of a violent deity. God's Spirit can and does bid us to be loving, generous, and to work for equity and justice, but divine threats and God's "power" cannot force us to be just. The result of my bad choices is that I miss out on abundant life and hurt others. The result of collective refusal of the Spirit's invitation can be catastrophic, not because of God's punishing violence but because our choices lead to war and not peace, inequality and not shared gifts, environmental stress and not health of the earth. The spiral of violence is unchallenged and unbroken.

Jesus associates abundant life with simple things such as daily food and community. Although the prophets often condemned riches as the fruit of violence, wealth was commonly understood to be a blessing from God. To be wealthy, at least in the minds of those who were or wanted to be rich, was to experience abundant life. Jesus saw things differently, and if even a small fraction of the headlines in the tabloids at any supermarket counter have a shred of truth, then we can see that wealth is no indicator of happiness or goodness. Jesus says to the surprise of many that riches are an obstacle to abundant life in the kingdom. In the story of the rich young man (Mark 10:17–25), Jesus looks upon a rich man who inquires about "eternal" life, loves him, and tells him to sell what he has, give the proceeds to the poor, and come follow. When the rich man slinks away despondently, Jesus tells the astonished disciples several times "how hard it is [for the rich] to enter the kingdom of God." The disciples still do not understand this reversal of expectations, so Jesus tries to get their attention with a startling analogy: "It is easier for a camel to go through the eye of a needle than for someone who is rich to enter the kingdom of God."

This, as in Luke's invitational judgment story, is another case in which abundant life is offered and rejected. Jesus loves the man and offers him abundant life. The invitation is refused because the man's priorities are wedded to his money. God is not understood as a coercive agent of punishment but as the one who invites us to experience abundant life. In a similar way, judgment is not understood as a punitive act of a punishing God heaped upon the disobedient but as the logical consequence of refusing the Spirit's invitation to live in accordance with the compassionate Spirit of God.

We can better understand this notion of judgment as refusal of invitation in the context of issues posed earlier. Recall that Jesus exposed injustices in the domination system but at the same time saw and experienced the abundance of God. Recall also that he rejected apocalyptic and messianic expectations that abundant life would come sometime in the future as a result of God's redemptive violence. We experience abundant life in the alternative kingdom, Jesus says, if and when we orient our lives to the Spirit of God. The Spirit invites us here and now and always to imitate and embody the compassion of God in our daily lives and in our

social systems. It is in this context that Jesus' radical antiapocalyptic saying concerning the kingdom should be understood:

> Once Jesus was asked by the Pharisees when the kingdom of
> God was coming, and he answered, "The kingdom of God is
> not coming with things that can be observed; nor will they say,
> 'Look, here it is!' or 'There it is!' For, in fact, the kingdom of
> God is among you" (Luke 17:20–21).

Jesus exposed the domination system in order to counter and change it
and in order to reveal its opposite, "the kingdom of God." Many Jews
expected the end of domination and the arrival of the kingdom through
dramatic events such as a successful violent revolt led by an anointed messiah or as the direct result of God's apocalyptic violence. In sharp contrast,
Jesus saw abundant life in the kingdom as a rather simple affair and as a
present reality. It is daily life lived in accordance with God's compassion.

I wish to make two important points about abundant life in the alternative kingdom. First, it is available to us now. Second, the rich and the
poor are invited to experience abundant life and each can miss it for more
or less the same reason. The rich think wealth is abundant life, and so
they do not pay attention to the Spirit prodding them to live differently.
"You cannot serve God and wealth" (Luke 16:13b), Jesus says succinctly.
The poor, on the other hand, often judge themselves by what the rich
have and what the domination system offers, which is what they do not
have but want. This makes it difficult for the poor to heed the Spirit's call
to find abundant life even in the midst of poverty in opposition and as
alternative to the domination system.

I am not saying that abundant life is possible when you are dying of
hunger. I am saying that, according to Jesus, abundant life is a gift of the
Spirit available to all, that it is part of an alternative way of life in the kingdom, that most rich people miss it because of their unfettered affluence,
and that many poor people who could experience abundant life in the
midst of relative poverty often miss it too. Why do the nondestitute poor
miss it? Because, according to Jesus, they internalize their oppression or
buy into definitions of abundant life propagated by the system itself
rather than definitions coming from the Spirit. In sum, Jesus invites both
rich and poor out of the domination system. We are to embrace abundant
life found in daily food, sharing, community, hospitality, and generosity.

The domination system robbed people of daily food. Abundant life
in the alternative kingdom involved shared meals and daily bread. The

domination system used debt to reduce peasants to destitution and to steal their land. Abundant life included debt forgiveness and a jubilee vision of restoration to the land (Luke 4:19). The domination system was held together by abusive patriarchal power even as families fell apart under the oppressive weight of both patriarchy and Roman commercialization. Jesus' alternative kingdom called forth new communities in which women were leaders, and people had assurances of "a hundredfold now in this age" of "houses, brothers and sisters, mothers and children, and fields" (Mark 10:30). The domination system defined people as insiders and outsiders, holy and unholy, clean and unclean. The abundant life of the alternative kingdom was inclusive and open, a place of healing, restoration, and wholeness. The domination system locked oppressed people into hostile relationships with each other, denied hospitality and eroded community mechanisms of mutual support. Abundant life in the alternative kingdom involved hospitality, including sympathy for hated toll collectors and safe havens for retainers who dared to take oppressive capital out of circulation. The domination system undermined communities, eroded hospitality, and pitted oppressed people against each other. Abundant life meant strengthened communities, solidarity, and cooperation. People were invited out of empire, out of the domination system, and into alternative communities that offered mutual support, hope, and a safe place to land.

The domination system fed a spiral of violence. It claimed divine legitimacy for itself or interpreted imperial domination as punishment for sin, and it crushed protests and rebellions with brutal violence. Abundant life in the alternative kingdom addressed daily needs and nonviolently challenged violent systems responsible for hunger, poverty, and destitution. It offered people ways to end the cycle of rebellion and repression by loving enemies, refusing to kill, encouraging creative nonviolent resistance (see below), and countering violent and punishing images of God that encouraged self-hatred and that fed illusionary and deceptive hopes of God's redeeming violence.

NONVIOLENCE AND THE STRUGGLE FOR JUSTICE

The Exodus understood as God's violent intervention to free an oppressed people from the oppressive Egyptian empire became the foundational story in Israel's experience. God's violence or human violence sanctioned by God was understood to be liberating violence in service to justice. Justice and violence, therefore, lived comfortably together within the character of God. Violence was understood to be the necessary means or instrument by which a just God established justice (defeated evil or the enemies of the people of God), punished justice's betrayal (disciplined the disobedient people of God), and reestablished justice by defeating enemies (salvation) after the disobedient people of God changed their inappropriate behavior.

The promise of a powerful God's liberating violence in service to justice was at the heart of the people's hopes and expectations of deliverance rooted in many prophetic and apocalyptic texts. Jesus was deeply concerned about the oppressive domination system and the many expressions of violence it spawned. Hunger, poverty, destitution, and pervasive violence at the heart of the system, he suggested, were mirror opposites of the just and compassionate order intended by the Spirit pulsating at the heart of abundant life. In short, it is clear that Jesus shared with much of his tradition and many of his contemporaries a deep commitment to social justice.

It is equally clear, however, that Jesus rejected the widely accepted notion that God's violence, employed directly or through human agents, was the necessary instrument for securing God's justice. In order to embrace Jesus' life as a revelation of God it is necessary to see the good news he announced and embodied as a bridge connecting his understanding of the domination system with his experience of God. What Jesus expected God to do in the midst of injustice and what he understood to be a faithful response to the spiral of violence that characterized the imperial situation clashed sharply with common expectations of God's redeeming violence. Some people expected a Davidic messiah to save them. Jesus told a parable about a messiah coming and nothing changing (Matt 18:23–35). Some embraced violent revolt as solution or at least appropriate response to injustice. Jesus told a parable depicting the destruction that inevitably followed rebellion, however tempting and justified violence might seem (Mark 12:1–12). Many clung to promises that sufficient holiness would activate God's action to crush enemies and assure Israel's glorious triumph. Jesus rejected standard explanations that Roman oppression was a punishment for sin and challenged the sin-based system's preoccupation with holiness both as a characteristic and as a requirement of God. Some created isolated, insular communities because they believed they could not be God's people within an unjust society. The Essenes, for example, lived holy lives set apart from the domination system and prepared for God's holy violence to end it. Jesus sought transformation and experienced the possibility and reality of abundant life within society, not apart from it. Some expected the end of the domination system as hated enemies were defeated. Jesus exposed and challenged the domination system, called forth alternatives, taught love of enemies in an effort to break the spiral of violence, and linked salvation to healing and wholeness. Some, including Daniel, John the Baptist, and the author of the book of Revelation, embraced apocalyptic promises of God's avenging violence to impose justice within or at the end of history. Jesus embraced but eventually rejected apocalyptic expectations of God and history, advocating instead the imitation of a nonviolent God. Some expected a glorious "kingdom" that would come with power through God's dramatic, redemptive violence. All the wealth of the nations would flow to Israel like a never-ending stream. Jesus spoke of tiny mustard seeds, subversive weeds, leaven in bread, Spirit within and surrounding us, daily food, and abundant life. Many understood God to be God because of superior violence. Jesus embraced the invitational, nonviolent power of a compassionate God.

Jesus was not the first Jew to promote or use nonviolence when resisting injustice. Hebrew midwives, Shiphrah and Puah, refused to carry out the deadly orders of Pharaoh (Exod 1:15–22). Esteemed teachers and their students pulled down the Roman eagle overlooking the Temple, and Pilate's introduction of images of Caesar on military standards prompted massive nonviolent protests. Jesus may have been the first, however, to specifically reject the violence of God as the foundation for nonviolent resistance. Rather than rooting nonviolence in the assurance of God's ultimate and redeeming violence, Jesus saw nonviolent action as a faithful embodiment of a nonviolent God, that is, as reflective of the very Spirit that is God.

Jesus' parables and other teachings and actions undermined messianic and apocalyptic expectations of God's redeeming or punishing violence. He illuminated and challenged each spoke in the spiral of violence, and he associated salvation with healing and restoration to community rather than defeat of enemies. His understanding of God's noncoercive, nonviolent power is reflected in the Lukan passage above in which everyone is invited to dinner. There is no threat of violent sanction but rather a lost opportunity because we miss the Spirit's open invitation to abundant life. This vision of a nonviolent God is reinforced in the prodigal story in which a father's compassion violates a brother's sense of justice. According to the logic of the oldest son, his irresponsible brother had forfeited his right to his father's love. The behavior of the father, however, illustrates that God's compassion is ultimately deeper than

God's commitment to justice, if by justice we mean that people get what they deserve or that in a well-ordered universe disobedience leads to sanction and obedience to blessing.

Jesus links compassion and justice together in opposition to the dominant tradition that saw God's violence or divinely sanctioned human violence as essential to God's justice. God's violence cannot be the instrument by which justice is established for the simple reason that God, according to Jesus, is nonviolent. God's power is invitational rather than coercive. Justice is the fruit of compassion. It is the vocation and logical outcome of those who embrace the infinitely loving Spirit's call to abundant life.

Jesus stressed both compassion and justice throughout the course of his life and faith while breaking with expectations of God's violence. This can be seen in the nonviolent practice he advocated in response to injustice in the domination system and is evident in a number of subtle ways within scripture. I noted previously that in response to an appeal for a sign, Jesus disappointed his conversation partners by referring to "the sign of Jonah," that is, to God's compassion. Early in Luke's Gospel, we encounter another example in which Jesus is said to have read from "the scroll of the prophet Isaiah" while visiting the synagogue.

> He unrolled the scroll and found the place where it was written:
>   "The Spirit of the Lord is upon me,
>   because he has anointed me to bring good news to the poor.
>   He has sent me to proclaim release to the captives
>   and recovery of sight to the blind,
>   to let the oppressed go free,
>   to proclaim the year of the Lord's favor" (4:17b–19).

Jesus may well have been illiterate, in which case this event is a Lukan creation. Its purpose, however, is clearly to place Jesus in continuity with Jewish traditions concerning justice and jubilee, the year of the Lord's favor. What I find intriguing, however, is that it also distances Jesus from the violence of God tradition. Luke's citation omits half of one verse from the original text in Isaiah. In its entirety, Isa 61:2 reads, "to proclaim the year of the Lord's favor, and the day of vengeance of our God." Jesus or Luke, depending on your assessment of Jesus' reading skills, communicates Jesus' commitment to justice but also his break with violent expectations of God.

A similar example concerns John the Baptist's perplexity concerning Jesus. Luke's Jesus reports that John heard many stories about Jesus from

John's disciples. "So John summoned two of his disciples and sent them to the Lord to ask, 'Are you the one who is to come, or are we to wait for another?'" Jesus responds by saying, "Go and tell John what you have seen and heard: the blind receive their sight, the lame walk, the lepers are cleansed, the deaf hear, the dead are raised, the poor have good news brought to them" (7:22).

This answer reflects images and expectations found in Isaiah (29:18–19; 35:5–6). Once again Jesus or Luke's Jesus, depending on your reading of these texts, has consciously drawn on healing and restorative images and rejected violent ones in defining his ministry. Of the many hundreds of violent, punishing images of God found in Isaiah, this Lukan text cites none. Isaiah 29, for example, includes threats that "you will be visited by the LORD of hosts with thunder and earthquake and great noise, with whirlwind and tempest, and the flame of a devouring fire" (v. 6). And while Isa 35:5–6 says that "the eyes of the blind shall be opened, and the ears of the deaf unstopped," and "the lame shall leap like a deer," verse 4 states, "Say to those who are of a fearful heart, 'Be strong, do not fear! Here is your God. He will come with vengeance, with terrible recompense. He will come and save you.'" When viewed in the broader context of Isaiah, Jesus' response to John's disciples clearly positions Jesus in continuity with justice, healing, and jubilee but in sharp opposition to vengeful, punishing, violent images of God and with expectations of salvation understood as defeat of enemies.

One other example in which Jesus breaks with violence is hidden subtly within Mark 3:1–6. Jesus performs an illegal Sabbath healing that prompts religious and political leaders to hatch a conspiracy to murder. I noted earlier that Jesus broke with expectations of God's violence when he associated salvation with healing rather than defeat of enemies. He also linked hardness of heart to unjust systems rather than to God, who in the Exodus account hardened Pharaoh's heart in order to create an opportunity to demonstrate God's power. What intrigues me in the present context is the provocative question Jesus poses to his adversaries prior to expressing anger and grief over their hardness of heart. "Is it lawful to do good or to do harm on the sabbath, to save life or to kill?" The controversy is about more than Jesus claiming the right to do good on the Sabbath. Recall that healing for Jesus embodies an alternative definition of salvation. The question invites us to revisit traditional notions of salvation understood as defeat of enemies. Although Jesus' adversaries are unwilling to allow healing on the Sabbath, they are perfectly willing to plot murder and to kill.

Killing on the Sabbath, even in warfare, had been disallowed until the time of the Maccabean revolt. At this time, a group of Israelites "refused to defend themselves on the Sabbath and were thereby slaughtered by the forces of Antiochus."[6] An exemption was then granted to soldiers so that they could kill on the Sabbath in defense of Israel. Other exemptions followed:

> [Permission to kill on the sabbath] was extended to permit the continuation of *offensive* warfare begun before the sabbath, a provision which the resistance fighters may have extended yet further. The topic of warfare on the sabbath was "in the air." Thus "to kill" on the sabbath may well have called to mind the exception necessitated by Israel's complex political situation in a hostile world.[7]

In the context of Jesus' overall critique of the spiral of violence and his earlier rejection of messianic and apocalyptic expectations, this biting question implies a flat-out rejection of violence as a means of national liberation and national defense. This is consistent with what we know elsewhere about Jesus. John Dominic Crossan comments on Jesus' admonition to love enemies found in both Luke and Matthew, "I can only interpret it as commanding absolute nonviolence."[8] Jesus urges us to pray for persecutors. He redefines salvation to mean healing instead of defeat of enemies. He warns of the dangers of rebellion and of the brutal consequences of state terror. He rejects messianic pretensions and expectations of God's apocalyptic violence. And he presents God as nonviolent and God's power as invitational rather than coercive.

NONVIOLENT RESISTANCE

Jesus' commitment to justice remained firm even as he embraced a nonviolent God. His rejection of violent images of God, however, including messianic pretensions and apocalyptic fantasies, broke with a longstanding tradition that understood God's violence and divinely sanctioned human violence as necessary for the establishment of justice. His embrace of God as infinitely compassionate and loving Spirit impacted how he resisted injustice and how he expected people of faith to live in the world. Two things stand out in Jesus' response to injustice based on his experience of a nonviolent God. First, Jesus invites us to imitate the Spirit of God here and now in the midst of and at the edges of the domination system. Jesus' "ethical kingdom" challenges life in the system and the system itself in fundamental ways. "It is," as Crossan notes, "a style of life for now rather than a hope of life for the future."[9] Jesus' ethical radicalism is understood as "a divine mandate based on the character of God." It is "nonviolent resistance to structural violence. It is absolute faith in a nonviolent God and the attempt to live and act in union with such a God."[10]

Jesus does not ground hope in promises that a violent God will act to replace the domination system in the near or distant future. He roots his life, his hope, and his nonviolence in the nonviolent character of God present in the world now. God's Spirit surrounds us every minute of every day and invites us here, now, everywhere, and always to abundant life in the alternative kingdom of God. The domination system is not compassionate, and participation in it makes compassion difficult or impossible. God is compassionate. We are called to challenge the system by imitating God and living compassionately here and now. Unjust systems produce poverty, inequality, and greed. God is infinitely giving and so we are called to undermine the system and build an alternative to it with generosity guiding personal and social priorities. God is infinitely forgiving. The Spirit forgives us before we ask; therefore, we are to be forgiving. Finally, in a world in which the spiral of violence threatens to engulf everyone and everything, and in the midst of violent domination systems that offer so many good reasons to hate, a nonviolent God loves enemies and so should we.

The second point based on Jesus' affirmation of a nonviolent God is that our resistance to injustice must reflect God's character and therefore be nonviolent. If the Spirit at the heart of all life is nonviolent and incapable of imposing justice, then human beings could well conclude that they are to be violent and that violence is essential to achieve justice. Jesus rejects this reasonable proposal. His embrace of a nonviolent God did not compromise his commitment to justice but it did lead him to practice creative nonviolent resistance. A key passage is Matt 5:38–42, in which, immediately prior to Jesus' admonition to love enemies, he says:

> You have heard that it was said, "An eye for an eye and a tooth for a tooth." But I say to you, Do not resist an evildoer. But if anyone strikes you on the right cheek, turn the other also; and if anyone wants to sue you and take your coat, give your cloak as well; and if anyone forces you to go one mile, go also the second mile. Give to everyone who begs from you, and do not refuse anyone who wants to borrow from you.

Walter Wink says that here Jesus calls for an alternative to "two deeply instinctual responses to violence: flight or fight. Jesus offers a third way: nonviolent direct action."[11] According to Wink, "Christians have, on the whole, simply ignored this teaching." Others have "understood it to mean nonresistance: let the oppressor perpetuate evil unopposed." "Cowardice," however, as Wink notes, "is scarcely a term one associates with Jesus."[12] If Jesus was not a coward, was not indifferent to injustice, and was not encouraging passivity, then what was he advocating? We need to clarify one word in the above translation and examine the three cases or scenarios (turn the other cheek, give your cloak, walk an extra mile) by which Jesus models nonviolent direct action. The Greek word *anthistémi*, translated above as "resist," is used most often as a military term. It refers to violent struggle or resistance in military encounters.[13] The translation "do not resist an evildoer" therefore is misleading. "Do not violently resist an evildoer" is a better translation. The Jesus Seminar captures the essence of this verse perfectly: "Don't react violently against the one who is evil."[14]

If we are not to resist an evildoer violently or use violence to fight injustice, then how are we to resist? Jesus offers three examples of creative nonviolent action in situations of oppression. Each is addressed to oppressed and exploited people in first-century Palestine. Slapping, suing, and forcing imply that someone with power is taking advantage of others who are vulnerable. The question in each, Wink notes, "is how the oppressed can recover the initiative and assert their human dignity in a situation that cannot for the time being be changed."[15]

Powerful people humiliating subordinates was apparently a common practice. Recall the landowner in the parable of the laborers in the vineyard, who paid workers starvation wages in reverse order and then dismissed the worker who dared complain. Humiliation was and is a fact of daily life for oppressed people. Many, for one reason or another, would have received a backhanded slap from their "superiors." If we pose the problem at the heart of the passage in Matthew in the form of a question, then Jesus might ask, "If someone with power over you gives you a backhanded slap in order to humiliate you, what would you do?" The most honest response was something like this: "I would cower at the feet of the one who delivered the humiliating blow, accept the humiliation, and try to go on with life as before."

Jesus in essence says, "Stand tall, look the one who slapped you in the face, and then offer your other cheek." Why turn the other cheek?

A backhand slap was the usual way of admonishing inferiors. Masters backhanded slaves; husbands, wives; parents, children; Romans, Jews. *We have here a set of unequal relations, in each of which retaliation would invite retribution.* The only normal response would be cowering submission. . . . There are among his hearers people who were subjected to these very indignities, forced to stifle outrage at their dehumanizing treatment by the hierarchical system of class, race, gender, age, and status, and as a result of imperial occupation. Why then does he counsel these already humiliated people to turn the other cheek? Because this action robs the oppressor of the power to humiliate. . . . The person who turns the other cheek is saying, in effect, "Try again. Your first blow failed to achieve its intended effect. I deny you the power to humiliate me. I am a human being just like you. Your status does not alter that fact. You cannot demean me."[16]

This unexpected behavior in a world of honor and shame "would create enormous difficulties for the striker." He could escalate the conflict by turning it into a fistfight, but this would make "the other his equal. . . . He has been given notice that this underling is in fact a human being."[17]

There are similar dynamics at play in the other nonviolent actions encouraged by Jesus. If they threaten to sue you and take your outer garment (they have probably already stolen your land), then give them your underwear. Stand naked before the court, shame the system, and humiliate all who look upon you. If a Roman soldier forces you to carry his pack one mile, then keep going and throw your oppressor off balance. Going a second mile could get *him* into trouble because having someone carry a pack more than one mile is against Roman law. This may not constitute a dramatic victory but it is something, and as Wink notes, it "is in the context of Roman military occupation that Jesus speaks" and with full awareness "of the futility of armed insurrection against Roman imperial might."[18] These concrete examples of creative nonviolence offer further and compelling evidence that Jesus rejected messianic and apocalyptic fantasies that linked the defeat, destruction, or overturning of domination systems to violent acts of God. Wink summarizes the significance of these nonviolent actions:

To those whose lifelong pattern has been to cringe before their masters, Jesus offers a way to liberate themselves from servile actions and a servile mentality. And he asserts that they can do this *before* there is a revolution. There is no need to wait until Rome has been defeated, or peasants are landed and slaves freed. They can begin to behave with dignity and recovered humanity *now*, even under the unchanged conditions of the old order. Jesus' sense of divine immediacy has social implications. The reign of God is already breaking into the world, and it comes, not as an imposition from on high, but as the leaven slowly causing the dough to rise.[19]

CONCLUSION

Dough rising brings us back to modest images of the "kingdom" and alternative visions of God's power rooted in mustard seeds and subversive weeds spreading throughout the landscape of the domination system. We see in and through Jesus glimpses of a God who is incapable of imposing justice, whose power is invitational rather than coercive, nonviolent rather than violent, a God whose very essence and character is compassion. A compassionate God desires justice, calls us to justice, and inspires resistance to injustice, but God cannot and will not impose justice. It is time to leave apocalyptic and messianic promises behind and throw images of a powerful, violent, punishing God who is capable of imposing justice into the dumpster. In faithfulness to a nonviolent God we must get on with our lives, recognizing that the Spirit of God invites all people to abundant life.

Jesus' humble claims concerning God's power and the alternative "kingdom" clashed sharply with grandiose expectations held by many people in his time and our own. This may explain why Jesus disappeared from Christianity, why he is not welcome in many of our churches, and why the New Testament writers embellished, distorted, and changed much of what Jesus said and did. The invitation to abundant life if embraced, however, can enrich our lives, our faith, our churches, and our world.

Notes

1. Robert W. Funk, Roy W. Hoover, and the Jesus Seminar, *The Five Gospels: The Search for the Authentic Words of Jesus* (New York: Scribner, 1993), 484.

2. John Dominic Crossan, *Jesus: A Revolutionary Biography* (New York: Harper Collins, 1995), 65.

3. Ibid., 63–64.

4. Ibid., 61–62.

5. Funk et al., *The Five Gospels*, 352.

6. Marcus Borg, *Conflict, Holiness, and Politics in the Teachings of Jesus* (New York: Edwin Mellen Press, 1984), 158.

7. Ibid., 159, emphasis in original.

8. John Dominic Crossan, *The Birth of Christianity* (San Francisco: Harper San Francisco, 1998), 391.

9. Crossan, *Jesus*, 56.

10. Crossan, *Birth of Christianity*, 287.

11. Walter Wink, *Engaging the Powers: Discernment and Resistance in a World of Domination* (Minneapolis: Fortress Press, 1992), 175.

12. Ibid.

13. Ibid., 185.

14. Funk et al., *Five Gospels*, 143.

15. Wink, *Engaging the Powers*, 182.

16. Ibid., 176, emphasis in original.

17. Ibid.

18. Ibid., 181.

19. Ibid., 183, emphasis in original.

25 TAKING JESUS SERIOUSLY

The world is fracturing under the weight of violence, injustice, greed, inequality, and religious distortions of God. Jesus is missing and we miss Jesus. His unmasking of domination, understanding and embodiment of a nonviolent God, and invitation to abundant life in his time are relevant to our situation and our time. I disagree with people who claim Jesus is unimportant to Christianity. To those who cite the obstacle of limited sources, I say we must do the best we can with the sources we have. To those who argue that it is to the Christ of faith that the Gospel writers speak, I say we can benefit from their rich testimony but we must receive it critically because evidence imbedded in the Gospels indicates that the Christ of faith betrays Jesus and God frequently. To those who warn that if you look for Jesus then you will find a Jesus in your own image, I say that is a potential pitfall anytime we speak about Jesus, Christ, or God and it is a realized danger in the work of the biblical writers themselves. In short, Christians must do the best we can to paint an accurate picture of Jesus set within the time period in which he lived and wrestle with the meaning of Jesus for our faith and time. If we take the life and faith of Jesus seriously and see Jesus as a revelation of God, then what does this mean for our lives, our priorities, our ways of being church, our rituals, and our actions in the world?

UNMASKING AND WORKING FOR ALTERNATIVES TO DOMINATION SYSTEMS HERE AND NOW

Christianity must be faithful to Jesus, whose experience and vision of God led him to oppose systems of domination and to embrace the alternative "kingdom of God." As followers of Jesus, we must unmask the mechanisms of abusive power in our own time and envision and embody alternatives consistent with Jesus. Economist Xabier Gorostiaga writes that our "world has become a 'champagne glass' [in which] the richest 20 percent of humanity hoards 83 percent of the world's wealth, while the poorest 60 percent of humanity subsists on 6 percent of the wealth." Millions of people are considered disposable, Gorostiaga says, because they are not needed as producers or consumers.[1]

According to the United Nations Development Program, the "three richest people have assets that exceed the combined GDP [Gross Domestic Product] of the 48 least developed countries." The richest 225 people have incomes greater than those of half of humanity. Nearly 3 billion people struggle to live on less than two dollars a day. Developing countries could achieve and maintain "universal access to basic education for all, basic health care for all, reproductive health care for all women, adequate food for all and safe water and sanitation for all" at a cost of approximately $40 billion a year. "This is less than 4 percent of the combined wealth of the 225 richest people in the world."[2]

Christians in the United States should be particularly concerned about the inequality, injustice, environmental destruction, and violence that are products of the present system. Inequality on a global scale is mirrored in our national reality. The United States is the most unequal of all industrial countries. One of four U.S. children is born into poverty. The richest 1 percent of households has more wealth than the combined total of the bottom 95 percent. In 1998, Bill Gates, whose wealth is more than the bottom 45 percent of American households combined, increased his net worth by more than $2 million an hour![3] The United States is also the most influential actor in the global economy and the largest exporter of weapons. Its militarized vision of policing the world distorts domestic and international priorities. Its leading export, however, is not weapons or computers or food. It is a vision of the "good life," a vision vastly different from the "abundant life" offered by Jesus.

A global economy built on the foundations of inequality generates unprecedented wealth for a small minority, affluence for a somewhat larger number, and insecurity, poverty, or destitution for many. The system has not only brought the world to the brink of environmental disaster, it feeds each spoke in the spiral of violence: problems of poverty and hunger worsen; social tensions spark rebellions; militarized societies and/or powerful nations working alone or in concert use superior violence, including in some cases the violence of economic sanctions, to impose "peace" or punish enemies; marginalized peoples vent frustrations or prey upon their neighbors; and many use God's name to bless the system or justify holy wars against it.

The economic system itself functions as a religion. MIT professor Lester Thurow criticizes "the theology of capitalism" that promotes the idea that "the distributions of wealth, income and earnings are of no consequence."[4] Overall, the global market economy functions as a god demanding ultimate allegiance. Economists are its high priests. Media outlets are intermediaries who control cultural images and project religious values worldwide through advertisements, TV, music, and movies. Malls are shrines where consumers go to worship and where they seek spiritual satisfaction. Retailing analyst Victor Lebow, writing after World War II, identified the foundational values of market morality:

> Our enormously productive economy . . . demands that we make consumption our way of life, that we convert the buying and use of goods into rituals, that we seek our spiritual satisfaction, our ego satisfaction, in consumption. . . . We need things consumed, burned up, worn out, replaced, and discarded at an ever increasing rate.[5]

As in any religion, the cult of the Market god has insiders and outsiders. Devotees need money to pay the significant tithes necessary for proper worship. Some have none and are excluded. Others have little and are marginalized. Some waste their lives and sacrifice their families by working longer and longer hours in an effort to pay for the endless and always changing series of icons available for purchase. Money is no object for the select few. The Market god, like many others, requires absolute allegiance and, like primitive gods, it demands human sacrifices as disposable people are left to die. The Market god is jealous and powerful and those who worship it use lethal violence in its defense. Few

Christians challenge its legitimacy. Many people, Gorostiaga says, think that inequality and destitution are inevitable:

> We are tempted by what I call a theology of inevitability: The world is like it is; economies just work that way; we can do nothing about it. From this perspective, Christians fumble, trying to prevent the poor from suffering too heavy a cost. Nongovernmental organizations devote themselves to charity; churches become like garbage pails, gathering up and caring here and there for those crucified by this historical context, trying to keep them simply from dying. What Christians and the churches need to be doing, though, is getting to the cause of this champagne-glass civilization, to the causes of this epidemic of impoverishment, of unemployment and of exclusion of the majority of humanity.[6]

The global order today is different from the Roman imperial system that dominated Palestine in the first century. There are many points of contact, however, between oppression today and the domination system that killed Jesus after he exposed it in parables and challenged it with the power of his vision and action. Jesus invites us to work against domination systems here and now. We must revisit Jesus' parables and write our own as we bring to light how the system functions and alternatives to it.

Jesus' faith, images of God, and his radical challenge to unjust systems require us to reritualize many aspects of our tradition. We might begin with baptism, which at present contains many images of God that Jesus rejected. Jesus undermined the links between God and redemptive or apocalyptic violence. It is hard to reconcile his experience of God with baptism services that draw on images of a "Holy God, mighty Lord" of whom it is written, "By the waters of the flood you condemned the wicked and saved those whom you had chosen, Noah and his family." More faithful to Jesus would be to understand baptism as symbolic death to oppressive systems, our acceptance of God's invitation to abundant life, our embrace of nonviolence, and our symbolic entry into communities of subversive weeds, communities of solidarity.

Taking Jesus' challenge to domination seriously could also help us make sense of the "Lord's Prayer." We should begin by acknowledging with Anglican bishop John Shelby Spong that the "definition of God implicit in the Lord's Prayer cannot be the operative definition for us today." God, as Spong points out, is not a Father, does not live in the sky, does not direct worldly events from heaven, and does not need or desire the flattery of humans.[7] Jesus as a first-century Palestinian Jew cannot be expected to have fully transcended the cosmological assumptions of his world. He did, how-ever, begin challenging them when he experienced God as the invitational, intimate Spirit at the heart of all life. What interests me here is that in the substance of the Lord's Prayer, Jesus addressed real debts and not spiritual-ized sins. Real debts were killing his people, and the complicity of the polit-ical and religious authorities and institutions in perpetuating indebtedness was a basis for Jesus' harsh critique of the oppressive system. In our world, real debts are the leading cause of hunger and death. Powerful nations use debt as leverage. Institutions such as the International Monetary Fund and World Bank coerce poor people and nations to worship the God of the international market. Structural adjustment programs place heavy bur-dens on the poorest of the poor and force vulnerable nations to participate in the global economy as junior partners in an oppressive system. It is a hopeful sign that hundreds of religiously based groups and organizations around the world joined together as part of "Jubilee 2000" to encourage debt relief for the world's poorest nations. Jubilee 2000 also continues to press for reform of agencies such as the World Bank and the International Monetary Fund.[8] Citizen, labor, environmental, and religious groups have also protested the abusive power of the World Trade Organization, which is dominated by large global corporations.[9]

Taking Jesus' challenge to the domination system seriously might also help us to see that nothing has distorted religion throughout history more than empire. The Gospels are riddled with contradictions concerning powerful Rome. There is evidence of Christian accommodation and there is counter evidence of a life and death struggle to undermine arrogant Roman claims: competing divine birth accounts, competing gospels, com-peting "sons of God," competing claims about how and through whom God was working in history. Arrogant empires claim, directly or indirectly, to be blessed by God. Our coins, like their Roman counterparts, read "In God We Trust." This impulse to appropriate God for nationalistic pur-poses is also evident in presidential speeches that call on God to bless America and in assertions that our nation's power is a sign of that bless-ing. The fact that we are Christians living in a powerful empire has undoubtedly impacted how we read scripture, understand Jesus, and live our lives. This is what Marcus Borg wants Christians to see when he writes that the "dominant values of American life—affluence, achievement, appearance, power, competition, consumption, individualism—are vastly different from anything recognizably Christian. As individuals and as a culture . . . our existence has become massively idolatrous."[10] Resistance to the historical Jesus is connected to our discomfort at being called out of empire and into an alternative "kingdom" that is at odds with domination of all kinds in all places.

READ SCRIPTURE CRITICALLY

Many professors, pastors, and church professionals do not challenge or reassess scriptural authority because they are afraid that knowledge of biblical inconsistencies and contradictions may lead people to abandon faith. One fear is related to the character of God. If God is as hateful, vindictive, and arbitrary as much of the Bible says, then people may abandon God and leave the church. People may be reluctant to commit their lives and money to a God who orders us to murder our disobedient children or to Jesus who repeatedly threatens people with weeping and gnashing of teeth. Better to censor such things or explain them away.

A related fear is linked to the reliability of scripture. If some things in the Bible are not true, then maybe none of it is. If Jesus was not born of a virgin, was not born in Bethlehem, was not from David's family line, and did not walk on water or turn water into wine as the Gospels or Christian creeds claim, then what else is not true? If Jesus, unlike Paul and the Gospel writers, rejected apocalyptic and messianic fantasies, and if Jesus did not proclaim himself the Messiah or utter any of the self-proclamation statements found in John ("I am the bread of life," "I am the light of the world," "I am the resurrection and the life," and so forth), then on what foundations do we base our faith? If the substance of faith is not that God sent Jesus to die for our sins so that believers will go to heaven, then what other "good news" may the Church proclaim? If, as many biblical scholars conclude, the resurrection of Jesus did not involve his physical appearance in bodily form among his disciples, and if "doubting Thomas" did not really stick his fingers in the wounds of Jesus, then how are we to deal with our own doubts about God, history, life, and death? How can we have confidence in eternal life or make sense out of the resurrection? If a focus on the historical Jesus erodes Gospel miracles as the foundation of faith, then what are the building blocks of a new foundation? Can we embrace the historical Jesus and still affirm and experience mystery? Can we deepen our spirituality? On what should we ground our Christian faith?

The fear implicit in such questions is understandable. There are two lamentable outcomes, however, of giving into rather than facing our fears. First, when we refuse to read scripture critically and to face biblical authority questions and scriptural contradictions honestly, we fail to see that for Christians Jesus' life in the Spirit *is* the alternative building block for faith. Jesus' life, faith, and revelation of an infinitely compassionate God are fertile fields within which to plant our hope and our lives. The Church still has a mission and a message, but the mission and message of God's unconditional embrace needs to be rooted in Jesus' life as a revelation of God. Jesus invites us to explore the mystery and meaning of abundant life lived in the midst of a beautiful, fractured world and lived in relationship with the Spirit of God at the center of life.

Second, we have legitimated terrifying images of God because of our failure to read scripture critically. Within the Bible and throughout human history, people have projected violence and hatred onto God with the claim that such sentiments and actions reflect God's actual character. Pathological images of God shore up men's abusive power, strengthen traditional associations between violence and power, and feed the spiral of violence that Jesus exposed and invites us to counter. Such images also help explain why fear and guilt are featured centrally within the life and theology of many churches and why many Christians are spiritually and emotionally wounded by their religious encounters with the church.

Questioning scriptural authority is taboo, and so many distortions of Jesus and God go unchallenged. Links between power and violence remain strong, and irreconcilable images of God and numerous biblical contradictions are downplayed or ignored. We end any and all biblical readings with high-sounding phrases such as "the word of the Lord" or "the word of God" or "Thanks be to God." Picture this scene and then hold it up to the light of Jesus' revelation of an infinitely compassionate God whose power is invitational:

> *Reading*: The LORD spoke to Moses . . . All who curse father or mother shall be put to death; having cursed father or mother, their blood is upon them (Lev 20:1, 9).
> *Congregational Response*: This is the word of God.
> *Reading*: If anyone secretly entices you—even if it is your brother, your father's son or your mother's son, or your own son or daughter, or the wife you embrace, or your most intimate friend—saying, "Let us go worship other gods" . . . [s]how them no pity or compassion and do not shield them. But you shall surely kill them; your own hand shall be first against them to execute them, and afterwards the hand of all the people (Deut 13:6, 8b–9).
> *Congregational Response*: The word of the Lord. Thanks be to God.

Although the full weight of human pathology projected onto God is carefully censored in our church lectionary, similar scenes are played out weekly in our churches. We end readings in which "villains" in the domination system are portrayed as God-figures who send people to the torturers, to outer darkness, to be cut into pieces with the words, "the Gospel of the Lord." This is both ridiculous and damaging. Embracing the pathology of God is the price we pay for cowardice and our failure to say honestly and openly that the Bible both reveals and distorts God.

Few people are willing to challenge distorted images of God's power or to say clearly and forthrightly that Matthew and other biblical writers often betray Jesus, for whom God is like the compassionate father in the prodigal story who forgives before being asked. In a similar fashion, P's merciless God and Jesus' infinitely compassionate Spirit somehow manage to cohabit our undifferentiated world of competing God talk. Jesus who threatens eternal punishments and weeping and gnashing of teeth is somehow in harmony with Jesus who teaches love of enemies and invites us into the embrace of an infinitely forgiving God. It is impossible to reconcile Jesus' images of God and his understanding of nonviolent power with biblical accounts in which God drowns most of humanity, orders us to kill disobedient children, sanctions or carries out genocidal violence, rejoices in reducing people to cannibalism, sends she-bears to maul boys who insult a prophet, sends bowl plagues to kill much of humanity as a matter of divine justice, and requires the sacrifice of God's child as the means to reconciliation with sinful humanity.

Many church officials are afraid that people may leave the church if scripture is approached critically and if contradictions are brought to light. It must be said, however, that many have left the church because they do not believe in a punishing, vindictive, all-knowing, almighty God capable of pathological violence. Many Christians choke on the creed, some recite it without meaning, and others sit on a reservoir of unasked questions. Perhaps most troubling, many who remain in the church have faith in a God who only remotely resembles the God revealed by Jesus.

Our unwillingness to redefine scriptural authority and to challenge numerous passages that link God's power to violence makes it nearly impossible for us to see that Jesus compels us to reassess God's character, violence, and power. It is time to let Jesus have a voice and to be honest about conflicting and irreconcilable images of God within scripture. It is also time to honestly face and purge our tradition of the many violent, punishing images of God that lie at the heart of many of our rituals, from baptism to the Lord's Supper. Jesus rejected vile and violent images of God that we reenact symbolically, consciously or unconsciously, week after week within our churches. We ground baptism rituals in a genocidal flood story (see above) and interpret the "Lord's Supper" in sacrificial terms (see below), thus betraying Jesus who revealed an infinitely loving God.

It is also time to acknowledge that the failure to approach scripture critically has many practical and troubling consequences. The biblical writers, for example, knew as little about homosexuality as they did about the dynamics of human reproduction, and yet scriptural passages continue to be cited today to shore up biases, deny rights, and prevent ordination of gay and lesbian people. In a similar way, a male-dominated Catholic hierarchy appropriates scripture to justify the exclusion of married priests and to deny women the right to be priests. Changing these very human and very wrong church decisions and policies depends on a critical reading of scripture and a long overdue reassessment of scriptural authority. An overreliance upon scriptural authority and church dogma concerning God and the Christ also prevents us from seeing that Jesus can shed light on but cannot dictate our own religious experiences.

CHALLENGING ATONEMENT EXPLANATIONS FOR JESUS' DEATH

Jesus rejected many distorted images of God that lie at the heart of many Christian rituals. Many Christians and Christian theologians, for example, embrace fundamental Gospel distortions concerning the meaning of Jesus' death. The idea that God sent Jesus to die for our sins makes sense only if you embrace punishing images of God rejected by Jesus. Vile and violent images of a powerful, punishing God were and are so widespread that many New Testament writers and those who follow their lead interpret the death of Jesus as an atoning sacrifice. Jesus, according to this logic, stands between sinful humanity and a wrathful deity. Jesus, who taught love of enemies and calls us to live in the presence of God's infinitely compassionate Spirit, is the "Son" of a wrathful God. More ironic still, Jesus (or the Lamb), according to many apocalyptic scenarios, will return as a punishing, violent judge to destroy enemies at the end of history. An infinitely loving God who forgives us before we ask does not need an atoning sacrifice.

This also raises questions about what it means to call Jesus our "Savior." From what, we must ask, does Jesus save us? The classic answer is that Jesus saves us from the consequence of our sin. God loved the world so much that God sent Jesus to die for us. If we believe this, then we will not be condemned (John 3:16). Many of us put on rose-colored glasses when we evaluate these words. We see a gracious God who loves us enough to send his only son to die in our place so that we might avoid our deserved punishment, go to heaven instead of hell, and have eternal life. Our rose-colored glasses prevent us from seeing brutal images of God, images rejected by Jesus, lurking behind this interpretation. If we believe that Jesus died for us so that we will not be condemned, then we should ask, "Condemned by whom?" The answer is God. What remains unstated in classic Christian statements of faith is that Jesus dies in order to save us from God, not from sin, or more accurately, Jesus' sacrificial death saves us from a God who punishes sin. Sin, both personal and social, is often destructive, but it is from a punishing God who threatens us with hell that we seek protection. The fearful images of God that are foundational to such views and to all sacrificial rituals are far removed from Jesus. Stephen Mitchell speaks of hell in this regard:

> This teaching about hell, which the church took over from a fierce, apocalyptic strand of Judaism, and which it . . . put into "Jesus'" mouth, proceeds from a very impure consciousness, filled with fantasies of hatred and revenge and of an unforgiving, unjust god whose punishments are insanely disproportionate to the offenses. There have always been theologians to justify this doctrine. . . . If hell means anything in reality, it is the world of torment that humans create for themselves and for one another out of their own greed, hatred, and ignorance. It is not a physical place; it is a psychological metaphor.[11]

Jesus and the compassionate God he reveals are the foundation and source of my life and faith. Our lives and the life of the world rest now and forever in the embrace of the Spirit of God in all times and places, in life and in death, in whatever comes. It does not make sense in light of Jesus, however, to understand "Savior" to mean that Jesus died to save us from our sins any more than it does to hold on to the promise of the Hebrew Scriptures that salvation is the defeat of enemies and the "Savior" is the one to implement God's redemptive or apocalyptic violence. This does not mean we are without sin or that there are no consequences to sin. Sin and evil are alive in the world and we see their ugly fruits in broken lives, environmental stresses, and deadly oppressions. It does mean that although the need for an atoning sacrifice is consistent with images of a wrathful, punishing God, Jesus experienced and revealed a *loving* God.

Perhaps Jesus saves us in the sense that he offers us a way into life in the Spirit and out of the deadly spiral of violence, including our imprisonment to violent images of God. Salvation, long associated with superior violence and defeat of enemies, is understood by Jesus to be the fruit of nonviolent love and action rooted in a nonviolent God. We are called to imitate a compassionate God as we seek to bring healing and wholeness to our communities and our fractured world.

The atonement theory, in which Jesus' blood sacrifice saves us from sin and the deserved punishment of a violent deity, is central to many Christian theologies and practices, as Spong notes:

> Most of the content of this faith tradition has been organized in such a way as to serve this rescuer mentality. The service of baptism presupposes the rescue operation. The primary eucharist worship of the Church, frequently referred to as "the sacrifice of the mass," reenacts liturgically this rescuing of Jesus. The entire corpus of the Bible traditionally has been read and interpreted in such a way as to undergird this particular understanding of Jesus as the rescuer. The presence of a cross or a crucifix as the central symbol of Christianity proclaims it.[12]

Doing away with atonement explanations of Jesus' death will require abandonment or revision of hundreds of hymns and liturgies. I suggest we acknowledge in all of our liturgies and rituals that God, who is infinitely gracious, forgives us before and without our asking. As Stephen Mitchell notes, "God's being is nonjudgment."[13] In this light it is important to replace rituals, confessions, and liturgies in which we ask for and receive forgiveness with ones in which we give thanks for the graciousness of God. This may seem a small point, but grounding what we do in the unsolicited graciousness of God is most consistent with Jesus. Confession, I would add, is appropriate and necessary for human beings. Reconciliation between individuals or groups is often impossible without it, and an honest accounting of our personal and social sins can open up the possibility of a different future. If graciousness is the very heart of God, then we can confess our personal and social failings more honestly to ourselves and to others, without fear and with commitment, confidence, and hope. The key point here is that *although confession is important for human forgiveness, it is not a requirement of God.* God, according to Jesus, is a gracious Spirit and there is nothing we can say or do or not say and not do that can stand in the way of God's graciousness.

I would also encourage us to set aside the notion that Jesus' death defeated the powers in favor of an emphasis on his crucifixion as a consequence of his life and faith. A hymn of praise sung as part of many Lutheran communion services is faithful to the book of Revelation but far removed from Jesus and the "mustard seed kingdom." The Eucharist, interpreted through an atonement lens, is "the feast of victory for our God." Christ, "the Lamb who was slain," is worthy because his "blood set us free to be people of God." Christ, unlike Jesus who revealed the Spirit of God through the abundance found in sufficiency of food shared and alternative community lived, is the recipient of power and privileges: "Power, riches, wisdom, and strength, honor, and blessing and glory are his."[14] These rewards come to Christ as payment for Jesus' blood sacrifice.

This Christian triumphalism, although meant to affirm Christ over empire, adopts categories of empire and embraces traditional characteristics of power projected by humans onto God. This is far from Jesus, who, living in the Spirit of God, risked his life and lost it as he exposed, challenged, and embodied alternatives to domination and the spiral of violence. Jesus' life and death should put to rest all speculation concerning God's redemptive violence. Jesus exposed the domination system, including its illusionary claims of divine favor, its false promises of peace and prosperity, its abuses of power, its confusion of riches with abundant life, and its claims to wisdom and glory. Systems that impoverish people materially and spiritually and that kill God's servants, whether Jesus, Gandhi, or Romero, cannot claim divine approval. Jesus lived an alternative to domination, and the Spirit at the heart of his experience of God invites us for all time to do so as well.

The resurrection of Jesus does not defeat the powers either, although this "surprise ending" should keep us from being immobilized by fear and should diminish the power of an oppressive system's ultimate sanction. We should approach humbly and minimize significantly our speculations concerning what happened at the "resurrection of Jesus" and the meaning of "life after death" because we do not and cannot know. The postresurrection narratives found in the Gospels are bizarre and contradictory. What we can celebrate in light of stories such as the prodigal son is that lives can be resurrected within history because the compassionate Spirit invites us always, each day, each moment, to new life. We can rejoice because abundant life rooted in the embodied life of Jesus is something to be built, discerned, and experienced here and now. Beyond this, it seems to me, the most we can do is *embrace the promise that death does not have the last word and get on with the business of living in faithful service to the*

Spirit revealed through Jesus' life and faith, a Spirit that thankfully neither a Roman crucifixion nor Church and biblical distortions can kill.

Fidelity to Jesus' images of God requires reritualization of the Christian Eucharist or Lord's Supper. Communion rituals need to be purged of all implications that Jesus' death was sacrificial. Insights from scholars are helpful but threatening to many people. The language "this is my body" and "this is my blood" is traceable to the early church and not to Jesus. More important, the images of God at the heart of this language betray Jesus' revelation of a loving God. These words and subsequent rituals surrounding them place the Eucharist or Lord's Supper in a sacrificial context. Just as the Jews were saved from God's slaughter in Egypt because their doorposts were marked with the blood of a perfect sacrificial lamb, so too Christians will be spared God's wrath by the blood sacrifice of Jesus. The Eucharist or Lord's Supper understood in a sacrificial light ritualizes appeasement of a bloodthirsty, punishing deity. It commemorates Jesus' blood sacrifice in which Jesus stands between sinful humanity and the violent judgment of God.

We need to reclaim the "Lord's Supper" as an actual, community meal shared in the context of bitter hunger and systemic violence. A ritual with Jesus at table probably emerged because of the centrality of food to Jesus' kingdom message and practice in the context of and as alternative to the widespread hunger resulting from the Rome- and Temple-dominated order. Jesus understood daily bread for all as a reflection of God's intent, a manifestation of God's justice, and a sign of the kingdom's presence. John Dominic Crossan questions contemporary practice:

> The Christian Eucharist is today a morsel and a sip. It is not a real meal. You may reply, of course, that such is sufficient to symbolize the presence of Jesus and God in the community of faith. But why symbolize divinity through a medium of food that is non-food? Maybe non-food symbolizes a non-Jesus and a non-God? . . . Of *course* the Eucharist is a symbolic meal. But does that mean it should be *a morsel and a sip symbolic of a real meal or a real meal symbolic of God's presence?*[15]

I suggest linking a ritualized meal to an actual meal in order to express symbolically the ongoing presence of Jesus or the Spirit that guided him within the life of the community and the world. When an actual meal is not possible, real food and drink can be used as part of a solidarity ritual or meal of remembrance. Through these rituals we remember and recommit ourselves to the powerful example of Jesus' nonviolent witness to the compassionate Spirit of God reflected in his public ministry of exposing oppressive systems, in his inclusive table practice of shared meals, and in his vision of an alternative order rooted in justice in which all would be fed. By sharing a meal communally or by receiving communion together we celebrate the nonviolent presence of God in daily bread and express our commitment to be in solidarity with those who hunger for real food and spiritual nourishment. We can preserve the tradition linking a community meal with the betrayal of Jesus by communicating clearly that communion is a solidarity meal in which we declare God's intent and our commitment that all be fed. Communion should always be understood as a risky, subversive act. It challenges systems that accept hunger as an acceptable cost of progress. As Crossan notes, *"it is in food and drink offered equally to everyone that the presence of God and Jesus is found.* But food and drink are the material bases of life," he continues, "so the Lord's Supper is political criticism and economic challenge as well as sacred rite and liturgical worship."[16]

If baptism is our initiation into a community of subversive weeds, then communion, the Eucharist, the Lord's Supper offer us bread for the journey. Communion builds community. It nourishes us along the way of the perilous path we have chosen, a path that places us in opposition to death, hunger, and domination. We re-member the community through a meal of remembrance and solidarity, recommit ourselves to justice, and get the nourishment we need to be communities of subversive weeds working for and embodying the alternative order of God.

I also find Trinitarian language confusing and limiting. The concept of the Trinity—God, Son, and Spirit—tries to convey the mystery of God. Although it attempts to communicate that Jesus incarnates God in unique and remarkable ways, it can easily fall prey to religious arrogance and distort the character of God. This is especially true when the uniqueness of Jesus is defined in sacrificial terms in which the blood sacrifice of God's only Son is what "saves" humanity or a select group of believers. The concept of the Trinity should be seen as one very human attempt to speak about the mystery of God. It should never be seen as immutable, dogmatic truth or be treated as a litmus test for authentic faith. Jesus never claimed to be God. He did claim to point us in the direction of God. I think Jesus would find it tragically ironic that he was elevated to the status of being one of three "persons" in the Trinity because New Testament writers and Christian interpreters defined his death in sacrificial terms.

Many of us who claim Jesus is God or the "Son of God" lose touch with the Spirit he embodies and lose sight of the God to which he points. Jesus reveals the Spirit of God at the heart of all life. The Spirit surrounds us with love, embraces us with compassion, invites us to abundant life, and accompanies us in our nonviolent action in service to justice. The Spirit, the compassionate source of all life, is incarnated in the life of the world and is reflected in the abundant life of the new community. Jesus apparently lived a life in harmony with his message to the point that others experienced and claimed that the Spirit of God was incarnated in his life.

In my own religious experience I feel the presence of God as Spirit. Spirit is for me the best word to describe God. I find it easy to relate to Jesus, however, because like each believer he has a faith journey and shares our humanity. Jesus, therefore, informs my experience of God as Spirit. It is impossible to say with certainty based on my religious experience that I know the "real Jesus" or that I have a personal relationship with the "living Jesus" or Christ. I am uncomfortable with reference to Jesus as Lord because even though it expresses something important concerning ultimate allegiance, abusive, patriarchal power is often attached to that designation. If there is a difference between life in the Spirit, faith in God, relationship to Christ, or experience of the "living Jesus," then I for one cannot differentiate between them. I am most comfortable speaking of God as Spirit. My experience and understanding of God as Spirit is shaped by my experience and understanding of Jesus' life and faith as revelations of a nonviolent God surrounding us with compassion and inviting us to abundant life.

ABANDONING TRADITIONAL IMAGES OF GOD'S POWER

We cling stubbornly to images of a powerful God associated with redemptive or apocalyptic violence for a variety of reasons including two to be named here. First, we want God to be powerful enough to insure life after death, to exclude or defeat enemies, to punish evil, and to establish justice. This hefty agenda requires an all-powerful God. Unlike Jesus, we have grandiose expectations concerning God's power, the nature of power itself, abundant life, and the "kingdom." This positions us with those who in the context of exile presented God as a divine puppeteer in control of all things. It also places us in close proximity to many of Jesus' contemporaries, including those who saw Roman domination as a just but temporary punishment for sin or as a blip on an apocalyptic screen that would soon be subjected to God's violent judgment. Many rejected the mustard seed and Jesus' invitation to be subversive weeds, to live resurrected lives in and as challenge to the imperial context. They expected God to send a messiah or apocalyptic judge to reverse their unfortunate plight, to defeat their enemies, to bring the wealth of all nations to Israel with foreign kings led in procession, to crush evil, to avenge wrongs, to vindicate the faithful, and to impose absolute justice within or at the end of history. Stephen Mitchell identifies some of the problems with such perspectives:

> All spiritual Masters, in all the great religious traditions, have come to experience the present as the only reality. . . . Passages about the kingdom of God as coming in the future are a dime a dozen in the prophets, in the Jewish apocalyptic writings of the first centuries B.C.E., in Paul and the early church. They are filled with passionate hope, with a desire for universal justice, and also, as Nietzsche so correctly insisted, with a festering resentment against "them" (the powerful, the ungodly). But they arise from ideas, not from an experience of the state of being that Jesus called the kingdom of God.[17]

Second, it is hard to reject violent images of God because they are featured prominently within the Bible. Most Christians are taught that if it is in the Bible, then it must somehow be true. Many passages and stories tell us that God is violent, punishing, and powerful. God is God because of superior violence, and God's violence is understood to be instrumental to God's justice. Jesus poses many challenges to scriptural authority and to Christianity. Jesus invites us to live according to his alternative vision and his experience of a nonviolent God whose power is invitational rather than coercive. Fidelity to Jesus requires us to rewrite the Apostle's Creed in order to, among other things, include his life and delete reference to "Almighty" God. Many liturgies, songs, and prayers project illusionary power onto God. They need to be revised, rewritten, or discarded. God, Jesus says, is nonviolent. The Spirit's power is invitational, available here and now. It is not punishing, abusive, and vengeful, as many messianic and apocalyptic voices within the biblical tradition contend.

EMBRACING THE NONVIOLENCE OF GOD

We live in a world, as Jesus did, that is characterized by injustice and violence. In such a world it is natural to want God to be powerful and to project violence onto God. We want God to be powerful enough to impose justice within or at the end of history. Even many nonviolent activists who embrace the nonviolence of Jesus root his nonviolence and their own in the violence of God. The God revealed by Jesus is incapable of violence. God is infinitely loving, giving, gracious, hospitable, and compassionate. God is not violent. God's power is invitational rather than coercive.

This vision of God leaves human beings in a difficult position, and it seems to be exactly opposite of what many nonviolent activists propose. We must choose how to live in a world of violence and injustice without the assurance that God's violent power will ultimately make things right. Our dilemma is this: If God is nonviolent and incapable of imposing justice now or in the future, then how are we to live? Jesus beckons us to embrace the nonviolent power of God. Few of us believe that nonviolence is powerful, but as Wink has written:

> We live in a remarkable time, when entire nations have been liberated by nonviolent struggle; when miracles are openly declared, such as the fall of the Berlin Wall, the collapse of communism in the Soviet Union and the Eastern Bloc, and the transformation of South Africa; when for the first time people are beginning to resist domination in all its forms. Yet these are also times of endemic violence, ethnic hatred, genocide, and economic privation around the world, as the super-rich hoard increasing shares of the world's wealth and the poor drown in poverty. It is a time of hope; it is a time of despair. I have seen enough of God's wily ways with the Powers to stake my life on the side of hope.[18]

EMBRACING THE NONVIOLENCE OF JESUS

The crisis of the world is rooted in the power of evil and our own reluctance to embrace nonviolence fully. Jesus understood that the Rome- and Temple-dominated order was unjust and that it was backed up by violence. He, like many of his contemporaries, was excited when he heard about a prophet in the desert calling for repentance in full expectation that God would act soon to destroy evil. He was baptized into John's movement, but the Baptist was killed and the expected apocalyptic violence of God did not materialize. Jesus knew well the ruthless efficiency of Roman violence. He was born and raised in the shadows of Sepphoris. Roman legions burned Sepphoris and crucified thousands of people in the aftermath of rebellions that greeted the death of Herod the Great. Popular kings and messiahs rose and fell during that time, and messianic promises lived on and apocalyptic expectations deepened in their aftermath. The land loss, indebtedness, poverty, and insecurity that accompanied Roman commercialization, heavy taxation, and Temple tithes would have left many people desperate and despairing.

We do not know exactly why or when, but somewhere along the way Jesus rejected expectations of God and history rooted in the violence of God. It is possible that repeated failures involving promises of violent redemption, centuries in which spirals of violence deepened, memories of the violent legacy of Sepphoris, and John's execution itself may have contributed to his changing understanding of God and history. We will never be able to pinpoint the reasons for these changes, but the Gospels contain compelling glimpses indicating that Jesus came to experience God as the nonviolent, loving Spirit at the heart of the world's life who invites us to new life.

This view of God as compassionate Spirit informed Jesus' critique of the domination system and guided his vision of the "kingdom" of God. Through his parables and other teachings and actions, Jesus exposed the inner workings of the oppressive system, including the spiral of violence. And all along the way, Jesus revealed, modeled, and called for the domination system's opposite: abundant life in the alternative "kingdom." The system produced hunger and indebtedness. The compassionate order of God stressed daily food and forgiveness of debt. The system claimed divine approval. Jesus saw it in opposition to God, and his execution exposed the system's lies. The system divided people and deflected hatred and violence onto toll collectors and retainers. Jesus called forth hospitality, solidarity, alternative family, and community. The system was maintained by violence, and those opposed to it saw God's violence or divinely sanctioned human violence as the means by which to overcome it. Jesus rejected images of a violent God, taught love of enemies, redefined salvation to mean healing rather than defeat of enemies, and modeled creative nonviolent resistance.

If Jesus had experienced and announced God to be nonviolent and then taken up arms in an effort to overthrow the Rome- and Temple-dominated order and to establish the alternative kingdom by force, then we would be left with a dilemma. The implication of his violent action would be that in a violent and unjust world, a world in which God is nonviolent and therefore incapable of imposing justice, human beings must use violence in pursuit of justice. This is not what Jesus did. Any illusion that God was violent or that human beings are to use violence in pursuit of justice should have died with Jesus on the cross. Burton Cooper writes:

> Jesus on the cross presents his failure to God. It is the failure of suffering love to coerce a loving response. But this defeat on the cross redefines failure for the Christian—and for the church. In his defeat, Christ denies the identification of God's power with coercion. Now it is a sign of failure to resort to coercive powers. In his defeat at the hands of the strong, Christ makes it a victory to identify with and care for the weak. Now it is a sign of failure to live with indifference to the suffering of the weak.[19]

Jesus portrayed God as nonviolent and the domination system as violent, and then he modeled creative nonviolent resistance, including a willingness to be killed rather than to kill. Jesus' nonviolent action, therefore, reflected his experience of a nonviolent God. Jesus' death on the cross testifies that God's power, whatever it may be, is invitational and not violent or coercive.

Embracing the nonviolence of God and Jesus would have far-reaching implications for Christians. First, Christians would not kill other human beings or be part of any military or police force expected to use lethal violence anywhere in the world, including for national defense. We would not use weapons to fight imperial or revolutionary wars, to work for justice or to resist injustice. Gene Sharp has developed strategies for nonviolent national defense and nonviolent resolution of international disputes that should be of great interest to Christians.[20] He outlines

> civilian-based defense [policies] intended to deter and defeat both foreign military invasions and occupations as well as internal take-overs, including executive usurpations and coups d'etat. Civilian-based defense applies social, economic, political and psychological "weapons" (or specific methods of action) to wage widespread noncooperation and political defiance.[21]

Second, Christians would support nonviolent defense efforts and be part of national and international nonviolent peace teams. These teams would be trained in conflict resolution skills and in strategies of noncooperation. Members would be willing to risk their lives to intervene in an organized, nonviolent way in domestic and international conflicts where injustice reigns, evil runs amok, or violence threatens. Such teams already exist in small ways funded and organized by various peace groups and nongovernmental organizations. If there are lessons to be learned from conflicts in Rwanda, Iraq, Bosnia, Kosovo, East Timor, Colombia, and many other places, they are that the world community makes little or no investment in peacemaking, that such national and international peace teams are desperately needed, and that without them nations and the international community will use military force and lethal violence as substitutes for diplomacy and creative nonviolent action. This feeds the spiral of violence.

Third, if Christians embraced the nonviolence of Jesus, we would become a major force within our nations and within multilateral institutions lobbying and working in a variety of ways for nonviolent alternatives to war and violence. Christians should be a principled constituency committed to nonviolent social change, mediation, and conflict resolution. Without such a constituency, nonviolent initiatives will continue to be marginalized.

Fourth, Christians would work in a multiplicity of ways to break the spiral of violence, including working to address in a systemic way the causes of hunger, poverty, indebtedness, and inequality.

Fifth, at educational institutions with ties to the church, ROTC would be replaced with peace and justice studies programs and nonviolent conflict resolution centers. The Justice and Peace Studies program at the University of St. Thomas where I teach creatively links peace and justice issues, includes courses in comparative religious perspectives, and stresses active nonviolence. [22] Programs such as this have tremendous potential to expand the links between Christianity and creative nonviolence nationally and internationally.

Sixth, Christians would reject the just war theory, which is often supported on the basis of images of God rejected by Jesus. In the context of the Gulf War, an editorial in *La Civila Cattolica* (widely understood to reflect the perspective of Pope John Paul II) noted that a "war cannot really be conducted according to the criteria required for a just war." The just war theory, the editorial said, is "indefensible and needs to be abandoned."

> War almost never ends with a true peace: it always leaves behind a remnant of hatred and a thirst for revenge, which will explode as soon as the opportunity offers itself. That is why the human story has been a series of unending wars. War

initiates a spiral of hatred and violence, which is extremely difficult to stop. War is therefore useless, since it solves no problems, and damaging because it aggravates problems and makes them insoluble.[23]

Seventh, Christians who take the nonviolence of Jesus seriously will work to dramatically reduce U.S. military spending. This could encourage demilitarization worldwide and could free up funds for global efforts to address issues of poverty and environmental collapse and to expand peacemaking teams and other initiatives aimed at encouraging creative nonviolence.

Eighth, Christians who fully embrace the nonviolence of God will offer a compelling example and invitation to all the people of the world to reexamine links between God and violence that infect many religions. Christians could help transform violent monotheism by embracing nonviolence and affirming the nonviolence of God.

Ninth, Christians committed to social justice and peace must continue to model nonviolent protest and social action because the majority of Christians will not adopt the nonviolence of Jesus and God overnight. In my view, however, many of these efforts will fail unless and until we root nonviolence in the nonviolence of God.

Tenth, taking the nonviolence of Jesus seriously means recognizing the relationship between inner and outer peace, between being at peace and being peacemakers. "To work for peace," Thich Nhat Hanh writes, "you must have a peaceful heart. When you do, you are a child of God. But many who work for peace are not at peace," he continues. "They still have anger and frustration, and their work is not really peaceful."[24]

> When there are wars within us, it will not be long before we are at war with others, even those we love. The violence, hatred, discrimination, and fear in society water the seeds of violence, hatred, discrimination, and fear in us. If we go back to ourselves and touch our feelings, we will see the ways that we furnish fuel for the wars going on inside.[25]

Finally, Christians who take the nonviolence of Jesus seriously can demonstrate with others that *nonviolence is God's transforming power in the world*. Few people believe that nonviolence is powerful and yet despite our reluctance and without conscious training, there is a good deal of evidence that nonviolence is not only right because it is the way of God but that nonviolence is also effective. The Gandhi-led independence movement, the U.S. Civil Rights movement, the People Power movement in the Philippines, and many others demonstrate the effective power of nonviolence. The key point is that rejecting violent power is not an exercise in futility, an abandonment of justice, or resignation in the face of evil. Jesus' nonviolence and the nonviolent power of God can be effective, if and when we take them seriously.

EMBRACING ABUNDANT LIFE

Jesus looked at the world and saw both injustice and the actual presence and future possibility of God's abundance. In contrast to many Hebrew scriptural passages rooted in the scarcity of both goods and God's blessing, Jesus experienced God as infinitely giving, compassionate, and loving. He invited all people to abundant life then and now. He was clear, however, that rich people would have a hard time accepting the invitation or experiencing abundant life because of the way they lived in the world. He lovingly called them to leave misguided priorities behind and to accept abundant life found in generosity, community, daily food, nonviolent action, and alternative families.

Jesus' invitation to abundant life has profound implications for many Christians in the United States for whom affluence or its pursuit is the very substance of life. We easily confuse comfortable lifestyles with abundant life. Many of us, however, know the poverty of affluence and feel there is something missing from our lives. I believe Jesus' invitation to abundant life found in sharing meals, community, healing, working for justice, and nonviolent action will resonate with many.

Abundant life is not only a question of how we earn and spend our money but how we spend our lives. Jon Sobrino, a Jesuit priest from El Salvador, once told a group I was with at the Catholic University in San Salvador that the world needs more liberation teachers, liberation plumbers, liberation doctors, liberation carpenters, liberation retirees, that is, more people who put their vocational skills to work improving communities and addressing pressing social problems rather than enriching themselves.

Jesus' invitation to abundant life poses equally radical challenges to the poor. Abundant life, Jesus says, is often possible in the midst of present difficulties. Poor people do not have to wait for the revolution or for God's violent intervention but can imitate the loving generosity of God in their own lives and communities. They can share food, forgive debts, maintain hospitality, work for justice, and reclaim dignity in situations intended to humiliate through creative, nonviolent resistance. The point is not to idealize poverty or let unjust systems off the hook but to keep focused on abundant life rooted in the Spirit and not on definitions and illusionary promises propagated by the domination system itself or by those who root hope in the apocalyptic or messianic fantasies of redemptive violence.

Jesus' invitation to *abundant life* is particularly relevant in a world fracturing because of empty promises of the *good life* rooted in market priorities within a global economy. David C. Korten notes this contrast:

> The leaders and institutions that promised a golden age are not delivering. They assail us with visions of wondrous new technological gadgets. . . . Yet the things that most of us really want—a secure means of livelihood, a decent place to live, healthy and uncontaminated food to eat, good education and health care for our children, a clean and vital natural environment—seem to slip further from the grasp of most of the world's people with each passing day.[26]

The Market god of the global economy and its accompanying religion fail us and undermine God's intent in three important ways. First, the global system generates inequality rather than equality. The system is so unjust that it fosters violence at every turn and defends itself with violence. Second, the present system threatens to undermine life as we know it because the production and consumption it requires in order to extend its vision of the good life to elites throughout the world is, environmentally speaking, catastrophic.

> No sane person seeks a world divided between billions of excluded people living in absolute deprivation and a tiny elite guarding their wealth and luxury behind fortress walls. No one rejoices at the prospect of life in a world of collapsing social and ecological systems. Yet we continue to place human civilization and even the survival of our species at risk mainly to allow a million or so people to accumulate money beyond any conceivable need.[27]

Finally, the Market god of the global economy fails because its flawed vision of the good life does not satisfy our deep and urgent spiritual longings. Ironically, our pursuit of the good life often leaves us empty and sends us searching for deeper meaning. Jesus invites the rich and economically powerful to abundant life. In order to experience it we must leave our privileges behind. The poor are invited to stay focused on the sufficiency vision of abundant life in the "kingdom" rather than place their hopes in illusionary promises of liberating violence, pie-in-the-sky promises of heavenly streets paved with gold, or deceptive promises of the glitter and good life promised by the dominant culture on billboards, and in television and movies. All of us are invited to embrace abundant life in the context of alternative communities rooted in the generosity, compassion, justice, and nonviolence of God. Such communities cannot simply withdraw from the world (like modern-day Essenes) but must seek to transform it (like modern-day followers of Jesus).[28] Churches in communities and countries throughout the world have the potential to be leavening agents of nonviolence and justice.

CONCLUSION

Jesus is missing. We miss Jesus. The mystery of Jesus' conflict with and disappearance from Christianity is rooted in our unwillingness to approach scripture critically, our reluctance to examine gospel distortions, and our refusal to let go of traditional notions of God's power. Images of God are important because they shape the content of our faith. The almost unlimited violence that humanity has projected onto God and Jesus has taken an enormous toll throughout history, making Christianity and other religions accomplices in the world's threatened destruction. I have tried to solve the mystery of Jesus' disappearance and to counter the tragic consequences of linking God and violence by calling attention to incompatible biblical claims about Jesus and God and by paying close attention to Jesus' life as a revelation of God.

Jesus can help us better understand God and historical injustice in Jesus' time and our own. Nonviolent images of God guided Jesus, grounded his faith, and informed his actions as he exposed and countered a deadly spiral of violence. His revelation of a nonviolent God and his invitation to abundant life rooted in the generosity of God offer us an alternative way to live. Abundant life is both present possibility and future promise. It is available to those who thirst for alternatives to despair and violence, those who accept Jesus' invitation to be communities of subversive weeds growing in and at the edges of imperial gardens. The important task for Christianity and Christians is to allow Jesus, and the God he reveals to us, back into our collective and individual lives. Jesus does not have to remain an invisible person symbolically absent from our creeds and actually missing from our lives. The God revealed by Jesus is available to us now and always. The compassionate Spirit is at the heart of all life and can be at the center of our lives and our journeys of faith. Thanks be to God.

Notes

1. Xabier Gorostiaga, "World Has Become a 'Champagne Glass,'" *National Catholic Reporter*, 27 January 1995.

2. Chuck Collins et al., *Shifting Fortunes: The Perils of the Growing American Wealth Gap* (Boston: United for a Fair Economy, 1999), 18.

3. Ibid., 5, 16, 18.

4. Ibid., 1.

5. Quoted in Alan Durning, *How Much Is Enough?* (New York: W. W. Norton, 1992), 22.

6. Gorostiaga, "World Has Become a 'Champagne Glass.'"

7. John Shelby Spong, *Why Christianity Must Change or Die* (San Francisco: HarperSanFrancisco, 1998), 138–40.

8. For more information contact Jubilee 2000/USA Campaign, 222 East Capitol St., NE, Washington, D.C. 20003.

9. According to the Institute for Policy Studies, of the world's 100 largest economic entities, 51 are corporations and 49 are countries. The world's top 200 corporations account for over a quarter of economic activity on the globe but employ less than 1 percent of its workforce. See www.ips-dc.org/top200.htm.

10. Marcus J. Borg, *Jesus: A New Vision* (San Francisco: Harper & Row, 1987), 195.

11. Stephen Mitchell, *The Gospel according to Jesus* (New York: Harper Perennial, 1993), 68.

12. Spong, *Why Christianity Must Change*, 85.

13. Mitchell, *Gospel according to Jesus*, 187.

14. *Lutheran Book of Worship* (Minneapolis: Augsburg Publishing House; Philadelphia: Board of Publication, Lutheran Church in America, 1979), 102.

15. John Dominic Crossan, *The Birth of Christianity* (San Francisco: HarperSanFrancisco, 1998), 424, emphasis in original.

16. Ibid., 444, emphasis in original.

17. Mitchell, *Gospel according to Jesus*, 12.

18. Walter Wink, *The Powers That Be: Theology for a New Millennium* (New York: Doubleday, 1998), 10.

19. Burton Cooper, *Why, God?* (Atlanta: John Knox Press, 1988), 123.

20. See Gene Sharp, *Making Europe Unconquerable: The Potential of Civilian-Based Deterrence and Defense* (Cambridge, Mass.: Ballinger, 1985); and Gene Sharp,

National Security through Civilian-Based Defense (Omaha, Neb.: Association for Transarmament Studies, 1985). See also his three-volume set, *The Politics of Nonviolent Action* (Boston: Porter Sargent Publishers, 1973).

21. Gene Sharp, *Self-Reliant Defense* (Cambridge, Mass.: Albert Einstein Institution, 1992), 8.

22. For information on this program, send a self-addressed, stamped envelope to: Justice and Peace Studies, University of St. Thomas, 2115 Summit Avenue, St. Paul, MN 55105–1096.

23. Quoted in John Dear, *The God of Peace: Toward a Theology of Nonviolence* (Maryknoll, N.Y.: Orbis Books, 1994), 128–29.

24. Thich Nhat Hanh, *Living Buddha, Living Jesus* (New York: Riverhead Books, 1995), 74.

25. Ibid., 19.

26. David C. Korten, *When Corporations Rule the World* (West Hartford, Conn.: Kumarian Press; San Francisco, Berret-Koehler Publishers, 1995), 18–19.

27. Ibid., 261–62.

28. My family is involved in an alternative, ecumenical Christian faith community in Minneapolis. For information send a self-addressed, stamped envelope to the Community of St. Martin, 2001 Riverside Avenue, Minneapolis, MN 55454.

Index